SIEGFRIED SASSOON

SIEGFRIED SASSOON

(1886-1967)

JOHN STUART ROBERTS

metro

Published by Metro Publishing,
an imprint of John Blake Publishing Ltd,
3 Bramber Court, 2 Bramber Road,
London W14 9PB, England

www.johnblakepublishing.co.uk

www.facebook.com/Johnblakepub 🔲
twitter.com/johnblakepub 🔲

First published in this hardback edition by Metro Publishing in 2014.
Originally published in hardback in 1999. Metro paperback
edition first published in 2005.

ISBN: 978-1-78219-912-0

British Library Cataloguing-in-Publication Data:
a catalogue record for this book is available from the British Library.

Design by www.envydesign.co.uk

Printed in Great Britain by CPI Group (UK) Ltd

1 3 5 7 9 10 8 6 4 2

Papers used by John Blake Publishing are natural, recyclable products made from
wood grown in sustainable forests. The manufacturing processes conform to the
environmental regulations of the country of origin.

Every attempt has been made to contact the relevant copyright-holders, but some
were unobtainable. We would be grateful if the appropriate people could contact us.

To
Dame Felicitas Corrigan, OSB
and the Benedictine Communities
at Stanbrook and Downside.

This new edition is dedicated
to my friend John Hefin
'whom I have loved long since
and lost – awhile'.

CONTENTS

ACKNOWLEDGEMENTS

I am grateful to Mr George Sassoon for permission to quote from the published and unpublished material of Siegfried Sassoon. I am also grateful to Max Egremont, Sassoon's official biographer, for the generous help and permissions he has given me.

It is a pleasure to acknowledge the contribution to Sassoon studies made by Dr Jean Moorcroft Wilson. *The Making of a War Poet*, the first volume of her full-scale biography of Sassoon, has rightly been greeted as a *tour de force*. My biography is on a lesser scale and has benefited from the engaging details and insights to be found in Dr Moorcroft Wilson's work.

A new critical study, *Siegfried Sassoon: Scorched Glory*, has been written by Paul Moeyes. Together with the critical study by Michael Thorpe published in 1967, this new work, full of ideas and interpretations, has widened my horizons and deepened my appreciation of Sassoon's prose and poetry.

It is impossible to measure the contribution made by Sir Rupert Hart-Davis. No one has laboured longer or harder than he to safeguard and enhance the reputation of Sassoon, whom he knew and whose friendship he enjoyed. His encouragement during the writing of this biography as well as his counsel has been one of the great sustainments during the last two years. Sir Rupert has placed important Sassoon material in the Archives and Manuscripts Room, Cambridge University Library, including the fine-edited copies of the unpublished diaries. The gesture enriched an already fine collection.

Every student of Sassoon will readily admit their admiration for and indebtedness to Kathleen Cann. Her knowledge of the entire collection and eager involvement in each project, large or small, is an example of librarianship at its highest level.

My gratitude is extended to the following libraries, collections and museums for their help: New York Public Library (Berg Collection); Harry Ransom Humanities Research Center, University of Texas, Austin; Bodleian Library, Oxford; St John's College, Cambridge; Clare College, Cambridge; Merton College, Oxford; St John's College, Oxford; Royal Archives, Windsor Castle; Royal Collection, St James's Palace; Osborne House, Isle of Wight; British Library, Colindale; BBC Archives Caversham; National Portrait Gallery; National Library of Wales; National Library of Scotland; Leeds University (Brotherton Collection); University of Wales, Cardiff; Henry Moore Institute, Leeds; Laing Art Gallery, Newcastle upon Tyne; Liverpool Public Library; Glasgow City Library; Westminster Library and Chelsea Library; Cardiff City Library; Pembrokeshire County Library; Neath Town Library; Kent County Library; Northampton County Library; Lambeth Palace and Fulham Palace Libraries; Public Records Office, London; Public Records Office, Trowbridge, Wiltshire; Imperial War Museum; Royal Military Academy, Sandhurst; Royal Welch Fusiliers, Caernarfon and Wrexham; Beaulieu Motor Museum; Marlborough College; Eton College; Christ's College, Brecon; St Mary Abbots Church, Kensington; Napier Institute of Technology, Edinburgh; New Beacon School, Kent; Local History Societies at Brenchley and Matfield, Kent, and at Warminster; Convent of the Assumption, Kensington Square, London, and Hengrave Hall, Suffolk.

Many individuals have given me their help, for which I express my gratitude. In particular I would like to thank the following: The Earl of Oxford and Asquith; Miss Rosemary Olivier; Claire Blunden; Mother Margaret Mary; Sister Jessica Gatty; Sir Giles Loder; Dennis and Diana Silk; Lady Helen Asquith; Heather James; Ian Davie; Andrew Pinnell; Carol Rothkopf; Kenneth Lohf; The Hon. Mary Morrison; Sarah Morrison; Hugo Vickers; Philip Hoare; Maureen Borland; Mark Amory; Jocelyn Galsworthy; Celia Liddington; Jane Seabrook; Dr Harri Pritchard-Jones; Euryn Ogwen Williams; Keith Williams; Howard Jones; Menna Phillips; Rhys John; Penelope Middleboe; Jane Tremlett; Richard Frost; Kostas Georgiadis; Raymond Jenkins; Joe Sassoon; Dr Paul Newgass; Roger Lockyer; Rachel and Brian Griffiths; Charles Wheeler; Sir Alec Guinness; Christopher Thornycroft; William Hethrington; Lionel Dakers.

This biography would not have been possible without the experience and support of Metro Publishing and its staff. Paul Singer – my indomitable researcher, Margaret Body – my guide through the wilderness of syntax, punctuation and spelling, Richard Cohen – my publisher and editor and Christopher Sinclair-Stevenson – my agent, have been unfailing in their patience.

My family has asked me not to thank them!

INTRODUCTION

Unveiling a memorial stone to Walter de la Mare in 1961, Siegfried Sassoon told his listeners in the crypt of St Paul's Cathedral how 50 years earlier he had first encountered the de la Mare magic in the poem 'All That Is Past'. His letter of thanks and the author's reply marked the beginning of a lifetime's friendship. It was while I was working in a second-hand bookshop in an effort to supplement a meagre student grant that the Sassoon magic first came to me as I turned the pages in a second-hand copy of his *Collected Poems* and found the hauntingly beautiful poem 'Alone'. The delight was cumulative; the effect permanent.

Simplicity of style, a tale well told (this applies to his poetry as well as his prose), humour and pathos are among the reasons why after 40 years his work still captivates me. He was a master of English prose whose appeal lies, for me at least, in the apologia which prefaces all his work: 'I have been true to what I have experienced.' Deeply emotional, he suspected the dispassionate – for him the heart always led the head. This priority showed itself in his response to the continuation of the Great War, to the economic deprivation which blighted the lives of so many in the 1920s, and above all in his personal relationships. Late in life he confessed his belief in the religion of the heart but he had practised it from his earliest years. It was a creed which brought him disappointments and periods of great unhappiness which, had he inhabited 'the cold altitudes of the intellect', might well have been avoided or at any rate mitigated. Like many another he learned that the emotional life has disciplines as demanding as the intellectual.

Throughout his long life Sassoon never lost the naïveté which typified the work of three of his literary heroes, Henry Vaughan, William Blake and John Clare. Like theirs, his work generates hope and affirms that to be human is an extraordinary gift, even when life would persuade us to the contrary. Sassoon was especially suited to offer this consolation. Materially, he lived a privileged and sheltered life, but like many of his generation he 'learned the loss of hope' through the devastation of war and through personal and domestic anguish. Hope was regained but only after false aspirations had been exposed and after a long, tortuous inner struggle. His most fierce arguments were with himself:

> To know myself – this fragment of today
> To pluck the unconscious causes of unrest
> From self-deceiving nature.

This was a hard road but it led to the inner harmony and peace of his last decade. Sassoon took himself seriously, too seriously sometimes, yet no writer was quicker at catching himself out in a pose and impishly laughing at his pretensions and piousness. Considering his abhorrence of intrusion and public display, it is remarkable how he offers so much of himself to his reader – remarkable but also deceptive. Although always truthful, Sassoon was not always candid.

During the last 20 years much has been revealed about Sassoon, which he and others might have preferred to remain unsaid, in particular his homosexuality and unhappy marriage. Discretion is more palatable sometimes than openness. Faithfulness to his memory has included preserving unsullied the picture of him as the innocent boy in the Weald of Kent, the sporting youth, the fox-hunting man, the brave warrior, the conscientious protestor, the amiable host and friend. He was all those things but he is not diminished by the more complex picture of him which is now emerging.

Sassoon's reputation as a poet rests in the main on the poetry he wrote during the First World War – but that is a fraction of his output. To understand what happened to him after the war one must read the poetry of personal exploration published in the 1930s and 1950s. Without these, any attempt at understanding his life would be incomplete. 'My real biography is my poetry. All the sequence of my development is there.' Sassoon is not one of the great poets but he is a significant one. Obviously the war poems and his influence on other poets have secured his reputation but so too ought his last three volumes of poetry, which were combined to form the single volume *Sequences*. They are reflections on his personal pilgrimage yet encompass universal longings and aspirations. Written during the Second World War and the years when the shadow of the atom bomb lay heavily across the path of the world, they have a prophetic quality and a timeless-ness. The rediscovery of these poems will, I hope, be one of the fruits of this biography.

His prose work has fared better than his poetry. His six volumes of autobiography, which, for convenience, I call the Sherston Trilogy and the Siegfried Trilogy, are not explanations of major world events or ideologies but rather an exploration of an internal universe through the experience of the writer. Sassoon's alter ego, George Sherston, tells his readers: 'Remembering that I had a bath may not be of interest to anyone, but it was a good bath, and it is my own story that I am trying to tell, and as such it must be received; those who expect a universalization of the Great War must look for it elsewhere. Here they will only find an attempt to show its effect on a somewhat solitary-minded young man.' Sassoon's subject was always Sassoon.

The personal nature of his work caused its decline in critical, though not in popular esteem. Pasternak's chilling phrase in *Dr Zhivago*, 'the personal life is dead – history has killed it', could well be applied to the years when Sassoon was at his most productive as a writer. He feared for the individual life in an orgy of collectivism and relativism. In his final years he was concerned that the scientific age would create a world which had no room for what de la Mare called 'the imagination of the heart'. Another friend, E. M. Forster, was equally engaged in the battle against busybodies, agencies and philosophies which threatened individual freedom and artistic expression. It is a pity that Sassoon is often thought of as a purveyor of nostalgia – there was so much more to him and his work than that. It has been written that one could 'condemn the whole of the twentieth century out of the mouth of Sassoon'; a large claim. A lesser but more sustainable one is that this century is better understood by studying his life, his work and his searchings. He was suspicious of the word 'progress' – 'modernisation' was another – when used as a general description. With wry humour he stated that he liked the horse because it was impossible to modernise.

Sassoon was also a tireless diarist. With few lapses he chronicled his life between 1905 and 1956. Sir Rupert Hart-Davis, who has edited and published three volumes up to 1925, gave me access to the fine copies of the diaries housed in his collection at the Cambridge University Library. Sassoon is here in all his moods – prickly, generous, taciturn, gossipy, juvenile and avuncular. Every life is complicated, riven with inconsistencies, but Sassoon's unevenness, as these diaries reveal, was extraordinary. Turning their pages and lost in the narrative one can hear his bass-baritone voice as clearly as though listening to the 1956 BBC recording of him. Unlike his published prose, the style and use of language are at times convoluted, especially when attempting to analyse his behaviour and attitude towards others. There are dramatic moments too when, recording an incident, a description or a conversation, the narrative is terminated with an abrupt tearing of the page. Affairs of the heart frequently fall prey to this treatment but there still remain many declarations of sexual confusion and of fulfilment.

Sassoon's correspondence, unlike his diaries, is housed in disparate collections, private and public. However, the letters share with the diaries an intimate, conversational quality conveyed in small, firm handwriting, occasionally illustrated with cartoons, well-rehearsed puns and schoolboy limericks. To sit in the New York Public Library handling a letter written by Sassoon from the Western Front to his mentor, Edward Marsh, is for a moment to sense the desperation and exhilaration of that awful place.

I was privileged to have access to a private collection of Sassoon's letters written to Dame Felicitas Corrigan OSB between 1959 and 1967. Although composed in the last decade of his life, the contents reach back to his 'earliest rememberings' and move poignantly through the troubled years to 'the faith that blest his pilgrim path begun'. These letters are his retrospective on the journey and form the basis of Dame Felicitas' 1973 book, *Siegfried Sassoon: A Poet's Pilgrimage*.

Sassoon's range of friends and correspondents was wide and he was a copious letter-writer. On occasions a sense of *déjà vu* comes over the reader: Sassoon was given to much repetition between diaries, letters and his autobiographies. From the major collections one turns to meet him in the single letter addressed to an admirer or in response to an enquiry, some old soldier or a schoolboy or a class of schoolgirls studying one of his books each receiving a considered and appreciative reply, which sometimes ended with the invitation 'If ever you're this way do look me up.' Despite his protestations to the contrary, nobody enjoyed fan mail more than Sassoon.

To this wealth of written material must be added the reminiscences and anecdotes of those whose lives were touched by Sassoon. I am grateful to those who shared their memories of him, occasionally with reluctance but always with a sense of pride and happiness for having known 'good old Sig'. In particular I am indebted to Doms Philip Jebb, Sebastian Moore, Martin Salmon and Aelred Watkin of Downside – monks have a gift for anecdote! So too did Miss Muriel Galsworthy of Warminster, who was the epitome of Aunt Evelyn in the Sherston Trilogy and whose stories of Sassoon's eccentricities and foibles were garnered from the afternoons she spent with him at Heytesbury. It is a matter of deep regret to me that she did not live to see the completion of this biography to which she gave so much encouragement and insight.

During his address at the unveiling ceremony in St Paul's, Sassoon imagined being asked three questions about de la Mare: 'Did you know him? What sort of writer was he? What was he like?' The poetry, the prose, the letters and the personal recollections have opened the way for me to come to know the man. But we know in part and relate in part. This is a personal response but I hope not a stereotype. So often the only Sassoon people know is the fox hunting man or the soldier poet forever frozen in the days before and during the Great War. This is a portrait of the person who went on to live for 50 years after that brutal catastrophe. It is a story which has not been told before.

John Stuart Roberts

1

WEIRLEIGH

1886–95

Siegfried Loraine Sassoon was born on 8 September 1886 at Matfield in Kent. Although Sassoon was described in his lifetime as a 'quintessential Englishman', it is incongruous that not one of his names is of robust Anglo-Saxon origin. His mother was responsible for the choice of the forenames. She admired the operas of Wagner, hence Siegfried. The middle name was given to mark the esteem in which she held a certain Canon Loraine, who had prepared her for confirmation and thereafter gave her spiritual guidance. There is no evidence that Siegfried was unhappy with the choice. Of his surname he was less enamoured. 'Sassoon is the name I go by, a mere susurration in eternity – to oblivion with it!' For him, in his formative years especially, the name carried nuances far removed from the joy which it denotes in Hebrew. It was synonymous with broken relationships and ostracism. 'Ever since I could remember, I had been remotely aware of a lot of rich Sassoon relations. I had great-uncles galore, whom I had never met, and they all knew the Prince of Wales, who sometimes stayed with them at Brighton. Never having received so much as a chuck under the chin from any of these great-uncles, I couldn't exactly feel proud of them for being so affluent but I was, as a matter of course, impressed by the relationship, and often wondered what they looked like.' He need not have wondered. His father's face and a look in the mirror would have revealed the exotic physical characteristics he shared with his forebears.

In 1858 Sassoon David Sassoon, Siegfried's paternal grandfather and known as S.D., became the first of the family to set foot in England. The

Sassoons had set their feet in many other places. Sephardic Jews, they had wandered over the centuries from Palestine to Spain and Syria. The branch from which Siegfried descended flourished first in Baghdad then in the city of Bombay, from whence in pursuit of their commercial interests individual members travelled afield, in particular to Asia and China. S.D. was one of nine children from two marriages, he being the eldest of the second brood. The names of his brothers and sisters are a mixture of their Hebrew ancestry and the family's deep respect for the British Empire – Albert, formally Abdullah, and Arthur balancing Reuben and Aaron, and the girls matching Kate with Rebecca. The children were well educated, confident, clannish and sagacious. Within the business, cultural and religious life of the Jewish community in India during the nineteenth century the Sassoons flourished under the founder of the modern dynasty, David Sassoon. Despite becoming immensely wealthy and influential he remained a modest man and possessed a generous spirit. Wealth was regarded as a means to an end. Hospitals, libraries and synagogues received substantial endowments. But however great their wealth or their commercial and social success, nothing was achieved at the expense of their loyalty to the Jewish faith.

Having developed the business eastwards, David Sassoon looked for new opportunities in England, where the cotton trade in the north was expanding. Of his sons he believed that S.D. was the best suited to further the family interests. S.D. travelled alone and established an office in Leadenhall Street in the City of London. Within a matter of months he was joined by his wife, Fahra, their three-year-old son Joseph and a three-month-old daughter Rachel. Fahra anglicised her name to Flora but, though an admirer of her adopted country, she arranged the household to reflect the customs and beliefs of Judaism. They bought a house called Ashley Park near Walton-on-Thames, which had once been the residence of that indefatigable builder of vast properties, Cardinal Wolsey. S.D. was as inveterate a bibliophile as Wolsey was a builder. He mined material from his extensive library for inclusion in his essays on aspects of culture and his study of languages. Preoccupied with business and immersed in learning, he was left little time to enjoy the fresh air of Ashley Park and its green slopes leading down to the Thames. Flora was not interested in commerce, nor the social scene. Small, outspoken and of a quixotic temperament, she found her main pleasure in her children and in music. In 1861 a third child and second son was born and given the names of Alfred Ezra. He would become Siegfried's father.

S.D. did not enjoy robust health. He was tall and thin, giving the impression of frailty. His father did not expect the demands of the London office to be onerous and, given his son's interest in Western culture, thought it an ideal location for his health and fulfilment. So it might have been, had not circumstances intervened. The Civil War in America and the blockade of the southern ports denied supplies of cotton to the factories in the north of England. All eyes turned to India and the East. Suddenly the Leadenhall Street office became pivotal and made demands on S.D. which he found difficult to meet. In the oppressively hot summer of 1867, as he waited to meet a business acquaintance in the foyer of the Old Langham Hotel, Sassoon David suffered a fatal heart attack. He was 35.

Reuben Sassoon was sent from Bombay to continue his late brother's work. Over the next decade he was followed by his other brothers. Each would achieve commercial success, social notoriety and royal favour. The Prince of Wales was not prejudiced against Jews, nor against those who had amassed fortunes through trade. His attitude was not entirely altruistic; he needed the Sassoons and others to underwrite his ceaseless demands for social distraction. House parties, horse racing, gambling and gargantuan dinner-parties required a constant flow of money. The Sassoons were more than able to meet the demand. Each son inherited £500,000 on the death of David Sassoon, to which were added the profits of the trading company. They bought houses in London and on the south coast of England, which were put at the disposal of the Prince and his social circle. They were given royal honours, including knighthoods; they were admired, no doubt they were envied, certainly they scaled the social heights of Edwardian England, but to Siegfried they were the great-uncles who never so much as gave him a 'chuck under the chin'.

Throughout his life Siegfried made few references to his Jewish ancestry and even fewer acknowledgements of his indebtedness to it. Indeed it was only in his last years and in response to a questioning friend that he recognised how his paternal side had given him religious, poetic and prophetic insights. 'You are right about my inheritance. I sometimes surmise that my eastern ancestry is stronger in me than the Thornycrofts. The daemon in me is Jewish.' The Thornycrofts knew the Sassoons of Ashley Park but neither family on first acquaintance could have guessed how their destinies would intertwine to produce a poet, a prose-writer and a quintessential Englishman.

Thomas and Mary Thornycroft were Siegfried's maternal grandparents. Both were descendants of English yeomanry – Thomas's roots lay deep in

Cheshire and Mary's in Norfolk. They were sculptors and met while studying and practising under the auspices of Mary's father, John Francis, who had moved from East Anglia to London. Mary, born in 1809, was nearing her thirtieth year when Thomas arrived at the Francis home near Regent's Park. He was seven years younger than Mary but this made no difference to the almost instant attraction they felt for each other. In 1840 they were married and ventured to Rome to pursue their studies before returning to England and establishing a home and studio first in Stanhope Street, then at Wilton Place in Knightsbridge. Sculpture was not an easy living but the Prince Consort was an enthusiastic patron, as was the Queen. Public commemoration and private decoration brought expanding opportunities from which Thomas and Mary benefited. The register of the Royal Collection contains an impressive list of the Thornycrofts' contribution. Osborne House, the private retreat of the Queen and Prince Albert on the Isle of Wight, contained numerous examples of Mary's work, many still there today. The greater part of Thomas's work was commissioned by public corporations to fill city squares and town halls with illustrious city fathers in effigy.

Between 1841 and 1853 seven children were born: two sons and five daughters, of whom Georgiana Theresa, the future mother of Siegfried, was the youngest. Contemporary accounts describe her as petite, with red hair and a shy smile. Although the last of the brood, she was not over-shadowed by her siblings. From an early age she showed an independent spirit and a witty turn of phrase. She was particularly close to her brother Hamo and remained so. All the children inherited the creative genes of their parents as painters and sculptors. Reading the list of admissions to the life classes at the Royal Academy one sees the names of Mary Alice, student May 1863; Helen, student January 1868; William (Hamo), student June 1869; then Theresa, June 1870. Thomas and Mary were enlightened parents. Hamo's daughter, Elfrida Manning, wrote that the 'girls would never have thought of themselves as advanced, yet they did everything that their modern successors, liberated by the bicycle, did in the next generation. They rowed, swam and when invasion threatened in 1871, learned musketry drill from their brother.' In writing of his mother, Siegfried expressed admiration for her as a daring diver into the swimming pool at the local baths, accompanied by her friend Nellie Epps, the future Mrs Edmund Gosse.

In a home where good conversation was encouraged, Theresa and her sisters developed strong opinions, which were expressed with crisp assurance and a hint of dogmatism. They were influenced by two movements – the Pre-Raphaelites and High Anglicanism. Theresa was never a radical in politics or in anything else and resisted her brother Hamo's attempts to persuade her to embrace the Socialist ideas of William Morris. The precepts and observances of the Christian religion were central to her view of life and in that orbit everything else moved and was judged. Decorum was a favourite and often-used word, reflecting her belief in an ordered and structured society. A household of artists the Thornycrofts most certainly were, but there was nothing Bohemian about them. Siegfried described their social attitude as the 'Thornycroft mentality' and on more than one occasion declared it to be their greatest gift to him.

To accommodate the artistic needs of the family, Thomas decided to leave Wilton Place and build a larger house with studios in Melbury Road, Holland Park, an area running north from Kensington. It was still open country and the homes of two renowned artists, Frederic Leighton and G. F. Watts, were situated there. In honour of his Cheshire forebears he named the new residence Moreton House. Thomas was by this time more engaged in engineering than sculpture and his eldest son John showed a similar inclination. Together they established a marine engineering works at Chiswick, to which John Donaldson came as manager. He married Frances, the third Thornycroft daughter, who became the mother of 10 children known as the 'little Dons' – Siegfried's happy cousins and over-active holiday companions. Mary Thornycroft, solid and matriarchal, was never happy unless she held a piece of clay in her hands. 'Stick with the clay,' she told her son Hamo. She never tired of encouraging her daughters to visit and to participate in exhibitions, especially at the Royal Academy. She was also in demand by rich patrons who desired sculpted representations of themselves and their loved ones. It was her reputation in this field which caused the initial acquaintance with the Sassoons, when in 1863 she was invited to Ashley Park to sculpt S.D. and Flora.

Following the death of her husband, Flora's life revolved around the rearing of the children. Her brothers-in-law offered assistance; Reuben was particularly solicitous, but each knew that Flora would brook no interference. She believed herself to be, and indeed was, more than capable of meeting the demands of widowhood. Supported by family wealth, strength of character and her entrenched cultural and religious convictions, she determined that the future would be propitious for her children, especially her favourite son, Alfred Ezra. He was full of charm, showing an early liking for music, particularly the violin. Flora was more than pleased and believed him to be a future concert artist. Never one to doubt her own judgement, she bought her prodigy not one Stradivarius but two. He was also fond of books, though not of reading them to any purpose. Alfred was not a robust child but, like his sister Rachel, he was a determined one. Flora did not encourage her sons to enter commerce. As far as Alfred was concerned this was a wise decision since he lacked the application required for success. This lack was not confined to commerce. Flora worried when her son began to exhibit signs of the dilettante rather than the purposeful student. He had passions for horses and cricket; he loved dancing and party-going. With his good manners and Sassoon winning ways he was attractive to women and attracted by them. Life for Alfred was to be measured in miles rather than fathoms.

Exeter College, Oxford, was a diversion for a few terms but proved too restrictive. The Continent beckoned; indulged by his mother he responded but went no further than Paris, where he tasted the delights of café society, the theatre, the boudoir and, if her autobiography is to be believed, an expensive dalliance with the actress Sarah Bernhardt. No doubt the gilded name Sassoon and its connections provided the entrée. This frenetic and undirected style of life continued when he returned to London but Flora's delight in her son was undiminished, as it was in her daughter. Rachel was of small build and a delicate complexion. In 1882 her mother commissioned Hamo Thornycroft to sculpt a figurine of Rachel. Hamo's fiancée, Agatha Cox, noted that the sitter was 'graceful, but not a pleasing face'. The remark has the undertone of fear that Hamo might be beguiled. At Melbury Road, Rachel met and liked Theresa: a friendship developed. It is possible that Alfred accompanied his sister to Hamo's studio and first saw Theresa there, but they did meet in Ashley Park, where Theresa was invited on several occasions by Rachel and welcomed by Flora, who did not suspect that the gaiety and boisterous laughter, always a mark of her son's presence in the house, was a prelude to bitterness.

Alfred became interested in modern art and sculpture in particular. The roll of entry for the life classes at the Royal Academy for the autumn of 1883 includes the following: 'Alfred Sassoon. Age 22. Walton-on-Thames. Recommended by H. Thornycroft.' Art and ardour were potent in the wooing of Theresa. She was eight years older than Alfred but this proved no impediment to the growth of their desire for each other. Impediments came, as might have been expected, from Flora. When Alfred's intention to marry Theresa was made known to her, this redoubtable woman was aghast. Despite being warned that his relationship to the Sassoons would be endangered if he persisted, Alfred was unmoved. It was now time for threats of disinheritance and the cessation of his allowance under his father's will. But Alfred was astute enough to check the terms at Somerset House. The money lay outside Flora's jurisdiction. A secret engagement was entered into in November and with the help of Hamo and Canon Loraine, a special marriage licence was issued. Theresa and Alfred were married at the Church of St Mary Abbots in Kensington on 30 January 1884. Hamo and Edmund Gosse stood witness. No parents or family were present.

The Thornycrofts were overjoyed when the news was revealed to them. Hamo had feared that his parents would have tried to prevent the marriage if told beforehand. Moreton House was in festive mood – not so Ashley Park. Flora called down a curse on the marriage and upon any issue proceeding from it. She forbade her other children to communicate with their brother: he had chosen a gentile for a wife and must suffer for his treachery.

In *The Times* on 23 April 1884, an advertisement appeared for the sale of a residence known as Weirleigh, Brenchley, Kent. Theresa and Alfred had decided that they would live in the country but within convenient reach of London. Alfred boarded the train at Charing Cross for Paddock Wood, from where he made a short journey and gained his first view of the house above whose door was emblazoned in Latin: *Vero nihil verius – Nothing is truer than truth*. Built in the 1860s, Weirleigh stands at the point where the road from the village of Matfield takes a sharp incline to Paddock Wood and the railway station. This strange pile of Victorian architecture had previously been the home of the nature artist and cat lover Harrison Weir. He had an obsession for adding to the house, with the result that it lacks symmetry. Theresa was critical of Harrison Weir's architectural ideas, which she constantly attacked as wasting so much space. Nonetheless the house enveloped her and for the next 60 years was the centre of her life. Of Weirleigh and its garden the adult Siegfried wrote, 'it is the background to all my dreams both pleasant and unpleasant.' Wandering through the rooms for the first time is like revisiting familiar surroundings, so accurate and vibrant are Siegfried's descriptions of them. This is especially true of the square, light-oak staircase, which rises past the room where he and his brothers were born. As one stands at the top and looks down the well, the spirit of place which he evokes in *The Old Century* and in his poetry, is almost palpable:

> Down the glimmering staircase, past the pensive clock,
> Childhood creeps on tiptoe, fumbles at the lock.
> Out of night escaping, toward the arch of dawn,
> What can childhood look for, over the wet lawn?

The documentary quality of his prose and poetry captures the essence of Weirleigh – the house, the garden and the distant prospect of the countryside: 'Looked at from our lawn, the Weald was, in my opinion, as good a view as anyone could wish to live with. You could run your eyes along more than twenty miles of low-hilled horizon never more than ten or twenty miles away. The farthest distance had the advantage of being near enough for its details to be, as it were, within recognisable reach. There was, for instance, a small party of pine trees on the skyline toward Maidstone which seemed to be keeping watch on the world beyond – a landmark on the limit of my experience they always seemed, those sentinel pines.'

At Weirleigh, Theresa created a typical upper-middle-class country home of the nineteenth century: Anglican, sociable, self-confident and organised. The staff, augmented by occasional help, comprised cook, scullery maid, parlour maid, nursery maid, gardener, groom and stable-lad. The grounds lay to one side and in front of the house. An upper, lower and bottom lawn were each separated by briar and clematis hedges; there was a peony walk, an herbaceous walk, a lawn tennis court, with an orchard to its right and, beyond, a kitchen garden fenced in by apple trees and gooseberry bushes. The perimeter of the garden was lined with rhododendrons, conifers and pine trees. Alfred and Theresa made few alterations. They did, however, extensively refurbish the stables and renovate Harrison Weir's studio near the house, which afforded space on the top floor for Alfred to set out his library and gave him solitude to play his violin, attempt some sculpture and paint landscapes of the Weald visible from the window. Theresa worked on the ground floor, filling her canvases with angels and seraphim, religious symbols and epiphanies of the spiritual world.

The Sassoons quickly established contact with the local gentry. Squire Marchant and his children, in particular his daughters May and Bessie; Major Horrocks and his sister Clara; Captain Ruxton, a gentleman farmer who was always ready to 'roll-up his sleeves at harvest time'. Theresa would order the trap and Richardson the groom would drive her hither and thither as she visited those who were within calling distance. Relatives and friends from further afield took the train and alighted at Paddock Wood to enjoy a day or even longer. The cavalcade of characters who worked at Weirleigh, or lived in the Weald, as well as those who came to visit, are immortalised in Sassoon's memoir of childhood, *The Old Century*, and also in his *Memoirs of a Fox-Hunting Man*. Theresa was an accomplished horse-woman and enjoyed a day's hunting. She was a country person who relished the rural life, much as her forebears had done in Cheshire and Norfolk. Alfred was not by nature or breeding a countryman. At Matfield he helped the local cricket team and added substantially to its batting strength. He was also a fine host and a somewhat frustrated entertainer, particularly in music and song. Theresa and he enjoyed the house being full of guests; but the dilettante in him was restless and the train from Paddock Wood to London became an increasingly regular means of escape.

Their three sons arrived in quick succession. Michael was born within the first year of the marriage, Siegfried in 1886 and the youngest, Hamo, in 1888. A nursemaid was employed, after the fashion of the day, a Mrs Mitchell from nearby Tunbridge Wells. The arrival of a nursemaid in many households meant that parents spent little time with their children. Not so Theresa and Alfred. They were attentive, even doting. The outward bliss, however, belied a growing tension. They were no longer in love. Alfred's excursions to London became more frequent. It gradually emerged that he was involved in an affair with the American authoress Julia Constance Fletcher. Writing under the name of George Fleming, she achieved her greatest success with *Kismet, a Nile novel*. In 1889, after five years of marriage, Alfred left Weirleigh to be with his lover in Kensington, in a house within a stone's throw of the church in which he had married. Theresa and Alfred never spoke to each other again.

Theresa faced the separation in a manner entirely consistent with her straightforward and practical approach to life. Her family helped, of course, being solicitous in both their visits and letters. Hamo, the brother closest to her, rounded on the faithless Alfred with unsavoury racist observations. At this time he was busy building his reputation as a sculptor. Recognition came quickly and his work eventually occupied central sites in London; Cromwell outside the Houses of Parliament, General Gordon on the Embankment and Gladstone in the Strand. One of his works, 'The Sower', exhibited at the Royal Academy in 1886, caught the eye of Gerard Manley Hopkins: 'I saw the Academy. There was one thing, not a picture, which I much preferred to everything else there – Hamo Thornycroft's statue of the Sower. A truly noble work and to me a new light.' John Thornycroft, the elder brother, was busy too, working with his brother-in-law, John Donaldson, in the marine engineering works at Chiswick, where according to Sassoon, 'Uncle John designed the boats and Uncle Don did everything else.' Hamo and his brother prospered and were knighted for their work. Their father, John Thornycroft, saw only the beginnings of their success. He died in the year of Siegfried's birth and four years before the break-up of his youngest daughter's marriage. His last sculpture, a vigorous representation of Boadicea and her daughters, was without a permanent situation in London at his death. In her last years Mary set herself the task of securing it a worthy and prominent position. Eventually it was erected at the Whitehall end of Westminster Bridge, directed threateningly towards the Houses of Parliament.

Theresa and the three boys were always of close concern to all the Thornycrofts and also to one other relative who, in the affections of Michael, Siegfried, Hamo and Theresa, stood almost supreme – Rachel Sassoon, Alfred's only sister. She had defied her mother's command to ostracise her brother. At first her defiance was furtive but then quite open. Flora, having registered her strong disapproval, did not proceed to make it a cause for estrangement. However, three years after her brother's apostasy Rachel, too, married out. Frederick Beer was a person of consequence, immensely wealthy and the owner of the *Observer* newspaper. He married Rachel in 1887 and as a wedding gift bought the *Sunday Times* for her. Ostensibly she became Editor of both papers. It is to be doubted that her lifestyle would have made possible any intense involvement. She took a particular interest in new publications, as her nephew, the young Siegfried, deduced from all the review copies which lay in piles around the house. Her qualities were many, notably defiance in the face of bigotry which fuelled her revolt against her mother and support for Alfred. She also campaigned for another Alfred – Dreyfus, her voice and that of her papers being among the first to detect and expose the anti-Semitism that sought to destroy an innocent man and would have done so, but for the voices of conscience and justice.

The Beers lived in grandeur at Chesterfield Gardens, Mayfair. Siegfried recalls visiting in the late nineties, having been met at Charing Cross Station by the brougham, complete with groom and coachman. Auntie Rachel showered the boys with gifts and treats. Frederick Beer is recalled by Siegfried as a shadowy figure meandering through the vast rooms, cigar in hand. On subsequent visits he vanished to an upstairs room and Siegfried never saw him again. Mr Beer was suffering from inherited syphilis about which his wife knew nothing. In fact she refused to believe he was ill in any way and went on arranging the house and domestic affairs as though her husband would at any moment walk down the marble stairs, cigar in hand, ready for whatever duty or pleasure life had in store for him. Auntie Rachel is portrayed in *The Old Century* as a wistful creature of contrasts and contradictions, symbolised by the beautiful diamond rings she wore on a grimy hand; a warm, affectionate aunt who yet offered her nephew a cold ivory cheek and smiled as though it were an afterthought. Through small explanations from Theresa and his innate ability to reach below the surface of things, Siegfried recognised the sadness in his aunt's life: the loss of the object of her love. If only, he mused, it could all be put right again; if only Auntie Rachel and Mr Beer could wake up and find that the threatening forces, now so destructive of their happiness, were but a dream and everything was as it had been.

If only the past could be undone – how he wished that for Weirleigh, too. Auntie Rachel used to visit them there. She was a shrewd judge of character and recognised in Theresa an unerring integrity and wisdom. Above all, she admired Theresa's discretion about the behaviour of Alfred. The anger, disappointment and sense of betrayal Theresa must have felt remained unspoken, especially at Weirleigh. Whether one can hide such feelings from every child is a matter of conjecture; what is beyond dispute is the heart-rending impact it had on Siegfried.

Alfred returned regularly to Weirleigh to see his sons. Before he arrived Theresa would lock herself away in her room. From the nursery window high up in the house the boys would watch for the village fly to arrive at the main gate and roll into the driveway. Laden, as Sassoon recalls, 'with guava jelly, pomegranates and funny toys which didn't need too much taking care of', Alfred would hurry to the nursery and spread his gifts before the boisterous trio. He knew how to entertain them with games on the nursery floor and out on the spacious lawns. The bond, already strong, was strengthened by each succeeding visit and deepened the desire for permanency. The depth of longing for all to be well again was recounted by Sassoon 50 years later with such artless intensity it is as though he had newly experienced it: 'One autumn afternoon we were out in the garden and he was giving us a ride in the gardener's handcart. We were all shouting and thoroughly enjoying ourselves when we came round the corner of some rhododendrons and met my mother. There she stood and we all went past her in sudden silence. I have never forgotten the look on her face. It was the first time I had seen life being brutal to someone I loved. But I was helpless, for my father's face had gone blank and obstinate, and the situation, like the handcart, was in his hands. All I could do was to feel miserable about it afterwards and wonder why they couldn't make it up somehow. For I wanted to enjoy my parents simultaneously – not alternately.' So much of the later Sassoon is revealed through that experience. The young, sensitive Siegfried adapted to circumstances but his 'memoried mind' retained the imprint.

Mrs Mitchell, the nursemaid, was an unsympathetic character, unable to enter into the world of the child. Discipline took precedence over affection and rules prevailed over imagination. Nonetheless she assumed an importance in Siegfried's young world, being the link between him and his absent father. Mrs Mitchell's allegiance was unreservedly given to Alfred. She was aware of a provision made for her in his will, but the legacy of £100 a year was dependent upon her remaining with the children until they attained an age when her services would no longer be required. Her relationship with Theresa was anything but cordial. However, the prospect of the annuity made her resolute.

What Siegfried did not know was the likelihood of Alfred dying a relatively young man. He had developed tuberculosis and was advised to leave London and move to Eastbourne. In 1893 he took rooms on the south coast in the hope of arresting any further physical decline. Keen as ever to see his children, he made arrangements for Mrs Mitchell to bring them there. The first visit was a happy one when the father and the three boys were photographed together. They are not stilted and formal as most Victorians look in photographs but portray a sense of closeness and affection. Obvious, too, is the shared Sassoon likeness, in particular the striking resemblance Siegfried bore to his father with his deep-set eyes and cleft chin.

Alfred's decline into acute tuberculosis was inexorable and by the end of the year he was confined to his bed. It is not known who told the boys of their father's condition and the reason for the terrible cough; probably it was Mrs Mitchell. How sensitively she did so can only be guessed at, but the picture Sassoon painted of her in his memoirs leaves room to doubt her capacity for gentle reassurance. Siegfried prayed for his father's recovery as fervently as he had desired the reuniting of his parents. Mrs Mitchell took Michael, Siegfried and Hamo for another visit to Eastbourne. It was to be memorable for more than one reason. Entering the room they saw, standing at the window, pensive and silent, a man who was introduced as their Uncle Joseph – Alfred's elder brother. Also in the room was the redoubtable and until that moment unseen Flora Sassoon, their grandmother. Although she greeted them with a smile, this small, brown-faced old lady created an atmosphere of menace for the seven-year-old Siegfried.

The portraits in *The Old Century* are kindly drawn; Grandmama

Sassoon and Mrs Mitchell are among the exceptions. Both had caused unhappiness to Theresa. Siegfried was not only the most sensitive of the three sons but also the most fervently protective of his mother. It is unlikely that he understood the complexities of the situation but children are instinctive in their loyalties. In the garden at Weirleigh he saw for the first time life being brutal to someone he loved and would never forget it.

In his father's sickroom, Grandmama Sassoon unrolled a chart upon which was described the Sassoon family tree. It was with an air of bemusement that Siegfried followed her finger down the succeeding generations to the place where his own name and those of his brothers were inscribed:

And it comes back to me, that sense of being among strangers, with Pappy being killed by that terrible cough, and the queer feeling that although this new grandmama was making such a fuss of us, it would make no difference if we never saw her again. I can see myself gazing at the Family Tree and wondering what all those other Sassoons were like, and how my great-grandfather had managed to produce so many of them. And I remember my miserable feeling that the only thing that mattered was that my mother ought to be there, and that these people were unfriendly to her who loved my father as they had never done and would have come to him with unquestioning forgiveness. Even Mrs Mitchell was against her; for I knew, with a child's intuition, how she had helped to keep them apart.

Such experiences explain why Sassoon preferred to think of himself as a Thornycroft. It was the last time he met his Uncle Joseph, the last time he met his Grandmama Sassoon and the last time he saw his father.

The Thornycrofts were fun to be with and so too were the Donaldsons, the family of Theresa's sister, Frances. The family bonds grew even stronger when Grandmama Thornycroft came to live at Weirleigh. Sassoon's description of this elderly lady is tender and admiring. Her black dress with white edges, her soft voice, stately walk, her serenity as she sat by the french windows and watched the seasons change in that year of 1894 are reminiscent of the later portraits of Queen Victoria. Age, too, can bestow an ethereal quality that summons up the past. This was an aspect of his grandmother which attracted Siegfried. He writes of watching her and seeing her transformed in his imagination into a beautiful young woman. One afternoon he watched her as she promenaded in the drawing room arm-in-arm with her son John. How grown-up, how dignified, how different in his young mind to the rent relationship between Pappy and Grandmama Sassoon: 'I bless the Thornycroft sanity which I inherited from my mother.'

And not only their sanity, but also their creative imagination: Sassoon liked to create worlds of his own to which he could slip away, unnoticed and undisturbed. These were not worlds he could share with his brothers. If, as he has said, 'My artistic side is derived from the Thornycrofts', then Michael and Hamo could claim that they had inherited the Thornycroft delight in making things, repairing things, designing things. Siegfried did wonder why he was so impractical. His brothers' interest in things mechanical isolated him. 'We were as different as chalk and cheese,' was how Michael described their relationship. Siegfried was fanciful and introspective: 'I was in an undisturbed world of my own, localised and satisfactory as such worlds always are.'

In the hard winter of 1895 Mary Thornycroft died. Siegfried went to see her in her coffin, surrounded by white lilies. His mother had told him that during her last weeks Grandmama had wandered into her past, where she had been happy with her husband and children in a kind of never-ending summer. Siegfried found this deeply consoling. The past should always be like that. The sad, the unattractive have no place in that kingdom. The past, however, cannot be so easily sanitised, as a much older Sassoon would realise – though even in 1938, writing *The Old Century*, he still clung to selectivity: 'I prefer to remember my own gladness and good luck, and to forget, whenever I can, those moods and minor events which made me low-spirited and unresponsive. Be grateful, therefore, and share my gratitude that I lived in such a pleasant region. For in those days I found no fault with the world, and did not foresee that it would, in my lifetime, alter much.'

Deprivations are, however, recorded and Sassoon is prepared to share the pains of childhood. In April 1895 Alfred Sassoon died: 'I thought I would never stop crying,' wrote his son. Siegfried's unrelieved grief may have been the reason why, unlike his brothers, he was not allowed to attend the funeral, or perhaps Theresa wanted him with her at Weirleigh. The wisdom of the decision is to be questioned on the grounds that it left Siegfried with a sense of incompleteness. His bewilderment was not helped by the reports of the funeral given by Michael and Hamo. Alfred was buried in the Jewish Cemetery in the East End of London. The whole affair had frightened the brothers by its strangeness, the Hebrew tongue and their lack of familiarity with Jewish ceremonies. They conveyed their fright to Siegfried with, no doubt, an inevitable measure of exaggeration.

Siegfried felt his father had been spirited away by strangers; buried in an unknown tongue, in a remote graveyard. Something else fed his grief – he would now never enjoy his parents simultaneously.

Within weeks of the funeral Mrs Mitchell left Weirleigh with her annuity. There were mixed feelings about her departure, regret mingled with relief. Despite her unpleasantness she belonged to the familiar world of Siegfried's first awakenings; the world of Weirleigh, when Pappy was still there and, afterwards, the link between him and his sons. As she went from Siegfried's bedroom for the last time, descending the glimmering staircase and past the pensive clock, he was aware that his daybreak world was changing. There remained one constant – Mamsy. 'Time teaches one to admire such people who refuse to pull a long face however deeply life may hurt them, and whose cheerfulness is born of courage as well as being the outcome of their abundant liveliness.'

2

TEACHERS

1895–1907

On the evening of Mrs Mitchell's departure, Siegfried developed pneumonia. Whether external events and inner tensions combined to bring on what, in those days, was often a fatal condition can only be surmised. He became delirious and his temperature reached 105°. The illness, and his long period of convalescence and of solitude marked a profound deepening of his awareness of aspects within and around him. Felicitas Corrigan writes of Sassoon that he 'belonged to that band of men and women to be found in every race, country and religion, who may be characterized as *homines religiosi*. They seem to be gifted by nature with a sense of the numinous, as lesser folk are with an ear for music or an eye for form.'

During the months of April to July 1895 he experienced a secret world carried to him by the familiar sounds of Weirleigh and the distant Weald of Kent. He had already discovered the solitary pleasure of fishing in the orchard pond and the enchantments of nearby Gedges Wood. Now intimations of his future vocation as a poet also came to him and the endless possibilities inherent in the word 'mystery'.

Throughout his illness he was nursed by Ellen Batty, a friend of Theresa. She had come to Weirleigh some time before the departure of Mrs Mitchell to help with the boys' education. Ellen represented a world full of hope and kindness in contrast to the harsh and suspicious world of Mrs Mitchell. Being the servant of hope and of endless possibilities, she opened up options rather than closed them down. She was also a born teacher, perhaps laying greater stress on exuberance than accuracy, but she knew how to enthuse, how to make knowledge accessible, how to bring alive the past in a way that was congenial to Siegfried. He confessed that he did not much like abstract thought, preferring to receive facts one by one, and each fact had to ignite his visual imagination.

He was also enjoying his life as an invalid and being the centre of attention. Fussed over by the family and the entire household, sleeping in the best bedroom, Siegfried was content. With the arrival of warmer weather he was carried downstairs to the garden, where Theresa had a tent erected. 'To be out of doors again at that time of year was indeed like coming back to life.' Alone all day he strained his ear to catch the gruff voices of the gardeners, the rumble of the wheelbarrow, the scythe being sharpened and the horses snorting at the front gate. Jays were squawking and pigeons cooing, and down in the valley the sound of the train on its way from Kent to unfamiliar worlds.

There was another sound which more than any other touched the depths of his being: 'In a crab-apple tree close to my tent there hung a small Aeolian harp that lent to the light summer breezes a local euphony which swelled and faded to a melodious murmur. The sound was like poetry; for even then poetry could just stir my mind – as though some living and yet mysterious spirit – touching me to a blurred and uncontrolled chord of ecstasy.' The experience of independence and security which the tent gave him was something he would seek throughout his life. A place apart, where he endorsed the belief of William Hazlitt, 'Never less alone than when alone.'

Prominent also was a preoccupation with time and the spectre of death. He was puzzled by them rather than frightened, a puzzle which grew out of the need to know who he was. What was his relationship to the world which existed before he was born and those events he was too young to remember? Here is the seed-corn from which grew the major themes of his poetry and prose: 'Can it be so far away – Yesterday, Yesterday?' In the early years of his marriage, Alfred Sassoon had given Theresa a bottle of perfume. Siegfried borrowed the now-empty bottle from his mother and sniffed the residual fragrance: 'I unconsciously made it a symbol of the time when they had been happy together.' The phial offered more: 'I supposed it to have come from Persia, where my ancestors had lived, so it seemed a sort of essence of my father's oriental extraction.' Was this a sign of deep bereavement, an attempt to reclaim a lost loved one and to erase the sadness of a broken relationship? The depth of his anxiety and grief over the death of his father and of the estrangement between his parents cannot be overestimated but it is equally valid to recognise here that Siegfried desired to 'remember and be glad'.

From the material of the past, Siegfried began creating his own version of Once-upon-a-time. In the best bedroom, where he had lain throughout his illness, there was an oblong photo frame which contained 10 photographs of relations and friends. These were visual records of times before Siegfried was born. The group projected, he said, 'a sort of happy past feeling'. They were all friends of Theresa and she had recounted to him days spent with them before her marriage. One of them was Helen Wirgman, known affectionately as Wirgie, who still came to Weirleigh for visits. Siegfried was fascinated by her, mainly because she belonged to the happy past but also because she shared the world of the young without making that world seem in any way trivial. An accomplished linguist, musician and traveller, she used anecdote, metaphor and the natural world around Weirleigh to open Siegfried's mind. 'I can see her sitting there in the schoolroom, telling me about Europe and making me imagine some of it quite clearly against the background of its mysterious immensity.' For Siegfried, Helen Wirgman and the mysterious were synonymous. He was, and always would be, attracted to such people, of whom Grandmama Thornycroft and Auntie Rachel were earlier examples.

For the first 11 years of his life, Siegfried lived in an environment that was predominantly adult and female. Although his relationship with his brothers was close, they remained divided by temperament. Michael and Hamo were extroverts, Siegfried an introvert. In *The Old Century*, the brothers are not as central as the many friends of Theresa, nor as prominent as the many neighbours who called to see her. In *Memoirs of a Fox-Hunting Man*, the brothers disappear and Siegfried dwells alone in a world dominated by older people. 'My childhood was not altogether a happy one. This must have been caused by the absence of companions of my own age.' Although he writes this as a complaint, as a deprivation, the fact is that by inclination Siegfried did not need companions of his own age because they did not belong to the secret world he relished as a child. It was the adult world that he desired, whose inhabitants fed and satisfied his deep desire for mystery, as personified by Wirgie. They possessed the ability to cast a spell – something which was always broken when his brothers 'came clattering down the corridor'. Neither were the brothers sympathetic to Siegfried's cherished belief in himself as a poet. They showed little appreciation of his juvenile attempts at poetic expression.

Siegfried was attracted to music from a very early age. Throughout his life he enjoyed playing the piano, going to concerts and listening to broadcast performances. Music affected him at several levels. Listening to Wirgie playing the Beethoven Sonatas, he sensed that she was not only interpreting Beethoven but imbuing them with autobiography, giving expression to her deep and complex personality. Seeking as he was an effective means to articulate his own complexities, the attraction of music was obvious. Its sounds allowed the imagination to roam freely; it created pictures in the mind. Music was a portent of the numinous; it summoned and fed the 'mystery' leading on to harmonies not caught by the natural ear. The middle-aged Sassoon could well have been describing the 10-year-old boy when he wrote:

> I think I'm fond of being alone
> With music and my past.

By the summer of 1896 Siegfried nursed the idea that he was born to be a poet. There had been some preconditioning of his mind by Ellen Batty, who had read in his palm undeniable signs of a poet in embryo. Theresa, too, was influential. In June 1925, Sassoon wrote, 'I have a copy of Coleridge's *Lectures on Shakespeare* inscribed by her to me on my third birthday. Very odd, as she was such a practical person, not the least high falutin. Whatever made her do it?' In posing the question Sassoon is being disingenuous. In *The Old Century* he supplies the reason: 'My mother had a strong maternal feeling that I was destined to be a great poet.' The late Victorian age was full of such tender, affectionate, sometimes destructive mother-son relationships. In the case of Siegfried there can be little doubt that it was Theresa's perspicacity that recognised early her son's talent for verse, often saying to him: 'Sig, go and write your poetry.' Theresa's influence was all-pervasive in these years. She encouraged him to read poetry, as well as compose it. His favourite poems were those of Shelley and Tennyson. The former offered memorable lines; the latter, particularly in 'The Lady of Shalott', a complete and entrancing narrative. Above all, both provided atmosphere and mystery in abundance. The meaning of a poem was always subservient to its capacity to enthral, all the better if the enthraldom was heavy with melancholy. He wrote in *The Old Century*, 'I have a tendency to expect all great poetry to be gloomy, at any rate serious.'

If there was a painter born to feed this passion for the darker side of life it was an old family friend, a neighbour at Melbury Road and godfather to young Hamo, G. F. Watts, or 'dear old Watts' as he was known to Theresa. Weirleigh housed copies of his paintings and a self-portrait hung on the stairs. Siegfried was thus familiar with his work when Theresa took him to view an exhibition of Watts' work in London. He stood, a dreamy and impressionable boy, 'gazing ecstatically at "The Court of Death" and "Time, Death and Judgement"'. He gazed at them, considered them and then went home to 'try and write poems about them'. The poems he wrote were collected into two small books and presented to Theresa as a gift of love, the first on her birthday in March 1897 and the second at Christmas the same year. The thought must have cheered her; whether the content did is questionable. 'Eternity and the Tomb were among my favourite themes and from the accessories of death, I drew my liveliest inspirations.'

There lay the lake of sleep: eternal sleep
That looked so still.
And far beyond, the palace of King Death
Who hidden lay:

And he spake thus: 'I hold the lives of men
From the beginning to the end.'
And, yea, behind him, angels stood
Guarding the things unknown, beyond the Tomb.

Edmund Blunden described such attempts as 'little sanctified verses' suffused as they all were by religious allusion and imagery. Theresa's commitment to the Anglican tradition – the Bible, the Book of Common Prayer and the Psalms – gave Siegfried a rich vocabulary rooted in religion and a mind preoccupied by death and judgement. The deaths two years earlier of his Thornycroft grandmother and his father also contributed to the preoccupation. Not all the contents of those 1897 volumes lacked humour, though. There is a short narrative piece entitled 'Something About Myself', in which, posing as a kitten, he tells a short family history. But even in this prose effort the Beatrix Potter element is mixed with helpings from the Brothers Grimm: his brothers get carried off in wicker baskets and his mother wiped out by invading cats! The story was illustrated by him as well. The whole production is remarkable for a 10-year-old.

Theresa found all this literary effort, even the lugubrious bits, greatly encouraging. Siegfried was very neat in his copying of each verse and totally concentrated on the poem in hand. His brothers found it all a reason for jest. On one occasion when Michael kicked the leg of the table on which Siegfried was writing, causing his brother's book to be smudged, he received a punch on the nose. He and Hamo had intruded on Siegfried's secret and tidy world.

It was an exuberant household. Theresa readily admitted that her three boys gave her 'a high old time', but she was resolute in her opposition to sending them away to public school at too early an age. 'She had a deep distrust of the feeding arrangements at schools and maintained that as we were all of us delicate, it would be a mistake for our brains to be overtaxed by conventional education.' Keeping the boys at home went against the norm, but Theresa was not intimidated by convention. Having the riotous trio at home, however, did mean a severe curtailment of time available to pursue her own painting. Uncompleted canvases lay around the Studio like unfulfilled promises. A decade earlier she had caused a sensation at the Royal Academy Exhibition with her painting, *The Hours*, in which some 24 figures floated across the sky, passing from darkness into light. Her work was full of religious symbols and motifs showing the influence of the Pre-Raphaelites. Consistent application, however, was impossible with the demands of running the house, raising the boys and the need 'to redeem the district from dullness'. Not all her efforts to do so were successful. The Poetry Society soon languished, but not before the boys disturbed proceedings. People liked to drive over to the house to visit Theresa and see 'the dear boys' and, having done so, would depart thinking how much easier it would be if Theresa were to send her sons away to boarding school.

These visits ended with a tour of the Studio. One picture in particular was always the subject of admiration. Painted in 1891, it depicted Christ and three boys: 'It was a picture which showed us in our angelic childhood and fully deserved their admiration for it was most touching and beautiful.' John Richardson, whose father was Tom the groom, saw the painting when he was a boy at Weirleigh: 'I remember standing beneath that elegant roof, gazing in awe-struck wonder at a huge canvas on which Theresa Sassoon had depicted a life-size figure of Christ; the kindly compassionate face looking down at three boys lying on the grass at his feet. The three boys were clearly her own three sons. At that time, I had never seen anything more beautiful and can recall that I tip-toed away, feeling as if I had intruded on something very private and intimate.' The painting conveyed the piety which underpinned Theresa's view of life and also her deep need of her sons and this perhaps, as much as her doubts about boarding schools, influenced her decision not to send them away 'too soon'. Until that point the boys' education had been haphazard, with friends being dragooned into helping. Now a more purposeful routine was needed. Tutors were employed, an arrangement which the three boys approved. They were content in their sequestered world, to which other children were rarely if ever allowed; its demands were far from onerous. Siegfried summed it up with typical conciseness: 'God in his Heaven and sausages for breakfast!'

The first tutor was a retired teacher who had settled in the village. Mr Moon took what might kindly be described as a wide-ranging approach – a bit of this and a bit of that, with some general background. Lessons were confined to the morning, the afternoon being for carpentry and cricket. Undemanding it certainly was, except for Latin. Siegfried could make no headway in the subject and never did. But he enjoyed English literature and listening to 'Moonie' reading extracts. Theresa kept an eye on their progress – or perhaps an ear would be more accurate. She was concerned that the boys were not advancing in languages and feared that Mr Moon lacked depth of knowledge. Thus Fräulein Stoy arrived at Weirleigh and Siegfried struggled with French and German. She also gave him piano lessons but, despite his love of the instrument, he failed to make it sound 'eloquent and eventful'. He liked the Fräulein, as he liked dear old stooping Moonie, but neither of them came near to Ellen Batty's imaginative and engaging approach. Arriving at Weirleigh with high ideals and intentions, Fräulein Stoy soon found herself succumbing to the overall atmosphere of informality and unhurriedness. With the arrival of a third teacher she was eclipsed and, according to Siegfried, became 'only a harmless appurtenance of the household'. It would be wrong to accept at face value Siegfried's account of his progress under Mr Moon and Fräulein Stoy. He had in full measure the tendency to self-deprecation and understatement. That acknowledged, he was aware of the basic problem: 'My brain absorbs facts singly, and the process of relating them to one another has always been difficult. From my earliest years I was interested in words, but their effect on my mind was mainly visual. My spontaneous assumption was that a mouse was called a mouse because it was mouse-like.'

The next tutor quickly understood Siegfried's tendency to disengage from subjects which were presented in too abstract a way. Mr Hamilton introduced a routine which Siegfried described as refreshing, particularly in English literature. He also widened the horizons and for the first time the possibility presented itself of a world of exploration beyond the garden, Gedges Wood and the sentinel pines on the horizon of the Weald. The Beet, so nicknamed for his ripe reddish complexion, was 'in every way an entirely suitable person to liberate us from the localisms of our over-prolonged and somewhat segregated childhood'. Clarence Hamilton had much more to commend him than his learning and piety (he was destined for the Church) – he was a cricketer of some merit. Being a student of the game, something he remained throughout his life, Siegfried knew details of the tutor's batting prowess, at his public school and then during the captaincy of his college team at Cambridge. Much was expected of him by his young admirer. Unfortunately, the Beet's cricket was to fall below the hopes of both Siegfried and the Matfield cricket team: on his first appearance for the home side he was dismissed after three deliveries. The putative hero and saviour had fallen victim not to the opponent's prowess but to the topography of the wicket and its vagaries, which confirmed the local wiseacres' opinion, 'them toffs never do no good on the Green'.

Someone who did know how to bat on the Green was Tom Richardson, the groom at Weirleigh. He loved cricket as much as Siegfried did and carried his bat for Matfield with all the ardour and pride of any England opener. His first loves, however, were horses and hunting. The Eridge Hunt under Lord Henry Nevill over the border in Sussex held a special appeal for him, being in his opinion the best. Tom was idealised by Siegfried in *The Old Century* and especially in *Memoirs of a Fox-Hunting Man*, where he is given the name Tom Dixon. It is clear in both how influential he was in Siegfried's early years. In all things he was conscientious, possibly a little dry and serious, but he took charge of Siegfried and taught him the art of riding and how to be a good judge of a horse. The appeal of the saddle was common to the three brothers, but Michael and Hamo preferred theirs on bicycles. By 1898 Siegfried had outgrown his pony. Theresa, on Tom's recommendation, bought a hunter for Siegfried called Sportsman. It was a memorable partnership from the moment he mounted and felt a shudder when seeing how far from the ground he now was. Tom took Siegfried in hand and taught him that slackness in the saddle was as reprehensible as slackness in appearance. 'He would have considered it a disgrace to have worn his stable clothes when taking me out, and I never saw him drive even a ponycart without looking as though it was a carriage and pair.' This was Siegfried's first real introduction to discipline, to which he responded. Tom was keen to involve Siegfried in hunting, especially to ride to hounds with the Eridge Hunt. The somewhat reserved, poetically inclined boy proved a fearless rider when stimulated by a high fence. Hunting also forced him into new company – not the most welcoming and sometimes rather stiff. Siegfried was not always at ease but he was always conspicuous, Tom having made sure that his pupil was immaculately turned out, especially with his clean bright yellow gloves. Riding out on Sportsman, high enough to see over the village hedgerows, Siegfried was elated but self-conscious. Tom observed him with a critical eye and pondered future successes and perhaps another hunter in the stables.

Buying and keeping horses placed a strain on Theresa's limited funds and Weirleigh was a costly house to maintain. Alfred had not been generous in his provision for her – she received £200, a life interest in Weirleigh and various possessions he had left in the house and the Studio. The bulk of the estate, which amounted to a little over £5,000, was for the benefit of the boys. Alfred had incurred a heavy penalty for marrying outside the faith. In 1899, Theresa and the trustees were preparing to meet the cost of the boys' education: Michael had already entered a nearby preparatory school and Theresa knew that come the new year, her two other sons must follow him. For them, the new century would be about the world beyond Weirleigh.

New Beacon School was new in the sense of having been moved to a fresh site on a hill overlooking the Kentish town of Sevenoaks. Siegfried and Hamo joined Michael there in the spring of 1900. The school specialised in preparing boys for entry into the major public schools of England. Michael and Hamo embraced their freedom from Weirleigh but their middle brother, who was now known as Sassoon minor, was nervous and tentative. It was his first experience of living in a community where privacy was at a premium and his first experience of being in an all-male environment which fostered the ideal of platonic companionship and commitment. Falling below such an ideal was a betrayal, but to exceed it was to be bestial. Homosexuality was an aberration, a deviancy which brought its practitioners everlasting condemnation – but only if they were discovered – sometimes through betrayal. Siegfried did not involve himself in its practices but 'the thoughts of youth are long, long thoughts'.

His uppermost thought was to be acceptable to the other boys and well thought of by the masters. The most important thing, he determined, was to avoid being gauche and not to fail in the subtle art of the done thing. The mores, customs and rules of the prep school, like those of public schools, were a maze, even for the most confident of boys. For the self-conscious, nervous and incautious, a careless moment could open up a pit of self-destruction. The forced gregariousness and the lack of privacy did nothing to boost the confidence of those whose inclination was to secret worlds of their own.

Then there was the difficulty of being a latecomer. He was approaching his fourteenth birthday. Boys would have spent at least five, if not seven, years in the system by the time they were his age. Theresa's eccentric attitude towards public schools obviously put her second son at a disadvantage. To have enjoyed so many years of informal and eclectic education at home made the transition to formality and regimentation difficult. Observing his brothers taking to their new environment with gusto created in Sassoon a sense of inadequacy: 'I stood alone on the edge of the playground, feeling newer than I'd ever done in my life.' To reach the age of 14 without having made a circle of friends must have blunted his capacity to mix freely with others. Sassoon would always be a nervous companion and a reluctant member of any group. At New Beacon School he laid the foundations of a life-long strategy to play the observer rather than the participant. The wisest course was to keep a low profile. This, physically at any rate, was difficult as he was tall for his age, precluding any possibility of slinking into a room or walking unobserved in a crowd.

There was also the challenge of keeping pace with the other boys in the classroom. He had no appetite and possibly no aptitude for the sciences. His gift lay in the arts, particularly poetry – a passion he hid from his fellow pupils lest he became the butt of ribaldry. He knew himself to be a citizen of a world where the imagination reigned supreme. Public schools, he believed, had little time for such temperaments. It was an incorrect assessment but a very convincing excuse. 'Abstract ideas were,' he has admitted, 'uncongenial to my mind.' In other words it was not so much a matter of ability but of aversion. Once Siegfried decided he did not want to do some-thing he would not do it. Won't do and can't do were inter-changeable terms for Siegfried and it required teachers of rare quality and imagination to evoke a response in him.

In the autumn of 1900 Michael went to Malvern School. In the tradition of the system his second brother became Sassoon major, with Hamo inheriting the minor title. This emancipation did little to help Siegfried academically but it did increase his self-confidence. He also adapted. 'I became a more or less ordinary boy, impulsive, irresponsible, easily influenced, and desirous of doing well at work and games.' An essential element required for a positive view of himself was to secure the good opinion of the masters and be regarded by them as mature and adult. Mr Norman, the headmaster, was kind, responsive and lacked stuffiness, but it was another master, Mr Jackson, who evoked Sassoon's greatest admiration, not only for helping him academically but for encouraging him to play golf. The game was not new to him. He had wandered over from Weirleigh to Lamberhurst and watched the players on Squire Morland's nine-hole course. Few, including the Squire, ever completed a round in under 50. As courses go, it had its own charm and challenges. In *The Weald of Youth* he recalled 'that it provided very poor practice for playing anywhere else. In fact, one could say it was a game of its own.' Mr Jackson, like Tom Richardson, was never content with the second rate. Only the best courses around Sevenoaks and Tunbridge Wells would suffice to meet his standard. Thus the third element was added to Siegfried's trinity of sports.

Mr Jackson was also a first-rate teacher and Sassoon major made significant progress in the classics and English, too, in which he reached the top of the list. It was not a brilliant academic performance but it was sufficient to secure a place at one of England's top public schools, Marlborough College.

Before going west to Wiltshire and the new school, it was home to Weirleigh for Christmas and the New Year. Nineteen hundred and two began with a heavy snowfall and the chance for Theresa and the boys to go tobogganing, all the more enjoyable now that they were all together again. There was, despite her conservative and fixed views, a certain physical recklessness about Theresa, some element of the tomboy which her sons must have loved as they watched her careering down a snowy slope on a tea tray. Then the laughter stopped. There was a telegram from Auntie Rachel begging Theresa to come to London at once – dear old Mr Beer had died. Sassoon recorded in *The Old Century* what happened next. It is an example of his gift for evoking humour and pathos:

We had long known that Mr Beer's death would be a happy release, but now, in that cheerful snowscape, we stood and wondered if we ought to go on with our tobogganing. The slide was in splendid condition, and it might thaw by tomorrow; and after all we hadn't seen Mr Beer since about 1897. Hamo suggested tossing up, but none of us had got a coin, so we resumed operations, feeling sorry for Auntie Rachel and rather hoping we shouldn't have to attend the funeral. We did; and the house in Chesterfield Gardens, never a festive one, seemed as though it had been waiting all its life for this mournful event. Auntie Rachel, when we got a glimpse of her, was murmurously distraught, and seemed to have ordered a vast quantity of white flowers which no one knew what to do with. Very few people were there, and most of them were strangers to us. There was a subdued grimness about the ceremony which made me unable to relax into feeling reverent. I knew that Auntie Rachel had been behaving very oddly. Since he died she had been continually telling my mother that Mr Beer wasn't dead, and at intervals she had protested against his being buried at all. My mother had been through a very trying time since the telegram was handed to her over the hedge.

Auntie Rachel's odd behaviour was due to her having been infected by the syphilis inherited by her husband. She would endure a long decline into dementia.

At the end of January, Theresa and her son took the train from Paddington to Marlborough. Sassoon felt 'pleased and rather important' at becoming a pupil of so illustrious a school, but at 15 he also felt quite capable of reaching any destination on his own. At the back of his mind, too, was the knowledge of Theresa's tenacity and eccentricity. Her suspicions of educational establishments, particularly their domestic and catering arrangements, would lead, he feared, to the unrelenting interrogation of those in charge. His fears were more than justified. Arriving at the school 'unpunctually early', Theresa proceeded to do her motherly duty via the headmaster, the Revd George Bell; the housemaster of Cotton House, Mr George Gould; and the matron, Mrs Bolt, to whom she handed extra blankets for Siegfried. Her son felt 'rather like a milksop'.

Whatever his feelings of exasperation, once they returned to the railway station Siegfried became conscious of impending separation. 'I believe I was my mother's favourite. She used to refer to me as her second self.' No relationship went deeper than his relationship with Theresa: he adored her. The pain of separation from his mother was something for which he was quite unprepared. 'My devotion to her was so comprehensive that I had never given any thought to it.' Returning to the college, pausing at the gates, he reaffirmed his strategy for survival: 'The safest thing to do, I thought, was to try and be as silent and inconspicuous as possible.' It proved an effective plan, so much so that he records with no small pride: 'By the time I was almost halfway through my first term I felt that I was getting on much better than I'd expected. No one seemed to have taken an active dislike to me and I was in Mr Gould's good books.'

There is something revealing in the desire to avoid being disliked, as opposed to any mention of active friendship, and his continued need to be on good terms with the adult world in the person of his housemaster. He worked hard and showed great application in order to achieve good results. Theresa had arranged special tuition in music and he threw himself into sporting activities. Given time and a little good fortune he might be, if not a distinguished Marlburian, at least a creditable one. So it might have been had not circumstances intervened.

Six weeks after arriving at Marlborough, Sassoon went down with measles, which developed into double pneumonia. The contagion had affected Cotton House and the rest of the school. Without being asked, Theresa hurried to Marlborough to nurse her son. No doubt her prejudices against public schools were confirmed by this calamity. Sassoon was in a serious condition and, according to Mr Gould, would have died but for the intervening hand of Theresa and her special brew of beef tea. Sassoon recalled in a letter that his mother's attendance at his bedside was 'considered a bit infra dig by the authorities. Parents of apparently good social position didn't do such things as a rule.' It was another triumph for Theresa's originality. Three weeks before the end of term he was well enough to go home to Weirleigh to convalesce. This was the first of many interruptions to his time at Marlborough. In the next autumn term he suffered heart strain and remained at Weirleigh until the following May. The following January of 1903 it was decided he should stay at home for the whole of the term lest another outbreak of measles at the school cause him to suffer a recurrence, perhaps a fatal one, of pneumonia. Out of a possible eight terms he should have completed between 1902 and the summer of 1904, he managed only four and a further six weeks of another two terms.

These absences inevitably impeded his chances of attaining academic credibility and the commendation of the masters. Marlborough was an uphill struggle, redeemed only by his talent as a cricketer. Mr Gould seemed suspicious of Sassoon's seriousness and application, accusing him of being a bit of a dodger who took soft options such as organ lessons instead of hockey. Despite his vow to keep his head down and avoid pitfalls, Siegfried walked straight into a situation which further reduced his standing in the eyes of Mr Gould. The pupil who usually played the piano at evening prayers cried off with a cut finger and asked Siegfried to take his place. The boy chose an easy hymn for the desperately nervous substitute. Mr Gould announced the hymn number and, without a modicum of confidence, Siegfried struck the opening chord, followed by a few bars and then came a deluge of boys' voices. It was unfortunate for Siegfried that he had not checked the words of the hymn. Its five verses lent themselves to 'facetious interpretation' and inferences about Mrs Bolt the Matron:

> How blest the matron who endued
> With holy zeal and fortitude,
> Has won through grace a saintly frame,
> And owns a dear and honoured name.

The remaining verses are a litany of anatomical allusions: 'As I struck the first chord for verse 2 (which began "Such holy love inflamed her breast"), I could only confusedly suppose that I had somehow blundered when Mr Gould practically bellowed "Let the music cease!"' Although later Mr Gould was heard to chuckle, it was from such incidents he divined Siegfried to be 'irresponsible and deficient in solidity of character'. His final report contained the crushing remark: 'lacks power of concentration; shows no particular intelligence or aptitude for any branch of his work; seems unlikely to adopt any special career'. It was a harsh judgement, made even worse when Mr Gould's last goodbye was accompanied by the words, 'Try and be more sensible.' Siegfried, however, took a more philosophical view of his time at Marlborough: 'moderately pleasant, but mentally unprofitable'.

Marlborough did one good thing for him, though: it nurtured the re-emergence of his poetic vocation. One of his masters, Mr O'Regan, encouraged the appreciation of poetry among his pupils and as a spur would occasionally offer a half-crown as prize for the best poem. The opposition was not fierce and Siegfried invariably won. Not that the editor of the school paper recognised any merit in his poetic endeavours – he rejected every poem submitted by Siegfried. Lying at home during his enforced absence from school in the spring of 1903, Siegfried composed what he called a parody, inspired by a debate current at the time about altering the height of the wicket, and sent it off to *Cricket* magazine. Entitled 'The Extra Inch', and having a Gilbert and Sullivan atmosphere and style, it appealed to the editor, Mr Bettesworth, who printed it.

> O batsman, rise and go and stop the rot,
> And go and stop the rot.

(It was indeed a rot,
Six down for twenty-three).
The batsman thought how wretched was his lot,
And all alone went he.

The bowler bared his mighty, cunning arm,
His vengeance-wreaking arm,
His large yet wily arm,
With fearful powers endowed.
The batsman took his guard. (A deadly calm
had fallen on the crowd.)

O is it a half-volley or long hop,
A seventh bounce long hop,
A fast and fierce long hop,
That the bowler letteth fly?
The ball was straight and bowled him neck and crop.
He knew not how nor why.

Full sad and slow pavilionwards he walked.
The careless critics talked;
Some said that he was yorked;
A half-volley at a pinch.
The batsman murmured as he inward stalked,
'It was the extra inch.'

This was Siegfried's first published poem. Mr Bettesworth took a shine to his poetry and published four more in the following 18 months. However, sustaining a belief in his vocation as a poet proved a difficult task. His success in *Cricket*, pleasing though it was, seemed more of an end than a beginning. But once again, in an unexpected moment, the hope was fed. He describes how in 1904, while in Cotton House library:

Idly I pulled out a book which happened to be Volume IV of Ward's *English Poets*. By chance I opened it at Hood's 'Bridge of Sighs', which was new to me. I had always preferred poems which went straight to the point and stayed there, and here was a direct utterance which gave me goose flesh and brought tears to my eyes. It wasn't so much the subject of the poem which thrilled me as the sense of powerful expression and memorable word music. For the first time since I had been at school I felt separated from my surroundings and liberated from the condition of being only a boy. As a child I had believed in my poetic vocation and had somehow felt myself to be a prophetic spirit in the making. Now my belief was renewed and strengthened.

Sassoon, Old Marlburian, in the summer of 1904, was 'bicycling' his way through his nineteenth year. He had decided to go up to Cambridge, but the University had yet to decide whether to accept him. Bridging the gap between desire and its fulfilment required the passing of an examination. In the village of Frant, near Tunbridge Wells and within easy cycling distance of Weirleigh, lay Henley House, a crammer establishment of some repute. The young adult on his bicycle was a 'happy-go-lucky sort of person, head in air and pleasantly occupied with loosely connected ruminations', who had thrown off much of the anxiety and nervousness of the schoolboy. He had crossed a boundary, much as he crossed the boundary between Kent and Sussex on the bridge by Dundale Farm, on his way to board at Henley House. His was a charmed existence. Under his father's will he was financially secure, the trust fund being administered mainly by the family solicitor, Mr Lousada. He was not wealthy and neither was Theresa; comfortable would be the best summary of his financial position. This meant, among other things, that there was no pressure to be successful; there was no family firm to enter and no call to find a profession. Mr Lousada and his alter ego Mr Pennett in *Memoirs of a Fox-Hunting Man* were more than willing to assist him into the Law. But what need of this to a bicycling youth, who was a poet? Inspiration lay all around him in the beauty of the Weald. The social order from the Squire down to the housemaids and stable-lads exuded permanence and its meridian prosperity seemed immutable. Sassoon was enjoying, like Sebastian Flyte of Brideshead, 'the languor of youth – a mind sequestered and self-regarding'. E. M. Forster, a contemporary and later a friend, in describing his own youth might well be describing Sassoon's: 'I belong to the fag end of Victorian liberalism, and can look back to an age whose challenges were moderate in their tone, and the cloud on whose horizon was no bigger than a man's hand.' Sassoon confesses of that time through his alter ego George Sherston: 'How little I knew of the enormous world beyond the valley and those low green hills.' Enlightenment would come in its own savage way; meanwhile it was still 'God in his Heaven and sausages for breakfast'. To which he might have added, 'horses in the stables, golf-clubs in the bag, and bat and pads by the door'.

Henley House had four teachers and 20 students: Sassoon thought it a vast improvement on Marlborough, where he had felt moody and unappreciated. Now he was considered lively and amusing, and was consistently cheerful. In *The Old Century*, Sassoon exudes a sense of relief as academic pressure is lifted off his shoulders and he settles into a routine, which, while unhurried, fulfilled what was required to pass into Oxford or Cambridge. Much of this was due to the 'quiet methods' and laconic style of the headmaster and proprietor Mr Malden – known as 'The Boss' – and his staff, all of whom are remembered and portrayed with affection by Sassoon. There would be little to say of Henley House and the year he spent there were it not for the friendships he made and which continued for many years after. The first of these was with his Classics teacher: all-round athlete, footballer and golfer, George Wilson. Sassoon's description of him is an illustration of his tendency to idealise older men, who acted as his mentors:

George was a man who was always glad to see someone else do better than himself, at golf or anything else. Even when I first knew him his selfless character was apparent in his fine resolute face. Eyes and voice had a shining quality of courage, humour and intelligence. He was, in fact, one of the paragons of my human experience – one of those men who go through life without being aware if it.

Only towards the end of *The Old Century* does Sassoon preface an introduction with a sentence about friendship: 'Among my contemporaries at Henley House I had found a friend.' The friend's name was Henry Thompson and he was known by Sassoon as 'Tommy'. There would be another Tommy in his life but Henry was the first. A native of Cumbria, he was cramming for a place at Oxford. As with Sassoon, his education had been interrupted by illness.

He was small, red-haired, and alert, with eyes which often had a look of being puckered up to encounter the wintry weather. He had very nice manners, which would take the form of behaving with sympathetic understanding of his elders. He had a delightful cronyish quality, and when I took him over to see my mother they became like one mind in their mutual interest in growing roses from the dissimilar soils of Cumberland and Kent. With me he shared an enthusiasm for golf.

His good manners apart, Tommy's appeal for Sassoon lay in his north-country shrewdness, his golf and in being the kind of person with whom Sassoon could share thoughts about the future: he and Tommy would together 'play every championship golf course in Great Britain, ending up at the Royal and Ancient'. Only with one other person did Sassoon plan a shared enterprise based on companionship and that was Robert Graves, more than a decade later.

Norman Loder was the third and the most important friend that Sassoon made at Henley House. He is not mentioned in *The Old Century*, as the other two are, but in *Memoirs of a Fox-Hunting Man*, with the pseudonym Denis Milden. Loder was a member of a well-connected county family, who lived at Handcross in Sussex. Theresa would almost certainly have been familiar with the name and it is probable that Sassoon had seen or met Loder before their encounter at Henley House. When he first appears in *Memoirs of a Fox-Hunting Man* he is barely into his teens and already the epitome of all that a rider should be.

> My memory fixes him in a characteristic attitude. Leaning slightly forward from the waist, he straightens his left leg and scrutinises it with an air of critical abstraction. All his movements were controlled and modest but there was a suggestion of arrogance in the steady, unrecognizing stare which he gave me when he became conscious that I was looking at him intently. Already I was weaving Master Milden into my day-dreams, and soon he had become my inseparable companion in all my imagined adventures, although I was hampered by the fact that I only knew him by his surname. It was the first time that I experienced a feeling of wistfulness for someone I wanted to be with.

Loder, alias Milden, is Sassoon's first admitted crush.

In autumn 1905 Sassoon went up to Cambridge. Loder went up, too, but there is no evidence that they spent much or indeed any time together. Sassoon was not short of company, however. His brother Michael had completed his first year at Clare, the college to which not only Sassoon was admitted that October, but also his brother Hamo. It was something of a record for three brothers to be in the same college at the same time, but the trio was dissolved when Michael went down at Christmas without a degree.

In addition there were and would be cousins, Donaldson and Thornycroft. There being no English Tripos at that time, Sassoon, or someone on his behalf, decided he should read Law. Considering he relied so heavily on the inspirational, the image and the evocative to scale the heights of learning, Sassoon's choice was a strange one – if it was his. Mr Lousada, no doubt, hovered with intent, knowing that Sassoon had not the faintest idea what subject he should read. As one who had known Alfred Sassoon, he may well have feared the adage 'like father like son'. The picture drawn of the solicitor in *Memoirs of a Fox-Hunting Man* is of someone for whom life meant commitment to seriousness and there was nothing more serious than the Law, certainly not poetry. When the moment came for a decision, all other options having failed, Lousada secured the verdict. If this is true, then Lousada did Sassoon a disservice, only partly redeemed by allowing him, as his Trustee, the sum of £80 a term.

Sassoon started well, but with his mind more on poetry than Jurisprudence, progress was slow and interest declined. What lay at the heart of the problem was, as he had already discovered at New Beacon School and Marlborough, his total inability to engage in what he counted as academic aridity. There was nothing dramatic or imaginative in the subject and he was, to say the least, disenchanted. The portrait he paints of himself at this time is of a young man determined to discover and enjoy his own world, the world of the imagination; he was a day-dreamer, though fully aware that disaster in the Tripos would be the inevitable consequence of his mental meandering. Life lived on one's own terms was the guiding principle. He wanted to be a poet, not a lawyer. At the suggestion of his senior tutor, W. L. Mollison, Sassoon switched to History: 'I tackled the History Tripos with a spurt of unmethodical energy. I had found Law altogether too inhumane and arid, but History was bound to be much more lively and picturesque.'

Not so. The underlying discipline necessary for success in his latter subject was the same as that required for the former. Soon he was equally in trouble with his History and was duly warned by his tutor. '"You really must put in some solid work on the struggle between the Empire and the Papacy," he remarked. To which I dutifully agreed and spent most of the next day reading *The Earthly Paradise* in a punt under a pollard willow with a light breeze ruffling the bend of the river and bringing the scent of bean-fields, while Cambridge, a mile or two away, dozed in its academic afternoon.'

William Morris, another Old Marlburian, was offering him an

'imaginative experience which provided an ideal escape from common-place actualities' such as tutorials and essays. Mollison, his tutor, was long-suffering and sympathetic to the earnest young poet. Sassoon was writing an epic blank-verse poem on Joan of Arc, in what he described as a 'state of rapt afflatus – a sort of first-love affair with blank verse. I really was bursting with poetic energy that year, though so immature.' He had also been bursting with golf – on the Mildenhall and Royston courses, among other diversions. Would 'Molly' have been so tolerant had he known? Sassoon was also working on an anthology of his favourite poems: 'Swinburne was the main influence at that time. I loved Tennyson but was incapable of imitating his distinctness. Dante Rossetti also, and I'd imbibed quite a lot of Browning, *Saul* being my prime favourite.' As for his own poems, he was collating them for a slim volume which, after much thought, he decided to publish in a private edition.

Publishing small private volumes of his work became his chosen method, of which Sir Rupert Hart-Davis has written: 'I think the explanation lay in a lifelong dichotomy in his nature. He longed for praise and recognition, but he was instinctively reclusive, so unsure of his gifts and afraid of making a fool of himself, that he preferred his poems to appear first in small and expensive editions, a sort of safeguard to prove their worth and test readers' reactions.' Sassoon admits to another reason, his total lack of experience with which to judge his work and awareness of its derivative quality, if not of content then certainly in style. His reticence did not prevent him sending occasional poems, which were accepted for publication in *Granta*, the university magazine. The poems selected for inclusion in the small volume were dense with metaphors, a good number of them of the mixed variety, and combinations of conflicting feelings expressing life's ups and downs in florid style. Occasionally there is a promising opening line. One of which he was particularly proud, as he confessed a half century later, declares boldly, 'Doubt not the light of Heaven upon the soul.' 'Not a bad start!' was his comment. If there is an underlying component in the collection, it is of life as pilgrimage, of seeking after some providential purpose. Sassoon spent the summer putting finishing touches to the proposed volume and on 20 September sent it to the Athenaeum Press. Within two weeks the first proofs arrived, with a second set in early November.

Having returned to Cambridge he was more than ever out of sympathy with his studies and was minded to go down without completing his degree. Theresa, he was confident, would support this; he might even have suggested it to her during the summer. She saw no point in her son pursuing matters in which he was not interested. Uncle Hamo took the opposite view and wrote urging him to persist. As a possible diversionary tactic, he suggested that his nephew enter for the Chancellor's Medal. The subject was Edward I and, although Sassoon thought it a strong theme for an epic poem, he became disillusioned with his efforts. Eventually he struck on a possible treatment and sent in the finished work. Convinced he would not win the prize, he went home to Weirleigh for Christmas. The 18th December was a red-letter day. Fifty copies of the presentation volume arrived. He noted in the proudest terms, 'no one knew about it, not even my mother'. Theresa was splendidly surprised with her Christmas gift.

In the New Year Sassoon had a slight chill which, turning into a mild case of flu, delayed his return to university till March, another of those convenient illnesses which enabled him to postpone the evil day. Uncle Hamo may have suspected as much and, unlike his sister, felt regret that his nephew would not complete his degree. Writing to his friend Edmund Gosse, he said that Siegfried jibbed at the idea of work and was determined to follow a line of his own; that he had his mother's support in this and must go his own way. He also appealed to Gosse to have a word with Theresa. Nothing came of his efforts. His idea of the Chancellor's Medal, or the Chancellor's Muddle as Theresa called it, also met with failure – his nephew did not win. Sassoon's undergraduate days at Cambridge came to an end. Well aware that his uncle was disappointed, he wrote to him on 19 May 1907:

Dear Uncle Hamo,
Cheque received: I must screw myself up to inform you that I intend to give up Cambridge. I see no use in staying there three years and not getting a degree, and am sure I should never pass the exams. I expect you will be very sick with me about it, but I don't think I should ever do anything there. I admit it appears rather idiotic, but I have quite made up my mind about it.
Your not at all truculent nephew
S.S.

Not truculent! And accompanied by a slice of imperiousness in the final sentence. Uncle Hamo accepted defeat, knowing that his nephew would be 21 that September and free to follow his own course. A few weeks before the birthday, Sassoon went in a semi-apologetic spirit to Uncle Hamo's studio. The trepidation he felt as he approached was dissolved by the ever charitable and gentle uncle, who showed himself quite reconciled to the decision. He was working on a statue of Tennyson and he encouraged his nephew to try on the Laureate's cloak and hat. It was something of a coronation, with Uncle Hamo's commendation of his nephew's work and faith in his future. 'Let us hope that some day you will have no need to borrow the mantle of greatness, old man. Let your thoughts ring true; and always keep your eye on the object while you write.' The advice was sound, though unfortunately Tennyson's outsize hat had slipped down to cover Sassoon's eyes.

3

POET AND SPORTSMAN

1907–14

Sassoon at 21 began to settle into the life of poet, sportsman and country gentleman with an income of £400 a year. He took possession of the upstairs floor of the Studio where his father had once played the violin, painted and browsed through his library. Sassoon's own library was begun during his frequent absences from Marlborough College. It was to be 'a real library – in which one went up a ladder and pulled out a dusty volume, to discover with delight that it was a first edition of somebody like Bunyan'. Nothing gave him greater pleasure than a good edition with a fine binding. A single volume or an author's complete works would be ordered from a favoured bookseller, usually in part exchange for one of his father's books, which the *Bookseller's Chronicle* informed him was being sought by some other bibliophile. The opening transaction involved a first edition of Gissing's *New Grub Street*:

> Heard from Brownish Bros. They are willing to give £1. 5s in cash for Gissing or £1. 15s in books. Have decided to accept the latter alternative, so wrote immediately for the *The Works of Samuel Johnson*, 12 vols., calf, 1801, 15s; Sir Dudley Digges's *State Letters*, folio, old calf, 1665, 6s; *Paul and Virginia*, 12 mo., calf, 1779, 2s.; Potter's Euripides, 2 vols., calf, 1814, 5s. 6d.; and the *Life of Queen Elizabeth*, 4to., panelled calf, 1738, 3s 6d. This leaves 3s. to my account.

These were the first of the thousands of volumes Sassoon collected during his lifetime and which he neatly arranged to show their bindings to best effect. Neatness and order were, he declared, 'a craving'. In his memoirs Sassoon creates the impression that he was, like his father, a browser. 'Most of my serious reading was undoubtedly done with my watch on the table, and my thoughts may have wandered away to the golf links over at Sevenoaks.' That is the confession of his youthful years; the mature Sassoon 'knew his books so well that he could spring up and pull one down and open it at the very page to make his point'.

Taking possession of the Studio in that September of 1907 had emotional resonances:

> If only the Studio could write reminiscences of its grown-up childhood how interesting they would be! My mother seldom spoke of those times, but the Studio had seen the happiness that came before those sad events which had so impressed themselves on my mind; and I would have liked to hear more about my father as he was at his best. The Studio must often have heard him playing his Stradivarius with that gipsy wildness which was the special quality of his fiddling. It had heard the light-hearted voices talking of the future without foreboding. The past had filled the Studio with vibrations that were one with my own history. For a moment I felt as if my father were in the room. So real had my meditations made him that I could almost smell his cigar smoke. But it was only the imagination of a moment.

For the next six years Weirleigh was the centre of Sassoon's life, from whence he ventured into the surrounding countryside of Kent and Sussex. There were trips to London, sometimes with Theresa to concerts or exhibitions and on to the old family home at Melbury Road. There were also visits to stock up with hunting gear. The six years have a dual theme: emerging poet and enthusiastic sportsman. His days were lived on two levels – the public life, as in *Memoirs of a Fox-Hunting Man*, and the internal, tranquil self of his second volume of autobiography, *The Weald of Youth*. These were also the years in which he formed a new friendship and strengthened an existing one. Both arose from Sassoon's love of hunting and point-to-pointing.

Stephen Gordon Harbord (known as Gordon) was born in 1890, the son of the Revd Harry Harbord, rector of East Hoathly, near Lewes in Sussex. Sassoon introduces him in *Memoirs of a Fox-Hunting Man*. In April 1911, Sherston goes as a spectator to a point-to-point meeting at

Dumborough in Sussex. The racing card informs him that one of the riders is a Mr S. Colwood: 'It can't be Stephen Colwood, can it? I thought, visualising a quiet, slender boy with very large hands and feet, who had come to my House at Ballboro' about two years after I went there. Now I came to think of it, his father had been a parson somewhere in Sussex, but this did not seem to make it any likelier that he should be riding in a race.' In fact S. Colwood is G. Harbord, and the passage is a good example of how Sassoon mingles circumstances, changes names and dates. Dumborough is the alias for Eridge; Colwood was the name of the Harbords' family home and it was Gordon's brother Kenneth Blair Harbord who was Sassoon's contemporary at Marlborough, but the experiences shared and the people portrayed are authentic, if at times heightened for effect.

The Harbords were a large family. In all there were nine offspring, of whom Gordon was the sixth and the third son. The father was regarded as a conscientious priest with a lively social ministry. He and his five boys were sometimes referred to as 'the Vicar and his sporting sons'. They were keen cricketers and accomplished riders. A family photograph taken about 1903 catches them in pensive rather than sporting mood, and Mrs Harbord looks careworn. In fact, the family was a happy and jovial one, with the boys exhibiting all the rumbustiousness of youth. Sassoon first met Gordon in 1908, after which Colwood Park became a second home for him and Gordon, whom Theresa liked, was a regular visitor to Weirleigh. Gordon was not academically inclined any more than Sassoon but he was conscientious and obtained a degree at London University. Also, and unlike Sassoon, he was practically gifted, with a bent for engineering, like Michael and Hamo. The common factor which drew Gordon and Sassoon together was sport, particularly horses and cricket. They also shared a quirky sense of humour, which colours their letters to each other but makes them unintelligible to the outsider.

Humour was not the outstanding characteristic of the person who exercised the greatest influence on Sassoon, the horseman and golfer, in the pre-war years. Although they had been together at Henley House and afterwards at Cambridge, Norman Loder was somewhat in the background up to 1907 but then he persuaded Sassoon to make a more serious commitment to riding and to golf. 'He knew that in most ways we were totally unlike, and was only dimly aware of my literary ambitions. If I had not been keen on golf and hunting our friendship could never have existed. On that basis he accepted me for what I was, just as I accepted him.'

He and Sassoon were virtually inseparable during the hunting and steeplechase season and, more often than not, Gordon Harbord made it a trio of enthusiasts. Weirleigh was a little too far from the meets frequented by Loder to make it a day's journey, so Sassoon would stay with the Harbords or with Loder. The friendship with the latter, whose prowess at hunting and matters equestrian was acknowledged and admired, brought out the adventurous, derring-do in Sassoon's character. His love of heightened excitement is obvious in the memoirs, as is the delight he took in the characters and the conventions of riding to hounds and point-to-pointing. Loder had no interests outside these things, not much humour and a plodding intellect. Sassoon, however, relied on him for companionship as well as instruction. He also admired his qualities. 'He was one of those people whose strength is in their consistent simplicity and directness, and who send out natural wisdom through their mental limitations and avoidance of nimble ideas. He was kind, decent, and thorough, never aiming at anything beyond plain commonsense and practical ability.'

With his other friend Henry 'Tommy' Thompson, the summers were filled with visits to golf courses, but not even golf was allowed to impinge upon Sassoon's commitment to cricket. He was proud of being a member of the Blue Mantles, who played their home matches on the county ground at Tunbridge Wells. It was a well-respected cricket club and Sassoon's inclusion on an almost regular basis is a pointer to his talent at club level. He fancied himself as a club player, both as batsman and as bowler, and the local teams of Matfield and Brenchley were glad to take advantage of his ability. Sassoon was very much an outdoor person, and having returned to Weirleigh he was keen to be out and about on a horse, on the golf course or enjoying the activity of a fine day's cricket. Walking and bicycling were activities he enjoyed for their own sake and could pursue alone. He exulted in the freedom of the open road and the natural world, which marks him out as a disciple of the author and poet George Meredith, whose books lined the shelves of his library and whose praises were extolled by Wirgie and Theresa. Since childhood Sassoon had been able to identify birds and plants, nursing a special enthusiasm for butterflies, Shelley's 'winged flowers'. The lanes and fields of Kent, the oasthouses, the orchards, the hedgerows and the gardens, were inspirational to him and his descriptions of his peregrinations bring colour and atmosphere to every facet of his work. It was a world which appealed to his aesthetic delight, his curiosity as well as his spirit of adventure. *Memoirs of a Fox-Hunting Man, The Old*

Century and *The Weald of Youth* catch the essence of Sassoon's musings in 1909:

> The setting sun was behind me. To the left of the high ground along which I was driving, the Weald lay in all its green contentedness. I was feeling fine, and had played quite a decent little innings in the match. But when I came to the cross-roads a mile and a half from home and caught that favourite glimpse of Kentish distance above the foreground apple orchards of King's Toll farm, the low-hilled blue horizon seemed luring me toward my heart's desire, which was that I might some day be a really good poet.

With all the splendour that surrounded Weirleigh, Sassoon was overflowing with celebratory and evocative verse, as was appropriate for a devotee of George Meredith. It was abundant but it was not focused. Uncle Hamo's advice about keeping one's eye on the object had not been taken. He worked on successive drafts of his poems and was still committed to the idea of small private editions. He also continued to send a selection to the editors of various literary magazines. One such was *The Academy*, whose editor immodestly but typically described it as 'the liveliest of literary journals'. He was T. W. H. Crosland, a charlatan on the literary scene, and in the habit of moving from one periodical to the next with regularity. But he had an eye for a poem, especially by young, inexperienced poets. Crosland was also a critic and polemicist in literary matters, sparing no one, however famous. Theresa disliked his stance and taste – mainly on the grounds that he had been brutal to the work of Sir Walter Scott. As she was a confirmed devotee of the Pre-Raphaelites, this was heresy. When Sassoon sent Crosland some of his work he received not an invitation but a summons to his office in London. He did not take to Crosland when they met but innocently jumped at the offer of a guinea each for the nine sonnets. The poems were published but the money never arrived.

Sassoon's most important contact with literary London was made in 1908 with Edmund Gosse. In that year he wrote and privately published *Orpheus in Diloeryum*, which he described as 'an unactable one-act play which had never quite made up its mind whether to be satirical or serious. Sometimes I was pouring out my own imitative exuberances; sometimes I was parodying the precosities of contemporary minor poetry; on one page I parodied Swinburne, (crudely, but to me it sounded rather fine).' When

Uncle Hamo read the work he, one must say loyally, thought it showed potential and suggested his nephew send it to Gosse. This eminent littérateur had been Uncle Hamo's friend since youth, just as Nellie his wife had been to Theresa, or 'Trees' as she called her. Gosse's response was that of a man who felt obliged not to be discouraging:

> It was very kind of you to send your delicate and accomplished masque *Orpheus in Diloeryum*, which I have read with pleasure and amusement. It reminds me of some of the strange entertainments of the early Renaissance and of Italian humanism generally. And I observe, with great satisfaction, your own richness of fancy and command of melodious verse. I hope you will make a prolonged study of the art of poetry, and advance from height to height.

Gosse could be pompous! Despite that and the reference to Italian humanism being 'over his head', Sassoon was encouraged by Gosse's note and pursued the connection. Gosse's real opinion is revealed in letters he exchanged with Uncle Hamo in May 1909. Hamo pressed the question first:

> Just on our leaving the other day you almost told us what you thought of young Siegfried Sassoon's attempts at verse. I am anxious that he should have any help and encouragement in this the difficult path he has chosen to follow. So if you can advise him, do please, if opportunity occurs. He is an interesting personage and spirit. I have been severely calling him to order lately for spending too much on hunting, golf, cricket and expensive editions of books, beyond what his income of £400 will stand.

Gosse responded within the week to say that Siegfried's work 'showed promise' but the need was for 'a distinct originality':

> Now I cannot truly say that I see as yet much evidence that Siegfried possesses this. So I think that to arrange his life from the point of view of his becoming a poet would be very rash. I think that if I was his Trustee, I should feel that he ought to have the chance of training for some other profession. Of course, if, in five or six years, he should feel his powers as a writer strengthening, and find that his vocation as a poet was irresistible, he could then retire and live on his modest fortune.

Sassoon was already finding his vocation 'irresistible'. Between 29 May and 14 August 1909, the initials S.S. appeared seven times beneath an assortment of verse in *The Academy*. On 26 June it published his sonnet 'The Travellers'. Sassoon was having a golden day, as on that day he also received a parcel from the Athenaeum Press containing copies of his latest venture, 'thirty-five in stiff white cartridge-paper covers and three on hand made paper bound in black buckram'. This private edition comprised 34 poems, of which 18 were sonnets. The title, *Sonnets and Verses*, was as predictable as the contents – loose descriptions of nature, early mornings, shepherds and goblins. The whole collection resembles fingers going up and down the keyboard, producing sound but no recognisable melody.

Helen Wirgman came for her usual long summer holiday. She was given a copy of the poems and Sassoon waited for her opinion before distributing copies of this latest opus. Meeting her in the garden and anxious for a response, he was deflated when none came. He sensed disapproval and disappointment on Wirgie's part. It was a reaction endorsed by his own opinion of the volume. Returning to the Studio, Sassoon was overcome with frustration and mounting annoyance with himself. The collection he now realised was immature and he was relieved that no one but Wirgie had seen the poems. Lighting a fire in the Studio grate, he burnt the entire edition, with the exception of the three buckram copies. 'When I confessed to Wirgie what I had done, she gave me one of her slow, sad looks.'

All was not lost in the conflagration. Sassoon had second thoughts about his precipitate action. He determined to salvage what he thought were the best of the sonnets and decided on another private edition. In a letter of May 1922 to his friend Sydney Cockerell, Sassoon says: 'I muddled along, making corrections; I had no one to whom I could show any poems in MS, and these little books were a sort of private hobby.'

Hobby is a strange description of an intensely felt vocation, highlighting the danger inherent in Sassoon's dividing his time between country pursuits and the pursuit of the Muse. As Uncle Hamo pointed out to Gosse: 'At present he is too much with the inferior country intellectuals and I should like him to meet literary men.'

Underlying Sassoon's disappointment over *Sonnets and Verses* was the suspicion that he had lost the naturalness of some of his earlier work. He was poetising, moralising and intoxicated with word-sounds. Influenced by Swinburne, he continued to explore the possibilities of the sonnet. Technique was a major problem, as was the question which opens one of his poems from the destroyed collection: 'What shall the Minstrel sing?' 'The question what exactly should I sing was one which I had not so far asked myself with any awareness of the circumstance that, like many minstrels of my age, I had nothing much to sing about.' There was, however, much to think about.

Sassoon at 25 years of age was not the happy-go-lucky person of earlier years. The absence of focus in his latest volume of poetry reflected the lack of focus in his life. There was an increasing awareness that life for him was 'an empty thing'. He was experiencing 'great perplexity and unhappiness'. It was while in this state of mind that he struck up a friendship with a brilliant academic named Nevill Forbes, Reader in Russian at Oxford. Sassoon first heard of Forbes nearly a decade earlier, when Fräulein Stoy arrived at Weirleigh. Her previous post had been tutor to Forbes and his sister. The Fräulein made it clear that Nevill was a pupil of prodigious talent, a polymath and a polyglot. So effusive and constant was the praise that Sassoon took against Forbes and dismissed him as a 'swot'. Forbes preceded Sassoon at New Beacon School and Marlborough College, after which he went up to Balliol, then to Leipzig, before returning to Oxford and an academic post. In addition to his facility with languages – of which he spoke 14 – he was also a brilliant pianist with a strong liking for the music of Debussy, Ravel and Chausson. Probably at the suggestion of Fräulein Stoy, Nevill Forbes was invited to Weirleigh. Despite his original dislike of him, when they met and spent time together, Sassoon reversed his opinion.

In June 1910 Forbes invited Sassoon to spend some days in Oxford. There is no record of their conversations but there is the strong probability that Sassoon shared with Forbes, albeit in a general way, his dissatisfaction with his latest volume of poetry, the lack of focus, the unhappiness which pervaded his life and his inability to settle. It is unlikely that Sassoon would have told Forbes that he attributed the cause to sexual frustration but it is clear that he told him enough for Forbes to guess the nature of Sassoon's difficulties because he suggested that he read the works of Edward Carpenter, whom Forbes knew and admired. During the autumn of 1910, Sassoon read Carpenter's pioneering work on sexuality, *The Intermediate Sex*, and his volume of poems published in 1883, *Towards Democracy*, part of which appeared under the title 'Who Shall Command the Heart?' Carpenter propounded the theory that masculine and feminine sexuality occupied different ends of a line. Moving towards the centre these absolutes lessen until at the midway point masculinity and femininity coalesce – each person is somewhere on that line, as opposed to the then held view that there was only unalloyed feminine and masculine sexuality. But there was more to Carpenter than theories on human sexuality. According to E. M. Forster, he was a socialist in the mould of Shelley and Blake, 'who saw from afar the New Jerusalem from the ignoble slough of his century'. Ordained into the priesthood, he afterwards found that he could not subscribe to the articles of faith and went to live among the working class in the north of England. The Socialist aspect in Carpenter's books did not engage Sassoon at that point but he was affected by his thoughts on homosexuality.

In May 1911 Sassoon went again to Oxford and stayed with Forbes. They made a sentimental journey to Marlborough and, no doubt, exchanged confidences, with Sassoon expressing gratitude for the introduction to Carpenter's work. Whether Forbes urged him to contact Carpenter is not clear but on 11 July a letter went to him from Weirleigh:

Dear Edward Carpenter,
... It was not until October last year, when I was just 24, that, by an accident, I read your *Intermediate Sex*, and have since read *Towards Democracy* and *Who shall command the heart?* I am afraid I have not studied socialism sufficiently to be in sympathy with what I know of it; but your words have shown me all that I was blind to before, and have opened up the new life for me, after a time of great perplexity and unhappiness. Until I read *The Intermediate Sex*, I knew absolutely nothing of that subject, (and was entirely *unspotted*, as I *am now*), but life was an empty thing, and what idea I had about homosexuality was absolutely prejudiced, and I was in such a groove that I couldn't allow myself to be what I wished to be, and the intense attraction I felt for my own sex was almost a subconscious thing and my antipathy for women a mystery to me. It was only by chance that I found my brother (a year younger) was exactly the same. I cannot say what it has done for me. I am a different being and have a definite aim in life and something to lean on, though of course the misunderstanding and injustice is a bitter agony sometimes. But having found out all about it, I am old enough to realise the better and nobler way, and to avoid the mire which might have snared me had I known 5 years ago. I write to you as the leader and the prophet.

The note of effusive thanks and admiration is followed by some details of Sassoon's life in the country, his love of music, commitment to poetry. He then, probably out of deference to Carpenter's Socialism, distances himself from the 'plutocratic' Sassoons and follows this with a quite extraordinary reference to his father who, he tells Carpenter, 'was intensely musical and I think had a strong vein of the homosexual nature in him'. Did Sassoon believe that showing intensity in the arts was a sign of homosexuality? What we know of Alfred Sassoon leaves little doubt that he bore no sexual antipathy to women. The letter ends with Sassoon in unctuous mood: 'May your reward be in the generations to come, as I pray mine may be. I am not religious but I try to believe that our immortality is *to be*, (in those immortals whom our better lives may lead to, and whose immortal ways are marred and kept back by the grossness of unworthy souls). I take as my watchword those words of yours – strength to perform and pride to suffer without sign.'

Carpenter must have worked hard to get any meaning from those florid final sentences, but he wrote appreciatively of the sonnets Sassoon had enclosed. Writing to him on 2 August, Sassoon suggested he might travel north to meet Carpenter, but in the event he stayed at Weirleigh and revised his poetry.

In November he sent a copy of the revised sonnets to Edmund Gosse and received, some three weeks later, a reply which opened on a note of encouragement and ended with a word of advice:

You show a firm advance beyond all verse of yours which I had previously read. You have the sonnet-spirit and something of the sonnet-touch. The picturesqueness of 'Autumn' and the tender melancholy of 'Evening in the Mountains' leave nothing to be desired. They achieve a rare beauty. You must, however, be careful to resist a mere misty or foggy allusiveness. The danger which lies before the poet who endeavours in a sonnet to capture one of those volatile and capricious moods of emotion which are particularly fitted for the sonnet is to resign himself to its haziness. Your sonnets are not firmly enough drawn.

Gosse's reply endorsed the advice Helen Wirgman had already given him in that summer of 1910, after she had read the revised work. Coming up to his study with the manuscript in hand, she said that this new edition was really no improvement on the original. In Gosse's words it was all 'haziness'. Wirgie described the weakness as a lack of physicality, of sharpness and definition:

> Wirgie had given me the clue that I needed, though I was unconscious of it at the time. She meant, as I now see it, that the feeling I put into my poetry was derived from delight in word-music and not from observation and experience of what I wrote about. She saw that my verbal imagery was becoming exclusively literary, while the opportunity for writing poetry was waiting for me all the time, as it were, in that view across the Weald from our garden. The vaguely instinctive nature-worship which I had sometimes tried to put into words needed to be expressed in a definite form.

Reading those poems now is to confirm Gosse's and Wirgie's assessment, and the poems which followed show the same deficiencies. Sassoon was slow learning the lesson and even slower in applying the advice. He continued, however, to be published in *The Academy* and in the more highly regarded *Westminster Gazette*, achieving 11 poems in print in 1911. In that same year, having revised many of the 1909 sonnets, and with some new additions, he ordered another private edition entitled *Twelve Sonnets*.

But his assiduity in working and re-working his verses and adding to their number did not find reward in solving the problem of the lack of concreteness. He remained sure of his vocation. Gosse continued to receive the fruits of Sassoon's endeavours and encouraged him to go on writing, despite the seemingly intractable nature of the problem, though Gosse's last sentence may suggest he was running out of kind things to say: 'I see progress. Try your hand at some objective theme. You must not spend all your life among moonbeams and half-tones. Better than all the listening to advice – go on writing hard and reading the old masters.' That letter from Gosse, dated 30 June 1912, came in response to Sassoon's latest effort entitled *Melodies*, a collection of 15 poems. It is difficult to see where exactly is the progress mentioned by Gosse. The Swinburnian inscription:

> The silence thrills with the whisper of secret streams
> That well from the heart of the woodland

sounds a warning note that what follows is still fanciful, disconnected and, as one observer noted of his earlier efforts, 'musical, grandiloquent and mindless'.

He was doing much better at cricket for his club, the Blue Mantles. His golf was also coming along, although here, as in his poetry, a lack of technique marred the possibilities of a good round. Theresa's busy social activity and the flow of guests through Weirleigh filled the summer. Autumn and winter brought the point-to-point and hunting, with time to enjoy the Harbords' liveliness at Colwood Park, the company of Norman Loder, country-house parties and dances. Here was the seemingly immutable rural England of cricket on the village green, church on Sunday, the cottage-garden, country lanes along which Sassoon would walk and enjoy his 'localised existence', where as he admits, the great affairs of the world seemed hardly to intrude. It was a world he evoked in later years, a partial world, romantic, sentimental and deeply loved.

There arose, however, doubts in Sassoon's mind about this rural existence and its value to him as an aspiring poet: 'Although I had always regarded the writing of poetry as a thing which needed to be kept to oneself, I now began to feel that it would be to my advantage if I were a little less remote from the literary world. I often wished that I could make friends with some other poets, but I never seemed to get any nearer to knowing any of them.' His most immediate connection with that world was Edmund Gosse and his wife Nellie. Gosse's most enduring work, *Father and Son*, had been published in 1907; he was a successful lecturer and arbiter of literary taste, who had introduced the work of Ibsen to English audiences. Returning with Theresa from London to Weirleigh after a visit to the home of the Gosses in Hanover Terrace, Sassoon was unsettled. 'To me it had been a tantalising glimpse which made the journey back to Kent not unlike an exodus from Eden.' He wanted recognition and was confident, given the right stimulus and a conducive environment, it would only be a matter of time before he 'stormed the heights of Hanover Terrace with a prodigious poem'. This aspiration reveals his ambition to be a poet of note rather than dissatisfaction with Weirleigh and the Weald; but the first signs are there that the rural idyll might have to be sacrificed for the goal to be achieved.

Early in December 1912, Sassoon's eyes wandered along the rows of books in his Studio and he randomly selected a copy of *The Everlasting Mercy* by John Masefield. Published in 1911, this long narrative poem was the first of its kind since Kipling's *Barrack-Room Ballads*. Its language was earthy and quite unlike the exalted expressions of High Victorian poetry. It created shock-waves with its realism and use of 'common and vulgar expressions'. Writing of the poem in *The Poetry Review* on 12 January

1912, Arundel del Re stated: 'Mr John Masefield is a revolutionary. His latest work is an assault upon cherished principles and venerable conventions. Its value lies not so much in sheer audacity, though this indeed had peculiar interest, as in the influence it may have on contemporary poets.'

Sassoon, who possessed a good ear for dialect, decided to amuse himself 'by scribbling a few pages of parody'. The result of this whimsical exercise was radical:

> Having rapidly resolved to impersonate a Sussex farm-hand awaiting trial for accidental homicide of the barman of the village ale-house, I began his story in the crudest imitation of Masefield's manner. After the first fifty lines, or so, I dropped the pretence that I was improvising an exuberant skit. While continuing to burlesque Masefield for all I was worth, I was really feeling what I wrote – and doing it not only with abundant delight but a sense of descriptive energy quite unlike anything I had experienced before. Never before had I been able to imbue commonplace details with warmth of poetic emotion. Wholly derivative from *The Mercy* though it remained, my narrative did at any rate express that rural Sussex which I had absorbed through following the Southdown hounds and associating with the supporters of the hunt. In other words I was at last doing what had been suggested by Wirgie in 1911 – writing physically. Far into the night I kept up my spate of productiveness, and next day I went on with unabated intensity. By the evening I had finished it. Reading it through again, I did not ask myself what use there could be in writing a poem so extravagantly unoriginal. Nothing mattered except the mental invigoration it had brought me. I felt that in the last twenty-four hours, I had found a new pair of poetic legs.'

The Daffodil Murderer, as the poem was subsequently named, relates the story of an altercation in a village pub. The narrator and his friend Ted are ejected after someone called Bill takes them by the scruff of the neck. They wait in hiding to give Bill his deserts:

> Bill seem'd hours and hours a-comin';
> 'Home Bill Bailey,' he was hummin';
> Kicking flints up with his toes,
> Back from his evening's work he goes –

I wonder now what Bill was thinking;
Belike 'twas nowt, for he'd been drinking,
And blokes that stumble home from boosing,
They haven't got no thoughts worth losing;
He pass'd me by, all strain'd and ready;
Thump went my heart, but I was steady;
I'd got the pluck as wants no bracing;
I tripp'd him up and kick'd his face in –
Bill blinked his eyes and gave a guggle,
And lay there stiff without a struggle;
'Here, Ted,' said I, 'I've clumped 'im fair,' –
Looked round, but Ted, he wasn't there.
Ted never had the guts to do it;
I done the job and got to rue it.

The style was a clear departure from the work he produced earlier that year, 'An Ode for Music':

Angels of God and multitudes of Heaven
And every servant of the soul's aspiring,
Be with me now, while to your influence bending
I strive to gain the summits of desiring;
Grant me in music's name
Your symphonies of flame.

Sassoon was not inhibited by the obvious disparity in styles and sent both poems to T. W. H. Crosland, who had moved from *The Academy* and then the *Athenaeum* and started a periodical called *The Antidote*. He published 'An Ode to Music' on 1 February, and then on 10 February he published a thousand copies of *The Daffodil Murderer* as a 30-page booklet, priced sixpence. The front declared the contents to be 'Brilliant Beyond Belief'. Sassoon's name did not appear, but a pseudonym, Saul Kain. Crosland, under the guise of someone called William Butler, wrote a spoof preface, introducing the author: 'Though a life-long abstainer, Mr Saul Kain is well acquainted with the insides of various public-houses.' Only one paper reviewed the work, the *Athenaeum*, whose hatred of Crosland was reflected in a hostile review, which employed this acerbic comment: 'The only conclusion we obtain from its perusal is that it is easy to write worse than Mr Masefield.'

Sassoon sent a copy of 'An Ode for Music' to Gosse but did not receive an immediate response. He sent him *The Daffodil Murderer* and waited. Three days after the publication of *The Daffodil Murderer*, Gosse wrote to Sassoon: 'I have given a copy of the D[affodil] M[urderer] to Mr Edward Marsh. Mr Marsh is most curious to see what else you have written, and I would like you to make up a parcel of your pamphlets and send them to him. I should like you to get into friendly relations with Mr Marsh, who is a most charming man.'

It was a propitious introduction to another of the leading names of literary life in London and a senior civil servant with access to Asquith, the Prime Minister; he was also Private Secretary to the First Lord of the Admiralty, Winston Churchill. Like Gosse he enjoyed the literary and political gossip of the day, but, more importantly, they were both great encouragers of emerging talent. To this end Marsh used a bequest he had inherited to support young artists, especially young poets: 'I should be ashamed of being comparatively well-off if I couldn't take advantage of it to help my friends who are younger and poorer and cleverer than I am.' Generous with his money and time, Marsh was also prepared to put his extensive network of well-placed friends and acquaintances at the disposal of his protégés. But he was not universally liked or trusted. Despite his sensitive position in the Civil Service, he could be indiscreet. Alan Lascelles, a future Private Secretary to the sovereign, records in his diary: 'Eddie Marsh chatted to me so indiscreetly about other people's indiscretions that I could have wrung his neck. He told me the last thing I should want to hear. I know why some people think it worthwhile hating him.'

Marsh was, however, a considerable literary critic and a generous friend. He was also, together with Harold Monro and Rupert Brooke, one of the prime instigators of the new movement of Georgian poetry. Recalling the genesis of the movement, he wrote:

> There was a general feeling among the younger poets that Modern English Poetry was very good, and sadly neglected by readers. Rupert announced that he had conceived a brilliant scheme. He would write a book of poetry, and publish it as a selection from the works of twelve different writers, six men and six women, all with the most convincing pseudonyms. That, he thought, must make them sit up. It occurred to me that as we both believed there were at least twelve flesh and blood poets whose work, if properly thrust under the public's nose, had a chance of producing the effect he desired, it

would be simpler to use material which was ready to hand. Next day we lunched in my room and started the plan of the book which was published in December 1912 under the name of *Georgian Poetry*.

The timing could not have been more providential for Sassoon, who wrote to Marsh as suggested:

Feb 14th 1913
Dear Sir,
Mr Edmund Gosse has asked me to send you my privately printed verses, and I have great pleasure in doing so.
Yours very truly,
Siegfried Sassoon

Marsh replied to this tersely diffident communication the following Monday with a long letter. Complimentary, perceptive and full of advice, it echoed the criticism given by Gosse and Helen Wirgman:

I think you have a lovely instrument to play upon and no end of beautiful tunes in your head, but that sometimes you write them down without getting enough meaning into them to satisfy the mind. I believe there is a good as well as a bad sense in which there must be fashions in poetry, and that a vein may be worked out, if only for a time. The vague iridescent ethereal kind had a long intermittent innings all through the 19th century, especially at the end, and Rossetti, Swinburne and Dowson could do things which it is no use trying now. It seems a necessity now to write either with one's eye on an object or with one's mind at grips with a more or less definite idea.

Sassoon agreed with the analysis and was encouraged by its tone. Here, at last, was someone who could help release him from the restrictive influences of the Victorians to 'emerge into an individual style' of his own. Sassoon wanted to discover that voice with which the younger English poets were speaking, especially the ones whose work appeared in the volumes of *Georgian Poetry* edited by Marsh and printed by Harold Monro at the Poetry Bookshop. But the thought came again: could he find that voice by remaining in rural Kent? Uncle Hamo had already expressed his doubts about the intellectual calibre of his nephew's country circle. Gosse, too, recommended exposure to the wider world: 'It would be useful to you, I think, as you lead so isolated a life, to get into relations with these people, who are of all schools, but represent what is most vivid in the latest poetical writings.'

Marsh and Sassoon met for the first time in London in March at the National Club in Whitehall. It was an affable beginning to their subsequent friendship. Marsh repeated his compliments about Sassoon's work, including *The Daffodil Murderer*, even though he was not certain what to make of it. Sassoon, as was his tendency in new situations and in meeting strangers, began to chatter away for all he was worth and assailed Marsh with views on poetry and poems. His host was an indulgent listener. Marsh liked people, especially young men and particularly artistic young men. His closest friendship was with Rupert Brooke, towards whom he acted almost as a father, certainly as an indulgent uncle. Possibly homosexual but more than likely asexual, Marsh was the centre of an extensive social and literary network in London and a frequent guest at the most exclusive country-house parties. He was entirely the right person to guide Sassoon out of the provincialism that was hindering his progress as a poet.

Throughout the spring and summer Sassoon worked diligently at his poetry. He went up to London in June to a dinner-party given by Edmund Gosse at which one of the guests was Robert Ross. Like his host and Eddie Marsh, Ross was a patron of emerging actors, writers, painters and poets, but his notoriety sprang from his friendship with Oscar Wilde, his loyalty to his memory and the jealousy this engendered in Lord Alfred Douglas, Wilde's nemesis. No one sitting around Gosse's table that evening would have been unaware of Ross's battles through the courts against Douglas's venom, to which was added the poisonous activities of Sassoon's erstwhile publisher T. W. H. Crosland. Sassoon liked Ross and, since his own declaration to Carpenter, felt solidarity with him. Ross's biographer writes, 'Robbie was instinctively drawn to the idealistic poet, who so obviously fulfilled all the spiritual and cultural elements he desired in a friend.' Despite this reciprocity of feeling, Ross made no effort to advance the aquaintance that evening.

Following his return to Weirleigh, Sassoon applied himself to his poetry, keeping Marsh informed of his progress or, more accurately, the lack of it. Theresa thought he should get more fresh air and he was inclined to agree with her. In September he forsook poetry and Kent for hunting and Warwickshire. Norman Loder had recently moved there to be Master of the Atherstone Hunt and Sassoon decided to scale the heights of his sporting ambition during the next six months. No one was happier with this move than Tom Richardson, who travelled north a month later in charge of Sassoon's four hunters, the purchase of which had warmed the groom's heart, thoroughly depressed Mr Lousada the trustee and placed a considerable strain on the combined resources of Theresa and her son. But Sassoon thought it all worthwhile as he breathed the morning air and in the evening played the pianola while Loder snoozed in a fireside chair. It was like the days they had spent together when Loder was Master of the Southdown Hunt in his native Sussex. 'There was something almost idyllic about those first weeks.'

Almost idyllic – Sassoon felt pangs of hopelessness about his poetry. Writing on 9 October he told Marsh: 'I don't suppose I shall ever publish any poems, the stuff I wrote last summer was utterly hopeless. Perhaps I will begin fresh in the spring.' But should that new start be in Kent? Marsh had already suggested not: 'But why don't you come and live in London? You can't expect all the interesting things to come down and stay with you in Kent.' Marsh was pushing on a half-open door.

Norman Loder had more than one reason for leaving Sussex for Warwickshire, as Sassoon discovered on his arrival. One of the prominent hunting families in the Midlands was the Fisher family of Amington Hall, Market Bosworth. One of the daughters, Phyllis, a keen and able horse-woman, had taken Loder's fancy. Their engagement was imminent. Sassoon could be diffident and awkward when meeting new people, but he liked Phyllis from the moment they met. She and Norman were among the central figures in Sassoon's life over the next decade, especially after the war when 'good old Sig' would move into their house for the hunting season.

It was during that 1913 season, the last before the war, that Sassoon formed another friendship which, on his part, awakened deep sexual passions. Robert Hugh Hanmer was born in 1895 and, like Gordon Harbord, was the son of a clergyman, the Revd Hugh Hanmer, sometime Rector of Market Bosworth and environs. The Hanmer family were landed gentry, whose estates were situated on the border between Flintshire and Cheshire. They, like the Harbords, were born into the world of the horse and the hound. Mrs Hanmer was a member of the Ethalston family in Sussex, who were prominent in the hunting fraternity there. She would certainly have been familiar with the Loders of Handcross and likely as not to have known the Harbords at Colwood Park. Through this network Robert and his sister Dorothy found themselves part of the Atherstone Hunt 'which prided itself on being quite like a family party'. Sassoon was well aware of the nature of his feelings for Robert. Their repression was essential if the friendship was to develop, which it did over the next year, mainly through Dorothy keeping up a correspondence from the Hanmer side: Bobby was not the letter-writing kind.

The hunting season was drawing to its close and Sassoon was getting restless for London and the company of Eddie Marsh. He had also resolved the matter of leaving home. Early in February 1914 he wrote to Marsh: 'I have quite made up my mind to live in London a good deal in the future. I shall never do any decent work buried alive among fox-hunters. So I want you to help me find somewhere to live and I don't want to say anything about it to my people, (at present), as I know they would kick up a fuss and spoil the whole venture!' In fact Sassoon had done some house-hunting during his occasional visits to the capital and, attracted to the idea of being near Marsh, had more or less decided on Number 1, Raymond Buildings, Gray's Inn. Marsh lived in Number 5. He moved to his new rooms in May, having secured a housekeeper, Mrs Fretter, whom, he told Marsh in a letter from Weirleigh, 'I engaged in spite of our first tremulous electric interview, [and who] appears to be economic'. Considering his sheltered upbringing, which hardly if ever called on him to engage with domestic concerns, Sassoon did well in organising the rooms, although he did run into difficulties with the upholsterers and also with the carpets: 'too big or too small I forget which'. It had not been easy persuading Theresa that this was the right decision. She was still upset over the sudden death of Miriam, her maid. It was not the best time to forsake Weirleigh, always at its most attractive in spring, Sassoon's favourite season: 'April in Kent has been quite lovely, orchards in blossom and sunlight.' But even these attractions failed to diminish the staleness he felt, or the aimlessness of his rural existence and, as he admits:

> I felt that I ought to set to work on a tremendous poem full of prophetic sublimity, spiritual aspiration, and human tragedy and that I needed to start my life all over again and give up everything except being noble and uplifting. I felt that my recent existence had been philistine and one-sided.

The move to London, he hoped, would provide the antidote. If his poetry was to achieve anything, then contact with the world beyond the 'sentinel pines' on the Weald's horizon was crucial. As an earnest of this fresh start he left all his books behind, taking only his Oxford Dictionary. On arriving in London he bought a folio of Gray's poems. The rooms, modest in size, were situated at the noisy end of Gray's Inn. This intrusive rumbling of traffic along Theobald's Road did not deter Sassoon, as he had made clear to Marsh: 'I shall certainly take the rooms, noise and all, I hope there will be noise of poetry in my head which will drown all other sounds.'

Sincere, as he undoubtedly was, about making a fresh start, he failed to keep to a routine in his new surroundings which would facilitate the writing of vibrant verse. But it was a liberation. Theresa, though doubting the wisdom or necessity of the move, came to inspect the place. Her approval, if guarded, was another worry out of the way. Conscious of the need to be a man about town, Sassoon acquired the necessary symbols of rolled umbrella, a bowler and a top hat, together with full evening suit. The outward appearance, however, did little to rekindle the muse and, instead of being the poet, Sassoon became a tourist.

Riding on the top of a London bus or walking nonchalantly through the streets, he filled his days with diversions. He was lonely. Marsh, busy with his political duties during the day and his social round in the evening, was rarely available. The Gosses were abroad and the expected social connections were non-existent. Wandering around London Zoo, Sassoon came unexpectedly on Helen Wirgman, herself as lonely as he felt. Their mutual situation, though unexpressed, provided the opportunity to renew their friendship with occasional concert and theatre visits, as well as Wirgie coming to tea in Raymond Buildings. Such visits could be a strain, as Wirgie was easily upset by an incautious remark or even an innocent one, but he always felt indebted to her and distressed by her circumstances.

Norman Loder and some friends from the Atherstone descended on London to sell horses at Tattersalls, including one of Sassoon's, which saddened him. Sauntering in St James's he met his old housemaster from Marlborough, Mr Gould. Such encounters did nothing to alleviate his sense of isolation which was deepened when, on attending the theatre or a performance by the Russian Ballet, he envied the exuberant friendships of the young people as they set off from the theatre to some dinner-party. Beyond the detail is the portrait of Sassoon the outsider, uncertain, awkward. He had reverted to the diffidence that marked his arrival into the world of the public school; at 28 years of age, he was still on the defensive.

Eddie Marsh invited him to breakfast with Rupert Brooke and W. H. Davies at Number 5, Raymond Buildings. Davies, loquacious but limited, was someone with whom Sassoon felt comfortable. His evocation of the countryside and gentle descriptions of the seasons were reminiscent of John Clare. Of the group of poets gathered under Eddie Marsh's wing, Davies was the odd man out in terms of birth and breeding – Welsh, working-class and poor. In appearance he was dark, swarthy and unkempt, so different from the blond, blue-eyed Brooke, who dressed with studied casualness. Davies was flannel but Brooke was gossamer. Sassoon liked Davies; his admiration he reserved for the younger poet in whose presence he felt a sense of inadequacy and under-achievement. He had read Brooke's work without understanding it: 'My unagile intellect was confused by his metaphysical cleverness.' Brooke was a successful poet, confident of his talent and self-possessed. He had travelled, garnered experience, involved himself in politics, while Sassoon had buried himself in rural Kent and struggled. Brooke's knowledge and assessment of other poets were expressed with assurance, while Sassoon had to grope around for something to say. Creating a right and good impression was all-important to Sassoon. On taking his leave, descending the staircase to the echo of the clicking lock, he knew what a feeble impression he had left on Brooke. 'When bidding me goodbye his demeanour implied that as far as he was concerned there was no apparent reason why we should ever meet again. He may even have breathed a sigh of relief at having got rid of me at last.'

Walking the short distance to his own rooms, Sassoon contemplated another situation which he found difficult to handle – his financial affairs. The cost of renting and decorating the rooms, together with other impetuous expenditure, had resulted in a significant overdraft. Mr Lousada once again shook his head in both disapproval and refusal of further advances of the quarterly allowance. Sassoon, only halfway through the year, was reconsidering his man-about-town adventure. Dire though the situation was, it did not deter him from buying tickets to hear Chaliapin and the Russian Opera. He did make the concession of opting for the upper gallery, but on the two occasions Helen Wirgman accompanied him, he booked the grand circle. 'These operas were a romantic discovery which appealed to my imagination more than any dramatic performance I had hitherto experienced.' Thus he consoled himself as he took the enforced return journey to Weirleigh.

He was despondent that money, or the lack of it, had curtailed his new, if undirected existence. While he lived free of charge at Weirleigh, the financial position would recover but the recovery of poetic inspiration seemed a forlorn hope. Meanwhile he played the music of the Russian Opera on the piano and revelled in the memory. The reverie was only disturbed by the constant talk and newspaper reports of war with Germany. In the last days of July rumours strengthened and people prepared for mobilisation. If war came and if, as the reports said, volunteers would be needed to swell the ranks, Sassoon was prepared to enlist. Although only half-believing that war, even at that late stage, was a possibility, he took a medical test and waited. Returning from a cycling trip to Rye, he ruminated on the beauty of the Weald, the place of his childhood imaginings and sporting adventures. What did all this have to do with war, he pondered. And what kind of war would it be? Would the Germans come marching down the Hastings road as the Normans had done in 1066?

Lit by departing day was the length and breadth of the Weald, and the message of those friendly miles was a single chord of emotion vibrating backward across the years to my earliest rememberings. Uplifted by this awareness, I knew that here was something deeply loved, something which the unmeasurable timelessness of childhood had made my own. The years of my youth were going down for ever in the weltering, western gold, and the future would take me far from that sunset-embered horizon. Beyond the night was my new beginning. The Weald had been the world of my youngness, and while I gazed across it now I felt prepared to do whatever I could to defend it. And after all, dying for one's native land was believed to be the most glorious thing one could possibly do!

4

WAR

1914–16

Sassoon went off to war on a hot August day without the remotest idea of what lay ahead. Caught in a fusion of fear and fascination about the unknown, he felt that something portentous was about to happen to him. Before leaving Weirleigh he looked around its rooms. Strangely silent rooms they were now, with Michael away in Vancouver and Hamo even further removed in Argentina. In the drawing room a slanting shaft of sunlight rested alongside the copy of dear old Watts' evocation of *Love and Death*. Departing the house was made easier by the seven months he had spent in Warwickshire and London. How long this next absence would be was an unanswerable question. The optimists were predicting that the war would be over by Christmas; which Christmas they did not stipulate. Lord Kitchener thought three years was the time-scale required to see off the Hun. Few guessed it would drag on for four years and fewer foresaw the changed world that would emerge at its conclusion.

Sassoon was more preoccupied with the past than the future. He was putting things behind him, especially the debt incurred by hunting and being in London. Then there was the empty and boring existence he was forced to endure at Weirleigh. His hope of storming Gosse's portals with the ultimate poem looked forlorn. Whatever progress he had made under the tutorship of Eddie Marsh was now sidelined into an unforeseen terminus. The Army, like public schools, had little time for poets and secret worlds. It was another fresh start. Sassoon felt ready for whatever challenges lay ahead; whether he was equal to them only time would tell. If asked what those challenges were he would have been hard pressed to explain, other than to say that King and Country expected it of him and that his neighbours, personified by Captain Ruxton and Squire Morland, expected him to square up to his responsibilities. Above all he would have stated that this war was inevitable and justifiable, after which the Captain would have clapped him on the back, Theresa shouted hurrah and the Squire called for three cheers. Sassoon, like them, believed in the rightness of the cause.

The nation was not united in support of the war; there was vociferous opposition as well as undercurrents of disapproval. Ramsay MacDonald, George Lansbury, Philip Snowden and Philip Morrell led the parliamentary opposition to any involvement and, outside parliament, Bertrand Russell began the first of his many crusades against war. How to prosecute the war became a cause of division, leading eventually to the removal of the Prime Minister, upheavals in the Cabinet and a change in the leadership of the Army, whose ranks were swollen by volunteers in what seemed an adequate supply for the task in hand. But the death toll rose beyond expectations and in January 1916 conscription was introduced. The Military Service Act contained clauses which allowed exemptions from military duty, but those who applied for exemption were called before tribunals to justify their motives. A new phenomenon appeared: the conscientious objector. There were periodicals which, if not pacifist, were prepared to give space to critical and questioning articles. One such was the *Cambridge Magazine*, whose editor was C. K. Ogden, another was the *Nation*, edited by H. W. Massingham. But the national press, like the vast majority of the country at the start of the war, was in favour of total involvement. It was only when the mounting lists of the dead and injured filled the pages of those newspapers; when the dreaded envelope arrived containing words of regret that another life had been extinguished; and when the first Christmas passed – and the war went on through three more – that many voices became less shrill and the mental stance more stoical.

When war was declared on 4 August Sassoon become a trooper in C Squadron, 1st Battalion, Sussex Yeomanry, the Royal Sussex Regiment. Three days later he was billeted at Hode Farm, near Canterbury. Choosing to go into the ranks rather than seeking a commission was unusual but not exceptional; others from a similar background followed the same path: 'Only one gent in the ranks, young Hope, son of J. E. Hope (the dullest man in Parliament isn't he?), and his son takes after his papa. The Colonel asked me to be an officer, but I don't feel equal to the effort, although it would be a more satisfactory existence.' Living in a tent with others had some compensations. His fellow troopers were 'kind and helpful, and there was something almost idyllic about those early weeks of the war. The flavour and significance of life were around me in the homely smells of the thriving farm where we were quartered; my own abounding health responded zestfully to the outdoor world.' His favourite horse, Cockbird, was with him. Being allowed, indeed encouraged, to bring one's own mount, had influenced Sassoon's choice of regiment. However, the burdens imposed on a trooper's horse were greater than those required from an officer's horse. Realising this, Sassoon sold Cockbird to one of the officers in C Squadron. It was a deprivation eased only by seeing Cockbird mingle with the élite. In a moment of anthropomorphic fantasy Trooper Sassoon, wandering down to renew aquaintance with him, detected an air of superiority in the newly promoted Cockbird.

There was nothing fanciful about being in the ranks. From a life of being served by maids and grooms, Sassoon was now fetching, carrying and grooming. Those officers and men who knew him before the war and were aware of his background must have wondered at his decision to be a trooper. At the end of September Sassoon was asking himself the same question.

In October, while giving the horses some field-work, he took a tumble and broke his arm. Progress was slow, as he complained in a letter to Marsh, a month later: 'I'm in the depths of despair and still spend my days in captivity. You can't think how dull it is here.' It was a miserable end to the year. Recuperating at Weirleigh he felt his spirits take a further plunge on seeing the stables empty – the horses had been commandeered by the Army; Tom Richardson, the groom, had enlisted in the Veterinary Corps. Gordon Harbord and his younger brother Geoffrey were awaiting embarkation. Norman Loder left the Atherstone to take up a commission in the cavalry; Bobby Hanmer was joining the Royal Welch Fusiliers and Hamo was coming home from Argentina to enlist. Sassoon, with his arm in a sling, was 'distinctly conscious of an anti-climax'.

He struggled through what he called 'the secret desperations of that winter', selecting 13 poems for another private edition under the title *Discoveries*. The poems are the first evidence of Eddie Marsh's influence on Sassoon's work and come nearer to Wirgie's demand that he write with greater physicality; the images are under greater control and Sassoon recaptures, albeit partially, that naturalness and directness, whose loss he bemoaned when he became 'rather Ninetyish':

Noah

When old Noah stared across the floods,
Sky and water melted into one
Looking-glass of shifting tides and sun.
Mountain tops were few: the ship was foul:
All the morn Old Noah marvelled greatly
At this weltering world that shone so stately,
Drowning deep the rivers and the plains.
Through the stillness came a rippling breeze;
Noah sighed, remembering the green trees.

Clear along the morning stooped a bird, –
Lit beside him with a blossom sprig.
Earth was saved; and Noah danced a jig.

The decision about the content of *Discoveries* was accompanied by another decision: Sassoon resolved to seek a commission in an infantry regiment. He believed that by so doing he would get to the Front more quickly than if he returned to the Sussex Yeomanry as a trooper. He wrote to the Adjutant of the Royal Welch Fusiliers, who sent a positive reply, suggesting he join the regiment in May. His friend, Robert Hanmer, was in the RWF and Sassoon hoped they would serve together. In *Memoirs of a Fox-Hunting Man*, Captain Ruxton is credited with suggesting the RWF because it was his old regiment and he could effect an introduction. It is more likely that Sassoon was following his heart and that the Hanmers, a highly influential family in Wales, smoothed the way for his commission. In *Memoirs of a Fox-Hunting Man*, the RWF is called the Flintshire Fusiliers. Hanmer is a Flintshire village under the patrimony of the Hanmers and within close proximity to the Regimental Headquarters at Wrexham.

Robert did not keep up a regular correspondence but Sassoon received news of him via his sister Dorothy. During the 18 months since Sassoon first met Robert and his sister, he had grown fond of her. At some point in 1915 they entered into what in those days was called 'an understanding'. Sassoon later described it as being 'dimly engaged' and Rupert Hart-Davis, in the published diaries, says it was a 'shadowy' engagement. Certainly there was nothing official in the arrangement.

Meanwhile spring was in the air, his arm had healed and, before joining the regiment, Sassoon took himself off to visit his Thornycroft relations at Bembridge on the Isle of Wight to regain his vitality. However, he could not shake off the sentiment that he had felt at Hode Farm that he was 'very much a man dedicated to death but the reality of war was a long way off'. The reality came closer when, in April, he heard of the death of Rupert Brooke. His first thoughts were for Eddie Marsh: 'I won't write anything about R.B. except that I know how much his loss means to you, (as indeed to us all).' The death of Brooke, as the bracketed words suggest, had more than a personal impact. The epitome of young England, romantic, patriotic and self-sacrificing, he became both icon and example. The style and subject of his poems set the tone for so many other young men who, with varying degrees of talent, sought through poetry to portray this war not as tragedy so much as heroic opportunity. For the first 15 months of the conflict Sassoon wrote in the Brookean vein and then found his own voice. But that Easter of 1915, because of his friendship with Eddie Marsh and his memory of the breakfast at Raymond Buildings, the death of Brooke became for Sassoon one of 'those things deeply felt'.

At the end of April Sassoon proceeded to the regimental training depot at Litherland, an area to the north of Liverpool and close to the mouth of the Mersey. It was a place markedly different from the rural beauty of his background and experience. The camp, like its surroundings, was bleak and singularly uninspiring. It had two redeeming features, however, its proximity to the golf course at nearby Crosby and an easy route into the centre of Liverpool. Sassoon took full advantage of both. Learning to be a second lieutenant did not pose an insuperable task for him; indeed he enjoyed the challenge and the camaraderie, but he adopted the same low profile and survival tactic which marked his conduct at public school and continued to play the observer of his surroundings. A cold wind blew off the Mersey and along the Liverpool–Leeds Canal, bearing the industrial smells of the Litherland Tanneries, the Bryant and May matchworks and Brotherton's dynamite works. The large Catholic cemetery nearby and the constant funeral processions were a daily reminder that the depot too was part of the intrusiveness of mortality; part of the boundary 'between the presence of life and the prospect of death'. The depot, like the surrounding factories, was about manufacturing. The constant, endless conveyor-belt produced trained, disciplined soldiers for dispatch to the Front. Nothing was permanent except the process, nothing more insistent than the need for more men as the news of losses came in. More men required, more men ready to fill the gaps in the line. 'Litherland was a manufactory of soldiers,' he records, and the place fed his death-haunted memory.

Then there were the medal-laden old officers who were responsible for preparing the young for conflict. A suspicion was planted in Sassoon's mind that their idealistic view of soldiering was not connected to the reality of the human toll war exacted. Theirs was the view from the club window and not the dug-out. This suspicion, one of the most powerful themes in Sassoon's war poetry, had its genesis at Litherland, as did another theme, the muddle war posed for organised religion. In *Memoirs of a Fox-Hunting Man* Sassoon tells the apocryphal story of troops lined up on the square ready for embarkation and the padre's final words to them: 'And now may God go with you; I will go with you as far as the station.' He had rejected institutional religion and the beliefs so precious to his mother. Rarely had he attended church after his confirmation and he admits that he never prayed. But he wrote prayers at this time and included 'A Child's Prayer' in his next private volume, *Morning Glory*:

> For Morn, my dome of blue,
> For Meadows, green and gay,
> And birds who love the twilight of the leaves,
> Let Jesus keep me joyful when I pray.
>
> For the big Bees that hum
> And hide in bells of flowers;
> For the winding roads that come
> To Evening's holy door,
> May Jesus bring me grateful to his arms
> And guard my innocence for evermore.

The air of impermanence which permeated the depot strengthened human attachments and deepened their intensity. The shared danger, the mutual involvement created bonds and released emotions which under other conditions would have remained dormant. David Cuthbert Thomas was the son of a clergyman from the small rural parish of Llanedi in Carmarthenshire, a former pupil of Christ's College, Brecon, and 19 years old when he joined the Royal Welch Fusiliers. Sassoon's description of their first meeting in May 1915 leaves no doubt that he was instantly attracted to him:

He had unpacked and arranged his belongings, and was sitting on his campbed polishing a perfectly new pipe. He looked up at me. Twilight was falling and there was only one small window, but even in the half-light his face surprised me by its candour and freshness. He had the obvious good looks which go with fair hair and firm features, but it was the radiant integrity of his expression which astonished me. While I was getting ready for dinner we exchanged a few remarks. His tone of voice was simple and reassuring, like his appearance. How does he manage to look like that? I thought; and for the moment I felt all my age. His was the bright countenance of truth; ignorant and undoubting; incapable of concealment but strong in reticence and in modesty.

Sassoon found in the 19-year-old Thomas an ideal companion – indeed an idealised one – and a substitute for the absent Robert Hanmer and Gordon Harbord. But there was something else, the latent sexual attraction which underscores the romantic description; the hyperbole of someone smitten by physical beauty, innocence and vulnerability. No previous friendship had stirred Sassoon so deeply. His friendship with Norman Loder emanated from admiration and hero-worship. The friendship with Gordon Harbord was founded in their mutual enthusiasm for cricket and in their passion for hunting, as too was his friendship with Robert Hanmer. But that friendship was, on Sassoon's part, more complicated. He was infatuated with Hanmer but there is no description of him which comes anywhere near that accorded to Thomas, of whom Sassoon also said: 'He made all the difference to my life.' Tommy, as he is called in the diaries, was the first of a series of young men whom Sassoon loved in a paternal way, the obverse of his own need for a father-figure.

In high summer Sassoon and Thomas were sent to Pembroke College, Cambridge, for the final part of their officer training. While there Sassoon began friendships which were to have their impact on his life after the war. Edmund Gosse had given him a letter of introduction to Sydney Carlyle Cockerell. Twenty years older than Sassoon, he had settled in Cambridge as Director of the Fitzwilliam Museum, a tenure which was an outstanding and radical success. His love was rare manuscripts and his knowledge in this field was unchallenged. Given Sassoon's bibliographical tendencies it was no wonder that a friendship began which lasted nearly half a century.

I spent several evenings at his house – evenings made memorable by the wonderful books he showed me – and from which I returned to my camp bed in Pembroke College in a trance of stimulation after having handled original manuscripts of D. G. Rossetti, William Morris and Francis Thompson. On those Sunday nights in the quiet candlelit room he seemed a sort of bearded and spectacled magician, conjuring up the medieval illuminated missals and Psalters on which he was a famous expert, and bringing my mind into almost living contact with the Pre-Raphaelites whom I had worshipped since my dreaming adolescence.

Cockerell also brought him into contact with Edward Dent, musicologist, biographer of Mozart and Scarlatti, and later Professor of Music at the university. Dent was homosexual and, Edward Carpenter apart, was Sassoon's first confidant. Cambridge had a circle of homosexuals, including two who also became friends of Sassoon – E. M. Forster and A. T. Bartholomew. Sassoon was struggling with his homosexuality. Dent had no such inhibitions and would, in due course, arrange for Sassoon to cross the boundary between desire and its fulfilment.

A decade had passed since his first arrival at Cambridge when he had found himself stranded on the shores of Jurisprudence. What a changed world now with uniforms more prominent than gowns. How distant the idyllic afternoon spent reading Morris's *Earthly Paradise* on the Cam. These were days of other rivers, the Marne, the Aisne, the Somme. It was at Clare College that Sassoon had resolved to be a poet. So what was that minstrel singing a decade later? Between April 1915 and the following September he worked on a poem which he called 'Absolution':

> The anguish of the earth absolves our eyes
> Till beauty shines in all that we can see.
> War is our scourge; yet war has made us wise,
> And, fighting for our freedom, we are free.
>
> Horror of wounds and anger at the foe,
> And loss of things desired; all these must pass.
> We are the happy legion, for we know
> Time's but a golden wind that shakes the grass.

There was an hour when we were loth to part
From life we longed to share no less than others.
Now, having claimed this heritage of heart,
What need we more, my comrades and my brothers?

In a bleak footnote to this poem, written in later years, Sassoon says: 'People used to feel like this when they joined up in 1914 and 1915.' Whether 'people' in general thought so is to be doubted but the class to which Sassoon belonged and the upper echelons of society certainly did embrace these sentiments. The heroic warrior, self-forgetting, spurred on by chivalry, attains the beatific vision vouchsafed alone to the 'happy legion'. It was a powerful myth and a costly ideal.

When Sassoon began to write the poem in April 1915, others were writing home about the reality. Raymond Asquith wrote to his wife Katharine at Mells in Somerset: 'How bloody everything is just now. I feel discouraged about everything, thoroughly tired of the war and utterly in the trough of the wave.' Sassoon had yet to cross the bridge of experience. Within a year he would know 'ecstasies changed to an ugly cry' but at Cambridge in 1915 with Tommy, his loved companion, he was surging with all the confidence bright summer days engender, and keen to seek the Holy Grail, 'Riding in armour bright serene and strong'.

Back at Litherland, and much to his delight, he was reunited with Robert Hanmer. Knowing that the threat of death hung over himself and the two loved companions, Bobby and Tommy, gave Sassoon feelings of elation rather than distress. The threat created an emotional bond, which in Sassoon's case had sexual undertones. And undertones they remained because neither Hanmer nor Thomas was homosexual. The consequences to Sassoon, had his sexual orientation been revealed, would have proved disastrous. Desires had to be suppressed; it was another strain. In October he was told that embarkation for France was on 17 November. Thomas, too, would leave at the same time but there was no certainty that after arrival in France they would be posted to the same battalion. Hanmer would not be going with them. Sassoon dreaded leaving him at Litherland and fretted, fearing that Thomas and he would be separated after their arrival in France.

On notice of embarkation, officers were given 'last leave'. Sassoon went home then went up to London to see Marsh. The year 1915 had not been kind to Marsh, with the death of Brooke followed by the death of Marsh's father. Brooke's mother was making life difficult for Eddie, who was the late poet's executor. As Private Secretary to Churchill he was caught up in the Gallipoli expedition and the increasing tension between members of the Admiralty Board about the wisdom of the enterprise. In a power struggle with Churchill, the First Sea Lord, Admiral Fisher, resigned. It was a first-rate crisis for the government made worse by the fiasco of Gallipoli and was only resolved by Asquith forming a coalition with the Conservatives. Their *bête noire* was Churchill. By mid-November he was out of office and into the Army. Eddie lost his high position – the price exacted for giving whole-hearted loyalty to Churchill.

There was little time for Eddie to entertain Sassoon. E. J. Dent came from Cambridge to London, where he kept a small flat in which to entertain his friends and young men. Maida Vale was one of London's discreet homosexual warrens. Sassoon had written to Dent about his 'angel' – 'the beautiful Bobby'; now he welcomed the opportunity to talk to Dent, perhaps telling him of how he liked to read his poems to Thomas and share with him the contents of his letters from Gordon Harbord. He needed to share his thoughts with men of experience who understood his longings and whom he could trust. Robert Baldwin Ross became the most important of these.

Edmund Gosse invited Sassoon to dinner at his home on 17 October, where he renewed his acquaintance with Ross. Eighteen months had passed since their first meeting under similar circumstances at Gosse's on 5 June 1913, when they had corresponded – Sassoon sent him some of his poems and Ross had invited him to call – but the start of their friendship was on the eve of Sassoon's embarkation.

Ross possessed an extraordinary capacity for friendship, particularly among painters, actors, writers and poets. Like Gosse and Marsh, he was an enthusiastic patron of young talent and placed his influence, insight and multifarious social connections at their disposal. A person of private but not extensive means, Ross delighted in entertaining his friends, particularly in the late evening, in the suite of rooms he occupied at 40 Half Moon Street, near the Ritz and even nearer Curzon Street, another clandestine meeting-place.

Ross was highly regarded as an art expert and literary critic. His reputation, however, lay in being the close friend and literary executor of Oscar Wilde. He was devoted to both Wilde and his family before, during and after the trial that saw Wilde condemned to two years' hard labour for sodomy. Following Wilde's death in 1900, Ross had, as mentioned, worked unstintingly to restore the artistic reputation of his friend with a single-mindedness that engendered admiration in some but in others contempt. Ross had enemies, in particular Lord Alfred Douglas, Wilde's erstwhile companion, and T. W. H. Crosland, the rogue publisher of Sassoon's early poetic efforts. These two conducted a vicious and persistent legal campaign against Ross over a period of nearly 15 years. When Sassoon first met him in that summer of 1913, Ross had newly finished another round of warfare in the courts with the prospect of more battles to come. That, to quote Ross's biographer, was the reason for the 18 months' gap between his first meeting Sassoon and the renewal of their acquaintance: 'with Douglas's prosecution threatening to engulf him, Robbie could not risk involving another young man in his problems'.

If indeed that was the reason, it was typical of Ross's generous and sensitive approach to friendship, a quality celebrated by Prime Minister Asquith, by his wife Margot and also by Sassoon: 'From the first I had found him one of the most attractive and amusing men I had ever met, and his spontaneous liking for me had been combined with an active interest in my poetic career. Although seventeen years my senior, his intuitively sympathetic understanding of youth made him seem a benevolent and impulsive bachelor uncle with whom one could feel on easy terms of equality, while consenting to be guided by his astute and experienced advice.'

Ross's rooms in Half Moon Street were part of single gentlemen's apartments under the supervision of Nellie Burton. Small, stout and worldly-wise, she had been maid to Ross's mother. Burton was not just a landlady or housekeeper in the mould of Sherlock Holmes's Mrs Hudson. She knew her gentlemen were part of London's homosexual network. Another of her tenants, a friend of Ross and subsequently of Sassoon, was Roderick Meiklejohn, a senior official at the Treasury. Nellie Burton was discretion itself and she expected her gentlemen to be so as well. When one of her tenants shot himself in the bath, with the resultant messiness, she told Sassoon that she couldn't understand why he hadn't gone down the road and shot himself in the park! As for Sassoon, he was taken to her ample bosom and he, in return, was always solicitous of her well-being. Half Moon Street for the next decade became a home from home, made possible by Ross's generosity and absolute commitment to friendship. He was one of the few whom Sassoon trusted and who never betrayed that trust.

The cold winds of winter came early to Litherland that year and Sassoon watched as more soldiers left for France and Flanders. The lists of casualties told their own grim story. But the grimmest news came in the form of a telegram which contained the news that Hamo Sassoon, his younger brother, had been mortally wounded at Gallipoli and buried at sea on 1 November. Their relationship had been close until Hamo, like Michael, followed different interests. The death of Hamo was another debt of honour, another reason for getting to the Front. When Sassoon and Theresa met at Melbury Road on 16 November, the eve of her favourite son's embarkation, she was tense both with grief for Hamo and anxiety for Siegfried. It was a wretched twenty-four hours. As the troop-train pulled out of Victoria, bound for France, on the afternoon of 17 November, Sassoon felt a sense of relief: 'To have finished with farewells; that in itself was a burden discarded.' By way of Calais and Boulogne, Sassoon arrived at the main base camp at Etaples at 11.30 on the night of the 18th. This was the main centre for the forces serving on the Western Front and near the General Headquarters at Montreuil. It was five days later that he received his posting to C Company of the Ist Battalion – as did David Thomas.

By the end of its first year the war was static, with the opposing armies facing each other in trenches stretching from the Belgian coast, across northern France, to the Swiss border. The main battlefields of the Western Front were concentrated in northern France, straddling its border with Belgium from the Channel to the River Somme. Throughout 1915, the Commander of the British Expeditionary Force, Sir John French, attempted to break the stalemate by a series of diversionary attacks, at Neuve Chapelle in March, Aubers Ridge and Festubert in May and at Hooge in June. The Germans took the offensive once at the second battle of Ypres in April. The toll of human life and suffering was out of all proportion to any gains made. In October General Joffre, the French Commander-in-Chief, called for a new offensive at the town of Loos. Sir John objected and had to be instructed by Lord Kitchener, Secretary of War, to co-operate. He did so but in his own way which, it is said, caused the failure of the battle. The slaughter was horrendous, with 15,000 British casualties on the first day. The battle of Loos marked the end of Sir John French; he was replaced in December by Field Marshal Sir Douglas Haig, who himself had connived against French.

Such was the state of things as Sassoon, together with Thomas, made his way on 25 November to join the Ist Battalion billeted at the town of Bethune, and then some two miles on to Le Hamel and C Company. There was never a good time to arrive at the Front and November was about the worst. Le Hamel was part of a network of supply depots behind the trenches and, as his diary records, Sassoon was given a platoon of 60 men, whose job it was to transport supplies through the labyrinth of communication trenches. His first week set the pattern for the next three months.

November 24
About 4.30, in darkness and rain, started up three-quarters of a mile of light tram-lines through marsh, with sixty men. They carried hurdles up the communications-trenches about three-quarters of a mile which took two hours. Flares go up frequently, a few shells go high overhead; the trenches are very wet; finally emerge in a place behind the first and second-line trenches, where we are digging new trenches.

November 27
Go out again, starting at 9.45 p.m. in brilliant moonlight and iron frost. Dig from 12 to 2. Home at 4.15. Up behind the trenches the frostbound morasses and ditches and old earthworks in the moonlight with dusky figures filing across the open, hobbling to avoid slipping, inhuman forms go to and from inhuman tasks.

November 29
Went with working-party 3 o'clock. Wet day. Awful mud up in trenches. Tried to dig till 7.30 and came home soaked. Home 9.45. A shocking night for the men, whose billets are wretched.

Life behind the trenches was bad enough; in the trenches it was worse. Rations were meagre, sanitation spartan; lice, rats and flies spread disease. Cold feet ploughed through muddy slime and everywhere was the stench of death. Along the communication trenches soldiers carrying supplies passed each other as silhouettes. Rupert Hart-Davis states, 'The War changed Sassoon from a versifier into a poet.' The change was almost immediate, as his first front-line poem, 'The Redeemer', testifies:

The Redeemer

Darkness: the rain sluiced down; the mire was deep;
It was past twelve on a mid-winter night,
When peaceful folk in beds lay snug asleep;
There, with much work to do before the light,

We lugged our clay-sucked boots as best we might
Along the trench; sometimes a bullet sang,
And droning shells burst with a hollow bang;
We were soaked, chilled and wretched, every one;
Darkness; the distant wink of a huge gun.

I turned in the black ditch, loathing the storm;
A rocket fizzed and burned with blanching flare,
And lit the face of what had been a form
Floundering in mirk. He stood before me there;
I say that He was Christ; stiff in the glare;
And leaning forward from His burdening task,
Both arms supporting it; His eyes on mine
Stared from the woeful head that seemed a mask
Of mortal pain in Hell's unholy shine.

No thorny crown, only a woollen cap
He wore – an English soldier, white and strong,
Who loved his time like any simple chap,
Good days of work and sport and homely song;
Now he has learned that nights are very long,
And dawn a watching of the windowed sky.
But to the end, unjudging, he'll endure
Horror and pain, not uncontent to die
That Lancaster on Lune may stand secure.

He faced me, reeling in his weariness,
Shouldering his load of planks, so hard to bear.
I say that he was Christ, who wrought to bless
All groping things with freedom bright as air,
And with His mercy washed and made them fair.
Then the flame sank, and all grew black as pitch,
While we began to struggle along the ditch;
And someone flung his burden in the muck,
Mumbling: 'O Christ Almighty, now I'm stuck!'

'What I have written,' he once recalled, 'is what I have experienced.' His experience of war, of course, was in its infancy as he was told by an officer who wandered into Sassoon's hut on 28 November:

I went to visit 'C' Company Mess, where I got a friendly welcome. I noticed *The Essays of Lionel Johnson* lying on the table. It was the first book I had seen in France that was neither a military text-book nor a rubbishy novel. I stole a look at the fly-leaf, and the name was Siegfried Sassoon. Then I looked around to see who could possibly be called Siegfried Sassoon and bring a copy of *Lionel Johnson* with him to the First Battalion. The answer being obvious I got into conversation with him and a few minutes later we set out for Bethune, being off duty until dusk, and talked about poetry.

The officer was Robert Graves and in this casual way his friendship began with Sassoon. It was never to be a smooth relationship, despite their closeness throughout the war and for some years after its conclusion. In his diary Sassoon writes of Graves as someone 'very much disliked. An interesting creature, overstrung and self-conscious, a defier of convention.' There is a fuller character reference in *Memoirs of an Infantry Officer*, where Graves is called David Cromlech:

At his best I'd always found him an ideal companion, although his opinions were often disconcerting. But no one was worse than he was at hitting it off with officers who distrusted cleverness and disliked unreserved utterances. In fact he was a positive expert at putting people's back up unintentionally. The Colonel was heard to remark that young Cromlech threw his tongue a hell of a lot too much ... he wasn't good at being seen but not heard.

Graves was by temperament the reverse of Sassoon; but the bond was poetry, not personality, and on their way to Bethune that was the subject of their conversation, as Graves remembers in *Goodbye to All That*.

Siegfried Sassoon had, at that time, published only a few privately-printed pastoral pieces of eighteen-ninetyish flavour, and a satire on Masefield. 'At this time I was getting my first book of poems, *Over the Brazier*, ready for the press; I had one or two drafts in my pocket-book and showed them to Siegfried. He frowned and said that war should not be written about in such a realistic way. In return he showed me some of his own poems. One of them began:

> Return to greet me, colours that were my joy,
> Not in the woeful crimson of men slain.

Siegfried had not yet been in the trenches. I told him, in my old-soldier manner, that he would soon change his style.'

Graves may have been outspoken but he had the measure that day of Sassoon the poet. He did not get the measure of the man. Sassoon was always sensitive to criticism, not because he overestimated his work but because he tended to underestimate it, evidenced by the dipping of his toe in the water with private publications. With Sassoon, as with so many sensitive people, saying the right thing is not always the right thing to say. Graves would always be an irritating enigma to Sassoon with his independent spirit, eccentric views, chaotic lifestyle and propensity for fusing fact and fantasy. Indeed, within a decade their friendship would founder on the rock of Graves' inaccuracies and insensitivity. But in November 1915, and for the first time, Sassoon had the company of a poet.

On 5 December the battalion was moved from Bethune and exchanged the fields of Flanders for Picardy, Amiens and the valley of the Somme. Sassoon was also crossing emotional boundaries. The war was forcing him to take stock of the past and of his present prospects. The fragility of life and the likelihood of sudden death threw him back on himself. His writings portray him experiencing a metamorphosis. Two days before leaving Bethune he writes: 'my inner life is far more real than the hideous realism of this land of the war-zone'. It would have been equally true to say his inner life was more real because of the hideous realism of the war. It is a strange paradox that war should bring him peace. His experience of the front-line trenches and the dangers of no-man's-land was still limited; but he was close enough to understand, as never before, depths of anguish, bravery and selflessness:

Men marching by, four after four, hideous, brutal faces, sullen, wretched. Strange to see, among those hundreds of faces I scanned, suddenly a vivid red-haired youth with green eyes looking far away, sidelong – one clean face, among all the others brutalised. The last fifteen months have unsealed my eyes. I have lived well and truly since the war began, and have made my sacrifices: now I ask that the price be required of me. I must pay my debt. Hamo went: I must follow him.

Crossing the bridge of experience and the boundaries of self-knowledge, Sassoon abjured the indulgence of his prolonged adolescence and regarded his man-about-town pretensions as inane. All that was captivity – this was freedom. As in August 1914, so now in the Somme valley the aspect of things was within him. Behind the lines he took to riding out to the surrounding countryside to restore his affinity with nature and to escape from the confines of company to the silence of his own thoughts. The valley was filled with winter sunshine; its contours, fields and trees evoked memories of Kent and Weirleigh. Fully convinced that he would be killed, he was garnering his memories like a Pharaoh taking his treasures with him to some nether-world. In his poem 'A Testament', dated 1 January 1916, he says:

> If, as I think, I'm warned to pack and go
> On a longer journey than I've made before,
> I must be taking stock of what I leave,
> And what I stand to lose, of all my store,
>
> Cries for completion. Things, that made me weep
> For joy of loveliness, come shining back
> Dazzling my spirit that prepares for sleep.

He was not indulging in morbidity but affirming his acceptance of death as the price for believing that 'dying for one's native land was the most glorious thing one could possibly do'. It was later that Sassoon qualified the belief with the words 'believed to be'. *Dulce et decorum est pro patria mori* was neither a young nor an old lie for Sassoon in 1916 but a truth that liberated him and enabled him to 'make an end to all things base'.

His spirits were high and he relished the company of David Thomas and Robert Graves. Graves's poems, however, impressed Sassoon as little as his did Graves. Sassoon expressed his doubts in a letter to Eddie Marsh: 'I am rather disappointed with his poems. Do you think it is wise of him to publish them? I am sure he will do much better work before long when he has recovered his balance.' In the same letter he asked Marsh if he had seen his verse in *The Times* of 18 January. The poem, 'To Victory', is an exuberant expression of the need Sassoon was feeling for the resurgence of the full colours and lustre of spring. 'I'm tired of greys and browns and the leafless ash.' The spring will bring the victory of colour over the monochrome world of war. He had sent the poem to Edmund Gosse who, on his own initiative, sent it to *The Times*, where it appeared with Sassoon's initials at the bottom.

The poem, unremarkable in itself, caught the eye of Lady Ottoline Morrell, wife of the Liberal MP Philip Morrell, who opposed the war. She was a half-sister of the Duke of Portland and an inveterate collector of people. Keen to discover more about the author of the poem, she wrote to the Editor of *The Times*, who passed on her enquiry to Edmund Gosse. His reply gave some biographical details of Sassoon and concluded: 'I am sure he will very much appreciate a letter from you.' Sassoon was indeed pleased. Arriving on 30 January as the battalion started out on a three-day march from its rest billets at Montagne to Morlancourt, 'Lady Ottoline's large sheet of beautiful hand-made note-paper seemed like something from another world.' Her effusive letter declared, 'It was such a delight to find in these dark prison-like days a sympathetic desire to fly out beyond into the beauty and colour and freedom that one longs for. It is only through Poetry and wild days in the country that one could escape.'

Sassoon concluded that 'she was a bit too intense.' But in his reply he expressed his pleasure at finding someone who was grateful for his efforts and promised to send her a small collection of his work: eight poems arrived bound in a green paper wrapper bearing the title *Discoveries:* he had also included his photograph. 'I wondered,' she wrote, 'if I should ever see this young poet with the handsome face, or would he too be soon blown to atoms.'

Sassoon was still positioned some miles behind the lines and went up to the Front to replenish supplies, starting out in the late afternoon as the sun set. The communication trenches extended for about 400 yards, connecting the reserve trenches at the rear to the support trenches some 200 yards further forward, and then the front-line firing trenches which looked across no-man's-land to the enemy lines. The communication trenches were as much a target as the rest of the trenches and difficult to negotiate in the darkness. Every kind of supply had to be brought up, from sand-bags to rations, and the constant flow of men moving up and down the lines resembled an ant-hill. But there was no advance, it was still stalemate. In his poem 'In the Pink' Sassoon writes of a soldier in the quarter-master's billet, half asleep and in a state of reverie thinking of happier times at home, then remembering that the next day he must return to the body-numbing, mind-numbing amnesia-inducing trenches where:

> Everything but wretchedness is forgotten:
> To-night he's in the pink, but soon he'll die.
> And still the war goes on – he don't know why.

The *Westminster Gazette* refused to publish the poem, believing it would adversely affect recruitment. Dated 10 February 1916, it was his first outspoken war poem.

Travelling between the trenches and his own billet, Sassoon felt excluded from the real action: 'The mare brought me home straight as a die across four miles of plough and mud. So I still see the war as a looker-on; catching a glimpse of the grim places, and then ride back to village lights and evening talk. But my time will come – never doubt it.' The intermittent pattern of his visits to the front line left him time to observe the contrast between the natural world and the world of men at war. The brown fields, the village houses, the churches, all exuded a permanence stretching back over the centuries. They had survived the other armies who had plundered and marched that way. The grass grows back, the crops are sown, the birds sing and the stars shine. The Cathedral at Amiens, which he visited on 25 January, embodied 'the great idea of religion, outshining all the formulae of office and celebration'. He was sensitive to whatever mystery lay behind the natural order of things and the beauty of its manifestation. The war was temporal; the rockets were 'brief lights soon burnt out – the stars wheeling changeless and untroubled, life and deathless beauty, always the same contrast'. This is the language of the mystic enriched by his reading of Blake and Henry Vaughan. He was not, however, professing or at this time practising any formal religion. 'My only religion was my vocation as a poet, and my resolve to do my duty bravely.'

The moral questions the war posed and the suffering it imposed could not be avoided. Rhetoric was the means he employed to express his perplexity, and the symbols of faith, particularly the wayside Calvary and the altar, provided the spark. The last five lines of his poem 'Prince of Wounds', written in December 1915, are a typical cry:

> Have we the strength to strive alone
> Who can no longer worship Christ?
> Is He a God of wood and stone,
> While those who served him writhe and moan,
> On warfare's altar sacrificed?

The front line had few advantages, but being there kept the mind so occupied with just surviving that the complex questions of metaphysics were forced into the background. Sassoon thought the best way to forget the war was to be at the heart of it. Staying alive outstripped the meaning of life as a priority; being at the rear had the reverse effect. This was even truer when on leave in England. At the end of February Sassoon left for home, having completed three months in France. In London he met Eddie Marsh, went to a concert at the Queen's Hall, spent two evenings with Robbie Ross at Half Moon Street and then went down to Weirleigh. Understandably his thoughts reverted to the war and his friends, particularly David Thomas, and he was keen to get back. Weirleigh was about the old life which had now lost its charm for him; it was about the past and his immaturity. What was once central became tangential. He still loved the place but as a memory, something to be folded away and looked at only as one looks at a photograph album.

When on 6 March 1916 Sassoon returned from leave, France was under snow. It was bitterly cold but within a week came the first signs that spring was returning. He was still acting as transport officer and therefore commuted daily to the trenches with supplies and spent time with his fellow officers, including David Thomas, before riding back to the rest camp to further thoughts and to write more verses. If only he could find a publisher! How terrible it would be if he were killed and so little poetry written and even less published. He wrote in desperation to Marsh to say that four new poems were on their way to him: 'Eddie, you must get my poems printed soon, it will be such fun to think of them when everything becomes horrid and people get sent away hurt.' Graves was well advanced with his plans for the publication of his first volume, *Over the Brazier*, with May being a possible date. Sassoon did not want to be left behind. They still reviewed each other's efforts and gave David Thomas a chance to read their work. Graves and Thomas, although in different companies, were together up at the Front and had became close. Thomas was fond of reading and Graves was attracted by his humour and gentleness.

On the night of 18 March Graves led A Company to the front-line firing trenches and met David Thomas, who was with C Company. He wrote:

About half past ten, rifle fire broke out on the right, and the sentries passed along the news: 'Officer hit.'

Richardson hurried away to investigate. He came back to say: 'It's young Thomas. A bullet through the neck; but I think he's all right. It can't have hit his spine or an artery, because he's walking to the dressing station.'

Then news came that David was dead. The regimental doctor, a throat specialist in civil life, had told him 'You'll be all right, only don't raise your head for a bit.' David then took a letter from his pocket, gave it to an orderly, and said. 'Post this!' The doctor could see that he was choking and tried a tracheotomy; but too late.

The news reached Sassoon the following morning. Convulsed with grief he rode up to the nearby woods and wailed for his fallen companion. 'Grief had its way with me,' he wrote:

Today I knew what it means to find the soul washed pure with tears, and the load of death was lifted from my heart. So I wrote his name in chalk on the beech-tree stem, and left a garland of ivy there, and a yellow primrose for his yellow hair and kind grey eyes, my dear, my dear.

The following evening, 20 March, Sassoon went up to the line:

Tonight I saw his shrouded form laid in the earth. Robert Graves beside me with his white whimsical face twisted and grieving. Once we could not hear the solemn words for the noise of a machine-gun along the line; and when all was finished a canister fell a hundred yards away and burst with a crash. So Tommy left us, a gentle soldier, perfect and without stain. And so he will remain in my heart, fresh and happy and brave.

Graves (who later commemorated Thomas in his poem 'Goliath and David') felt 'empty and lost but it did not anger me as it did Siegfried'.

A week after Thomas's death Sassoon was relieved as transport officer and for the first time went with the battalion into the trenches. His grief and anger blunted any reticence he might have felt about killing the enemy. He was out for vengeance and determined to repay them for the death of Thomas, Hamo, his cousin Norman Donaldson and all the others. Personal safety was discounted, 'hate has come and the lust to kill'. At dusk he went under the wire and into no-man's-land in search of prey. His aim with a grenade was accurate, something his brother Michael attributed to his deftness as a fast bowler. He often heard the enemy but only saw them either as retreating shadows or as mutilated bodies stuck in the murky water and enfolding mud of the craters. There was an urgency to all this daring because the anger he felt was something which by nature he knew he could not long sustain; it would ebb away but the grief, the deprivation would remain, undiminished.

His diary entries betray a distempered mind which engendered recklessness and bravado more than cool courage and bravery. His fellow officers began to call him Mad Jack. He was overwrought and suicidal, something they noted with concern. 'They say I am trying to kill myself. Am I? I don't know.' The attractiveness of death, of being killed in a 'decent show' out there in no-man's-land, was infinitely preferable to death by a stray bullet or a grenade thrown into the trench. And would it not show that the poet was no cringer but courageous and self-forgetting? The death of Thomas triggered thoughts which were the fruit of a deep emotional bruising; the tiredness of living on a knife-edge and knowing that, despite all the sacrifice, the war was getting nowhere; 'I was angry with the war,' an anger so fierce that killing Germans was the only way it could be assuaged. 'I used to say I couldn't kill anyone in this war; but since they killed Tommy I would gladly stick a bayonet into a German by daylight.' Such an extreme and violent vocabulary is totally out of character and antipathetic to Sassoon's nature: it stands as prime evidence of the impact upon him of the war. The outburst was inevitable; indeed it was necessary if he was to know sanity again. But there in the trenches Sassoon believed he would never again know peace until his 'feckless course was run'. He wrote on 2 April in his poem 'Peace':

> In my heart there's cruel war that must be waged
> In darkness vile with moans and bleeding bodies maimed;
> A gnawing hunger drives me, wild to be assuaged,
> And bitter lust chuckles within me unashamed.

He was as desolate and disconsolate as the ruined villages and countryside around him:

> Down in the craters the dead water took a dull gleam from the sky. I stared at the tangles of wire and the leaning posts and there seemed no sort of comfort left in life. And here I was staring across at the enemy I'd never seen. Somewhere out of sight a bird had begun to sing. Without knowing why, I remembered it was Easter Sunday. Standing in that dismal ditch, I could find no consolation that Christ was risen.

On the evening of Easter Day Sassoon left the Front and travelled by bus from Mericourt to Flixécourt, a small town between Amiens and Abbeville. He was going on an officers' training course, although he suspected it was the Army's way of giving officers a respite from the Front. The journey took him through a countryside bursting with resurgent spring. The contrast between the drabness of the trenches and the colours of spring was, he said, 'like coming back to life warm and serene – it was to feel how much there is to regain'. As before in his life, nature and spring proved the effective antidote to despair. They brought relief but not consolation. To have time to himself was always restorative to Sassoon, and never more so than the month at Flixécourt. He enjoyed the company of a fellow Marlburian, Marcus Goodall, and in conducive surroundings buried himself in his books. His feverish mind was quietened and the physical exercise restored a sense of well-being.

One incident at Flixécourt, however, threatened his equanimity. He attended a lecture on the effective use of the bayonet. The lecturer, a Scot called Major Campbell, used a phrase which disturbed Sassoon: 'The bullet and the bayonet are brother and sister.' Of the enemy he said, 'If you don't kill him, he'll kill you. Stick him between the eyes, in the throat, in the chest, or round the thighs.' And so the Major went on as one possessed, employing graphic anatomical descriptions and vehemence until 'all who listened caught fire from his enthusiasm'. After the lecture, Sassoon went for a walk to the woods with the uncompromising language reverberating in his head. He understood full well, and could not deny the intrinsic logic of the lecture. What else was war about but killing? Battles are not decided on the toss of a coin. Respect for the enemy was only possible when he lay as a mutilated corpse at one's feet, and the more corpses, the nearer came victory. Although the logic was seemingly unassailable, Sassoon felt he could not affirm it in his heart. In *Memoirs of an Infantry Officer*, he records his ambivalence: 'Whatever my private feelings may have been after the Major's lecture, the next morning saw me practising bayonet-fighting. Obviously it would have been both futile and inexpedient to moralise about bayonet-fighting at an Army School.' But that is Sassoon speaking in 1930, and one detects that he is rationalising the past – 'futile and inexpedient' are the words that betray him. The allusion to his 'private feelings', however, though not elaborated upon, has a different ring about it. What in the lecture disturbed him so deeply? Could it have been hearing his own intemperate language of revenge after the death of David Thomas echoed in the words of Major Campbell? Uttered in a moment of retaliatory hysteria the words were shocking enough, but hearing them declaimed as orthodoxy, as normal and right, struck a deep discord in Sassoon. The war was threatening his sanity; next it would destroy his innocence. War was not chivalrous defence but aggressive revenge, which unleashed barbaric instincts. On the evening of the lecture Sassoon wrote a poem entitled 'The Kiss':

> To these I turn, in these I trust –
> Brother Lead and Sister Steel
> To this blind power I make appeal,
> I guard her beauty clean from rust.
>
> He spins and burns and loves the air,
> And splits a skull to win my praise;
> But up the nobly marching days
> She glitters naked, cold and fair.
>
> Sweet Sister, grant your soldier this;
> That in good fury he may feel
> The body where he sets his heel
> Quail from your downward darting kiss.

He returned to Morlancourt and the Front on 22 May. Three nights later he was part of a raiding party on the enemy front line. In the dark and rain of no-man's-land the party's advance was halted by the enemy's wire. At the rear Sassoon waited; all was quiet: then the Germans opened fire. Sassoon went forward to the craters where the party was pinned down by enemy fire and bombs. The Germans were only yards away and Sassoon, darting from crater to crater, was in point-blank range. He went back and forth to his own line, leading out the rescuers and dragging back the wounded until all were accounted for as night gave way to dawn. Five days later he wrote to Eddie Marsh: 'A dead secret; my name has gone in for a Military Cross. Probably shan't get it, so don't tell Robert or it might get round to the Depot that I told someone.'

Sassoon had seen little of Graves since the death of David Thomas. Graves had gone back to England for an operation on his nose to repair a childhood accident which made breathing through a gas mask almost impossible. Then he went to his parents' home in Harlech. In June Graves was posted from the Ist to the 2nd Battalion at Litherland. There, as in

France, all the expectation was about a major assault on the German positions in the Somme valley. Sassoon too had been in England during June and, although pleased to get into everyday clothes, have a decent bed to sleep in and the luxury of a bath, he wanted to get back to France. There is something perverse in the way he thought of France when in England and when in France spent hours dreaming of English summers and reading Thomas Hardy.

The battle of the Somme began on 1 July, preceded by heavy bombardment of the German lines. Field Marshal Haig, the Commander-in-Chief, believed that this had broken the defences around the Germans, giving the British forces a clear run across no-man's-land towards the enemy. He was wrong. His troops, mainly inexperienced volunteers led by inexperienced officers, went forward at walking pace and were mowed down. On the first day nearly 58,000 were either wounded or dead. The battle of the Somme lasted four months. By the time it petered out, in November, over 600,000 of the Allied troops were dead or injured. They had forced the Germans to retreat five miles.

Sassoon was in the Fricourt sector, near to where David Thomas lay buried. He did not take part in the attack but, situated some 500 yards behind the front trenches, he could see the theatre of battle. Between him and the village of Fricourt ran the road from Albert to Peronne, the road along which, in 1415, Henry V had travelled to Agincourt. The village of Mametz lay to Sassoon's right, with Mametz Wood on the horizon and Montauban further across. Throughout the day he watched as the German front line was gradually pushed back; the day had gone well. On 3 July the battalion moved down the Peronne road to a point outside the village of Carnoy. The taking of Mametz Wood was their objective for the next day. As the troops bedded down for the night, Sassoon captured the scene in a poem called 'At Carnoy':

> Down in the hollow there's the whole Brigade
> Camped in four groups; through twilight falling slow
> I hear a sound of mouth-organs, ill-played,
> And murmur of voices, gruff, confused and low.
> Crouched among thistle-tufts I've watched the glow
> Of a blurred orange sunset flare and fade;
> And I'm content. To-morrow we must go
> To take some cursèd Wood ... O world God made!

Mametz Wood proved a more difficult objective than was first thought. The attack strategy was confused. Sassoon, although ordered back, went forward with some of his men and occupied a trench; not content with this, he advanced on his own and attacked another one still occupied by the Germans: 'I chucked four Mills bombs into their trench and to my surprise fifty or sixty ran away like hell into Mametz Wood.' This Mad Jack episode would have gained for him another decoration but for the overall attack being a failure. Sassoon was in high spirits when he wrote to Eddie Marsh on 14 July: 'I got the M.C. all right. Our 2nd Battalion are near here – Robert is with them.'

Sassoon was now based away from the front line and was able to contact Graves by letter, expressing his hope that his friend could come to see him. Graves got a horse and rode over but, failing to find Sassoon, in the end sent a note. Although Sassoon had just returned from England, that leave had only served to fuel his disillusionment. He was tired and despondent; he wanted to go home, in one piece if possible, but a wound would be welcome if that was his passport out of the war. The next day, 14 July, Sassoon records in his diary that he and Graves met: 'The Second Battalion are bivouacked three hundred yards away by the Besordel road. I had a long chat with Robert Graves, whimsical and queer and human as ever. We sat in the darkness with guns booming along the valleys, and dim stars of camp fires burning all around in the dark countryside.' The day of their meeting was also the day when the Big Push began. The Allied strategy was to overwhelm the enemy by a massive assault on their position. On 15 July Graves went up with the 2nd Battalion to the front line near Mametz Wood and prepared for an attack on High Wood.

Sassoon was consumed by a sense of futility. The rain began to fall, keeping time with the booming guns over Albert. Thinking of the future deepened his depression, so he thought of the past, of England and especially Kent and of walking to the crease to open the innings for the Blue Mantles. What a world it had been, now it was all dead and done with, as far as he was concerned. 'If I'm lucky and get through alive, there's another sort of life waiting for me. Travels and adventures, and poetry: anything but the old groove of cricket and hunting, and dreaming in Weirleigh garden.' He also ruled out the prospect of marriage and acknowledged the impossibility of the understanding with Dorothy Hanmer: 'The Hanmer engagement idea was a ghastly blunder, it wouldn't work at all. That charming girl who writes to me so often would never be happy with me.' Then he adds, 'It was my love for Bobby that led me to that mistake.' The statement is as enigmatic as it is incongruous. Indeed, the diary entries for the days between the 16 and 22 July suggest a mind assailed by a mounting fever. The thought process is erratic, disjointed and despairing. It was Sassoon's lowest point since the death of David Thomas.

On the 19th the Germans lashed the Allied positions with their artillery and forced a retreat. Graves was seriously wounded. News from the Front came in disconnected bits of information; and so Sassoon heard that Graves had died from his wounds on 20 July. In his diary he said of Graves: 'In him I thought I had found a lifelong friend to work with.' In a letter to Eddie Marsh he asked, 'Won't they leave anyone we're fond of?' Within two days Sassoon was taken ill with a respiratory infection. An examination conducted at the New Zealand Hospital in Amiens also revealed patches on his lungs. Within the week he was sent home to England. Six months would elapse before he saw France again. The war and the suffering would change little in that time; but not so Sassoon.

5

GARSINGTON

1916–17

Sassoon reached Southampton on 2 August and was transferred to a Red Cross train destined for Oxford. Glad to have France behind him, his only sense of guilt was in forsaking the battalion. The war seemed to have less and less purpose and he, like many others, believed it would go on for ever. Personal losses – particularly the loss of Graves – added to his feeling of dejection. This mood of gloom was lifted somewhat as the train passed through the Hampshire countryside and the rolling fields of Oxfordshire. The ripening harvest under the August sun, the occasional wave from some stranger as the train went by, even the familiar hoardings, all came upon him 'with an irresistible delight', as he describes in his poem 'Stretcher Case':

> There shone the blue serene, the prosperous land,
> Trees, cows and hedges; skipping these, he scanned
> Large, friendly names, that change not with the year,
> Lung Tonic, Mustard, Liver Pills and Beer.

Somerville College, Oxford, became a military hospital for the duration of the war, and Sassoon was soon settled in one of its ground-floor rooms. Despite the memories, he resolved to enjoy the last of summer and write poetry. 'Christ and the Soldier' was the first poem, written on 5 August. It takes the form of a dialogue between a soldier 'dumped down on his knees' before a wayside Calvary and Christ. The soldier seeks through a series of questions to make sense of his life and the hideousness of war in the light of Christian precepts. The dialogue peters out into silence:

'O God,' he groaned, 'Why ever was I born?'
The battle boomed, and no reply came back.

This poem was not published until 1973, six years after Sassoon's death. An explanatory note written many years after its composition gives an insight into its genesis:

> I intended it to be a commentary on the mental condition of most front-line soldiers, for whom a roadside Calvary was merely a reminder of the inability of religion to co-operate with the carnage and catastrophe they experienced. The dilemma of an ignorant private is demonstrated. But I was a very incomplete and quite unpractising Christian, and understood little more than he of the meaning of Our Lord's teaching. I was anti-clerical, and the Churches seemed to offer no solution to the demented doings on the Western Front. The poem cannot be read as showing any clue to my own mental position, which was altogether confused, and became increasingly disillusioned and rebellious.

He was also aware that intellectually he had bitten off more than he could chew:

> My carefully contrived attempt at a potent parable certainly wasn't worth printing. Could anyone from a fully informed religious understanding have made a success of the subject?

The central question remained with him for the next 40 years and much if not all of his poetry is the chronicle of the struggle to find an answer.

Threading the other Oxford poems together is the pathos of war, but all was not gloom. Good news arrived in the form of a telegram from Eddie Marsh saying that Robert Graves was alive. The whole episode was a tale of confusion. Graves had been seriously wounded by an exploding howitzer shell on 20 July near High Wood. An Army doctor attended to him but expressed the view that there was little or no hope. The prediction became an assumption and so the news spread. Graves was moved to the field hospital, where the regimental doctor confirmed that the now-unconscious Graves was breathing his last. Anticipating the inevitable, the Colonel wrote an official letter and Graves was put in a quiet corner and left. The following morning the orderlies responsible for clearing the corpses noticed that he was breathing. He was moved to the 8th General Hospital in Rouen and then to the military hospital in Highgate, London. Unfortunately, the official letter had reached his parents and an announcement appeared in *The Times*. In the meantime Graves had written to his parents assuring them that he was alive and well. They were totally confused and scurried around London trying to find out the real situation. He also wrote to Marsh on 26 July giving an account of his injuries and recovery. Graves wrote from Highgate to Sassoon on 4 August, sending the letter to the Battalion Headquarters in France. Sassoon, of course, was now in Oxford. The irony of the situation was that while Graves was in the 8th Hospital in Rouen, Sassoon was in the 2nd Hospital in the same city. This comedy of errors was resolved by Marsh's intervention. 'How I'll pull his leg about it when I see him,' Sassoon wrote to Marsh. He was elated by the news.

Within days of this good news, another message arrived, this time from Robbie Ross saying that he intended to travel to Oxford to see Sassoon, who remembered that his enthusiastic correspondent Lady Ottoline Morrell lived near Oxford. On asking Robbie if he knew anything of the lady, he was surprised to find that his friend was on intimate terms with her. With the minimum of delay Sassoon and Ross were in a taxi and on their way to Garsington.

'We drew up outside the tall iron gates and stood for a moment in the shadow of some lofty elms. Within the gates was a green forecourt, walled on either side by high yew hedges. Across the court a paved path led to the manor house … my only words for it were the obvious ones, an absolute dream of beauty.' If the exterior beauty of Garsington took Sassoon by surprise, his first encounter with Lady Ottoline was even more startling. She was not in the house itself but having her portrait painted in a nearby garret: 'My first view of her was somewhat disconcerting. Always original in her style of dress, which was often extremely beautiful, she happened on this occasion to be wearing voluminous pale-pink Turkish trousers; and these garments, as she descended the ladder backwards, were, unavoidably the first part of her that I beheld.' The rest of her body took a time before coming into view because she was unusually tall for a woman, a good six foot. The natural colour of her hair was red with a strong hint of gold, but when Sassoon met her she had adopted the colour purple. With a penchant for large and elaborate hats, high-heeled shoes, flowing garments and a liberal use of make-up, she was striking rather than beautiful. This tendency to eccentric appearance was, Sassoon admits, off-putting to him and he was never comfortable with it during the years of their friendship. He did, however, recognise immediately that this new acquaintance was a person of rare distinction.

Ottoline's first impression of Sassoon was formed as she observed him over tea. His face and mode of speech gave the impression of a shy, even sullen person. She saw the features of a stag or a fawn in the wide nostrils, the green eyes, the protruding ears, the jerky moving of the head from side to side. The longer she observed this poet, the greater became her desire to know him. 'His coming had fallen into our midst and it was still unreal,' she confided in her journal. The following Sunday Sassoon returned to spend the day with the Morrells. Their home was a refuge for pacifists. The Conscription Act exempted those who for reasons of conscience refused to join the Army, providing they contributed in some other way to the war effort. Farmwork came within this description and so the Home Farm at Garsington in 1916 was full of conscientious objectors. Philip Morrell was a leader in Parliament of the anti-war faction and resolutely carried a banner for the cessation of hostilities. Ottoline was unswerving in support of her husband's stand and he was supportive of Ottoline's efforts to 'live life on the grand scale'. This mutuality, it would appear, did not prevent either of them from having intense affairs with others. At the time of Sassoon's first visit to Garsington, the philosopher Bertrand Russell was central to Ottoline's life. He too was dedicated to the pacifist cause. Contact with such a milieu at a time when he was confused about the war, its conduct and purpose, when he was physically, emotionally and mentally on the verge of collapse, fed Sassoon's uncertainties.

Walking around the grounds of Garsington that Sunday afternoon, Sassoon recounted to Ottoline his experience of the war which he was 'beginning to realise as horrible and cruel and tragic'. Such sentiments struck a chord with Ottoline but what pleased her most was the empathy of their views generally. Apart from Lytton Strachey, none of her other Garsington intimates 'entered into that chamber of my being whence springs the fountain of romance, where a strange and magical coloured light plays upon the intruder'. Sassoon for his part was flattered to be the centre of Ottoline's attention and to be discussing his poetry in surroundings so different from those in which it had originally been written. As someone who throughout his life enjoyed 'hob-nobbing', he was impressed by her aristocratic connections and by the fact that Lady Ottoline considered his visit 'an event of exceptional significance for her'.

While at Somerville, Sassoon went for a day-trip to nearby Burford, where Hamo Thornycroft was staying. Uncle Hamo enjoyed the countryside and, faithful to his farming roots, enjoyed working in the fields during the harvest. As he walked up to the Bull Inn to meet him, Sassoon felt that his good service at the Front and his Military Cross had wiped out the disappointment he had caused Uncle Hamo by leaving Cambridge without a degree. Burford, Garsington and Weirleigh were islands of peace in a troubled and confusing world and seemed immutable, an impression confirmed as uncle and nephew walked through the village in the direction of the Priory. Emslie John Horniman, who owned the Priory, was the epitome of the Victorian English gentleman; well mannered, well travelled, a collector of well-made and refined objects and a believer in serving one's country. As he gave Sassoon a tour of the house, Mr Horniman and Uncle Hamo exchanged views on the war in a way that left Sassoon with 'strange stirrings of perplexity'. 'How had Uncle Hamo and Mr Horniman managed, I wondered, to make the war seem so different from what it really was? Their attitude was to insist that it was splendid to be in the front-line. So it was if one came out of it safely.' There was a time when he himself believed in the romance of war – being at its centre cured him of that illusion.

The visit reminded him of the difference between the romantic view of war and war as he had experienced it on the Somme. He was at a loss to understand how two intelligent men could possibly speak of the nobility of this war when daily the casualty-lists testified to the contrary. They were deluded and he believed that, had he tried to explain the reality to them, it would not have impinged upon their views: 'I felt that no explanation of mine could ever reach my elders – that they weren't capable of wanting to know the truth. I resented their patriotic suppression of those aspects of war which never got into the newspapers.' Six months earlier, when the *Westminster Gazette* had refused to publish his poem 'In the Pink', he should have recognised the way things operated on the Home Front. Patriotism not truth is the nation's first line of attack and of defence in any war. His innocence, which received such a bruising when Major Campbell extolled the virtues of the bayonet, was bruised again.

Sassoon left Oxford during the last week of August and went home to Weirleigh. The impact of the war on rural villages like Matfield was manifested in the grief caused by the loss of young men. There were other signs; the neglected cricket pitch at the heart of the village, the overgrown tennis court at Weirleigh and the redundant stables. Then there was Theresa whose social round, though curtailed, provided her with only a momentary distraction from grief and worry. For her own sake and for the sake of her son, the war rarely featured in their conversation. When it did arise, Theresa summed up her views succinctly by declaring Britain to be engaged, like St George, in a crusade against the Prussian dragon. Sassoon was seeing it differently. In fact his belief in the war as a righteous crusade was ebbing away. It was now a matter of loyalty to the battalion and to his men.

His main preoccupation was with the notes and jottings he had kept while at the Front and the possibility of transforming them into poems. What he had seen and heard in France had been recorded with a technical and descriptive accuracy quite unlike anything he had achieved previously. The peaceful interlude at Weirleigh was the ideal opportunity to add new poems to those already completed. Sassoon noticed with satisfaction that with some of this new work he was 'providing a thoroughly caddish antidote to the glorification of the supreme sacrifice and such-like prevalent phrases. These performances had the quality of satirical drawings. They were deliberately devised to disturb complacency.' The desire to disturb complacency was in part the result of Robbie Ross urging him to write with greater candour about the war, the conduct of which, particularly by the military mandarins, was a constant object of criticism by Ross. The visit to Burford added fuel to the fire. Sassoon knew that he was in danger of crossing the line of acceptable comment: 'Although I didn't want to upset Uncle Hamo, I should like to give some of the comfortable civilians a few shocks, even if they were to accuse me of being wrong-headed and ungentlemanly.'

Ross was not the only one to commend this approach. Robert Graves was just as enthusiastic. Sassoon shared the contents of the manuscript with him when he visited Graves' home near Harlech and immediately afterwards when Graves came to Weirleigh. This was the high point of their friendship as they encouraged each other in their work and planned for the good days they would enjoy together when the war ended. Although both men were outwardly relaxed, they were inwardly tired and strained. There was no escape from the war, even in the quietness of Meirionydd and Kent. Graves, on the first night at Weirleigh, was disturbed from his sleep by loud voices and banging. He thought he recognised the voice of Theresa and believed that she was trying to contact her dead son. The following morning he remonstrated with Sassoon, declaring Weirleigh to be 'worse than France' and that his already shattered nerves could not cope. Sassoon, so Graves recalled, 'explained the situation, and admitted that he too was irritated by his mother's behaviour'. This helped Graves to calm down and immediately reversed his decision to leave.

Graves was revising his memorial poem to David Thomas entitled 'Goliath and David', while Sassoon was fine-copying his manuscript which would eventually be published as *The Old Huntsman and Other Poems*. Its contents ranged from a long autobiographical poem of an ageing and ailing huntsman to the savage realities of war. Sassoon also included many of his pastoral compositions and early lyrical evocations of his youthful experience. The 72 poems, many of which had already been privately published or had appeared in periodicals, constitute a progression from callow youth to 'happy warrior', to the confused soldier and angry man of 1916. Reading the poems in chronological order is to recognise the maturing of technique, the sharpened ear, the perceptive eye and the emergence of his individual voice. There is the ringing authenticity of the war poems which, Sassoon declared, 'I wrote in a period of rapt afflatus', but the volume as a whole underscores Sassoon's remark, 'My real biography is my poetry. All the sequence of my development is there.'

The manuscript was destined for Robbie Ross, upon whose contacts Sassoon relied to secure a publisher. Together with Graves, he left Weirleigh for Garsington. Lady Ottoline had extended an invitation to him for the middle of September. Sassoon wrote asking her to include Graves. It was a dangerous time for two officers perplexed about the war to visit one of the centres of dissent. Ottoline, however, was more concerned about securing the friendship of Sassoon than persuading him to join the cause; that might come later. Never frivolous in her idealism and 'lofty but vaguely-formulated ideas', she was intent upon knowing more about her guest. For his part Sassoon was flirtatious but also cautious, resisting any temptation to cross uncongenial emotional frontiers. Friendship was one thing but the intensity of interest Ottoline showed posed a threat. He enjoyed the attention she lavished upon him but recoiled from her zealousness. Sassoon must have communicated his unease because, writing in her journal after the visit, Ottoline was both elated and depressed:

> Siegfried and his friend Robert Graves have been staying here. I find
> Siegfried very sympathetic and attractive, and my instinct goes out to
> him for he seems so intimate to me, as if he were a twin brother. He
> is natural and full of fun and perceptive of all things around. I find it
> a great joy to be with anyone so human and aware of ordinary life,

after the intellectuals who walk along half-blind. Sometimes I feel that in him I have found a wonderful companion that I have so much desired, who would drink of the fountains of many colours that spring up in my inner self, but he is aloof and obviously doesn't need my friendship. Robert Graves is an odd fellow with the face of a prize-fighter. He is very possessive of Siegfried and I think he resents any friendship between us.

Ottoline was inclined to singularity in her friendships and openness. This made her vulnerable to criticism and caricature, particularly from those to whom she showed the greatest generosity, such as D. H. Lawrence in *Women in Love* and Aldous Huxley in *Crome Yellow*. But Ottoline was a sexual and cultural vulture and more than a little absurd.

The intensity of his hostess was matched by the intensity of the pacifists and intellectuals who were staying at Garsington alongside Sassoon. It was his second experience of anti-war thoughts expressed by so many in one place at one time. 'At Garsington the war was described as being waged for unworthy motives, and it was the duty of a courageous minority to stand out against the public opinion which supported its continuance and prolongation. I was impressed by Mr Morrell's parliamentary connection, and listened to his judicially expressed opinion with the feeling that I was at last learning the truth about what was happening behind the political scenes.' One piece of information especially disturbed him. The Germans had sought peace negotiations, which the Marquis of Lansdowne and other Cabinet members saw as the only way left to stop the slaughter of the male population. But Asquith and Lloyd George were at loggerheads and the opportunity passed. 'That this should have an unsettling effect on my mind was not surprising. It was the beginning of a process of disillusionment which afterwards developed into a fermentation of confused and inflamed ideas.'

Despite his empathy with Ottoline and those at Garsington, Sassoon felt that much of the high idealism and the abstract arguments seemed inappropriate to his mental and emotional state. If war had taught him anything it was to live while he had the chance and do so in as much comfort as possible. Being sent to oblivion by a bullet or a shell mattered little; what concerned him was that such an exit would happen before his poetry was published. His anxiety was calmed by a letter which arrived at Weirleigh in October from the publisher William Heinemann expressing his willingness to publish a selection of the poems. Robert Ross, who had now assumed the role of Sassoon's literary 'producer', effected the introduction to Heinemann, endorsed the contractual offer and promised to advise him on the poems to be chosen. Sassoon wrote on 3 October to Uncle Hamo relaying the good news; it was further proof that his vocation as a poet was genuine.

The letter marks the point at which Uncle Hamo began moving towards the wings, as did Edmund Gosse and, to a lesser degree, Eddie Marsh. The centre stage now was occupied by Graves, Ottoline Morrell and Ross. Sassoon's developing resentment and anger caused these changes. Uncle Hamo was an obscurantist where the war was concerned; Gosse saw the Hun poised to strike at the heart of England and therefore could brook no diminution of resolve. As for Marsh, a civil servant at the centre of government, he could not be expected to sympathise with outspoken criticism of the military and political leadership. Rupert Brooke and his evocation of heroism still ruled Marsh's affections. Sassoon had moved on from Brooke to another poet whose reflections on the war were nearer his own. Charles Sorley was killed in 1915, the same year that Brooke died. Brooke celebrated the pride in being an English soldier, Sorley wrote of the price exacted by war.

Ross encouraged Sassoon's new-found satirical voice. 'There was an element in his nature which delighted in provoking opposition; he hated the War, and was unable to be tolerant about it and those who accepted it with civilian bellicosity and self-defensive evasion of its realities.' Between Garsington and Half Moon Street, Sassoon was imbibing a heady concoction of anti-war sentiment. There was, however, a difference between these two sources of influence. Ottoline was intense and cerebral, Ross relaxed and sardonic. Ottoline at Garsington was challenging, but Ross in Half Moon Street 'provided an oasis in the confusion and uncertainties of the War'.

Ross's urbanity also appealed to Sassoon, as did his sophisticated taste with its touch of the exotic. The circle of friends was catholic and the conversation witty, gossipy and expansive. It is to be doubted that Sassoon ever felt truly comfortable while at Garsington but in Half Moon Street he was at ease, indulged and guided by the avuncular and generous Robbie and the all-male society. The ease of his surroundings made returning to the Front a miserable prospect. The Medical Board had extended his leave to the end of October. Sassoon took full advantage of this, hunting, golfing and, above all, writing poetry, which he composed with ease: the irony and satire flowing freely. He was also being noticed by the public as his work appeared in the *Cambridge Magazine*, the *Westminster Gazette* and the *Saturday Review*. The only minus was the letters he received giving news of the battalion and its continuing losses in all ranks.

Graves was still on sick-leave, which he spent mostly at Harlech. He came to London at the end of October and made arrangements to meet Sassoon for luncheon on 2 November. Graves' attitude to the war changed considerably during his leave. He was revolted by the jingoism and the glorification of suffering and death at the Front. His religious faith evaporated and with it any semblance of regard for its institutions. The damage his lungs had sustained in his near-death escape from High Wood was slow to heal and this added to the sense of anger and hopelessness. Paradoxically Graves believed, as did Sassoon, that the only escape from the agonies of war was to be at its centre where there was no time to rationalise. But how to continue when his conviction about the rightness of the current conflict had died? Sassoon offered a resolution when he remarked at their luncheon that they were poets first and foremost. It was a vocation and, representing all poets, they should prove by their own courage that poets were not idle dreamers. The killing of the enemy was not their primary objective, but doing everything possible to ease the burden and suffering of those they commanded. Graves grasped this fragile and tenuous lifeline.

Declared fit for service by the Medical Board, Graves and Sassoon were reunited at Litherland, the regimental depot outside Liverpool, where Sassoon arrived on 2 December. The last thing either had desired was to be in that 'dreary drab flat place of fogs and bleary sunsets'. Few of the officers were known to Sassoon and the depot was full of conscripts. 'What in earlier days had been drafts of volunteers were now droves of victims. I was just beginning to be aware of this.' Sassoon resented the loss of silence and privacy which hindered the flow of his work; sharing a hut with others, including Graves, made him tetchy. He escaped by riding with the Cheshire Hunt, playing golf at Formby and dining at the Adelphi in Liverpool. Here he ordered his meal and wine with a nonchalance designed to impress the other diners. What a surreal world in which to live!

The surreal was evinced further by Ottoline, who was determined to keep her hold on Sassoon. To relieve the drabness of his hut she designed and made a rug that she then drenched with perfume. Her letters with their hyperbolic emotional sentences frightened Sassoon. It was becoming clear that unlike the other women he had known, Ottoline was not easily deterred. He decided to formulate each reply as though it were a joint offering of thanks from himself and Graves. With women, platonic friendship was the only kind Sassoon could handle – apart from that he was not available. When asked at this time why there were no women in his verse, he replied, 'They are outside my philosophy.'

The week before Christmas Graves was declared fit for active service and would be sent to France in January. Sassoon, when he attended the Medical Board after Christmas, was told that his posting to the Front would be delayed until February. He was in no rush to go: 'four months away from the Army blotted out the sense of discipline I had managed to acquire, much against my will. I want to go off and play golf and be independent and alone, all the time. My absurd decoration is the only thing that gives me any sense of responsibility at all. And the thought of death is horrible, where last year it was a noble and inevitable dream.' The last day of the year he went off to play golf with Graves, whose tomfoolery on the course 'rather annoyed my serious golfing temperament'.

Sassoon was not the only patriot from whose eyes the scales had fallen. In May 1916, H. G. Wells published his latest novel, *Mr Britling Sees It Through*. The eponymous hero is a writer and renowned observer of world events. Britling had been a theorist about the conflict but as the war came nearer home in its effects, culminating in the death of his son Hugh, he was forced to face its realities. At the commencement of the war he had believed it to be a final 'clearing up' of man's irrational past before he moved on to a saner and more civilised world, a kind of purification. But Hugh's letters from the Front convinced him that this war, like every other one, 'was madness'. Far from securing the future, it was destroying it by killing off a generation of young men. The jingoism of intelligent men, the egotistical and inept leadership of monarchs, politicians and military commanders all combined to shatter Britling's belief in the inevitability of liberal progress:

When it began I did not believe that this war could be like other wars. I did not dream it. I thought that we had grown wiser at last. It seemed to me like the dawn of a great clearing up. I thought the common sense of mankind would break out like a flame, an indignant flame, and consume all this obsolete foolery of empires and banners and militarism directly it made its attack upon human happiness. It was all a dream, the dream of a prosperous comfortable man who had never come to the cutting edge of life. Everywhere cunning, everywhere small feuds and hatreds, distrusts, dishonesties, timidities, feebleness of purpose, dwarfish imaginations, swarm over the great and simple issues. It is a war now like any other of the mobbing, many-aimed cataclysms that have shattered empires and devastated the world; it is a war without point, a war that has lost its soul, it has become mere incoherent fighting and destruction, a demonstration in vast and tragic forms of the stupidity and ineffectiveness of our species.

This is not only Mr Britling 'seeing it through' but Mr Britling seeing through it. Sassoon copied part of the above extract into his diary on 27 December 1916. He too had come to the cutting edge of life from a comfortable and prosperous background, the 'old inane life', as he describes it. He too had believed in the noble cause of the war; now the war was 'sheer madness'.

On 4 January 1917, Sassoon picked up a translated extract from a Danish newspaper, which Graves had left lying around. He records the following in his diary: 'A Copenhagen paper says, "The sons of Europe are being crucified in the barbed wire enclosures because the misguided masses are shouting for it. They do not know what they do, and the statesmen wash their hands. They dare not deliver them from their martyr's death." Is this true?' On 16 December Lloyd George had succeeded Asquith as Prime Minister and he was against any repeat of the Somme catastrophe. There would be no major offensive of that sort unless there was the certainty of major territorial benefits. But neither would there be any halfway-house peace settlement. Sassoon was given some inside information by the ever-faithful Ottoline. 'I heard from old Birrell that the Germans had made definite peace proposals and he hoped they would come to something.' She began her letter with the same sentiment as that expressed by Mr Britling: 'The spirit and purpose of the war, that kept it fine and clean at first, dwindles and gets fainter, leaving it utterly ghastly.' Sassoon could only agree. All these elements taken together were adding to his discontent but they did not help him form a coherent counterblast, even though his poetry was becoming more strident in its criticism and personal in the use of satire. This brought him a rebuke from Edmund Gosse, who wrote to him on the 17 February:

I have just been reading with admiration your striking verses called 'Conscripts' in *The Spectator*. But there is a phrase in them which

I hope you will modify before you republish them. You say 'many a sickly, slender lord went home'. This is a cruel and unworthy libel. No section of the whole community has shown more courage or devotion than the class you so gratuitously sneered at. The House of Lords has sacrificed, in proportion, more of its members and connections than any other in the country. I am unable to guess who 'the many slender sickly lords' are whom you have met on their skulking home. I have heard of none, and I think your attack on the class, in order to butter up 'the common ones', is a very unworthy one.

Gosse was Librarian of the House of Lords. It must have been galling for him that the young man whose poetic talent he had helped to refine; whom he had entertained at his home just four nights before, should turn and rend him. The offending poem appeared two days after Sassoon boarded the train for France at Waterloo. Two days later he was in a Rouen hospital with German measles; Gosse's indignant letter reached him there.

Sassoon was faced with a real dilemma: Gosse was someone whose support he had received in consequence of his mother's and his Uncle Hamo's friendship. The last thing he wanted was for his mother to know of Gosse's displeasure. To the ever-patient Uncle Hamo he wrote a letter on 27 February, the contents of which can only be described as a disingenuous attempt at extraction:

Mr Gosse has written to me complaining of my 'cruel and unworthy libel on the House of Lords'. He refers to two lines – 'Many a slender, sickly Lord who'd filled my soul long since with lutanies of sin, Went home because they couldn't stand the din'. Of course I meant my own precosities of pre-war days – that was the whole point of the phrase 'lutanies of sin', an obvious decadent cliché. I wish you to tell him how sorry I am that he mistook my meaning. But it's thin ice for me. I can't refer to his well- known liking for people in Debrett! Oh it's too funny that a man of his attainments should put his foot in it so badly, and to a youngster like myself, a mere lad of 30!

The poem is based upon a scene on the parade ground in which it is difficult to avoid the conclusion that the offending words are an indictment of certain aristocrats shying away from their patriotic duty. In any case, the 'decadent cliché', if that is truly what it is, introduces confusion. The reader would have to be very familiar with the pre-war Sassoon to understand the allusion. Uncle Hamo wrote to Gosse attempting to explain the background. Gosse regarded the explanation as impugning his judgement:

> I did not in the least 'misunderstand' the passage about 'many a slender, sickly lord', but I blamed it and I blame it still. It is a blot on his work, and it shows his mental limitation, that he should be unnable to perceive it. He is a dear and attractive creature, wonderfully loveable but as I say, strangely undeveloped for his age.

Adjectives like attractive, wonderful and loveable would have been eliminated if Gosse had seen Sassoon's letter to his uncle. The whole incident, however, has another significance in that it marks a further step in Sassoon's disenchantment with, and estrangement from the older generation as represented by Gosse. This would not become apparent until after the war but the seeds were sown during it and in many ways because of it.

Sassoon was marooned in Rouen for almost a month. On his own admission he was mentally and physically in no state 'to face the hardship and nerve-strain'. It would have been better if he had gone to the Front sooner. Not being in the thick of things left him time to ruminate. He was morose and negative about everything. That world of certainties in which he had been raised; the England he loved; the beauty and pieties of simple religious faith; the unquestioning self-forgetting sense of duty – qualities he admired in friends like Robert Hanmer – all these had been taken from him. Even his tenderness was gone, his innocence and joyous optimism about life. The war was taking him apart, slowly, piece by piece. It was a lacerating process. He could see no end to the slaughter. Shout as loud as he may 'Oh Jesus, make it stop', the Heavens were as brass. Like all weary men, he wanted to go home or else be shot dead, the ultimate release:

> My brain is so pitifully confused by the war and my single part in it. There is no tenderness left in me; only bitter resentment and a morbid desire to measure the whole ignominy which men are brought to by these fearful times of sanguinary imbecility. For the

soldier is no longer a noble figure; he is merely a writhing insect among this ghastly folly of destruction. God is a buffoon, who skulks somewhere at Base with tipsy priests to serve him. The agony of armies will be on every breeze; their blood will stain the flowers. The foulness of battle will cut off all kindliness from the hearts of men.

His loathing of those who desired and conspired for the war to continue became the object of further satire. In 'Base Details' he wrote about the professional officer class who hung around Rouen, safe from the real conflict, their self-indulgent lifestyle lived out in hotel dining-rooms; older men careless of younger lives:

> If I were fierce, and bald, and short of breath,
> I'd live with scarlet Majors at the Base,
> And speed glum heroes up the line to death.
> You'd see me with my puffy petulant face,
> Guzzling and gulping in the best hotel,
> Reading the Roll of Honour, 'Poor young chap,'
> I'd say – 'I used to know his father well;
> Yes, we've lost heavily in this last scrap.'
> And when the war is done and youth stone dead,
> I'd toddle safely home and die – in bed.

The cant of organised religion was pilloried when he visited Rouen Cathedral and watched some histrionic priest deliver himself of irrelevancies. Sassoon had written a swingeing satirical poem the previous October, which underlines the depth of his disillusion:

> The Bishop tells us: 'When the boys come back
> They will not be the same; for they'll have fought
> In a just cause: they lead the last attack
> On Anti-Christ; their comrades' blood has bought
> New right to breed an honourable race,
> They have challenged Death and dared him face to face.'

> 'We're none of us the same!' the boys reply.
> For George lost both his legs; and Bill's stone blind;
> Poor Jim's shot through the lungs and like to die;

And Bert's gone syphilitic: you'll not find
A chap who's served that hasn't found some change.'
And the Bishop said: 'The ways of God are strange!'

When Eddie Marsh read this poem he could only say, 'It's too horrible.'
Marsh liked gentility, but he did not condone censorship and included the
poem in his anthology *Georgian Poetry* of 1916–17. There was no
diminution in their mutual affection but Marsh, unlike Ross, was not
really enamoured of such biting satire. This may account for *Georgian
Poetry* being parodied as 'Gorgeous Poetry' by J. B. Morton and Eddie
Marsh christened 'Freddie Mush' by H. G. Wells.

Sassoon wandered around Rouen absorbing and observing. One
incident at the Base is captured in a poem called 'Lamentations':

I found him in the guard-room at the Base.
From the blind darkness I had heard his crying
And blundered in. With puzzled, patient face
A sergeant watched him; it was no good trying
To stop it; for he howled and beat his chest.
And, all because his brother had gone west,
Raved at the bleeding war; his rampant grief
Moaned, shouted, sobbed, and choked, while he was kneeling
Half-naked on the floor. In my belief
Such men have lost all patriotic feeling.

This description of an actual event exposed that ugly side of the war of
which the general public was ignorant. Sassoon's aim was to enlighten
them. The soldier, a private, either had deserted and been caught or had
suffered a breakdown and been removed lest he affect the other soldiers.
His real crime was being human in 'that zone of inhuman havoc'. The
soldier as hero was the public's expectation. Sassoon was angry. The
common soldier in his eyes had become the real hero of the war, one of
the 'droves of victims' sacrificed by incompetent leaders, such as 'The
General':

'Good morning, good morning!' the General said
When we met him last week on our way to the line.
Now the soldiers he smiled at are most of 'em dead,
And we're cursing his staff for incompetent swine.

'He's a cheery old card,' grunted Harry to Jack
As they slogged up to Arras with rifle and pack.

But he did for them both by his plan of attack.

Arras was Sassoon's destination when he left Rouen on 11 March. The nearer he got to the Front, the better he felt. He found himself moved between two stages of emotion, resentment and acquiescence. Although he had lost his belief in the war, he was still in thrall to the feeling of sacrifice. Writing of himself in the third person, he recorded: 'He doesn't know for what he is making the sacrifice; he has no passion for England, except as a place of pleasant landscapes and comfortable towns. He despises the English point of view and British complacency. Some day he will be able to explain this feeling of unreasonable acquiescence.' The duality was due in part to his 'being drawn back into the machine' which 'took away the responsibility for life'. Philosophical and moral questions would be left in abeyance for the duration of the war. If he survived there would be plenty of time to ponder and analyse the inconsistencies. For the present he would act sponge-like, soaking up each and every experience presented to him by Fate. The journey to the spring offensive was slow. It was on 8 April, Easter Sunday, nearly a month after leaving Rouen, that he reached the village of Basseux, some seven miles from Arras. In March the Germans had withdrawn from the Somme to the Hindenburg Line, which they called the Siegfried Line. The Battle of Arras began on 9 April but Sassoon was not involved in the first wave. He remained in his dug-out reading *Far from the Madding Crowd*.

Thomas Hardy had been a constant companion, through his poetry and novels, especially *The Dynasts*. A parcel arrived from Ottoline containing a 'little paper edition of Keats bound in green vellum'. Keats, who had forsaken the vocation of medicine for the vocation of a poet, was an early favourite of Sassoon. The gift could not have been more welcome. Graves, in a letter 10 days earlier, gave Sassoon the latest on Garsington, where he had been warmly received by Ottoline despite her previous doubts about him. After a month in France, Graves had been declared unfit for any further active service, sent home and was about to take up an instructorship post based at Wadham College, Oxford. Sassoon was glad to know that his friend was out of the war safely, and free to enjoy the pure air of Wales and the comforts of Garsington.

The snow in the Somme valley was melting, turning the ground into a quagmire made worse by rain. It was bitterly cold at night, there was little or no room to lie down and rations were reduced to one meal a day. Progressing towards the Hindenburg Line on 13 April, he saw the bodies of those who had fallen in the earlier advance. Next day he was at the Line itself, marvelling at this exhibition of Teutonic engineering. There were other sights:

> The dead bodies lying about in trenches and in the open are beyond description especially after the rain. Our shelling of the line and subsequent bombing etc has left a number of mangled Germans – they will haunt me till I die. And everywhere one sees the British Tommy in various states of dismemberment – most of them shot through the head – so not so fearful as the shell-twisted Germans. Written at 9.30, sitting in the Hindenburg underground tunnel on Sunday night, fully expecting to get killed on Monday morning.

He was not killed but sniped through his right shoulder. Recklessly Sassoon had stood up above the lip of the trench, making himself an easy target from the German line. It was a clean wound with little loss of blood. He felt he could carry on leading his men, and so he did until he was replaced and ordered back to the aid-post. It says much for his strength that despite the injury and the after-effects of a tetanus injection he was still able to trudge through the mud for four miles until he reached the field-hospital. He had been at the Front for eight days and seen horrors that exceeded even those of the Somme, a year earlier. Now it was time to journey home through the mud-soaked fields of northern France to an England bursting with spring again. 'The Front Line was behind us; but it could lay its hand on our hearts, though its bludgeoning reality diminished with every mile. It was as if we were pursued by the Arras Battle, which had become now a huge and horrible idea. We might be boastful or sagely reconstructive about our experience, in accordance with our different characters. We were the survivors; few among us would ever tell the truth to our friends and relations in England.' That April, Sassoon wrote 'To the Warmongers':

> For you our battles shine
> With triumph half-divine;
> And the glory of the dead

Kindles in each proud eye.
But a curse is on my head,
That shall not be unsaid,
And the wounds of my heart are red,
For I have watched them die.

6

THE STATEMENT

1917

'This is Lotus-Land,' Sassoon wrote to Uncle Hamo about the 4th London Hospital, Denmark Hill, in South London. The visitors came in a constant stream to see him. Theresa, now 60, failed to make the journey from Weirleigh because of rheumatism, but Nellie Gosse, his aunt Frances Donaldson and her children, Robbie Ross and Edward Marsh, were among those bearing gifts. Robert Graves at Oxford did not know that Sassoon had been wounded and his long letter to him, which included more news of Garsington and Ottoline (whom he nicknamed Lady Utterly Immoral), was sent to France. Ross got a message to him and Graves wrote again on 22 April. His sister Rosaleen was a nurse at the hospital, so he could visit by proxy. An advance copy of *The Old Huntsman* was now in his possession and he enthused over its contents and suggested changes. Sassoon at this time was ready and willing to accept Graves' opinions. It was part of their commitment to each other.

Letters, gifts and visitors did much to lighten Sassoon's mood but they also left him exhausted, especially if they touched upon the war. Sleep and rest were difficult in the ward, particularly after the lights went out and gruesome imaginings assailed him:

The floor is littered with parcels of dead flesh and bones, faces glaring up at the ceiling, faces turned to the floor, hands clutching neck or belly; a livid grinning face with bristly moustache peers at me over the edge of my bed, the hands clutching my sheets. They are not here to scare me; they look at me reproachfully, because I am so lucky, with my safe wound. One boy, an English private in full battle order, crawls to me painfully on hands and knees, and lies grasping at the foot of my bed; he is fumbling in his tunic for a letter; just as he reaches forward to give it me his head lolls sideways and he collapses on the floor; there is a hole in his jaw, and the blood spreads across his white face like ink spilt on blotting-paper. I wish I could sleep.

Spring mornings brought relief as the early light reached through the high windows of the ward. Sassoon's rudimentary pantheism which brought such comfort to him while in France offered respite again from the horrors of the night. There it had been trees, fields and larks, here in the ward it was the daffodil, the primrose and the lily. Such release was temporary, as were the excursions into London from 1 May to meet with Ross and others at the Reform Club. A week later he was at the Reform again, dining with Arnold Bennett and the editor of the *London Mercury*, J. C. Squire. Sassoon was in town celebrating the publication by Heinemann of *The Old Huntsman and Other Poems*. This was his first major book of poems and dedicated to Thomas Hardy. 'The Wessex Wizard', as Sassoon called him, was delighted when in January his permission was sought in a letter from France. On receiving his copy in May he wrote to Sassoon:

I was going to wait till I could send you an elaborate letter of commentary, after a thorough reading of the poems, but then I felt you would prefer, as I do myself, just this simple line to tell you how much I like to have them. I should say that I am not reading them rapidly. I never do read rapidly anything I care about ... I don't know how I should stand the suspense of this evil time were it not for the sustaining power of poetry. May the war be over soon.

The letter, Sassoon told Uncle Hamo, 'was the great event for me. It affects me more than any review could do, because he praises the grimmer verses which I know to be the most significant ones. And who but he can say whether such things "come off or fail"?' Uncle Hamo's opinion mattered, too. He thought it all 'stunning throughout but especially the first half'. This pleased his nephew because that half contained the acerbic war poems. Virginia Woolf, reviewing for the *Times Literary Supplement* on 31 May, praised Sassoon's portrait of war's reality: 'It is realism of the right, the poetic kind.' Sassoon wrote to Ottoline saying how highly he prized such commendation. His delight was passed to Mrs Woolf by a purring Ottoline. Edmund Gosse, who had so recently admonished Sassoon for his poem 'Conscripts', also lent his praise, even though Sassoon had not altered the offending reference to 'many a slender, sickly lord'. More importantly for him, the letter from Gosse meant that the door to the critic's home was still open. All in all, Sassoon was pleased with the reception accorded the book. The only review that annoyed him was in *The Times*, which underplayed the strong war poems in favour of the more innocuous ones and described their author as 'a devout and amiable amateur'. 'Never mind,' he reposted, 'I will be a wicked poet, I will! just to spite them.'

The reviews reached him at Chapelwood Manor in Sussex, where he arrived on 12 May. The Earl and Countess Brassey had opened its doors to convalescing officers. The venerable lord belonged to the old world-order; his wife to some other world from where the glorious dead, the heroic dead, gave their help to England. Both represented an age that was passing, certainly one at odds with the tenor of Sassoon's thoughts as he pondered his future in the arcadian atmosphere and surroundings of their estate. The news of continued losses sustained by his old battalion bore down on him. He admits that each morning as the dawn chorus wafted across the Sussex Weald, or he opened his eyes in a sun-filled bedroom, other men, men he knew, 'were dying, fifty yards from their trench'. He listened as the rain fell at evening, 'the steady, whispering rain, the voice of peace among the summer foliage', and remembered the men who 'are cursing the downpour that drenches and chills them while the guns roar out their challenge'.

Sassoon understood now that his commitment was no longer to the war but to those whom he regarded as its living victims. They became his cause, his motivation. The comfort of Chapelwood Manor was a hindrance to the pursuit of that cause, and self-indulgence blunted the edge of motivation. Leaving the Manor on 4 June, he had rejected the idea of using poetry as his sole means of protest. Also rejected was the principle he had enunciated to Graves about being of succour to those under his command at the Front. If the cause were to be effective, it must be fought on the Home Front. The idea of such a protest had been on the agenda when he spent time with Graves at Harlech and Weirleigh, but then rejected. Graves, in a letter to Sassoon dated 22 April, suggested a softer option, that of obtaining a post as an instructor, which would be home-based. Sassoon was tempted, especially when others endorsed the idea. He kept the option open but his instincts were for something bold and challenging. During the next two weeks he began to write a statement for publication in which he would declare 'on behalf of soldiers' that the continuance of the war was no longer justified. The only people who knew about this course of action were Ottoline and her husband Philip. He was negative about the whole scheme and left Sassoon in no doubt that in his own opinion nothing could possibly come of it. According to Sassoon, Philip was beginning to show signs of the inevitable exhaustion following his four-year campaign against the war. Ottoline was fully behind the move. What Sassoon needed was help to draft the statement to achieve maximum effect. According to Ottoline's journal, it was Philip who advised Sassoon to seek the assistance of H. W. Massingham, Editor of *The Nation*, John Middleton Murry, the writer and critic, and Bertrand Russell. When writing of these events in *Memoirs of an Infantry Officer*, Sassoon says he met Massingham as a result of his own initiative on two occasions; on 7 June at the Reform and again at the offices of *The Nation*. On this second visit Massingham recommended a meeting with Russell. The Morrells are not mentioned and neither is Middleton Murry. This is a further example of how Sassoon rearranged events when writing his fictionalised autobiography. In *Siegfried's Journey*, which is not a fictional account, the only person omitted is Massingham. The major role is given to Russell, who oversaw the statement Middleton Murry and Sassoon composed and arranged the contact with the pacifist MP H. Lees-Smith, who agreed to raise the matter in the House of Commons at a later date.

Russell, of course, saw immediately the possibility of a powerful publicity coup for the anti-war movement. It was an absolute gift; here was a decorated officer, unassailable from any accusation of cowardice, who, through the publication of his poetry, was known to the discerning public. Russell discounted the consequence of publication. He was always ruthless on himself and others in pursuit of every cause he undertook. The Statement was completed in Middleton Murry's home in Kensington, approved by Russell and dated 15 June. Sassoon went back to the United Club in St James's Street where, in the library he read and pondered the Statement.

I am making this statement as an act of wilful defiance of military authority because I believe that the War is being deliberately prolonged by those who have the power to end it. I am a soldier, convinced that I am acting on behalf of soldiers. I believe that this

War, upon which I entered as a war of defence and liberation, has now become a war of aggression and conquest. I believe that the purposes for which I and my fellow-soldiers entered upon this War should have been so clearly stated as to have made it impossible for them to be changed without our knowledge, and that, had this been done, the objects which actuated us would now be attainable by negotiation. I have seen and endured the sufferings of the troops, and I can no longer be a party to prolonging those sufferings for ends which I believe to be evil and unjust. I am not protesting against the military conduct of the War, but against the political errors and insincerities for which the fighting men are being sacrificed. On behalf of those who are suffering now, I make this protest against the deception which is being practised on them. Also I believe that it may help to destroy the callous complacence with which the majority of those at home regard the continuance of agonies which they do not share, and which they have not sufficient imagination to realise.

He was content that his deepest feelings had been so succinctly expressed. His concern now was whether or not he had the courage and stamina to endure the inevitable consequences. As he confessed later in *Memoirs of a Fox-Hunting Man*: 'Possibly what I disliked most was the prospect of being misunderstood by my fellow officers. Some would regard my behaviour as a disgrace to the Regiment. Others would assume that I had gone a bit crazy. How many of them, I wondered, would give me credit for having done it for the sake of the troops who were at the Front?' It was also for those with whom he had served and were dead. That evening he wrote a poem which he called 'To Any Dead Officer'. The last verse echoes the spirit of the statement:

> 'Good-bye, old lad! Remember me to God,
>   And tell Him that our Politicians swear
> They won't give in till Prussian Rule's been trod
>   Under the Heel of England. Are you there? ...
> Yes ... and the War won't end for at least two years;
> But we've got stacks of men ... I'm blind with tears,
>   Staring into the dark. Cheero!
> I wish they'd killed you in a decent show.'

Sassoon now entered into what he called his 'double life'. Family and friends were not told of the Statement. He went to Cambridge to attend an interview board for a post as Cadet Instructor and was accepted. Returning to London, he sought out Robbie Ross and told him only about the Cambridge posting. It pained Sassoon to deceive so close and loyal a friend. He also, together with Russell, met the Member of Parliament for Northampton, H. Lees-Smith. The strategy was for Sassoon to return to Weirleigh and deliberately overstay his leave. The next step would be taken when he received the summons to report for duty. Leading a double life created tensions between Sassoon and his mother. He wanted to tell her about his intended course of action but was restrained from doing so mainly because she was not sympathetic. Theresa believed in the war and those who opposed it were 'mad with their own self-importance'. He could not disabuse her of what to him were wrong notions lest, in an unguarded utterance, he reveal his imminent intentions. The imposed silence on this subject led to morose and prolonged intermissions in any conversation. Theresa's attempt at diversion was small talk and parlour games, which only added to Sassoon's impatience and the desire to escape to the garden or his bedroom. Doubts assailed him and the effort to find distraction through reading or walking did not relieve them. The newspapers were another irritant, spreading their propaganda and misrepresentations about the war and the glory and the sacrifice of the soldier, all of it swallowed by a generation old enough to know better but 'insatiable in their desire for slaughter, impenetrable in their ignorance'.

> Soldiers conceal their hatred of the war.
> Civilians conceal their liking for it.

It was the press who fed the 'liking', particularly Northcliffe. It seemed that authors, press barons and politicians were singing the same tune of English rectitude and the need to fight to the finish, whatever the cost to others. Sassoon was incensed by those who were doing well out of the war, the profiteers crying into their expensive handkerchiefs and dining off the best tables, and the servants of Christ, like the Bishop of London, Winnington-Ingrams (who had confirmed Sassoon), and who went around Fulham, Southwark and the East End of London in army uniform, recruiting men and assuring them that killing Germans was a Christian act. The world, or at least England, had gone mad in an orgy of inverted values.

Weirleigh, which from his earliest rememberings had been a haven of joy and peace, laughter and discovery, had lost its magic. Everything about it, around it and within it seemed organised to remind him of the war. His state of mind during those two weeks at Weirleigh is caught in his poem 'Repression of War Experience'.

> Now light the candles; one; two; there's a moth;
> What silly beggars they are to blunder in
> And scorch their wings with glory, liquid flame –
> No, no, not that, – it's bad to think of war,
> When thoughts you've gagged all day come back to scare you;
> And it's been proved that soldiers don't go mad
> Unless they lose control of ugly thoughts
> That drive them out to jabber among the trees.
>
> You're quiet and peaceful, summering safe at home;
> You'd never think there was a bloody war on!
> O yes, you would ... why, you can hear the guns.
>
> Hark! Thud, thud – quite soft – O Christ, I want to go out
> And screech at them to stop – I'm going crazy;
> I'm going stark, staring mad because of the guns.

Doubts about the value of his intended protest came and went. Resolution would have been easier to maintain had Sassoon been in the company of those who shared his convictions. As it was, the people who visited Weirleigh had different sympathies, in particular Captain Ruxton, their neighbour, who represented the old voice of military England. Freed from the curse of age, he would stride out again in her defence.

There was no room in the Captain's world for the conscientious objector, whom he judged to be 'the antithesis of an officer and a gentleman'. He found no fault or contradiction in bishops endorsing the war – 'For him the Church couldn't be too militant.' Theresa was in total agreement with him. Affection for them both kept Sassoon from including the Captain and Theresa on his list of war villains; they spoke without guile and the war brought them no profit. They spoke, however, believing that in Sassoon they had a sympathetic ear: he was the guileful one. If only they knew what 'young Siegfried' was about to do. The irony appealed to the poet; the deception distressed him. Many years before he had told a lie about Mrs Mitchell, his nurse, and he believed as a consequence that he was damned eternally. Ellen Batty drew the poison from his wounded conscience and told him that as the lamp on the front of his bicycle sends light into the darkness before him, so too the conscience, but to be effective it must be kept clean. The lesson of 1895 had its resonance in 1917.

'July 4. JOIN LITHERLAND IMMEDIATELY.' The telegram was signed by the Adjutant, 3rd Battalion, Royal Welch Fusiliers. Sassoon had already overstayed his leave by a week. He wrote a covering letter to accompany the Statement, addressed to the commanding officer:

> I am writing you this private letter with the greatest possible regret. I must inform you that it is my intention to refuse to perform any further military duties. I am doing this as a protest against the policy of the Government in prolonging the War by failing to state their conditions for peace.
>
> I have written a statement of my reasons, of which I enclose a copy. This statement is being circulated. I would have spared you this unpleasantness had it been possible.
>
> My only desire is to make things as easy as possible for you in dealing with my case. I will come to Litherland immediately I hear from you, if that is your wish.
>
> I am fully aware of what I am letting myself in for.

Does conscience make cowards of us all? Sassoon had second thoughts but within forty-eight hours of the telegram arriving his response was on its way to Litherland. While in London with Russell he had ordered copies of the Statement from the Pelican Press and now he sent them to friends and to those who, upon reading it, might endorse its contents and his action. Some friends he knew would be shocked and to these he felt further explanation was due. To Eddie Marsh, he wrote on 7 July:

> I feel I must send you the enclosed document, although you will not approve of my action. So I won't say any more, except that I have sent it to my commanding officer at Litherland, and shall proceed thither in a day or two. It's a bloody performance altogether. But I could do nothing else.

Marsh's response came on 11 July:

Thank you very much for telling me what you have done. Of course I am sorry about it. As a non-combatant, I should have no sort of right to blame you, even if I wanted to. But I think you are intellectually wrong – on the facts. We agree that our motives for going to war were not aggressive or acquisitive to start with, and I cannot see that they have changed. But now, dear boy, you have thrown your die, and it's too late to argue these points. One thing I do beg you. Don't be more of a martyr than you can help. You have made your protest, and everyone who knows that you aren't the sort of fellow to do it for a stunt must profoundly admire you for doing it. But for God's sake stop there.

Robbie Ross wrote from Brighton on 8 July in a state of panic:

I am quite appalled by what you have done. I can only hope that the C.O. at Litherland will absolutely ignore your letter. I am terrified lest you should be put under arrest.

Robert Graves was convalescing at Osborne on the Isle of Wight. He was staggered by the news, and he knew who to blame: those Garsington pacifists who had taken advantage of Sassoon when he was in a serious nervous condition. He knew and feared that if Sassoon persisted he would be 'court-martialled, cashiered and imprisoned'. For the next 10 days Graves became the key player in diverting Sassoon from such an ignominious and crushing fate. He wrote to the Assistant Adjutant, Major Macartney-Filgate, stressing that Sassoon's Statement, read in the light of his war record, could only be an aberration which itself was the result of war weariness. He urged Macartney-Filgate to use his good offices with the CO, Colonel Jones-Williams, suggesting to him that the case should be treated as medical rather than as rebellion and Sassoon be sent home on indefinite leave. As it happened, the Colonel was on leave and Macartney-Filgate acting CO. Graves' next letter went to the Hon. Evan Morgan, whose passing acquaintance he had made some months earlier at Oxford. Morgan was the Private Secretary to W. C. Bridgeman at the Ministry of Labour. When Macartney-Filgate, following protocol, sought advice up through the chain of command until it reached the War Office, Bridgeman's influence, according to Graves in his memoirs, ensured that the matter would be treated on medical grounds. Graves then successfully sought from the Medical Board his own discharge from Osborne. On 12

July he wrote to Marsh, telling him that the real problem was going to be persuading Sassoon to drop his protest and to extricate himself by way of a Medical Board. What he wanted to avoid was quarrelling with Sassoon and exacerbating the situation.

Marsh was working at Number 10, having moved there when, on Churchill leaving the government and enlisting in the Army, he lost his highly placed position as Private Secretary. His influence on and direct access to high ministerial rank was reduced. According to his biographer, Marsh did visit the War Office and presented a defence of Sassoon, though by this time the War Office was already aware of the case through Macartney-Filgate's enquiries. Marsh, having done what he could, waited on the sidelines for the matter to be resolved; he felt powerless to do more. Then, on 16 July, Marsh's phone rang. It was Winston Churchill. Lloyd George had recalled him to the Cabinet as Minister of Munitions. He was phoning to ask Eddie to be his Private Secretary: Marsh was back at the centre of influence. On the same day Graves left Osborne for Litherland via London.

Meanwhile Sassoon had, on receipt of a second summons, returned to Litherland, unaware of the machinations being conducted on his behalf. The account of his reception at the depot is recorded in *Memoirs of an Infantry Officer* and, although it is fictionalised, there is no reason to doubt the essence of the description of events which occurred over the next days. The first surprise was finding in charge not the Colonel but Macartney-Filgate, who greeted him warmly and invited him to his room. The high tension that Sassoon had predicted to himself on his journey to Litherland was absent. The Colonel had left clear instructions that Sassoon be asked to withdraw his Statement and the matter would be dropped. It was a tempting offer but Sassoon was resolute in his reply. His main concern was to remain poised and convinced of his argument and thereby avoid any suggestion of mental breakdown or emotional exhaustion. There must be no reason for being sent before a Medical Tribunal and his protest explained away. The next step after this refusal must be, Sassoon assumed, his arrest. But Major Macartney-Filgate, in what Sassoon thought a sympathetic tone of voice, said he should book in at the Adelphi Hotel in Liverpool and await further instructions.

So I trundled unexpectedly back to Liverpool and although, in all likelihood, my troubles were only just starting, an immense load had been lifted from my mind. I thoroughly enjoyed my tea, for I'd eaten nothing since breakfast. After that I lit my pipe and thought how nice it was not to be under arrest. I had got over the worst part of the show, and now there was nothing to be done except stick to my statement and wait for the M.P. to read it out in the House of Commons.

But events moved differently. He was handed written instructions to attend a Medical Board, which had been specially arranged. Tempted again by the possibility of ending the affair, Sassoon toyed with the idea of attending the Board, but his resolution returned and the instructions, together with the accompanying travel warrant, were torn up. The authorities at Litherland, on hearing from the Board of his non-appearance, explained it away as a misunderstanding of the instructions on Sassoon's part. The Army's patience was wearing thin but higher authorities were determined to prevent the affair from becoming a public cause. Sassoon was given more time to consider his position.

In some ways Sassoon's patience was also wearing thin. Playing it long, the Army had taken a lot of the sting out of the protest, and Sassoon was irritated by the lack of action. The amiability of Major Macartney-Filgate and others proved that a gentle answer turneth away wrath, but this delay Sassoon had not foreseen and it began to exasperate him. He took himself off to Formby, walked along the golf course and upon reaching the mouth of the Mersey, ripped off the Military Cross ribbon from his tunic and let it float on the surface of the current – 'the poor little thing fell weakly on to the water and floated away as though aware of its own futility'. Most reports of this incident say that Sassoon threw the medal itself into the water. This is not correct, if only for reasons of gravity: the medal and its attached ribbon would have sunk immediately instead of bobbing to obscurity in the way Sassoon describes. At the Adelphi Hotel he was informed that another Medical Board had been arranged, but Sassoon still had no intention of complying. What he wanted was a court martial.

On Wednesday, 18 July, Graves arrived at the hotel intent upon persuading Sassoon to conform to orders. In London he had met Marsh, who advised him that the only way of solving this matter was to make it absolutely clear to Sassoon that he would never be granted a court martial and that if he persisted in his present frame of mind he would be declared insane and incarcerated in a lunatic asylum. At Litherland Graves found Sassoon adamant and tense. He stuck to his agenda, beginning on a note of solidarity as far as the foolishness of the politicians was concerned and agreeing:

that everyone was mad except ourselves and one or two others, and that no good could come of offering common sense to the insane. Our only course would be to keep on going out until we got killed. I expected myself to go back soon, for the fourth time. Besides what would the Battalion think of him? How could they be expected to understand his point of view? They would accuse him of ratting, having cold feet, and letting the regiment down. The army could only read it as cowardice, or at best a lapse of good form. The civilians would take an even unkinder view, especially when they found out that 'S' stood for 'Siegfried'.

Graves had personal experience of this last calumny. His maternal grandfather was German; his full name was Robert von Ranke Graves and he had suffered as a result at the hands of fellow officers. His statement about going back for a fourth tour of duty was an exaggerated hope, given the state of his lungs, but it was a good try. His threat of social ostracism did not persuade Sassoon to change his mind. It was then that Graves played his last card. He told Sassoon that he had it on the 'highest authority, that the military would never give him a court-martial' and that, should he continue to refuse a Medical Board, they would lock him up in a lunatic asylum. There would be no publicity for his cause.

This revelation shook Sassoon; he asked Graves to repeat what he had just said, swearing to its veracity on the Bible. Knowing that he had lied about the highest possible sources and their intentions, he placed his hand on an imaginary Bible and swore that he was speaking the truth. The chink in Sassoon's armour which Graves' perjurious statement revealed was, he believed, sufficient justification for this deliberate falsehood. Sassoon agreed to a Medical Board. Graves went in to testify on Sassoon's behalf. It was a courageous act of friendship and loyalty from someone who was himself on the verge of a nervous breakdown. He burst out crying three times during the interview and members of the Board felt that Graves should have been before them in his own right. After questioning Sassoon, the Board declared that he was suffering from neurasthenia and referred him to Craiglockhart Hospital, near Edinburgh. He journeyed north on 23 July. Graves, deputed to escort him, missed the train.

7

CRAIGLOCKHART

1917–18

Craiglockhart was a hydro until the war came. For 50 years people went there to take the waters. Large rooms, high windows and long corridors were its main interior features. Externally the grounds were extensive: rockeries, walled gardens, lawns and meadows which stretched away to the village of Swanston and the Pentland Hills. The winds blew over it from the Firth of Forth and everything combined to engender a sense of bracing well-being in the well-to-do guests. Now it was a war hospital with some 150 officers, whose nerves and minds had been affected to varying degrees.

When, on a fine July afternoon, Sassoon arrived there by taxi from nearby Edinburgh he found it 'a gloomy cavernous place … a live museum of neuroses'. Some of the amenities of the old hydro remained for the use of the patients. Among such were the large but jaded common-rooms and a decently equipped library, where it was possible to find silence. Outside in the gardens, officers could potter around or go for walks. Many of the activities were designed by the medical staff as part of the therapy. Some of the patients formed clubs around a common interest, as people do in such circumstances. Sassoon preferred the outdoors and relished the chance to stride out in the direction of the Pentlands, where Robert Louis Stevenson had roamed before him. Also, to his abundant joy, there was a golf course. In all his memoirs he rarely mentions mixing with the other inmates. His shyness, however, would not have in any way diminished his capacity for sympathy. He needed privacy and he needed peace; the outdoors alone could satisfy that need.

Sleep did not come easily at Craiglockhart. Many were assailed by nightmares. Screams made their anguish audible. Suppressed and denied by day, the memories took their revenge in the night. Guilt about not being at the Front duelled with the fear of being sent back there. The sense of personal failure nibbled at the roots of self-esteem and self-confidence. Accepting rather than denying the reality of their experience was the keystone in the bridge that connected past and present. Fleeing their past they could find neither present nor future, only no-man's-land.

Sassoon was required to share a room, something he disliked. He was not free from his own dreams and nightmares. His therapy was his poetry, and the notes and outlines for more poems. For the first few days he also had the company of Robert Graves, who had arrived four hours after him. In some ways Craiglockhart was similar to Osborne, Graves' last hospital, in both its structure and its patients – injured solders, bewildered men. The following day, 24 July, was Graves' twenty-second birthday. Sassoon, in a letter to Ross two days later, said, 'It was very jolly seeing Robert Graves up here. We had great fun on his birthday, and ate enormously.' The meal was in Edinburgh whither, under the relaxed rules of Craiglockhart, he could travel at will; it was the promise of freedom, as were the golf course and the open countryside. With plenty of books to read as well, he was able to assure friends like Ottoline that he had a spring in his step and that he regarded Craiglockhart, which he nicknamed Dottyville, as simply an opportunity for marking time and reading steadily – 'The Pentland Hills are glorious. I leap their ridges like a young ram.'

That letter to Ottoline is dated 30 July. Just before seven o'clock that evening Mr Lees-Smith rose in the House of Commons. His intervention was part of a wider debate about the alleged use by the government of underhand means to suppress opposition to the war. The previous Saturday soldiers in mufti had, it was claimed, broken up a pacifist meeting with the connivance of the authorities. This was contrary to King's Regulations. The men were not punished. Lees-Smith contended that for every soldier who supported the continuance of the war there was one who disagreed; but the latter was denied the right to protest, and if he did so, the government made sure it was kept from the public and the offender dealt with surreptitiously. This created the opportunity for Lees-Smith to read out Sassoon's Statement.

He was forced to appear before a Medical Board, and the Board, having heard the opinions he had expressed in his letter, informed him that he must be suffering from the effects of a passing nervous shock due to his terrible experiences at the Front. He was sent to a hospital for officers suffering from shell-shock. I read that letter, because I think, however profoundly Honourable Members may disagree from it, that it contains no indication whatever of having been written by a man suffering from any kind of nervous shock ... that the decision of the Medical Board is not based upon health, but based upon easily understood reasons of policy. It is quite clear that it was to avoid publicity.

The Under-Secretary of State for War denied any such motive and confirmed that it was health grounds and not the avoidance of publicity that determined the decision of the Medical Board. The predictable answer was irrelevant. Lees-Smith had secured what he wanted. Next day the exchange was national news. Graves wrote to Sassoon, 'Well, you are notorious throughout England now, you silly old thing.' Not everyone welcomed the publicity. One such was Uncle Hamo and Sassoon thought it best to get a letter off to him post-haste:

I am very sorry if I have caused you worry and annoyance by my recent actions. Of course you don't agree with me, but I hope you won't rely on the people who wriggle out of the situation by saying I'm dotty. I talk about the war to a doctor Captain W. Rivers – a very good chap. If you think there's anything wrong with my nerves you can write and ask him!

W. H. R. Rivers was a doctor of medicine, an anthropologist and a psychologist. His work at Craiglockhart, and that of his colleague, Dr Brock, was experimental rather than tried and tested. As with all pioneering work, it was viewed with suspicion by the authorities, who belonged to the 'pull-yourself-together' school of thinking. Sassoon himself, in a letter to Ottoline at the end of the first week, described some of his fellow patients:

A great many of them are degenerate looking. A few are genuine cases of shell shock etc. One committed suicide three weeks ago. The bad ones are sent to another place.

The letter continues with remarks about Rivers:

My doctor is a sensible man who doesn't say anything silly. But his arguments don't make any impression on me. He doesn't *pretend* that my nerves are wrong, but regards my attitude as abnormal. I don't know how long he will go on trying to persuade me to modify my views.

The note of resistance could be construed as Sassoon assuring Ottoline that he had, and would keep the faith. Russell and the other pacifists had concluded otherwise and regarded his presence at Craiglockhart as a betrayal. From the longer perspective of *Sherston's Progress*, Sassoon's account of the hospital, of the patients and of Rivers is mellower and more acquiescent. Most of the sessions with Rivers were held in the evening for about an hour. Sassoon took to him at once and the feeling was reciprocated – 'He liked me and he believed in me.' Rivers had the gift of ease, which remained unalloyed, despite the distressing and demanding nature of his work. One of the best descriptions of him was written by the writer and critic Frank Swinnerton, who met him through Sassoon after the war:

Once or twice I must have run into him alone, and it was on those occasions that I felt the comfort of his unaffected agreeableness. He was not a tall man, was, indeed, an unimpressive figure. He wore what I remember as black-rimmed glasses, and dressed with a sort of inconspicuous shabbiness. Always, across his face, there spread a wide smile. I doubt whether he ever accepted any idea without considering it with the greatest care. He gave the impression of being one of the most evenly tempered and kindly creatures I have ever met; and this with no suggestion of softness. Moreover he was not ridden by a theory and was not afraid of reality.

Behind the affability lay a singleness of purpose, the understanding of the human mind and consciousness through neurophysiology and psychotherapeutic methods. At Craiglockhart he adopted the Freudian tenet, that what and why we forget are more significant than what and why we remember. The war patients gave him an unequalled opportunity to pursue his theory that the unconscious played its part in causing mental and functional nervous disease.

Sassoon counted himself lucky to be under the care of Rivers, who allowed him to talk about himself, the Statement and what he thought might be his future. The conversations followed their own momentum.

Tired at the end of a long day, Rivers listened. He was never judgemental, although some of Sassoon's inconsistencies in logic were the cause of mutual laughter. He became 'a kind of father-confessor to me'. From the outset Rivers did not believe that Sassoon was suffering from shell-shock:

> There are no physical signs of any disorder of the Nervous System. He discusses his recent actions and their motives in a perfectly intelligent and rational way, and there is no evidence of any excitement or depression. He recognizes that his view of warfare is tinged by his feelings about the death of friends and the men under his command in France. His view differs from that of the ordinary pacifist in that he would no longer object to the continuance of the War if he saw any reasonable prospect of a rapid decision.

Rivers soon found Sassoon different from other pacifists and different also from the other patients who *were* suffering from shell-shock. He wanted to explore this difference and through the exploration help Sassoon to unburden himself. For his part Sassoon needed to talk – 'I am no exception to the rule that most people enjoy talking about themselves to a sympathetic listener.' Sassoon was a very private person, who did not easily or readily share his confidences. Rivers, however, possessed the right criteria:

> There was never any doubt about my liking him. He made me feel safe at once, and seemed to know all about me. What he didn't know he soon found out. Forgetting that he was a doctor and that I was an 'interesting case', I answered his quiet impartial questions as clearly as I could, with a comfortable feeling that he understood me better than I understood myself. Rivers never seemed elderly; though there were twenty years between us, he talked as if I were his mental equal, which was very far from being the case. I was really very ignorant, picking up my ideas as I went along, but Rivers always led me quietly past my blunders.

That amalgam of disparate references to Rivers in *Sherston's Progress* shows clearly not only the method Rivers adopted but also his purpose – he wanted Sassoon to think as well as to feel. Rivers recognised that Sassoon was emotionally and intellectually immature. Edmund Gosse in the altercation over the 'sickly, slender lord' reference had made exactly the same point. To quote Sassoon's own description of himself at this time, he was a 'shy and callow youth'; this at 30 years of age. Observing Sassoon 'the happy warrior' in the light of this callowness affords a different view from the one generally given of him during the war. The exploits which earned him the epithet 'Mad Jack' were in a particular sense those of an adolescent – bravado rather than bravery. His dashing forward to capture an enemy trench, occupying it and then proceeding to read a book was irresponsible and hindered further advance. It was a bit of a devil-may-care attitude in which personal and collective consequences were discounted or not counted at all. Brave men do not seek martyrdom, self-destruction or death – three terms Sassoon uses about himself. They hover nervously on the thin line that divides self-preservation and self-sacrifice in the hope that finally the course may be altered. 'If it be possible, let this cup pass from me, but ...' Brave men do not count the cost but they do consider the options. They hold the subjective and objective in balance. What Rivers recognised in Sassoon was the imbalance. It was all subjectivity, as though the world turned on the axis of his ego. In consequence his view of the war and the world was one-sided and emotional, lacking any objective content.

Ottoline perceptively wrote in her diary: 'Siegfried is terribly self-centred, and it seems almost as if when he does a valiant action, such as this protest, that he watches himself doing it, as he would look into a mirror.' Nothing in his background had prepared him for the reality of war. In fact, it had not prepared him for life outside his privileged and introverted world. The war, through its brutality, the suffering it wrought, its physical and emotional deprivations, brought Sassoon to a crisis that he could not comprehend, and he lacked the objectivity to deal with it. Twenty years on, he could speak with greater self-knowledge in *Sherston's Progress*:

> The weak point about my 'protest' had been that it was evoked by personal feeling. It was an emotional idea based on my war experience and stimulated by the acquisition of points of view which I accepted uncritically. My intellect was not an ice-cold one. It was, so to speak, suffering from trench fever. I could only see the situation from the point of view of the troops I had served with; and the existence of supposedly iniquitous war-aims among the Allies was for that reason well worth believing in – and inveighing against.

In *Siegfried's Journey*, published in 1945, he relates the circumstances in which he made the protest of 15 June 1917:

While at the Front I was able to identify myself with my battalion. But, once I was back in England, I had to do something to relieve my state of mental tension. In my note-book there is an entry dated May 21st: 'I still think that I'd better go back as soon as possible unless I can make some protest against the War.' Had there been the chance of my getting passed for general service at the end of my June leave, I might conceivably have tried for it in the spirit of self-destructive bravado. But there seemed no likelihood of my being sent out again for several months, so I plunged headlong into my protest.

Sassoon said that he never regretted making his protest, but the above quotations show the confused and ambivalent state he was in when he decided to proceed. Fifty years on, he wrote that his war poems 'were improvised by an impulsive, intolerant, immature young creature, under extreme stress of experience'. The same could be said of the Statement. Reflecting on those sessions at Craiglockhart, Sassoon writes: 'My definite approach to mental maturity began with my contact with the mind of Rivers.'

One of the few consolations the war had so far brought Sassoon was the company, albeit intermittent, of Robert Graves. He was also a faithful correspondent, and through his letters kept Sassoon informed of army gossip, his latest poetry endeavours and humorous tittle-tattle about the literati. There is an irrepressibly boyish quality in their mutual and frequent exchanges. Sassoon was now following the advice of Rivers and 'marking time' at Craiglockhart. There were signs of improvement in his golf and he was working at his poetry. There was also good news about the sales of *The Old Huntsman*, of which new impressions were being printed. The aggressive anti-war spirit which produced the Statement had evaporated and Sassoon was 'psychologically passive' about the war. Even the old feeling of guilt at being comfortable and safe had lost some of its sting. Only once did he feel his anger rise against the waste and loss. Reading the casualty lists in *The Times* on 21 August he saw:

HARBORD. Killed in action on 14th August. Lt. (Temp Capt.) Stephen Gordon Harbord, M.C., R.F.A., third son of Rev. H. and Mrs Harbord, Colwood Park, Bolney. Aged 27.

Gordon had been his first real companion and his family at East Hoathly, in Sussex, had welcomed Sassoon as one of their own. Gordon and he had ridden out together with the Southdown Hunt, talked horses and cricket; 'He was indeed my greatest friend before the War,'

> The dearest of them, and the last
> Of all whose gladness linked me with the past.

Gordon and his younger brother Geoffrey had kept up their correspondence with Sassoon throughout the war. Geoffrey wrote to Sassoon:

Dear Old Sig,

I have kept trying to write to you ever since I heard about it, but damn well couldn't and tore my letter up each time. Of course it's what we've all been dreading ever since August '14 but that doesn't soften it much, in fact it is an irreparable calamity to every soul who knew the old lad. I know you'll feel it a lot. He was awfully fond of you as you know and I think you were easily his best friend.

I don't know how the poor old guv'ner and mother are taking it but I should be awfully grateful old boy if you could find time to go down and see them sometime. I am still getting letters from him but almost dreading coming back home now. His last letter enclosed one of yours, rhapsodizing on hunting.

If we both live to be a hundred we shall never again meet such a sportsman with such an extraordinary personal charm and such a loveable old creature in every way. I can't write anymore. Good luck old son.

Yours

Geoffrey Harbord

Sassoon expressed his own loss in the poem 'A Wooden Cross (To S.G.H) August 14 1917':

> I cannot call you back; I cannot say
> One word to speed you on your hidden way.
> Only I hoard the hours we spent together
> Ranging brown Sussex woods in wintry weather,
> Till, blotting out to-day, I half believe
> That I shall find you home again on leave,
> As last I saw you, riding down the lane,
> And lost in lowering dusk and drizzling rain,

> Contented with the hunt we had, and then
> Sad lest we'd never ride a hunt again ...

The war was 'a sham and a stinking lie'. The loss was irreparable but the anger was momentary. Three factors subdued it: his psychological passivity, the sessions with Rivers and a new friendship with a fellow patient, whose passion for poetry was as intense as that of Graves. The friendship began in the middle of August:

> There was a gentle knock on the door of my room and a young officer entered. Short, dark-haired, shyly hesitant, he stood for a moment before coming across to the window, where I was sitting on my bed cleaning my golf clubs. A favourable first impression was made by the fact that he had under his arm several copies of *The Old Huntsman*. He had come, he said, hoping that I would be so gracious as to inscribe them for himself and some of his friends.
>
> He spoke with a slight stammer, which was no unusual thing in that neurosis-pervaded hospital. My leisurely, commentative method of inscribing the books enabled him to feel more at home with me. He had a charming honest smile, and his manners – he stood at my elbow rather as though conferring with a superior officer – were modest and ingratiating. He gave me the names of his friends first. When it came to his own I found myself writing one that has since gained a notable place on the roll of English poets – Wilfred Owen.

Owen had arrived at Craiglockhart a month earlier than Sassoon, suffering nervous prostration. The St Quentin area of the Somme was the place where, after pursuing the Germans in their retreat to the Hindenburg Line, Owen fell asleep near a railway line, totally exhausted. An exploding shell blew him into the air – he survived, but his nerves were shattered. Stammering and trembling, back at the Headquarters of the 2nd Manchester Battalion, he was obviously in a state of neurasthenia. The decision was to send him to Craiglockhart for treatment. He was under the care of Dr Brock who, through a combination of investigative conversation and activity, began to restore Owen's self-confidence and mental balance. Among the various activities he undertook was that of Editor of the *Hydra*, the bi-weekly hospital magazine. But despite his busyness, and the care given by Dr Brock, the underlying experiences of war were all-pervasive, as evidenced by disturbing dreams and the stammering speech. He was also deeply unhappy and isolated.

The copies of Sassoon's *The Old Huntsman* which he carried that afternoon to the author's room became his passport into the world that he loved and desired most – the world of the poet. He had taken two weeks to summon up courage to make the acquaintance of Sassoon. There was about Owen an innate reticence. The poetry of Sassoon had revealed to him a new and different way to write about the realities of the war. His desire to capture its essence and infuse his own poetry with it was a sufficient antidote to any reluctance.

The description of their first meeting strikes the note of master and disciple or, at least, hero and ardent admirer. When they became more certain of each other that did not change. Owen always felt inferior and indebted. This was not due exclusively to Sassoon being first in the field of a new poetic realism: Owen was conscious of their social differences. Sassoon made no effort to ameliorate the situation and, to judge by his memoirs, their initial contact had more of the aura of an audience than a meeting. Owen's letters to Sassoon were always adulatory. Their friendship worked because both were happy with the relationship. Then there were the commonalities. Both were repressed homosexuals; the most important relationship was with their mothers; both had lost their religious faith, certainly in its institutional form; jingoistic civilians were their sworn enemies. Shelley and Keats were a shared delight and both in their pre-1916–17 poetry reflected the sentimentality and lyricism of the Romantic poets. Above all, in the desert that was Craiglockhart, they needed each other.

Owen was a willing and eager pupil. Sassoon taught him that poetry had a social purpose – to convince people of the brutish nature of the war. This could be achieved by writing from their experience, writing from the heart. The soldier-poet alone was qualified and capable to speak of war's reality and to expose the lie that the sacrifice of a generation was necessary for the securing of a better world. Sassoon introduced Owen to the work of Henri Barbusse, *Under Fire*, a penetrating description of war at the Front, of war as class exploitation and nationalistic barbarism. Poets who evaded this prophetic challenge betrayed those whom they had led on the Somme and those who at that moment were being sacrificed at Passchendaele. Owen's understanding of the poetic vocation was deepened by Sassoon, who also encouraged him to read Thomas Hardy and the works of H. G. Wells and Bertrand Russell, which pointed to a world of international understanding and social change.

Such things, essential and desirable if future conflicts were to be avoided, however, must await their day; the immediate call was to address the war through the voice of poetry. The vocabulary of that poetry should be vigorous and direct, emanating from experience. Sassoon helped him discard 'over-luscious writing' and 'embarrassing sweetness' – all the lessons that he himself had learned. Within the influence there lurked the danger of imitation and Owen's first attempts fell prey to it. However, within weeks he was emerging as a singular voice. 'Anthem for Doomed Youth' marked the beginning of his emancipation and Sassoon's appreciation of his talent: 'It dawned on me that my little friend was much more than the promising minor poet I had hitherto adjudged him to be. This new sonnet was a revelation. I suggested one or two slight alterations; but it confronted me with classic and imaginative serenity.'

The imprint of Sassoon was obvious to the experienced eye of Robert Graves, who arrived at Craiglockhart on 13 October, but he also recognised that Owen was a genuine and original talent. These two friends of Sassoon could not have been more different in their relationship with him – Owen respectful and subservient, Graves pugnacious and familiar. The friendship between Owen and Sassoon was in the ascendant; the friendship between Graves and Sassoon had passed its zenith. Graves was not a good judge of another person's mood. On meeting Sassoon that day he failed to temper his remarks to meet Sassoon's irritability. There was dispute in the air about the war and what were the right attitude and action. Graves did not approve of the war any more than Sassoon, but the war was a fact and therefore must be fought. Not to do so was to dishonour one's comrades and the regiment. His guiding principle as ever was 'he that endures to the end'. Rightly or wrongly, Graves had found a reason to sustain him. Sassoon, on the other hand, resented Graves for alluding to honour and duty in a war that was based on lies and deception.

The one point of amicability was Owen, whom Graves was more than willing to help. Writing to Graves on 19 October, Sassoon expressed his thanks for this gesture of friendship and generosity. The letter offered an apology wrapped up in an explanation: 'Seeing you again has made me more restless than ever. My position here is nearly unbearable, and the feeling of isolation makes me feel rotten.' He went on to tell Graves of a decision he had made – 'I have told Rivers that I will go back to France if they will send me (making it quite clear that my views are exactly the same as in July – only more so).'

Sassoon was desperate to get away: 'I would rather be anywhere but here.' He desired to be at the Front, with the battalion. He wanted to identify with the men who were there; those on whose behalf he had made the protest in the first place. The protest had failed, but he did not regret the attempt. Now he must return. He had no remit to remain and the authorities no right to detain him. Despite this period at Craiglockhart of marking time and putting the war behind him, the reality of war still held him in a tight grip, his thoughts ever revolving around the men he had left behind at the Front: 'Those men, so strangely isolated from ordinary comforts in the dark desolation of murderously-disputed trenches, were more to me than all the despairing and war-weary civilians.' In more than one of the poems he was writing for his next volume, *Counter-Attack*, he confesses guilt for their plight and his need of forgiveness for deserting them, despite his having 'cried to those who sent them out into the night'.

> The darkness tells how vainly I have striven
> To free them from the pit where they must dwell
> In outcast gloom convulsed and jagged and riven
> By grappling guns. Love drove me to rebel.
> Love drives me back to grope with them through hell;
> And in their tortured eyes I stand forgiven.

This decision to return was not made in any 'spirit of self-destructive bravado' or over-wroughtness; he had considered his options and taken an objective and practical position. He was clear in his mind that being at Craiglockhart was not bearable, but the authorities would be reluctant to allow a dissident to return to active service. He had not changed his views, as expressed in the Statement. The task was to obtain his release by a Medical Board. Rivers had confirmed from the outset that Sassoon was not neurasthenic, and he would, if the word of Rivers needed endorsing, seek a second opinion. The weight of medical evidence would make it impossible to refuse his release. He would declare his willingness to return to active service with the rider that he be sent immediately to the Front. In the meantime he must do nothing which would give reason to the authorities for locking him in a padded cell for the duration. He had matured enough to resist being used again by the Garsington pacifists; but there was no need to alienate them – especially Ottoline, to whom he wrote on 17 October:

> I have told Rivers that I will not withdraw anything that I have said or written, and that my views are the same, but that I will go back to France if the War Office will give me a guarantee that they really will send me there. I hope you and others will understand what I mean by it. By passing me for General Service (which Rivers says is 'the only

thing they can do') they admit that I never had any shell-shock, as it is quite out of the question for a man who has been three months in a nerve-hospital to be sent back at once if he really had anything wrong.

To confirm his continued alliance with the pacifists, he said that if his conditions were rejected he would let them pass him 'for General Service and then do a bolt to London – and see what course they adopt'. None of this cut any ice with the Garsington people. What they wanted was another public gesture of defiance. Sassoon was not swayed.

Rivers was supportive, convinced that Sassoon's return to the Front was the best and only solution, but a successful outcome would not be accomplished easily. Sassoon knew that too and was nervous but resolute. He was also busy with his poetry. Craiglockhart saw an extraordinary outpouring of work, which includes some of his finest war poems, 20 of which, including the title poem, were published in *Counter-Attack* in 1918. Eight of them were published in the *Cambridge Review* and one in *The Spectator* while he was at Craiglockhart. A quarter of his war poems between the commencement of the war and November 1917 were written there. He told Wilfred Owen: 'sweat your guts out, writing poetry' – he himself was sweating out his experience. The old enemies are there – the press, the clergy, the comfortable and the benighted, but so too are the ghosts, what Sassoon calls 'spiritual presences'. His poems from Craiglock-hart are a mixture of the lyrical and the pensive, as well as the acerbic.

The relationship with Owen deepened during October and Sassoon was now showing his young disciple the latest poems. Owen's confidence had grown and he was prepared to suggest amendments. They were careful not to discuss their traumatic experiences at the Front; Sassoon in particular feared such recounting would be injurious to Owen. The theme was always the nature and the place of poetry in war. Sassoon had managed to secure a room to himself and this facilitated writing, and conversations with Owen. However, their time together was short. At the end of October, Owen was passed for general service and left Scotland on 3 November after a sumptuous dinner and happy evening. Sassoon gave him a letter of introduction to Robbie Ross and a ten-pound note.

Sassoon was concerned that his determination to return to the Front was upsetting to Ottoline. He did not want to forfeit her friendship. Letters, he felt, were not the best means to convey his reasoning; it would be easier if they talked. Ottoline, too, worried that Sassoon was moving in the wrong direction. Given her views on the war, that was to be expected. She offered to come to see him but Sassoon tried to dissuade her: 'It isn't worth you coming all the way to Edinburgh in this awful weather, wait a bit – I may be getting out soon.' And again on 29 October he wrote: 'It would be jolly nice to see you: but it seems a terrible long way for you to come, especially if you are rather broke, as I gather you and Philip are. However if you decide to come, let me know what time you arrive.' Ottoline regarded this and the other letters as being a plea for her to make the journey.

The whole episode was a disaster due mainly to Sassoon's lack of thought and Ottoline's expectations:

> When I arrived I looked everywhere for Siegfried but he was not at the station to meet me; he had been playing golf and was late, but I took a cab to the hotel where he had engaged rooms for me. I felt rather aghast at the grand rooms which I found, knowing I should have to pay a fortune for them.

At dinner that evening it was clear to her that Sassoon was determined to return to the Front and was not open to argument. The next day they went for a long walk and Sassoon talked incessantly about himself:

> He had been engaged to a girl at the beginning of the war, he 'felt he ought to be as all his brother officers had a girl', but he soon found it impossible, as he really only liked men, and women were antipathetic to him ... he rather surprised me by telling me that he found me very complicated and artificial and could not understand me and that I ought to become simpler. He seemed to come quite near in his confidence and then the tide turned and went far out, leaving me alone on the beach. He always had an odd way of going off without a word and without attempting to say good-night or good-bye. I left Edinburgh the next morning. Siegfried did not come to see me off or say good-bye. He preferred to play golf.

Even allowing for Ottoline's possible over-dramatisation, this is an extraordinary account. Sassoon was preoccupied, but the purpose of seeing Ottoline was to discuss the reason for that preoccupation. His offensiveness and gratuitous lack of consideration put him in a very unpleasant light. He had behaved similarly to Ottoline the previous February in London, walking away without looking back. Her first instincts about him were right, 'I think he can be cruel.' The incident is instructive. Sassoon wanted sympathetic listeners for company, not for any contribution that they might make, and especially if they questioned his conclusions. He liked talking about himself but he also liked talking to himself. He seems to have preferred monologue to dialogue but he needed an audience. Rivers understood this, Graves did not and neither, it seems, did Ottoline.

Her reference to his saying that he was 'antipathetic to women' echoes his own remark at Litherland that women were outside his philosophy. These are classic overstatements on his part and evidence of his struggle to contain his homosexuality. Not being sexually attracted to women is different from being antipathetic to them. In his early life, and indeed throughout his life, some of his most treasured and influential friendships were with women. What he could not cope with were complicated and intimidating relationships. Ottoline in 1917 came into that category, as he says in *Siegfried's Journey*, when recalling their meeting earlier that year: 'My own comprehension of her fine qualities did not begin until some years later. The situation was too complex for the shy and callow young man I was on that dreary February afternoon.' Ottoline never came to terms with Sassoon's self-obsession and complained about it in her correspondence, but their friendship survived because of her own generosity of spirit: 'He is a man who has so much natural charm and good looks, which makes nearly all who know him idealise him; but in spite of the many things he has done to hurt and annoy me, I always remain fond of him.'

Two weeks after the visit Sassoon appeared before a Medical Board in Craiglockhart. As influences had been employed to ensure his arrival there rather than at a military prison, so now they were employed to ensure his release. Rivers had worked on his behalf, and Sassoon too had been in London. The War Office knew of the condition he was trying to impose, that he would return to duty only if he was sent to the Front at once. They and the authorities at Craiglockhart wanted the matter over and done with as quickly as possible. On 26 November he was passed for general service and was, he sardonically remarked, 'once again an officer and a gentleman'.

Sassoon did not return immediately to the Front. By way of Litherland he went home to Weirleigh, where for the first weekend he was joined by a new friend, Robert Nichols. Nichols had been discharged from the Army, having been diagnosed as neurasthenic and unlikely to recover sufficiently to make any return to active service. Of the younger Georgian poets he was regarded as the most promising. His first volume, *Ardours and Endurances*, was received with great acclaim in May 1917 and was the best-selling poetry book of that year. He did not sustain the success. Graves had introduced his work to Sassoon earlier in the year and they corresponded; it was Ross who arranged for them to meet at Half Moon Street, when Sassoon made his trip down from Craiglockhart a few weeks before his release. Ross was good at accomplishing and encouraging the meeting of poets. He had welcomed Wilfred Owen to his rooms at Sassoon's instigation and introduced him to some of the leading literary figures in London. Both he and Marsh acted as catalysts in this regard. Sassoon and Nichols took to each other. Nichols had character similarities to Graves, especially in his open and garrulous mode of conversation.

Graves was stationed at Rhyl in North Wales and Sassoon, on his return to Litherland in December, went over to visit him. Since last seeing him, Graves had become engaged to Nancy Nicholson, the daughter of William Nicholson the painter, who was a neighbour at Harlech. Graves had not been open with Sassoon about the development of this relationship, which accounts for the incongruous entry Sassoon made in his diary: 'Went to Rhyl to see Graves, and received his apologies for his engagement to Miss Nicholson.' Graves may have felt the need to apologise for his lack of candour and also for the fact that this commitment to marriage put paid to their travelling together after the war and their other plans of co-operation. Graves was confident that Sassoon would like his fiancée and everything would be as before. He was wrong: Sassoon did not take to Nancy's formidable, not to say strident, manner and opinions. The greatest obstacle was in her being an interloper. The former intimacy began to cool and the friendship, already dented, drifted on for another decade or so, with Graves making most of the running. Nineteen seventeen ended with Sassoon at Litherland, feeling 'healthy beyond measure' and making New Year resolutions: 'I intend to lead a life of light-hearted stupidity. I have done all I can to protest against the war and the way it is prolonged. At least I will try and be peaceful minded for a few months – after the strain of the last seven months. It is the only way by which I can hope to face the horrors of the front without breaking down completely. I must try to think as little as possible – and write happy poems. (Can I?)'

The Army gave him plenty of time to think and also to write poetry by choosing for him a circuitous route back to the Front – Ireland for a month and Palestine for three months. He returned via the south of France to the old battlefields of the north, where the Germans were mounting the last phase of their summer offensive in what proved to be their final attempt at victory. The first anniversary of the Statement, 15 June 1918, found him in reflective mood and considering the tension between being a soldier and a poet with pacifist tendencies. Since returning to France he had been too busy training his Company to think of other things. Those duties completed, the ensuing lull revived his detestation for the mind-numbing stupidity of soldiering and the price of so-called 'patriotism' exacted from 'sensitive gifted people'. These thoughts were not the result of an exhausted and tired mind – he was in the best of health, mentally as well as physically. Freedom from nightmares was not total but these apart, he stood assuredly astride the line where mind and emotion meet. Concern for, and commitment to those under his command, the central element in his decision to return to the Front became the prominent theme in the diary entries and are more personalised. He felt a new sense of well-being. *Counter-Attack*, his second volume of war poetry published on 27 June, was selling well. He had also been joined by a new Company second-in-command, Vivian de Sola Pinto, who was a poet.

When the company moved up to the Front, Sassoon's musings on patriotism disappeared; what then reappeared was the old self-destructive bravado. He made an unaccompanied excursion into enemy territory, came upon a manned machine-gun post and saw for an instant, for the first and only time in the war, the living face of the enemy. On 13 July he took a party on a patrol towards the enemy lines and, returning to his own line with his helmet in his hand, was shot in the head. The bullet came from a British gun – he had been mistaken for a German by a member of his own company. Sassoon was invalided out and taken back to England. This bizarre end to his military career can safely be judged as totally appropriate.

It was only a scalp graze. In the hospital at Lancaster Gate, Sassoon was fussed over and received letters and visitors. It was all too much for him. He hated being separated from his Company, which he believed gave some semblance of purpose to his life. England, and London in particular, was full of jingoistic nonsense. It was Rivers who came to the rescue, persuading Sassoon that he need feel no sense of failure or disloyalty at being out of the war. Sassoon became reconciled, indeed was relieved that he could enjoy liberty. Then there was Robbie, who bustled into the ward with press cuttings about *Counter-Attack*.

Of all his published work this was the most widely reviewed. As might be expected, the anti-war writers lauded not to say larded the volume with superlatives. There were surprises in the reviews published by the pro-war lobby, which included the *Morning Post*. It did not endorse the contents of the poems but commended their author's right to express his experience in so powerful a way. But the greatest surprise came in the review penned by the man who had helped Sassoon to put the finishing touches to the Statement –

John Middleton Murry. In *The Nation* he attacked the volume for its lack of any intellectual content, which reduced the poems to an unbridled emotional outburst. Sassoon's reaction was to admit the charge – he had never aspired to intellectual rigour. Ottoline was outraged. She had written to Murry, urging him to give the volume a solid, favourable review; she and Philip now let the critic know of their displeasure. Virginia Woolf, in a letter to Clive Bell, expressed her surprise; she thought the 'tone of the review a little superior' and stated that in her eyes 'there's some merit in the war poems. Still Ottoline's methods are monstrous, and I'm glad Murry didn't bow down.' Robbie Ross took the more practical approach that criticism, positive or adverse, helped the sales, which quickly mounted to 3,000 copies.

Wilfred Owen, who after leaving Craiglockhart was stationed at Scarborough, also wanted to get back to the Front. His friends were against this move but he persisted. On Thursday, 15 August he met Sassoon in London and again on the Saturday. It was a glorious summer day made memorable through the kindness of a new acquaintance, Osbert Sitwell, who was based at Chelsea Barracks just round the corner from his home in Swan Walk. Sassoon and Owen enjoyed a 'sybaritic afternoon'. Sitwell had arranged for them to visit the home of the harpsichordist Violet Gordon Woodhouse, who mesmerised them with a two-hour virtuoso performance; then back to Swan Walk for a splendid tea, followed by a visit to the Physic Garden. There was not a cloud in the sky as they walked back to Lancaster Gate, where they said goodbye on the steps of the hospital.

Sassoon boarded a train for Scotland on 17 August. His first destination there was Craiglockhart, where he spent three days, then down to the Borders and the town of Coldstream. The next month was a period of convalescence at the home of Major Walter and Lady Clementine Waring. Ever one to explore his surroundings, Sassoon enjoyed bicycling and walking in the Cheviot Hills. In the first week of September he received a letter from Owen. Much to Sassoon's surprise, his 'little friend' was in France. Sassoon had supposed that after their meeting in London, Owen had returned to Scarborough – 'The news caused me consternation, but I did my best to be impersonal by telling him that it would be "good for his poetry".'

Sassoon did not write many poems at Coldstream but he did find a poet. Frank Prewett arrived there from Craiglockhart, where he had been a patient of Rivers. This 25-year-old Canadian, who received the nickname 'Toronto', became a friend almost at first sight. Sassoon took to him, finding him physically attractive and a boon companion on excursions into the countryside. Prewett's experiences at Passchendaele had marked him, leaving him subject to depressive moods and withdrawal, but when these passed, his conversation and company were engaging. This encounter might have been a re-run of the Owen and Sassoon meeting at Craiglockhart. Sassoon gave lessons to him in the art of poetry, but the genius of Owen and the burning passion of a vocation were not present; Prewett was someone who wrote poetry as opposed to being a poet. This new friendship was one of many that Sassoon was making. For someone who four years earlier had been rather solitary, his circle in the autumn of 1918 was quite wide. In the first week of October, when he returned to London for a few days, he wrote names in his diary that were to be part of his postwar world. The Sitwells, Osbert and Edith, featured prominently; at the ballet and dining in the London clubs he met some of the Bloomsberries – Lytton Strachey, Mark Gertler, Duncan Grant and Maynard Keynes. It was a different world from his 1913 experience when, all togged-up in white tie and tail-coat, he went to the opera on his own or with Helen Wirgman; but in those days he was not a celebrity.

His poetry was reviewed and admired, even if the admirer did not always agree with the underlying sentiment. One such was the Minister of Munitions, Winston Churchill. On 3 October, Sassoon met him at his office in Northumberland Avenue. Sassoon was taken aback when Churchill paced the room, quoting his verse with ease and admiration. Two months earlier, while on a visit to the Front, Churchill had shaken members of his staff in the same way when he copiously recited the anti-war poems from *Counter-Attack*. Lord Esher, who was with Churchill at the time, was so puzzled by the enthusiastic performance that he wrote to a member of Haig's staff asking, 'Who is Siegfried Sassoon? Winston knows his last volume of poems by heart, and rolls them out on every possible occasion.' The person to whom Esher directed the enquiry was Philip Sassoon, the poet's cousin. Churchill told Eddie Marsh, who was with him in France, that he wanted to meet Sassoon and Marsh, thinking ahead, saw the opportunity to secure a position for his friend in government service for the duration of the war. Siegfried was not sympathetic to the suggestion – but he was flattered by the attention of Churchill.

That evening he went round to Half Moon Street to take his leave of Robbie Ross on the eve of Ross's departure for Australia. What Sassoon had hoped would be a quiet and intimate evening was interrupted by the arrival of two visitors, Charles Scott Moncrieff and Noël Coward. The latter was unknown to Sassoon, but the former was known and disliked. Sassoon made an earlier than planned exit: 'I said goodbye to Robbie with tormented abruptness, and when I was downstairs and about to let myself out of the front door, he came quickly down and stood beside me. He said nothing, but took my hand and looked up at me for a long moment.' Two days later, on 5 October, Sassoon returned to Scotland; on the same afternoon Robbie Ross died from heart failure.

In the weeks that remained before the Armistice, Sassoon formed a new friendship – with T. E. Lawrence. They met on 5 November and Sassoon recalled: 'The impression left on me by Lawrence was of a pleasant, unassuming person, who preferred to let other people do most of the talking. As he often did, he was subduing that power of stimulation which could lift others above and beyond their habitual plane of thought and action by communicating his mysterious and superlative vital energy. Had I been told that I was meeting one of the most extraordinary beings I should ever know and idolise, I should have refused to believe it.' Not since prewar days had Sassoon ascribed the word 'mysterious' to someone.

Lawrence engendered recollections of those halcyon days when he admitted to admiration of C. M. Doughty, whose works *The Dawn in Britain* and *Arabia Deserta* had brought delight to the young Siegfried and to whom in 1909 he sent one of only three specially bound volumes of *Sonnets and Verses*. Lawrence and Sassoon shared a passion for another man of letters, Thomas Hardy. Sassoon came to 'idolise' Lawrence and to 'venerate' Hardy.

The day after his lunch with Lawrence, Sassoon journeyed to Dorset and Max Gate. Throughout the year they had corresponded and Hardy wrote in September to say that he was, according to his habit, slowly reading the contents of *Counter-Attack*. 'One cannot read poetry straight-off – at least I cannot – so I look into them. I like the title pieces, and 'To Any Dead Officer' so far the best.' Arriving late because he had sat in the wrong part of the train and been shunted off to Bournemouth, Sassoon had his first view of his hero against the background of a flickering fire and subdued lighting. This added to the venerability of the sage but it was Hardy's ordinariness and lack of any pretension that first impressed his admirer. Sassoon became a firm favourite. Florence Hardy said that her husband referred to him as his 'adored Siegfried Sassoon'. Of course Sassoon had a head start through his connections with some of Hardy's old acquaintances: Uncle Hamo, Gosse and Robbie Ross. But Sassoon was winsome and people, especially women, found him attractive. Florence Hardy was no exception.

His poet's progress continued with visits to John Masefield and to the home of the Poet Laureate, Robert Bridges. The ageing poet gave Sassoon a somewhat frosty welcome. Bridges was virulently anti-German and disapproved of volumes like *Counter-Attack*. Sassoon was hurt. Ottoline welcomed him again to Garsington and was introduced to Sassoon's new friend, Frank Prewett. On that same day, 9 November 1918, the Kaiser fled to Holland, where in subsequent years he was befriended by Ottoline's family, the Bentincks. Sassoon heard the news to the music of Beethoven and Brahms being played on the piano.

Two days later, Sassoon was near Oxford.

November 11
I was walking in the water-meadows by the river below Cuddesdon this morning – a quiet grey day. A jolly peal of bells was ringing from the village church, and the villagers were hanging little flags out of the windows of their thatched houses ...

I got to London about 6.30 and found masses of people in streets and congested Tubes, all waving flags and making fools of themselves – an outburst of mob patriotism. It was a wretched wet night, and very mild. It is a loathsome ending to the loathsome tragedy of the last four years.

How much deeper would that loathing have been, had he known that a week earlier Wilfred Owen had been killed in action and was now part of

> The unreturning army that was youth;
> The legions who have suffered and are dust.

8

AFTERMATH

1918–20

Sassoon took no part in the Victory celebrations. He was not in any mood for what he regarded as primitive gregariousness. This was an arrogant attitude on his part. Many of those celebrating had endured as much as he and were relieved that the whole cursed business was ended. Besides which he was amenable to the more sedate pleasures of select dinner-parties at which the guests often represented a view of the war that he found abhorrent. On the evening of Armistice Day he attended a dinner-party in Chelsea, where he assumed an attitude of moral superiority towards the other guests, particularly those whom he suspected of not pulling their weight during the war. Sassoon was being adolescent and used his celebrity status ('being trotted out' is his description) as a licence for ill-tempered remarks which created embarrassment for both guests and host, including on one occasion Eddie Marsh. Caught up in 'a vortex of invitations' during the weeks following the Armistice, Sassoon played the radical with the self-satisfied and the snob with the proletariat. Of the two he preferred the company of the former.

Dining at Marsh's club he recalls: 'At Brooks's, of course, we found a sanctuary of comfort and decorum, and the dinner was such that I felt myself to be celebrating Victory with delectable exhilaration, reminded that there was more to be said for privileged than for proletarian standards of behaviour.' He and Marsh also went to an after-dinner party at the home of Lady Randolph Churchill, where her son Winston again affirmed his admiration of the poet. Sassoon basked in the adulation: 'Nothing, of course, could have been pleasanter than the contrast between such a civilised assemblage and the rampant rowdiness of the mob in Trafalgar Square.' Sassoon was playing a part, changing his mood to suit the occasion. He found the role of the celebrity difficult to handle; as was being part of the scene, fêted by excitable middle-aged matrons, who admired the hero-poet and flirted with this latest find. It was a flimsy world, which both attracted and repelled him during the early post-war years.

He behaved better when he visited the Gosses and displayed none of his impatience, despite the adverse review Gosse had published of his poetry. (On reading Gosse in the *Edinburgh Review*, Robert Graves had written to Sassoon: 'he's a bit sick with you evidently.') The sense of indebtedness he felt towards Gosse played its part and Sassoon was anyway genuinely fond of him. The welcome was as warm as ever. Sassoon had a way with him that could disarm his severest critic; he could be perceived as a loveable scamp by the older generation, who looked upon his errant behaviour as youthfully irritating but harmless, well intentioned but misguided. Despite his lapses from consideration for others, his irritability in company and occasional sarcasm, he could be the epitome of courtesy and gentlemanliness.

There were also deep convictions which, when violated, brought a sharp riposte that gave no quarter. The lapses from the norm, occasional as they were, owed much to a tired and distressed mind. The Sassoon of December 1918 was a disturbed person, whose belief in the structures which enabled him to form a benevolent view of the world had been eroded. Like many others he had been radicalised by the experience of war. The generation of Gosse, Uncle Hamo and, indeed, his mother, was seen as an impediment to progress; they were the defenders of a discredited social structure. Sassoon's affection for them was not impaired but his respect for, and confidence in their values was undermined. He had not formed a coherent political view but instinctively he opposed any return to the values of the pre-war world of his elders. Above all he felt that the causes of war must never again achieve the ascendant. Influenced by the writings of Henri Barbusse and H. G. Wells, he looked to world government and mutual co-operation to secure the peace. In particular he subscribed to President Woodrow Wilson's vision of nations sitting in harmonious conferences reasoning together for a new world order. Patriotic nationalism, monarchies and imperialism were destructive and divisive. Sassoon was unequivocal about this, as he told Marsh in a later outburst: 'I hate the bloody British Empire.'

Such sentiments did not intrude upon the enjoyment he derived from meeting John Galsworthy or dining with Walter de la Mare. Literature and poetry were the sole agenda. Sassoon's moods oscillated between the iconoclastic Socialist and the quiescent guest. This chameleon tendency arose from his emotional approach to life. Many years later he wrote: 'Blake said that "a tear is an intellectual thing", but I can't agree with him. Mine aren't, anyhow. And as for my intellect, I regard it with deep distrust. Those cold altitudes are not for me. Give *me* the homely pastures of the valley.'

At the beginning of December it was the homely pastures of the golf course at Rye that raised his spirits. He wrote to Marsh, 'I am happier than I ever was before.' Rye was his favourite course and the pleasure of being there again was enhanced by the company of George Wilson, his classics teacher at Henley House, whose friendship Sassoon valued highly. But there was another reason for his happiness – a young officer.

William Park Atkin was 21 and from South Shields. Before the war he had shown promise as a water-colourist and had studied briefly at Newcastle. With the outbreak of hostilities he enlisted and spent most of his service on the south coast. Atkin, who adopted the forename Gabriel, was no angel; he was hedonistic and dissolute, into drugs and undisciplined but he had charm and good looks and knew how to use both to advantage. In the summer of 1915 he was sent to Cambridge for officer training and fell into the orbit of E. T. Dent and Dent's friend A. T. 'Theo' Bartholomew and therefore into the homosexual coterie. His time at Cambridge nearly overlapped with the visit there in the August of Sassoon and David Thomas, when Sassoon made the aquaintance of Dent. Gabriel was not just of passing interest to Dent and Theo; they wanted to help his artistic talent: they had also discerned a tendency in him to dissipation. In the days of the Armistice, Theo told Dent:

we must use every effort to get him started upon some *work* as soon as possible. You know I deplore this incessant alcoholism and never tire of telling him so. I think he probably ought to go to the Slade; but it would be extremely difficult to keep a hold on him in London. Everything will depend on the people he gets 'in' with. He likes the best in people and in life generally I believe but he is very weak and easily led. He is much too good to be wasted. I had a wonderful surprise on Sat. As I was dreaming in front of my fire, who should come in but Siegfried. He put down his very heavy suitcase on my right foot and said he had come to stay. I hope on Wed he is going to Margate. It was a very good idea of yours to make those 2 meet. I told him a lot about Gabriel and I think he will do G. a lot of good.

'Gabriel Atkin sounds all right,' Sassoon told Dent.

'I am excited by the possibility of meeting Siegfried Sassoon,' wrote Gabriel from Margate.

'I wish Margate was nearer,' complained Sassoon to Dent.

'I can't get to Paddock Wood because of my meal times,' complained Gabriel to Dent.

Their first meeting, arranged for 12 November, did not happen. Gabriel told Dent that he was 'devastated' with disappointment. Then, on the 20th, Sassoon took the train to Margate. Gabriel wrote to Dent afterwards: 'Siegfried is the most amazing, gorgeous man in the Universe; he is the most wonderful thing that has ever happened.' Amazing, gorgeous, wonderful – but no longer 'unspotted'.

Six days later Sassoon wrote to Theo, 'Have you heard from Gabriel since I went there? He is one of the divinest things that have happened to me. I am going to see him again.' Gabriel went home to the north and Sassoon to Lewes, from where he informed Eddie Marsh on 4 December: 'I will be in town Dec 16–18th with someone who will be on leave. He's a half-fledged painter. I am going up to Blackburn and Glasgow for the Election.'

While at Rye, Sassoon had received a letter inviting him to speak in the election campaign of Philip Snowden, a leading figure in the Independent Labour Party. David Lloyd George had called a snap election, intent upon taking full advantage of his popularity as the man who had won the war. Snowden, who had opposed militarism, supported pacifism and defended conscientious objectors, was fighting a near-hopeless cause to retain his parliamentary seat. Though hesitant at first, Sassoon accepted the invitation because of Snowden's pacifist stance during the war. For one with little public-speaking experience and even less political awareness it was a brave decision. He had been assured that what he might say was of less importance than his presence. Public endorsement of Snowden by an officer of proven courage could only enhance his candidature. In the event it did not save Snowden but Sassoon had nailed his political colours to the mast.

Gabriel and Sassoon spent the Christmas holiday together at Weirleigh and at Half Moon Street. By the 27th Gabriel was back in Margate and reported to Dent that he didn't know whether he had been in the town or the country, the way Siegfried rushed around. He was going to turn over a new leaf by 'permanently avoiding whisky, which will be a good test of my strength of will, and I am becoming convinced that I have one. I have already started by giving up promiscuity.' Sassoon was back at Weirleigh, where he sensed his mother's disapproval.

'She did her best to be tolerant of my new interests and experiences but I was often aware of disagreements looming up between us. My association with Snowden had pained and displeased her, and it wasn't possible to speak about him. She looked upon many of my recently acquired acquaintances with disfavour, suspecting that if they weren't Socialists they were at any rate Radicals!' Here was a generation gap with a difference – the experience of a war that rent the old world from the new. Many middle-class, public-school-educated young men who had served as officers carried forward their concern for the servicemen they had commanded into peacetime. Systems had to change; the values of capitalism be replaced by social and economic justice for the working man and his family.

The season of goodwill and generous feelings might have degenerated further had it not been for the presence of Dr Rivers. Rivers was a Socialist, and a radical one at that. This should have been enough to make any mutual respect between himself and Theresa a nigh impossibility but Theresa liked him and Rivers in turn was taken by Theresa's penetrating and informed comments on life. With not a little pride Sassoon wrote: 'My mother had what I can affectionately describe as a weakness for the medical profession. For her any doctor was difficult to disbelieve in. Rivers had earned her gratitude by curing me of being a militant war-resister and she could discuss my general health with him to her heart's content.' Her contentment might soon have evaporated had she been aware that Rivers was actively encouraging her son in his Socialist ideals. He suggested to Sassoon that, in order to give those ideals a firm foundation, he should study Socialist theory and political economy. Given Sassoon's antipathy to academic discipline it was not the best counsel, but Rivers recognised that Sassoon's idealistic and fluid views, which owed more to William Morris than to Karl Marx, needed a good handful of starch. As at Craiglockhart, Rivers wanted him to think as well as to feel. Sassoon liked the idea and decided upon Oxford as the apposite place for informal and independent study.

Lady Ottoline, ever faithful, useful and available, was asked to scour

Oxford for a suite of rooms, a task she accomplished with brisk efficiency, securing lodgings at 14 Merton Street. The dawn of 1919 saw the earnest but green revolutionary set upon the path of knowledge and the road to Oxford. But first he was to gain some practical experience of revolution. During the last week of January 1919 the Association of Shipworkers and Engineers on Clydeside began a strike in pursuance of their demand for a 40-hour week. Over the next four days their employers and the government resisted their demands. The crisis point was reached when the workers, assembling in mass protest in Glasgow's George Square on 31 January, tried to prevent the movement of tramcars on the south side of the square. The police drew their batons and in the altercation a number of strikers were injured. The situation was such that the Lord Provost read the Riot Act and the leaders of the strike, who included the young and fiery Emmanuel Shinwell, were arrested.

The following day, 1 February, Sassoon was sitting in the safety of the Reform Club in London having an early dinner and musing upon the activity of his fellow diners as they read the latest news from Glasgow. He was joined by H. W. Massingham, Editor of *The Nation*, the radical Liberal weekly. Massingham, who had been supportive of Sassoon and his anti-war views, bemoaned the fact that he did not have someone who could cover the Glasgow story for the following week's edition. Sassoon, though unproven in that kind of journalism and ignorant of the issues, volunteered his services. Massingham agreed and Sassoon left London on Monday 3 February. That same day the shipworkers and the engineers drifted back to their work and the strike was over. Although he had missed the main story and had to search around for some decent copy, the visit left a deep impression on him, as had the visit to Snowden's Blackburn constituency a few weeks earlier. These were his first contacts with life as lived by the working classes in the densely populated industrial towns and cities of postwar Britain. He recalled the experience in *Siegfried's Journey*:

> That the 'Reds' of the City Corporation had reason to be indignant was grimly impressed on me when I was conducted through the worst of the slum areas. I had thought of slums as wretched and ramshackle, but had imagined them mitigated somewhat by some sort of Dickensian homeliness. These courts and alleys were cliff-like and cavernous, chilling me to the bone. The few unfortunates who scowled at us from doorways looked outlawed and brutalized. Here the thought of comfort never came, and there was a dank smell of

destitution. Cold as the stones we trod was the bleak inhumanity of those terrible tenements. Appalled, and more than willing to ask why such things should be, I felt thankful to get back into the thriving city streets. I had no wish to enter the Cowcaddens again.

The idea that 'some Dickensian homeliness' could possibly mitigate the squalor underlines the gulf separating Sassoon's Socialist imaginings from brutal reality. It was a divide he never bridged. Studying politics at Oxford was also part of a sincere but dislocated ideal. In fact he did not study there any more than he had at Cambridge, 15 years earlier.

Sassoon shared with Robert Graves his earnest intent to shake Oxford out of its slumbers and welcome the Revolution. Ought not the Bolshevik leaders be raised to the status of icons? Graves was committed to Socialism but eschewed extremist views. Demobilised in February 1919, he had laid plans to return to Oxford in the autumn. Now married to Nancy Nicholson and the father of a daughter, Jenny, he was living at Harlech, writing poetry and working on a new literary magazine, *The Owl*. The prospect of joining Sassoon at Oxford and pursuing with him the causes of poetry and Socialism filled him with optimism, but he was concerned about Sassoon's more exuberant and extreme pronouncements and warned him: 'Despotism and cruelty have gone too far in Russia: they are solving the question in their own way. But I think that despite Lloyd George, Clemenceau and the Capitalist, we can save Western Europe from so deep an operation and at least keep the bourgeoisie alive.'

Graves' parents were dismayed by his Socialist leanings and his and Nancy's unorthodox views on religion and domesticity. It was another example of the rift between the generations. The October Revolution in Russia and the execution of the imperial family; the rise of the Communist party in Germany; industrial disturbances in Britain, all seemed to the older generation a portent of their known world crashing around them. That their children should be agents of such catastrophes was beyond their comprehension. Graves' parents identified the culprit – Sassoon. He was exercising too much influence on their son. Such an accusation caused Sassoon no loss of sleep. He was prepared to defend the new against the rotten and discredited old system which had plunged the world into chaos. It was his generation that had paid the price and therefore had the right to shape a new world order. He was not alone in that belief, and at Oxford he found several kindred spirits.

Like that of many of his contemporaries, Sacheverell Sitwell's university education was delayed by the war. On its cessation he went up to Balliol. The Oxford of 1919 was full of mature, serious men back from the war rather than frisky young undergraduates, ripe for revolution and eager for diversion. For Sacheverell and Sassoon this was a disappointment. Osbert came to visit his brother in February. He was the newly defeated Asquithian Liberal candidate for Scarborough, but his mood was buoyant despite the defeat. Time did not stand still when Osbert was around. The Sitwell brothers, together with their sister Edith, were intent upon revolution through the arts as well as politics. Painters, musicians and poets, all must be liberated from the clammy hands of the predictable: the new age demanded new sounds, new images, new metaphors. On the day war ended Osbert, returning to his house in Swan Walk, Chelsea, knew his future must be 'divided between the creation of beauty and giving shape to ideas, and an effort to improve the conditions of life for the workers and to prevent the recurrence of slaughter'. Edith, Osbert and Sacheverell were devoted to each other and were out to make their mark on the world. Sassoon first met the brothers through Robbie Ross in 1917, and Edith had written a letter of support when he issued his Statement against the war in that same year. Osbert had been influenced by that protest and by Sassoon's poetry.

Sassoon described 1919 as a period of 'rootless rebeginnings and steadily developing disillusionments'. His Oxford revolution advanced but a little and soon became a movement without a move. The three months were, however, creative in the friendships and alliances he made there. In fact it marks the beginning of more than a decade of personal exploration, the search for companionship, amusement and travel. While at Oxford, he took full advantage of the hospitality on offer at Garsington. Ottoline and Philip were still filling their home with such as D. H. Lawrence, the Huxleys, the philosopher George Santayana and of course Bertrand Russell. Then there was Boar's Hill, where Robert Nichols lived, frittering away his early promise as a poet and inclining his thoughts towards teaching. John Masefield lived further up the hill and was quite amenable to Sassoon's invitations to speak at undergraduate meetings. Also studying at Oxford was Toronto Prewett, the Canadian whom Sassoon had met at Coldstream in the Scottish Borders. Prewett invited Sassoon and Masefield to the Oxford Musical Club for a performance of contemporary music. At the end of the concert he introduced a young man to his two guests. William Walton wrote to his mother the next day: 'Went to the Musical Club last night. I met John Masefield and Siegfried Sassoon, the poets.' At

17, Walton was besotted with modern music, in particular, Stravinsky, Prokofiev, Debussy and Ravel. This passion made him a kindred spirit of the Sitwells, to whom Sassoon introduced him. Walton's background was far removed from that of the Sitwells and Sassoon. His place at Christ Church had been won through a scholarship when he was nine and he survived there only because of the generosity of patrons such as the Dean of the college. His mature years would be dependent upon the continued financial backing of those who recognised his genius, among whom was Sassoon. The Sitwells adopted him as their protégé and when Walton failed his examination at Oxford, Osbert and Sacheverell gave him a room, first in Swan Walk, then in Carlyle Square, their new home in Chelsea.

Sassoon's role in introducing Walton to the Sitwells was repaid at once by Sacheverell's introducing Sassoon to the novelist Ronald Firbank. This exotic fantasist was a link with the world of the nineties and Oscar Wilde. Sassoon was bemused by his 'genius for subtle silliness' and although Firbank's writing held no appeal for him, he nonetheless entertained him on two other occasions. Sassoon's willingness to do so was an indulgence to Gabriel Atkin, who came on a visit to Oxford. He was a devotee of Firbank and was an eager and contented guest when Sassoon, the Sitwells, Toronto Prewett and others invited Firbank to dinner at the Golden Cross Hotel in Oxford.

Gabriel took his place with ease in that company, with not only his delight in Firbank but also his enthusiasm for all that the Sitwells wanted to achieve through the arts. Osbert formed a close and supportive friendship with him and admired his independent mind and taste, such as his liking for Rossini and Verdi at a time when their music was disdained. Above all, the Sitwells commended his self-belief as an artist and his aversion to conformity, writing: 'There is nothing intellectual in his approach to art; it is sensual, visual; from the heart and eye rather than from the head.' What was true of his art was also true of his approach to life; Gabriel was very much his own person. This made him difficult to handle in both a personal and a social context, something Sassoon found a constant source of irritation.

At the end of March Sassoon received an unexpected invitation to become the Literary Editor of a new national daily newspaper. The letter was signed by Cyril Gould in his position as Deputy Editor of the *Daily Herald*. The paper was launched as a daily in April 1912, becoming a weekly, bearing the title simply *The Herald* during the First World War. Now restored to a daily, it maintained its commitment to espouse and explain the Socialist cause. The Labour movement had no allies among the newspaper barons of Fleet Street; under the editorship of George Lansbury the vacuum was to be filled by this revival of a daily paper with 'its face towards the future' – a Socialist future. Sassoon hesitated, albeit momentarily, then admitted that Oxford was for him a dead-end. He embraced the challenge with his usual enthusiasm for a new adventure, in this case made attractive by the opportunity to promote the Socialist cause through literature. His responsibilities were not onerous; he was required to produce a weekly page of book reviews and some literary notes of a discursive nature. The paper was launched on Monday, 31 March and on 2 April, Sassoon made his debut as its Literary Editor.

'BOOKS OF TODAY AND TOMORROW' – thus the reader was introduced to the world of books that would feed and nurture the Socialist dream. He decided to make the opening column a résumé of the duties of a literary editor: 'The life of a literary editor is like a fairy-tale. He gets up at a not unreasonable hour; on his way to work he pops in to see a few eminent and sympathetic publishers. Finally he drifts down Fleet Street like a ray of sunshine and arrives at the office, where he finds that people have sent him presents of lovely books. After glancing at a few of these, he writes some literary notes and goes away to spend his salary.' It was vintage light-hearted Sassoon. In fact he had worked hard to establish contact with publishers and had thrown his net wide to secure a team of reviewers – Bertrand Russell, E. M. Forster and Walter de la Mare among them. The side columns carried the latest advertisements from publishers: Chapman & Hall, Martin Secker, Chatto & Windus and Macmillan. Noticeable by his absence was Sassoon's own publisher, Heinemann.

Mr Heinemann was implacably opposed to supporting a paper which he regarded as a social menace, a view shared by most of Sassoon's older friends. Theresa shuddered and described the *Daily Herald* as 'that rabid and pestilent rag'. She did not utter this criticism directly to her son, being aware that any adverse remarks about the paper would provoke unpleasant silences. Sassoon was a doughty defender of this 'weapon against the privileged classes and vested self-interest'. He saw little reason for objectivity in the contents of the page. This was a crusading paper with an agenda of its own.

Sassoon underestimated the workload. As the weeks proceeded the column-inches increased, as did the correspondence. Eager at first to engage with writers and readers, he began to view with growing dismay the ever-mounting number of letters and enclosures. So it was with no great expectations that he opened and began to read 'a small privately printed book of verse – evidently one of those amateur productions which so often depressed me by their sub-mediocrity. Impatiently opening this one at random I was instantly startled by a felicitous line. Within five minutes I knew that I had discovered a poet.'

The covering letter was modest and respectful.

Sir,

In the hope that you will notice them in your literary notes, I enclose two chapbooks of verse about which a slight explanation is required. The poems were written at school but not printed until 1916 when I was in France, and I have had no opportunity to issue them until now.

With gratitude not only for your vivacious criticism in *The Herald*, but also for your great efforts throughout the war to bring the ferocity of the trenches home to a public more disturbed about rations than Passchendaele,

I am,

Yours truly,

E.C. Blunden (Scholar-elect, Queen's College, Oxford.)

Edmund Blunden was born in London in November 1896. His father and mother were teachers in a school just off the Tottenham Court Road. They decided, however, to raise their children in rural Kent, settling eventually in the village of Yalding, some eight miles northeast of Matfield, the birthplace of Sassoon. Growing up in the same environment as Sassoon, Blunden shared his love of everything belonging to the English countryside, particularly the Kent and Sussex border. It was their evocation that caught Sassoon's eye and heart in the small privately printed volume that arrived, and might so easily have been missed, in the office of the *Daily Herald*. Without delay, Sassoon replied:

Dear Mr Blunden,

Send me your *Pastorals*, plus two more copies of the chapbooks. I have only glanced at them for a few minutes, but got an impression of freshness and originality in spite of your juvenile word-crowding and humdrum-rhythm. The opening of 'Silver Bird' is delightful and gave me quite a thrill of surprise – I have had so much bad verse sent

149

to me lately. Come and see me when you're in London – that is at *The Herald* office. I'm usually there on Tuesday and Friday in the morning. In the meantime I will have another look at your poems, and hope they will continue to grip my attention.

When are you going to Oxford? And how old are you? And what did you do in the Army?

Blunden had fought with the Royal Sussex Regiment at Passchendaele, Ypres and on the Somme. Like Sassoon he found difficulty in returning to a peacetime life: his nerves were shattered, he was plagued by insomnia and unable to lose himself from the memory of those who had died. But Blunden was physically and emotionally resilient, although this was belied by the fragility of his outward appearance.

It was this seeming frailty that first struck Sassoon when they met and Blunden became the third friend to whom Sassoon attached the adjective 'little'. David Thomas was the first, followed by Wilfred Owen. As with Thomas and Owen, Sassoon took Blunden under his wing in an act of protective friendship, the impulse for which he later described in his diary: 'It is the frailty of Blunden which makes him unique. Perhaps my vanity is flattered by my protective feeling for him. His spirit burns in his body with the apparent fragility of a flame. I want always to be imposing the bulk of my physical robustness between him and the brutish threatening winds of the outside world.'

The friendship with Blunden was among the most important and enduring of Sassoon's life, spanning nearly half a century, although, like most of Sassoon's friendships, there was a period of estrangement. They had so much in common over and above poetry and the war. Both were avid collectors and hoarders of books – special editions or a neglected volume that needed a home. Their knowledge of books was surpassed only by their encyclopaedic knowledge of cricket – village, county and Test. Then there was their eye for the detail of rural life and nature's endless variety and mystery. Deeply susceptible to the melancholic, Blunden and Sassoon developed a harmonious relationship. Blunden possessed the qualities to be one of Sassoon's ideal companions.

Little Blunden makes me more inclined to label myself 'literary'. For he brings with him his aura of enthusiasm for literature. He creates a special atmosphere which inspires me with certainty that I am a privileged person sharing the mysteries of the noble craft of letters.

When I am with him I rejoice to think that, after all, I have an appreciative palate for the vintages of fine verse and well-languaged prose. When I have spent an hour or two with Blunden I am agreeably conscious that I have added something to the treasury of my earthly experience.

Despite being busy with the literary page and nurturing his new friendships, Sassoon found time for his own poetry. He had decided just before the Armistice to publish another volume but the final content was not settled – indeed not written – until April 1919. This new collection, published under the title *Picture Show*, contained poems written after January 1918. The 34 poems are not exclusively about the war and the ones that touch upon that theme lack the immediacy of those in the two previous volumes, *The Old Huntsman* and *Counter-Attack*. In *Picture Show*, the underlying theme of the war poems is the danger of forgetting and the danger of remembrance. Time, grief and memory sanitise, sentimentalise and warp the reality.

Aftermath

Have you forgotten yet? ...
For the world's events have rumbled on since those gagged days,
Like traffic checked while at the crossing of city-ways:
And the haunted gap in your mind has filled with thoughts that flow
Like clouds in the lit heaven of life; and you're a man reprieved to go,
Taking your peaceful share of Time, with joy to spare.
But the past is just the same – and War's a bloody game ...
Have you forgotten yet? ...
Look down, and swear by the slain of the War that you'll never forget.

Picture Show also included love poems, some of the few he ever wrote: 'Idyll', 'Parted', 'Lovers', 'Slumber-Song' and 'The Imperfect Lover'. The object of the poet's love is not revealed. Though not impossible, it is unlikely to have been Gabriel as their affair only started six months before the publication of the poems. The quintet is almost certainly homoerotic, given that women were excluded from Sassoon's philosophy. He was exercised through the 1920s with his attempts both to find and to be, if not the perfect lover, then certainly an acceptable and contented one. Sassoon was never comfortable with the physical side of homosexuality, what he calls 'the gross elements'. This ambivalence created problems within his relationships generally. He was deeply attracted to 'Toronto' Prewett who, like Robert Graves, regarded homosexuality as a deviancy; Blunden in his friendship with Sassoon was neither physically attracted to him nor desired by him. It is one of the reasons why he was such an ideal companion: 'He is one of the rare people in whom I recognise beyond all doubt some comradeship of the mind which leads me outside the exhausted atmosphere of my introspections. With Blunden I am my better self; I feel an intense sympathy and affection for him; but it is a kinship of mind; the gross elements of sex are miraculously remote.'

Sassoon preferred the platonic but the physical desire was persistent. Gabriel was almost certainly his first sexual encounter and by then Sassoon was 32. Many were the reasons for that comparatively late initiation: his own inexperience, the fear of being found out, his inability to make the first move, hence the Dent and Bartholomew mediation. Perhaps more than anything else it seemed a denial of his masculinity. But he needed the physical: in the war years the urge was sublimated, while in earlier years it had been repressed. The hindrances brought frustration. When the hindrances were removed he found physical release and emotional relief but he was not satisfied. The critical point in his commendation of Blunden is in the words 'With Blunden I am my better self'. Six months earlier he declared that Gabriel was 'one of the divinest things that have happened to me'. Sassoon was unable to resolve the war within himself between reality and the ideal; he wanted the one, but he needed both.

There was another element in his perplexity and another poem in *Picture Show* is an expression of it: 'To a Childless Woman'. Observing a woman praying before a statue of the Virgin Mary, 'the enhaloed calm of everlasting Motherhood', the narrator whispers:

> You think I cannot understand. Ah, but I do ...
> I have been wrung with anger and compassion for you.
> I wonder if you'd loathe my pity, if you knew?

The narrator had noticed her before holding:

> Another's child. O childless woman, was it then
> That, with an instant's cry, your heart, made young again,

152

Was crucified for ever – those poor arms enfolding
The life, the consummation that has been denied you?
I too have longed for children. Ah, but you must not weep.
Something I have to whisper as I kneel beside you ...
And you must pray for me before you fall asleep.

Sassoon believed that through his homosexuality he too had been denied what he most wanted – paternity. There would be protégés but no progeny. The ultimate consummation was tendered impossible by his sexual orientation.

Picture Show was published in July as a private limited edition of 200 copies. It contained almost the last of Sassoon's poems, whose genesis lay in the war. In the autumn of 1919 Heinemann published *The War Poems of Siegfried Sassoon*. Two thousand copies were printed, followed quickly by another 1,000. But Sassoon knew that people would soon tire of war poets and he himself was already played out as far as that subject was concerned. Edmund Gosse sent a letter of encouragement after reading *Picture Show*: 'You have it in your hands to decide whether you will go right up among the notable English poets. Now work away, don't be distracted by anybody or anything from the direct call of your own spirit and heart.'

In warning Sassoon against distractions perhaps Gosse knew of his possible visit to the United States on a lecture tour at the beginning of 1920. E. P. Dutton in New York published an edition of *The Old Huntsman*, *Counter-Attack* and, to coincide with Sassoon's visit, *Picture Show*. The caravan of English writers and poets on the American circuit, popular before the war, was starting again. Among them were John Masefield and Robert Nichols, who urged various poetry groups and literary societies to invite Sassoon. Financially, such tours could be rewarding, were rarely heavy on preparation and were very good for book sales. A letter of invitation arrived from a lecture agency under the management of a Mr Pond. Sassoon pondered, then refused. The offer was renewed some weeks later when the indefatigable Mr Pond arrived in London and persuaded Sassoon to undertake a series of poetry readings and 'make a few informal comments' mainly in New York and some major locations around New England.

Indefatigable Mr Pond may have been, but he was equally ineffectual, so much so that when Sassoon arrived in New York only two engagements in February were settled, although he had stirred up the

New York press, who flashed their bulbs and filled their pads at Sassoon's hotel, and his photograph was displayed in a window on Fifth Avenue. That evening, with W. B. Yeats as a fellow speaker, Sassoon addressed the annual dinner of the Poetry Society of America. The challenge of public speaking and the knowledge that a successful speech could fill the ominously empty diary had a wondrous effect on the normally shy and inexperienced Sassoon. He entered into the spirit of American journalese by telling his audience that 'he had come with a toothache and would leave with a heartache'.

Mr Pond was beside himself, declaring Sassoon's debut had been 'a great little hit'. It did not, however, fill the diary and it was only by Sassoon's own efforts that the phone began to ring and letters to arrive, offering definite engagements. He had prepared some notes on the futility of war to which he added selections from his poems. From an uncertain initiation in Bryn Mawr College, Pennsylvania, he refined his performance as he visited Chicago, Yale, Princeton and Harvard, as well as the numerous and worthy clubs, groups and societies peppered in and around New York and throughout New England. Wherever he went, the press were keen to interview and quote him and the publicity sometimes generated more invitations. When reviewing the number of speaking engagements and the fees, Sassoon knew the venture would not make him a fortune. On the other hand, he would cover his costs with somewhat to spare.

Despite the slowness of bookings, life for Sassoon was hectic. He had come with a pocket full of introductions, which created an avalanche of invitations and encounters ranging from the poets Robert Frost and Amy Lowell to the world of the theatre and one actor in particular, Glenn Hunter. Sassoon was smitten by this handsome 25-year-old leading man, who was appearing on Broadway in a play long forgotten, *The Country Flapper*.

It was an encounter in which Sassoon made a fool of himself, allowing his infatuation to become obvious and his excitability to be embarrassing. Hunter disdained him, leaving him with the humiliating memory of being led 'such a devilish dance up and down West 44th Street'. Hunter was 'talented, good looking and absolutely empty' – Sassoon found him irresistible and the rejection wounded him. He failed to escape from the infatuation, even when he left New York for Chicago and Toronto. 'Going away from N.Y. makes my G.H. trouble much worse,' he wrote from Cambridge, Massachusetts, and a week later from Lake Forest, Illinois:

'The whole machinery of my intellect seems to have given out. It is simply idiotic. I have heard nothing from the origin of it all. I must just pull through somehow and try not to make an exhibition of myself (more than I've already done).' The recipient of these confessions was Sam Behrman, who wrote of Sassoon's emotional drubbing and its cause, 'I don't know how Siegfried met him … at that time I knew so little about this variety of love that I was bewildered, horrified and shocked. I really hate to think of it because it seems to be that I never saw such suffering, such unmitigated agony as Siegfried endured over a thoroughly commonplace young man. Well, why is it stranger than when we see a gifted young man go nuts over a perfectly commonplace girl?'

Sam Behrman in the early twenties was making his way through the publicity and newspaper world of New York. He was 26, a graduate of Harvard, and lived in an apartment in Westover Court on West 44th Street. Shortly after arriving in America, Sassoon moved into the same block and became friendly with Sam, who occupied the next apartment. 'During my first few days in Westover Court I knew of him only as a rather too diligently clacking typewriter in an adjoining flat. Tired and irritable, I probably resented the noise as a bit of a nuisance. If so, it was the only time Sam Behrman has been anything but a blessing to me.' Sam was just what Sassoon needed: easy-going, useful and a Jewish New Yorker who knew his way around and was capable of showing Sassoon a path 'through the perplexities' that surrounded him. He made one important contribution to Sassoon's literary development, as it was he who pointed him in the direction of the novel and the possibilities of fictional prose. Sam himself was a gifted writer, who within a few years would achieve distinction as a major dramatist. For the last three months of his stay in America, Sassoon leant on this friend, for whom no task on his behalf was too difficult or too onerous.

Dr Rivers visited New York in February. He had encouraged Sassoon's expedition to America, telling him that a lecture tour would help him escape the aftermath of war and that talking about his poetry would be cathartic. To a limited extent, the aim was achieved but the gains had to be set alongside the emotional bruising and his general feeling of being adrift. A year later he was craving to be in New York again, but for the last eight months he had been craving for London. It was all symptomatic of his confusion – sexual and artistic. Boarding the liner in August for the voyage home, he had no definite plans, only vague hopes. Would inspiration come and breathe new life into his poetry? Would he find inspiration to write a great novel? Everything was uncertain and until he next reached dry land, that is how everything could stay.

9

TUFTON STREET

1920–1

'The existence to which I was returning after seven months' absence was unencumbered by material complications. I had only to convey myself and three suit-cases to a small house near Westminister Abbey.' The small house was 54 Tufton Street – a new, but limited development amid much older houses. That part of Westminster was not fashionable in the 1920s, and much of its housing comprised tenements built by charities for poor and low-wage families. But at its periphery stood the Abbey Church, the Houses of Parliament and Lutyens' Whitehall. For Sassoon, Tufton Street had the advantage of being a brisk ten-minute walk across St James's Park to Pall Mall and the Reform Club, while in the other direction along the Embankment was Cheyne Walk and Chelsea. Gabriel Atkin had found a studio flat down there in Tite Street, and in Carlyle Square the Sitwell brothers were living on 'the bare luxuries'.

Sassoon had made an arrangement with Walter J. Turner and his wife Delphine to rent two small rooms. Turner, a native of Melbourne, had arrived in London in 1907 and was making his way as a music and theatre critic. He was also one of Eddie Marsh's Georgian poets, having made his debut in the anthology of 1916–17. Sassoon liked him and was partially responsible for ensuring that Turner followed him in the post of Literary Editor of the *Daily Herald*. Turner and his wife survived on a low and shaky budget, which made it impossible for them to buy a house without the help of a third party. Sassoon, not wishing to live on his own, loaned them £1,800 towards the purchase price of the house; the loan, together with his rent, solved the housing problems of both parties.

The two small rooms which Sassoon was to occupy for the next five years were sparsely furnished with some small tables, two chairs and a bed. He regretted that his piano could not be accommodated but the Turners readily agreed for it to be in their part of the house. The minimalist attitude towards furnishings reflected Sassoon's current belief that possessions were an encumbrance to the artist and that the limited space was irrelevant to one who desired above all else to live in the world of the imagination, the world of the poet. In 1949 he wrote:

> I regarded my room with approval, indifferent to its deficiencies. For after all, the room in which one lives and does one's concentrated thinking is something more than cubic feet of space. Unknown to others, it can become saturated by the presence of its occupant and permeated by the intensity of his mind-working solitudes. And that cell-like room was indeed destined to be, for several years, the hermitage of my private self, in contrast to the life I was to lead when away from it.

Sassoon determined to establish a line of demarcation between the public man and the contemplative:

> In that room I should be a single-minded poet. Elsewhere I should be the person who went about experiencing things and reacting in different ways to the various people he was with. Wherever I went, I should leave my private self behind in that room.

There were good reasons for this strategy:

> I wanted to revert to being my unpublicised self. I was aware of the need to take that self in hand and remedy his irrational inconsistencies.

Celebrity and 'temporal trophydoms' had blown him off course and he was now at a point where his future lacked any discernible direction. The war, which had left him physically and emotionally drained, had at least provided his life with a focus and his poetry with a subject; could peacetime do the same? And the war had also struck what he now recognised as a decent balance between activity and reflection – indeed, the one had fed the other. Could he again secure such a partnership? What would be the external stimulus?

When formulating a procedure for the cultivation of my private and poetic self I gave no thought to the future functionings of the energetically occupied one. It could be assumed, however, that circumstances would continue to keep me on the move.

And so they did throughout the autumn but they did nothing to rouse the dormant muse, as Sassoon bemoaned to Eddie Marsh in November and again in a letter dated 7 December: 'I seem to have lapsed into my pre-war sterility. I feel no impulse to write at all.' In fact, he was writing but none of it was acceptable to him, nor indeed to anyone else. His poetry had last appeared in the *New Statesman* in January 1920, just as he left for America. Entitled 'Passing Show', it was a limp spectator piece of a lover's tiff in Leicester Square. Now a year later, on 23 January 1921, he posted a poem to *The Nation* which, on re-reading, he recognised as 'nothing but an exercise in intellectual word-weaving'. The poem, 'On Reading My Diary', was rejected by the paper.

Not everything was negative on the artistic front. As he struggled to recapture the 'feeling and the fluency' of his earlier poetry, another facet of his literary talent emerged. Apart from his literary notes for the *Herald*, Sassoon had not hitherto felt any inclination to write prose; his vocation was poetry. But 1921 was to be the starting point for him as prose writer. The day before he posted his poem to *The Nation* an article of his was published in the *New Statesman* under the title 'A Sporting Event'. The subject was the final of a major billiard competition between 'Messrs Smith and Inman, for a stake of five hundred pounds'. The article quickly takes the reader from the foggy exterior of Saturday night Leicester Square into the smoke-filled hall:

Then the ceiling lights were extinguished, leaving an intense illumination on the vivid green flatness of the table. Beyond and above it rose a steep receding uniformity of blurred faces emitting tobacco of varying quality. The referee, a dour, sandy-haired gentleman with a pencil behind his ear, assisted in the replacing of the balls on the table and sank into his seat. The combatants entered. Their appearance evoked a burst of applause. Smith grinned; Inman bowed. Those four words represent the contrast in their characters.

Sassoon transformed a sporting event into a short story. He was pleased that others found merit in the article and he too acknowledged the skill of his prose, although before submitting it he thought it 'futile and worthless'. But that judgement was part of the general depression he felt about his private and poetic self: 'I have been ruthlessly criticising the results of my work since August, and it is a very unsatisfactory affair. I have written between thirty and forty poems, of which less than half are worth publishing, and I am not satisfied with any of them.' The private self was in the doldrums.

The public self was faring better. His relationship with the Turners was good and he enjoyed their friends, who came, usually after the theatre, for conversation and gossip, which sometimes passed for insight and knowledge. Hardly a day went by without Sassoon visiting a gallery or going to a concert, sometimes two in a day. Meals were taken at the Reform Club, where invariably he would fall in with Arnold Bennett, H. G. Wells, Massingham from *The Nation* or J. C. Squire of the *London Mercury*. At the theatre he might encounter W. B. Yeats, Aldous Huxley, St John Irvine and other luminaries.

In February he went to Oxford for the first time since returning from America. Here he renewed his friendship with Toronto Prewett, John Masefield and T. E. Lawrence and met Richard Hughes and L. P. Hartley. He had his first meeting with Robert Graves in two years, their correspondence having become irregular. Graves and his wife Nancy were keeping a grocery shop at the bottom of Masefield's garden on Boar's Hill. When Sassoon visited them, this pioneering effort by Nancy was in serious financial trouble and soon they had to make their way to another house and more domestic challenges. Sassoon had given Graves financial help more than once, not always willingly, but always out of affection and loyalty, both of which were now wearing thin. Nancy was never amenable to Sassoon and it was only with the greatest reluctance that he later stayed with them at Islip, a village to the north of Oxford. Graves, with his gift for getting on the wrong side of people, had upset even the gentle and unassuming Edmund Blunden, who had been a neighbour on Boar's Hill between October 1919 and May 1920. Blunden complained to Sassoon about the overweening and proprietorial attitude Graves took towards him and his poetry. By then, Blunden was working in London on the *Athenaeum*, commuting from Suffolk, where he lived with his wife and their two children. Sassoon was quite fond of Mary and enjoyed visiting their home. Taking Blunden around London to meet the famous was something else he enjoyed and he was amused by Blunden's unaffected manner.

The constant gadding about, which included a five-day visit to Hardy, meals with the Sitwells, meeting T. S. Eliot, writing reviews and attending concerts, left little time for his intended 'confederate silences'. Indeed the whole of March was spent in frenetic activity, including a visit to Rivers at Cambridge, hunting with the Loders in the Cotswolds, theatre-going with his mother, spending time with Turner, Blunden and de la Mare and endeavouring to steer Gabriel in the direction of mature behaviour. Sassoon found Gabriel's liking for riotous company and excessive drinking totally uncongenial, as too his disorderliness and extravagance. It was not without trepidation that during the first week of April he bought expensive train-de-luxe accommodation for Gabriel and himself to travel to Venice. Gabriel's unpredictable behaviour, which Sassoon found more and more tiresome, might well turn their Italian holiday into a disaster. In the event it was not Gabriel who caused the holiday to be cancelled but the miners, the railwaymen and the transport workers of Britain.

The coal-owners of the country announced a reduction in the wages of the miners in order to meet foreign competition. In sympathy, the other unions joined with the miners to fight the owners and formed a triple alliance. Sassoon detected a deeper significance to the confrontation: 'The issues are of more than insular significance. Organized Labour is being tested; and, whether it wins or loses, the way is being opened up for a further and palpable advance into the battlegrounds of the future.' Sassoon's sympathies were completely with the miners and organised labour. His post-war left-wing ideals, expressed in apocalyptic language, owed much to the company he kept at the 1917 Club, a Socialist watering-hole in Gerrard Street, Soho, named in honour of the Russian Revolution and founded by Ramsay MacDonald. Inevitably the Sitwells were members, so too Leonard and Virginia Woolf, the Huxleys and E. M. Forster. A different atmosphere prevailed at his other club, the Reform, at least among those with whom he dined on the evening of 8 April. Sassoon alone defended the miners' cause. On returning to Tufton Street, 'thoroughly upset', he composed a satirical poem, rather heavy-handed, about those who sit in comfortable places denying a better life to others:

The Case for the Miners

Something goes wrong with my synthetic brain
When I defend the Strikers and explain
My reasons for not blackguarding the Miners.

> '*What do you know?*' exclaim my fellow-diners
> (Peeling their plovers' eggs or lifting glasses
> Of mellowed *Chateau Rentier* from the table),
> '*What do you know about the working classes?*'

So the first verse ends with a perfectly fair question, which put Sassoon on the spot and revealed the paucity of his experience, which could not be covered by slogan and jargon. Sassoon's Socialism owed nothing to intellectual analysis and everything to his innate sense of justice. This quality survived when his political activity ended. Angry with the supercilious and annoyed with his own ignorance, the next day he persuaded Massingham to send him down to South Wales for *The Nation*.

April 9:
Slipped away from the Reform after dinner with bag, and caught the 9.15 from Paddington. Arrived Neath 4 a.m., had a carriage to myself all the way, and read Trotter's *Instinct of the Herd in Peace and War* – very stimulating, and suitable! Knocked at hotel door for twenty minutes, and finally was admitted by yawning manager and yapping dog.

After a couple of hours' sleep the first port of call was the home of his former army servant, John Law. Sassoon kept in contact with Law and helped him financially to set himself up in business, first in Neath and later in Croydon. Commitment to the well-being of friends and comrades was one of Sassoon's most attractive qualities.

For the next week he travelled around the coal-field meeting miners and colliery officials, comparing what the establishment press was saying with what he was finding at the pit-head. The result was three articles, laced with irony and satirical bite, an echo of the war poetry. The first was published in the *Daily Herald* on 13 April and three days later, a second appeared with his poem 'The Case for the Miners' in *The Nation*. The article was a straightforward account from the pit-head at Tonypandy, which the paper described as 'usually a storm-centre of the mining camp'. Sassoon rebutted in forensic style the allegations of the government and the owners that the miners were engaged in acts of sabotage by not manning the pumps and thus causing the mines to be flooded. But what incensed Sassoon was a comment that likened the miners to the Hun: 'I have only to add that I have watched the men whom the Recorder of

London officially designates as *"a foe perhaps quite as serious as the Germans, whom we spent four years in fighting"*. They have, so far, committed not a single irresponsible act of violence and the behaviour has been all their wisest leaders could wish.' The piece was heavily edited in London, but the act of placing it alongside the satirical poem 'The Case for the Miners' strengthened both. Reading the poem and the article after watching a football match between Merthyr and Bristol Rovers, Sassoon regretted some of the wittiest pieces had been removed, but he felt content. Merthyr and the mining valleys held little appeal for him, but the miners did and he recovered for the first time since the war a sense of being at one with others in a common cause; the experience was therapeutic: 'A week since I left London; very much alive in the last seven days.'

A general strike was averted, mainly through the collapse of the unions, and Sassoon returned to London, where in Tufton Street he worked on a final article about the Welsh miners with the title from George Borrow's classic *Wild Wales*, and published it in *The Nation* on 23 April. The article was a foretaste of what became Sassoon's prose technique, combining anecdote and polemic, written from his personal standpoint and directly expressed. There are touches of irony, feigned surprise and understatement. First there is the union official, whose welcome for Sassoon 'the reporter' is lukewarm:

[he] was evidently suffering from an over-dose of newspaper men, in addition to other and more serious worries. So I found no difficulty in forgiving him when he referred to THE NATION as 'a paper that caters for the ultra-respectable'.

Since then I have been asking myself who are the ultra-respectable people to whom he referred. A middle-aged commercial told me one night last week that the South Wales miners invariably eat strawberries out of season. 'The labouring classes must learn to be more affable,' he boomed. 'That's what's wrong with the country! We must get back to a ten- or twelve-hour day and lower wages for the workman.' He drank up his 'double-rum-hot', and toddled upstairs to bed. But he will never read my article.

The Welsh miners did *not* enter the dispute with full stomachs and high hearts. They were locked-out after three months of unparalleled depression in the industry. The miners may have enjoyed a previous period of comparative affluence but I can vouch for this – that it is useless for the ultra-respectable people to write to the 'Morning Post' from Torquay, asking why the miners' wives don't pawn their pearls: because the miners' wives have been sending their children to the relief soup-kitchens for the last seven weeks. Nor is early asparagus on sale in Merthyr Tydfil, or even in the grim village that contains the four ex-soldiers who wrote to the Prince of Wales and 'received a courteous acknowledgment'. There are no strawberries and cream visible in the Rhondda. At the top of this valley, between Treherbert and Hirwain, lies the richest unworked coalfield of South Wales. Who is going to inherit those riches? Will the cheeky young Marxian develop into a second Lord Rhondda, and, in the labyrinths of successful organisation and profitable speculation, forget that he was ever a Communist? Or will that unexploited region be a field for just enterprises and equitable rewards?

The article ends with a subtle allusion to Martin Luther, who challenged the status quo of his day and to the revolutionary spirit of a young Wordsworth:

It is fifty miles from Tonypandy to Tintern Abbey. When Jack Jenkins makes his summer excursion to the Wye Valley, he stares at the monastic ruins, listening, perhaps, to the 'soft inland murmur' of the river that travels through that 'wild, secluded scene'. But when the young collier of 1921 scribbles his name on a door-post in the Abbey garden, he is writing his semi-articulate claim on his fellow countrymen for fair and decent conditions of existence. And he is not altogether satisfied with the propagandist calculations issued for his edification by the Secretary of the South Wales Coalowners' Association.

The essence of Sassoon's Utopia lies within a circle whose circumference is described by 'fair and decent'. In his more aggressive moments he may have wanted the whole edifice of capitalism to come crashing down, but the most consistent flavour of both his Socialism and that of the Sitwells, the Woolfs and E. M. Forster was the reputed English sense of 'fairness'. They were not political revolutionaries: they specialised in teasing and provoking, albeit to the point of outrage, but none of them then or later would forgo the privileges that went with being who they were. These years were thought of by many as 'the ante-chamber to the millennium', recalled a mature Sassoon, 'too much was expected of it'. It all stemmed

164

from the idea of a bright and beautiful new world in which 'Everyone was a bird; and the song was wordless; and the singing will never be done' – Utopia's national anthem.

Fraternity and friendship – and the lack of them – featured prominently in Sassoon's London world for the next year. He enjoyed the constant social demands and yet continued to crave solitude so that his private self might flourish. Despite his stated resolve to take that 'private and poetic self' in hand by turning the rooms in Tufton Street into a cell, the public self was ceaseless in its need for distraction. True, he was collecting raw material for his poetry, which increasingly struck a note of social comment. Working through the night; rising mid-morning; lunch at the Reform or some restaurant; a gallery or a concert in the afternoon; dinner and another concert in the evening; late nights with Gabriel or solo meanderings around Westminster, Chelsea or Victoria; such became the routine. Outside London he made the misleadingly named Hut at Bray, near Windsor his country retreat by permission of its owner, Frank Schuster. Born in 1840 of German-Jewish descent, Frankie, as he was known, lived entirely for music and muscians. He was among the first to recognise and support the genius of Edward Elgar, upon whom he bestowed his friendship and patronage, much as his sister Adela had done for Oscar Wilde. Frankie's house in Old Queen Street, Westminster, was the venue for parties on the grand scale: a veritable extension of the opera house and concert hall. Sassoon wrote of him: 'Unable to create anything himself, he loved and longed to assist in the creation of music. He wanted to create artistic history; but could only do so by entertaining gifted people. He was a social impresario of "artistic events".'

Sassoon's first experience of Schuster's world was at a party in Old Queen Street, which he attended 'elaborately rigged-out as a Tartar prince'. Schuster was well advanced in years, but nothing would deter him from a performance or a party. Travelling across the country or the Continent in his chauffeur-driven Rolls-Royce to concerts, opera and ballet, he left the much-younger Sassoon breathless. Schuster was a companion for the travels of the next few years, as indeed was another friend, Gerald, Lord Berners. An epigram he composed for himself gives a hint to his personality:

> Here lies Lord Berners
> One of the learners,
> His great love of learning

May earn him a burning,
But, praise to the Lord
He was seldom bored.

Berners was a practitioner of the arts in the enthusiastic way that Schuster was a patron. He was a musician, writer and painter. Like Schuster he seemed to be endowed with energy quite out of the ordinary. Faringdon, his country mansion in Berkshire, was another retreat from London for Sassoon. Visitors approaching the house would be greeted by pigeons on the wing, their plumage variously dyed, pointing to the exotic tendencies of Berners and his singularity. He was avant-garde, as befitted a friend of Diaghilev, Salvador Dali and Igor Stravinsky. In every aspect of his life, Berners was indisputably a man of unusual taste.

Inevitably Schuster and Berners were known to the Sitwells and quite friendly with them. It seemed to Sassoon that Osbert, Edith and to a lesser extent, Sacheverell were inescapable. Whether it was a concert, ballet, dinner-party or literary event, the trio was usually in voluble evidence. Impervious to contradiction, they aired their views, pronounced their judgements, engaged in merciless invective and took no hostages in print or in debate. This desire for infallibility was a family trait which reached its apotheosis in their father, Sir George: 'I must ask anyone entering the house never to contradict me or differ from me in any way, as it interferes with the functioning of the gastric juices and prevents me sleeping at night.'

After a short vacation in Holland and a visit to Garsington, Sassoon spent part of August 1921 at the Sitwell country estate, Renishaw, in Nottinghamshire. He was still in his anti-possession mode and was not happy with the command to look at this and look at that. An 'atmosphere of nerve-twitching exhaustion' filled the house as a result of the tension between father and offspring. Sassoon had never been comfortable in their company. Osbert was all right in small doses but he detested his swaggering certainty. Edith had been troublesome about the editing of Wilfred Owen's poems – a task Sassoon had abandoned in order to go to America and which Edith accomplished. He admired her poetry and she was, like others, a little infatuated with him, but she, like her brothers, had an unsettling effect on him, their self-assurance highlighting his self-doubt. Unlike him, the Sitwells never retired hurt. Their greatest strength was their unity.

Sassoon had no such emotional and creative support uniquely shared with another. Indeed much of the twenties was a search for such a comforting and sustaining relationship. Theresa was the nearest. She, it seemed, existed almost exclusively for him and in the past had made Weirleigh a sanctuary and the Weald an encircling Elysium. But their relationship was not as close now. Michael had moved into Weirleigh with his wife Violet and their children. Sassoon felt excluded. The tension between Theresa and her daughter-in-law pervaded the house, as did the noise of the children. His visits to Weirleigh became fewer. When mother and son met they did so in London, Sassoon, dutiful and attentive, accompanying Theresa to a concert or an exhibition. She also stayed with him at Frankie Schuster's house at Bray, where her views were expressed in that direct and incisive manner that made Sassoon proud and embarrassed at the same time. Theresa never sought the good opinion of her son's avant-garde friends or felt it necessary to endorse each new fashion in the arts. This stubborn self-assuredness was a quality Sassoon admired, but it underlined how each was travelling away from the other. The former intimacy and mutual delight had disappeared.

Some weeks before going to stay with the Sitwells at Renishaw, Sassoon took Gabriel to a concert of chamber music. The players, by both their appearance and their performance, created 'an incongruous and amateurish effect, as though they'd just "dropped in" for a bit of music'. Sassoon suddenly recognised one of the players as a former violin teacher to his brothers and a close friend of Theresa's. He was startled again when he saw his mother sitting some six rows in front of him and Gabriel:

There was a gulf of more than six rows of seats between us. She belongs now to a different life from mine, a remote worn-out life from which I've escaped into the adventurous uncertainties and perplexities of active experience. Mother seemed indigenous to the mechanical serenity of the dull classical music. I could anticipate every phrase, as I can when she talks about the weather and the servants and the doings of relatives. I knew exactly how each movement would end. I'd heard it all before. It was a futile echo of something which had long ceased to interest me. I prefer to be harrowed by dissonances of Schonberg and Stravinsky. If I'd been alone I'd have moved up and spent the rest of the evening with Mother. But I was with G. G represents green chartreuse and Epstein sculpture. Mother is G. F. Watts and holy communion. They can't be mixed.

Time would teach Sassoon that his emotional attachment to both Theresa and her world was deeper and more resilient than he had realised. That time was passing quickly, and the fear that he was being prodigal with it, depressed him. On the eve of his thirty-fifth birthday he felt his mind sluggish and on the day itself 'as dry as a biscuit'. Working best at night, he attempted to transfer to verse those impressions and experiences of his outer public self; but the fruit of these labours, he believed, lacked verve and authenticity. He was in a state of disgruntlement when he left Renishaw at the end of August. Gabriel's presence there did not help. In fact it was a definite irritant and Sassoon was not happy with the friendship between Gabriel and Osbert: 'I seem to suffer from a poisoned mind: an unwholesome unhappiness pervades my healthy body. Is it pride – conceited pride – that makes me crave to alienate everyone?'

Travelling west to Hereford and the Three Choirs Festival, he was genuinely disconsolate. The music of Dvořák, Holst and Elgar on 8 September made it a golden day but the thought of those composers achieving so much beauty and profundity served to cast down his already dismal spirit. By 14 September he was once again with Thomas and Florence Hardy, but for the first time the restorative power of their company was unable to lift his sense of isolation and aridity. 'Stick to the old trade,' Hardy counselled as Sassoon took his leave but the 'old trade' of poetry was becoming more and more difficult. Reviewing the last six months and his 'developments through successive stages of muddle-headedness and midnight-maunderings', he deduced that he had been 'ruminating the final flavours of my prolonged youthfulness'. It was time for being serious, for becoming intense; time to discard those elements of his youthfulness which could not cross the border with him into maturity. This was the land of betwixt and between, where looking back evoked regret and looking forward engendered apprehension. Turner told him that all these thoughts were the fruit of the year Sassoon had spent getting to know himself. At 35 years of age it would not have been unreasonable to have found him further along the path but Sassoon always thought of himself as being seven years younger than he really was.

At the end of September Sassoon, accompanied by Toronto Prewett, made his first visit to Italy. It was the delayed excursion from before the miners' strike. The intended companion then was Gabriel but he was back now at his painting. Given Sassoon's mood of introspection, that was fortunate. Prewett was reliable and unobtrusive, which would leave

Sassoon time to himself and free from the clamour that seemed to arise whenever Gabriel was around.

He was fond of Gabriel but his lover's flimsy attitude to life was becoming more and more unattractive: he lacked background, he lacked breeding and he lacked sensitivity. Sensitivity was not a quality required at the riotous Café Royal of an evening, where he spent his time and Sassoon's money. Sassoon had written about this to Dent in the months after he and Gabriel had met, when the older man observed the social ineptness of the younger. Gabriel also had a sadistic streak, which he indulged by provoking Sassoon with outrageous statements and behaviour. Sassoon was both angry and sad, oscillating between being lover and father, comforting himself with the occasional sign of improvement. Why bother? was a question he often asked on the road between Chelsea and Westminster. The answer was always the same – he needed Gabriel. The nature of that need was complicated and on Sassoon's mind before he left for Rome. He questioned whether his unsettledness and general irritability might not be connected to his 'animal passions' and the 'cursed business of sex'. He was not promiscuous: his eye appreciated physical beauty, wherever and whenever he saw it, but 'thankfully it never went further'. What he desired was a relationship – not only physical, but also a sharing of life. Paternal by nature, he was inclined to younger men but he also needed maturity and stability, qualities that Prewett possessed, as did Edmund Blunden. Sassoon did not share with E. M. Forster, J. R. Ackerley and others any desire to get involved with men from the working class, nor to set them up in Maida Vale, Hammersmith or Shepherd's Bush.

The Hotel Angleterre was their base in Rome but waiting to greet and entertain them at his apartment, 8 Via Varese, was Gerald, Lord Berners. Few hosts excelled Berners' welcome which, like his table, was always ample and the company engagingly cosmopolitan. Sassoon enjoyed Rome although, as with most first visits, it was at times tiring. It was the confusion and frustration in his mind that really plagued him – the 'cursed obsession of sex-cravings' being the main cause. He was becoming increasingly attracted to Prewett but knew that if his travelling companion guessed the nature of that attraction as Sassoon feyly put it, 'he would be less happy than he was at that moment'. Sassoon looked from his hotel window at the eternal city stretched out before him and he remembered New York. There too he had been heart-sick and frustrated but those emotions had been part of his aliveness; here such feelings were part of the deadness caused by his failure to find love.

It was then he found Philipp. Of medium height, with dark hair, square face, strong build, an upright bearing, light of foot and 25 years old, he captivated Sassoon. His personal qualities – the amiability of his demeanour, the impeccable manners, the social assurance – were, Sassoon discovered, as attractive as his lineage was impressive. This was Prince Philipp of Hesse, grandson of Emperor Frederick the Third of Prussia. Like the rest of the German royal family, Philipp had fallen on hard times. His nation had lost the war and he had lost his inheritance. He resented both, as he did the terms of the Versailles Treaty. His circumstances were reduced but not his pride. Philipp was grateful to have found Sassoon. Sassoon was happy to have discovered Philipp. Letters from the Prince, when he went home to Germany at the end of October, were full of romantic allusions inspired by his 'dear Sig'.

> Home again at last finding your dear letter waiting for me here. It brought back everything more vividly than ever: you, your voice, Rome with all its beauty, the murmuring of the fountains, some vague melody of Bach played by small untrained fingers, two small rooms in a little hotel and all that happiness ... I had the same feeling a few days ago in Munich when I heard Kreisler play and told him so when the concert was over but I didn't tell him the real reason.

Sassoon in Tufton Street awaited each letter. Unsettled and craving human warmth, he could not regard Philipp as anything other than a gift. A few weeks earlier Osbert Sitwell had remarked that Sassoon was 'quite the worst judge of character he knew'. It was an indictment of Sassoon's innocence, or what he himself described as his 'unworldliness'. Gabriel was not told about Philipp or the letters. What difference would it have made? He was unlikely to forgo the £300 a year Sassoon was allowing him and unable to repay the £380 he owed him. Sassoon was generous with his £1,200 a year, too generous, and only kept within limits by scrimping on himself. Friendships were valuable to him – some were expensive as well.

From the promises in these new friendships Sassoon, on returning to London, was confronted by the demands of old ones. Blunden had written on 31 October, complaining about Robert and Nancy Graves. To Blunden's annoyance, Nancy had been influencing Mary with ideas about the selfishness of men, husbands in general and Blunden in particular. But the real root of Blunden's irritation was Graves's betrayal of a confidence. Blunden had mentioned to him that his father had 'overdone the pint system'. Through a series of hints Graves suggested to Mary that her husband had inherited the family trait. Blunden was not present, having gone into Oxford for the afternoon. When he returned to the house it was obvious that Mary had taken the hint. Perhaps she already knew about the drinking problem but, even if she did, Graves' indiscretion was unforgiveable and injurious. The betrayal left its mark. The same letter contained the pleasant news that Blunden's latest collection of poems, *The Shepherd*, was to be inscribed to Sassoon. It was a gesture of esteem but more especially of friendship.

At this time, Sassoon received a letter from the mother of Wilfred Owen asking him to help her son Harold advance his ambition to be a painter. Sassoon arranged some introductions but the greatest need at that juncture was money. In his memoirs Harold Owen is critical of Sassoon for what he regarded as the older man's aloofness. It is clear from Sassoon's diary, however, that he made considerable efforts to raise funds for him. He wanted to contribute upwards of £150, but generosity to family and friends was threatening to outstrip his resources. Owen's criticisms were more justified when he mentions the long silences in their conversations, the sullenness that seemed to envelop Sassoon and which made their initial meetings so difficult.

On his own admission Sassoon was at this time in the grip of a 'self-lacerating irritability' which made writing or publishing almost impossible and socialising a trial. Periods of depression, irritability and despair were the consequence of the war, something Harold Owen recognised as part of his own experience. He also suspected that his presence raised the spectre of his brother Wilfred, whose loss was still painful for Sassoon. It was a wound that never healed, as Sassoon once told Blunden: 'I have always suffered from an obscure difficulty in clarifying my friendship with him, perhaps because the loss of him was a shock which I never faced squarely, coming as it did at the most difficult time when I was emotionally and physically without foundation.' Three years after the death of Owen, the lack of emotional security was still a torture for him. His sexual ambivalence, the desire to free himself from the ties of his pre-war life, the memories of the war, his grief for the dead and the guilt for surviving, all these impinged upon his capacity to work and to establish solid relationships. 'I am a cantankerous creature,' was his verdict on himself and some of his actions exhibited a touchiness verging on paranoia.

In November Edith Sitwell published another edition of her literary magazine *Wheels*. Osbert contributed a typical Sitwellian knock-about article using the pseudonym Augustine Rivers and bearing the title 'The Death of Mercury'. The pseudonym could only have been another ruse to upset the 'philistines', as most people knew it to be the pen-name Osbert regularly used. The article was a blast against J. C. Squire, founder and Editor of the *London Mercury*. Squire, a brilliant satirist and critic who played a leading part in the literary life of the day, was one of the conservatives whom the Sitwells despised and were determined to dethrone. Sassoon held Squire in high regard and had dined with him at the Reform. If Osbert's article had been an assault on Squirearchy alone, all might have been well but Osbert fired broadsides at W. J. Turner and Robert Graves, and added a dig-in-the-ribs to Edmund Blunden for good measure. It is doubtful whether any of those whose artistic reputation was impaled on Osbert's nib was over-concerned, but Sassoon was outraged, interpreting this latest Sitwellian foray as a covert attack upon him. The article was 'a mean and spiteful outburst'. All links with the trio were severed.

Reasons for the severance had, however, causes beyond the offending article, as Sassoon confided in his diary on 1 December: 'Much of my morosity is due to my inability to write anything which pleases me. I feel a want of vitality. Being with people of strong vitality gives me a sort of restless satisfaction. One reason why Osbert's naughtiness affects me so much is that he is such a vivid (though unsympathetic) character. I can't hope to blot him out of my life and thoughts.' Two months later his diary continues the explanation. At a concert in the Wigmore Hall he had noticed Osbert moving towards the exit. Sassoon left his seat and followed him with the sole intention of cutting him: 'On my way home I suddenly realised that my attitude toward O. is strongly sadistic. I saw, quite calmly, that my (supposed) stab at his feelings this afternoon aroused in me acute sexual feelings toward him.' Sassoon wanted to control and to dominate; there was no chance of that with Osbert or his siblings. While he clung to the shallows, they sailed on in their man-o'-war. How he envied them. More than three years would pass before Sassoon spoke to them again – but Osbert would often send his regards and assurances of unchanging affection!

10

FRIENDSHIPS

1921–2

The Sitwells had failed the test of friendship as set by Sassoon; others were to follow. It has been written about Sassoon that, like Edmund Blunden, 'he was absolute for friendship' but the claim is not sustainable for the Sassoon of the 1920s. He placed a high price on loyalty but failed to match his expectancy with a realistic estimate of human constancy, including his own. Some friendships withered on the vine, that natural decay attributable to changing place, passage of time, lack of proximity or, as in the case of Norman and Phyllis Loder, the loss of a shared interest. The friendship with the Loders had begun over a decade previously, being a natural progression of the earlier friendship between Norman and the youthful Siegfried in the optimistic and carefree days before the war. Then Norman the accomplished horseman was the epitome of what Siegfried considered sophisticated. Now the hero of youth had lost his appeal and the paradise of sport had been displaced by a more sophisticated world – supposedly. This friendship fell victim to Sassoon's rush away from his old life of fox-hunting and the point-to-point. That appeared superficial now, such a waste of time, compared to the new world peopled by intelligent friends with whom he could share his 'socialistic ideals and communistic tendencies'. What point now the world of the 'Fernie-Goldflakes', the nickname he gave the hunting set, who were:

> Crassly unconscious that their Reynardism
> Is (dare I say it?) an anachronism.

Further he judged the Loders were by temperament and inclination incapable of wrestling with fundamental questions about life. What mattered to them was their own world, the challenges of which were limited, as was their vision, to the next fence. 'How easy it is to be alive when we demand of life only the simple and crude reward of success in a steeplechase,' records Sassoon unsympathetically in his diary.

On his return from America he had resolved to break his ties with those who were antipathetic to his career as an artist. He also felt that, as a 'Labour Movement intellectual', he ought to give up fox-hunting. The visits to Cirencester were unhelpful and unsettling. The Loder friendship, their company, their conversation, like Theresa's, held no surprises, everything was predictable. Sassoon was unable to confess his homosexuality – the attempt would damn him forever. He was aware that a gulf was opening that could not be bridged, as he hid his secret life: but what else could he do? Unlike his enlightened and sophisticated friends, the Loders would not understand, neither could they see that he was not the same person as the 'good old Sig' of former days. Affection remained, but intimacy waned and they gradually drifted away from each other.

Not that everything and everybody in London matched what Sassoon regarded as good and profitable company, engaging him in witty, elevated conversation. In the twenties he was one of the most sought-after party and dinner guests. He was flattered by being in such demand but soon discovered that the wages of flattery were boredom and vexation; he even took to leaving dinner-parties early, if he became bored. Such behaviour cannot all be attributed to the war. Sassoon could be dismissive and inconsiderate, not to say on some occasions priggish, as his poem 'Grandeur of Ghosts' bears witness:

Grandeur of Ghosts

When I have heard small talk about great men
I climb to bed; light my two candles; then
Consider what was said; and put aside
What Such-a-one remarked and Someone-else replied.

They have spoken lightly of my deathless friends,
(Lamps for my gloom, hands guiding where I stumble,)
Quoting, for shallow conversational ends,
What Shelley shrilled, what Blake once wildly muttered ...

How can they use such names and be not humble?
I have sat silent; angry at what they uttered.
The dead bequeathed them life; the dead have said
What these can only memorise and mumble.

Only one person still came near the ideal – Edmund Blunden. He was 'the living emblem of all that is finest in this hazardous world of dust and dreams'. Against him and his completeness everyone else was measured. Of Toronto Prewett, Sassoon wrote: 'I have established a very solid and sympathetic understanding, which ranks very high among the amicabilities of my existence. But Toronto's character lacks that homely sweetness which makes little Blunden so delightful.' Graves, who once topped the league as the most stimulating of companions, now made Sassoon 'self-conscious, whereas Blunden takes me out of myself'. Graves was in disgrace anyway for treacherous disloyalty by accepting an invitation from Edith Sitwell to attend her Anglo-French Poetry Society. Graves could see no reason to ignore Edith because Sassoon was in dispute with the Sitwells. The whole incident became the subject of bitter letters between them, with Graves always offering the hand of reconciliation and wanting 'to start a new show'. Of course the root of the problem remained Nancy and Graves' loyalty to her. Sassoon, who was free from any domestic or marital responsibility, could never understand why Graves was not available on demand. Then there was the problem of Graves' independent streak, striking out confidently into pastures new and complex, and assimilating them into his work with bold assurance. Ironically, given Sassoon's judgement on the failure of Norman and Phyllis Loder to recognise that he was no longer their 'good old Sig', he totally failed to recognise that Graves in 1922 was no longer his 'dear old Robert'. Of course there was still Gabriel, who was not ideal but was responding to Sassoon's guidance and showing signs of social improvement. They proved short-lived; that was something Philipp did not require. Sassoon read his letters avidly, especially when the young prince spoke of his worries and sought his friend's advice and assistance.

Dependency, or even its appearance, was a vital ingredient for any intimacy with Sassoon; he needed to be needed. He had a propensity for protective concern, which was quick to discern vulnerability and respond to a need. Those he helped tended to be younger than he but when in need of support he turned to those older than himself. In the past there was Uncle Hamo, Edmund Gosse, Eddie Marsh and Thomas Hardy. Rarely did he turn to his mother: she was among those to be protected. In the twenties these counsellors, honoured still by him, were not capable of understanding any more than could the Loders the causes for much of his unrest. In a sense they were on the sidelines shouting encouragement rather than giving advice.

He was fortunate that Turner and Delphine provided for him in Tufton Street a haven of intimacy without intrusion. They were 'the rock on which my lighthouse is being built. Turner more than anyone I know imposes sanity and half-humorous self-scrutiny on me,' Sassoon wrote in his diary. Turner was allowed to read it, an amazing concession granted to only one other person, E. M. Forster, who, in turn, showed Sassoon the manuscript of his clandestine novel *Maurice* and other erotic short stories. Sassoon and Forster shared the same sexual orientation, Turner did not. Such was the growing intimacy between them that Turner became almost another W. H. R. Rivers.

Rivers was 62 years old in 1922 and living in Cambridge. After the war he had returned to St John's and a college post with the title Praelector of Natural Science Studies. Freedom to follow his own studies was without doubt the great benefit which the post offered and he took full advantage of the opportunity to engage with a variety of scientific disciplines and students. To this he added active party politics, becoming the prospective Labour candidate for the University of London. When accepting the nomination he declared in apocalyptic words, 'Entering practical politics can be no light matter. But the times are so ominous, the outlook, both for our country and the world, so black, that if others think that I can be of service in political life, I cannot refuse.'

Rivers remained attentive to his friendships. He and Sassoon spent many days together at Weirleigh, at the Reform Club and in Cambridge. What they discussed is not known: unusually, for Sassoon anyway, there is no correspondence. Given Rivers' engagement with anthropology and psychology, subjects which begin to be reflected in Sassoon's poems from this time onwards, it is probable that theories of who and what is man were on their agenda. Increasingly over the succeeding years Sassoon meditated on the human journey, its origins, its purpose, its destiny, turning in on himself to search for clues. In his three volumes of poetry published in the twenties, *Recreations*, *Lingual Exercises* and *The Heart's Journey*, there are poems which one can imagine as the fruit of conversations between Sassoon and Rivers. The older man was more than a father-figure – there were a number of those in Sassoon's life – he was the father-confessor. This role set him apart from all the others in the years following the war, the years in which, on his own admission, Sassoon was in a chaotic state, desperate to find some semblance of peace and harmony. Rivers could not bestow them as gifts, but he could and did lend a tutored and sympathetic ear. Sometimes the healing was in the talking.

In the first week of June 1922 Sassoon escaped from London to the cooler air of Bray-on-Thames, where Frank Schuster, genial and generous as ever, had invited his friends from far and wide. On 6 June *The Times* announced in bold letters, 'Dr Rivers, the famous anthropologist, died suddenly at Cambridge at 7 o'clock last night.' Sassoon, who had been told the news earlier, walked around the gardens stupefied for hours after. The suddenness, the finality of this death were chilling; it was different from death in the war. This death was totally unexpected. Two thoughts came to him: the first a reproach, the other a comfort. He remembered Rivers' full and intensely lived life. Despite his robust appearance he was not healthy and became quickly exhausted, but he worked with a passion and Sassoon had benefited from those labours. He felt chastised by thoughts of his own indulgence and soon romanticised the man he knew: 'He is gone forever, but I see him in all his glory of selfless wisdom and humane service. I suppose this is the inevitable effect of death on the living, when the living have loved the dead; it is the victory of life over death.' Sassoon was consoling himself with thoughts of his own making; there was no consolation for him in Christian promises.

Sassoon was bereft, but almost immediately a new father-figure appeared: Dr Henry Head, a distinguished neurologist and early collaborator and colleague of Rivers. His wife Ruth also took a part in the supportive role rendered vacant by death, and their home in Montagu Square and later their home in Dorchester became havens for Sassoon, whom Ruth described as 'the goodest and bestest of men'.

It was fortuitous for Sassoon that he had arranged to spend part of June with the Blundens in Suffolk and the Hardys in Dorset: two homes which offered the solace he needed. Despite the difference in their ages, Edmund and Hardy bore a striking resemblance to each other. Physically there was a bird-like quality in their build and movement; temperamentally they were of a gentle and unaffected demeanour. In addition, Sassoon admired their attitude towards poetry in particular and literature in general. Allied to a spirit that eschewed ostentation and the encumbrances of possessions, they exuded a 'sublime freedom from sophistication'. 'This affinity between B and H is one of the strangest things I have experienced. Also both are modest and unassuming.'

Two pieces of good news also helped to revitalise Sassoon as June drew to a close: Blunden won the Hawthornden Prize for his collection of verse, *The Shepherd*, which was dedicated to Sassoon. Although he counted such prizes as 'bunkum', Sassoon realised that the £100 that came with it would be very handy for Blunden. While visiting Hardy, Sassoon received the second piece of good news. Waiting for him at his hotel in Dorchester was a letter from Philipp of Hesse, the German prince whom he had met the previous August in Rome. Sassoon had written to him at the beginning of May, suggesting they meet in Munich in the summer and do the opera season together. Philipp's delay in replying had left Sassoon with the impression that he was no longer interested in continuing the friendship. Without Philipp, the idea of going to Germany was not attractive and Sassoon's heart sank at the thought of being there with Frankie Schuster and others for weeks on end. This belated letter of acceptance made the prospect of the German visit 'alluring again'.

Going to the Continent for three months needed attention to detail: passports, hotels, luggage and trains. Having no appetite or aptitude for such things, Sassoon struck on the idea of offering Turner, who excelled at such tasks, an all-paid-for holiday. Henry and Ruth Head encouraged Sassoon to put the strain of the last months behind him and, being friends of Turner, endorsed the idea of him as a good, steady companion and more likely than most to withstand the undulating nature of Sassoon's moods. On 20 July the two left Victoria Station for Munich, breaking their journey at Paris, Frankfurt, Nuremberg and Cologne, before arriving on 1 August in Munich and installing themselves at the Park Hotel. The 12-day journey from London saw a deepened intimacy between them. Free from London and the daily deadline, Turner gave his attention to Sassoon, especially over dinner and the late evening. During the day Sassoon kept his own company, which made the evening meetings fresh and lively, rather like some of the evenings in Tufton Street, except that here their conversation was unlikely to be interrupted by visitors. Turner was aware of what Sassoon called his 'sex problem' and their discussions were never inhibited by the need to be coy or evasive. He knew all about the friendship with Philipp, as he did about the Gabriel relationship and its difficulties. Turner also rendered up a few secrets of his own in a demonstration of mutual need.

The expectation of meeting Philipp after an interval of 18 months took on greater intensity as Sassoon neared Munich. In Paris the thought brought 'serenity' but within the week:

26 July: I am getting more and more emotionalized at the prospect of seeing P again.

27 July: My brain has been busy with fantasies.

29 July: These days are only a prelude to the 'world-without-end hour' when I meet P.

1 August: Nuremberg. We leave at 1.40 on the train that comes from Berlin and Leipzig. Quite possible that P. will be on the train.

Philipp was not on the train and neither was he in Munich, when Sassoon arrived there five hours later – 'No sign of P. which was a relief, in a way, although I was greatly excited at the idea of seeing him.' His relief, which seems a strange reaction considering the build-up, was occasioned by seeing and being seen by people who knew him – Frankie Schuster for one, and Adrian Boult. Anxiety about the delicacy of the situation had troubled Sassoon some days earlier. He loathed the idea of his 'idiotic enchantment' with Philipp becoming gossip; and feared the other 'distractions': 'Perhaps the prelude will have been more delicious than the banquet. Much depends on P himself.'

A telegram message was received that evening from Philipp: he would be arriving on Saturday – that was four days away: 'I think it is a very good thing, the wire made me quite happy again, and Saturday will be heavenly.' The burden of the intervening days was lightened by the music and the city, having some time to himself, and Turner being 'extremely sagacious and sympathetic'. On the eve of Philipp's arrival Sassoon was more relaxed, and on the day itself 'full of confident expectation'. In the evening he went to a Mozart concert and returned to his hotel just before midnight, expecting to see Philipp or at least to have a message confirming his arrival. There was no Philipp and no message. 'Train from Homberg due at 12.20 (ninety minutes late), so I went to the station in the rain, and waited till the train came in at 12.50. Lots of people but no P. Came back very disconsolate and slightly indignant.'

Next day he was distraught and angry. Schuster got on his nerves and the first two acts of *Siegfried*, to which he had so looked forward, were an anticlimax but the last act was 'rapturous'. On Monday, with the rain falling, he decided that Philipp would be true to his promise – 'he will turn up all right'. The next day – Tuesday, 8 August – Philipp arrived at the Regina Hotel and suddenly everything 'seemed like Elysium'.

Sassoon records the succeeding days as ones of 'intense happiness'. The visit had begun well and continued so until Schuster, hearing Sassoon speak lightly of a German edition of his poetry 'making his reputation', could not resist the rejoinder, 'Take care you don't *unmake* it in Munich.' It was the kind of remark that Sassoon dreaded. Neither did he like it when two days later Turner spun a yarn about Sassoon having a quiet meal with some 'red-haired woman'. 'Quite unnecessary and clumsy,' was Sassoon's verdict. For the first time he was getting weary of Turner. Sharing a bedroom with him was irksome enough, but Turner walking off with his fountain pen was just too much. 'It is always the little unimportant things that upset one's temper,' he wrote.

Sassoon was incapable of social compromise if it in any way threatened what he wanted at a given moment. In Munich that was to be alone with Philipp, unseen by prying eyes and free from wagging tongues. But it was impossible to achieve. At the peak of the opera season, Munich could not offer the privacy of a desert island, especially to the nephew of the last Kaiser. Being in a different hotel meant that his visits to Philipp's room and the length of his stay required discretion. All spontaneity was lost. He was also vexed by unexpected traits in Philipp's behaviour and the realisation that there were other attachments. There was the mature American woman, referred to as Baby, to whom the ubiquitous Philipp played the gigolo. Then the classic slip-of-the-tongue when Philipp called Siegfried by the name 'Maurice', and the slipping away to other places to enjoy licentious talk and heavy drinking. 'It doesn't enter his mind that I might be rather disgusted by such goings on. He evidently keeps me in a separate compartment of his mind.' It was so reminiscent of Gabriel and ran counter to the hope Sassoon had nursed that his weeks with Philipp in Germany and Italy would put their friendship 'on a firmer basis than mere sensualism'. Philipp for his part lost none of his poise as Sassoon's moods oscillated; he attributed it all to 'nerves'. Prussian coolness under provocation, however, was a further irritant.

It was Turner who struck at the heart of the problem when he told Sassoon 'that he'd never known anyone who had such a strong desire to dominate people's lives – a sort of half-paternal instinct, he called it. Adding that I put an almost impossible strain on the people I'm fond of, by demanding an intensity equal to my own.' Sassoon was fully aware that his shortness of temper, tendency to sulk and his demanding nature strained personal relationships but that was the way he was – emotional and intense, demanding that affection be exclusive and fully reciprocated. His sometimes violent reaction when ardour was threatened or thwarted meant that time after time he became 'the self-appointed executioner' of his own happiness.

There was, however, virtue in Sassoon's earnestness and it stemmed from his experience of young lives wasted. He held a deep antipathy to what he describes as 'a low view of life', 'worldliness' and 'hollowness' – vapidness, as exhibited in dinner-parties and the soirée world of hostesses like Sybil Colefax and Emerald Cunard. It was an aspect of Eddie Marsh's character about which he wrote in July 1965: 'Dear old Eddie was hollow inside – a prime example of what Belloc wrote in *Portrait of a Child* about people who discard sacredness. He did many good services to the arts; but was inwardly frivolous, and ended in despair – all his social world having collapsed.' He recognised and recoiled from the same shortcoming in the character of Frankie Schuster, who took music seriously but regarded everything else as unimportant. When writing of him in *Siegfried's Journey*, he strikes a chilling note: 'For a moment I saw him with the mask of social sprightliness discarded, and as though he were comparing this latest evocation of festivity with those many others which had gone their way of impermanence with the caravan that starts for the Dawn of Nothing when the door is closed behind the last departing guest. It was a face world-weary and saddened by the pursuit of pleasure, yet still in love with life, still demanding stimulation from the spectacle of youth in action.'

When the serious side of Sassoon asserted itself against the superficial, shockwaves were the result. He was strongly of the belief that life was 'a sacred trust' and something which ought to be 'kept as a holy thing' by constant reaffirmation. Dealing in the currency of superficiality, be it work, affections or attitude, was to deny that sacredness. What Turner described as 'a sort of half-paternal instinct' revealed itself in Sassoon's desire to prevent Gabriel and Philipp from falling into the abyss of hollowness. It was part of the wish to 'put my friendship with P. on a firmer basis than mere sensualism'.

By the middle of August, the party began to break up. Turner returned to England and Philipp went to Frankfurt to see his parents, then to Homburg and his American lady. Sassoon travelled to the Bavarian resort of Berchtesgaden, enlivened by the prospect of days spent in mental isolation. On reaching the Hotel Post, he was surprised to find both the hotel and the town so full of visitors. Mercifully, few were English. For the first week Schuster was also there but after 28 August, having seen him safely entrained for Munich, Sassoon was 'genuinely alone for the first time since 20 July'. The weather, which ranged from the sultry to chilly rain, kept him confined to his room. Ordering a meal seemed to take an eternity and the food left much to be desired. However, there were good days and he took to striding about the Bavarian countryside. Inwardly his moods reflected the weather.

Greetings for his birthday arrived early. The one from Theresa touched a sensitive nerve by its simplicity and earnestness: '*God bless you, dear*'. 'I read it as I was walking uphill, and it hit me rather hard.' Having spent so much time with people whose sole focus was on the ephemeral, his mother's solidity and sincerity reminded him 'of all things rich and true': things that prevail over impermanence, complacency and vapidness. The greeting from Gabriel was the other extreme, being 'quite amusing and futile'. Since Philipp's departure his mind had been frequently occupied by thoughts of Gabriel. He was probably on his way back to London after weeks of miserable exile in Newcastle with his aunt, a penance for his indulgences in the Café Royal and the Chelsea Arts Club. Gabriel, unlike Philipp, made no secret of his waywardness; he revelled in the shocking and the uncouth, whereas Philipp hid his feelings and preferences under the cloak of good manners. Philipp's response to Sassoon's emotional demands, however, had echoes of Gabriel: 'P. seems to take love, and everything else in life, in the same way as he takes his meals. He has smashed all the romance out of me in the last three weeks. And as in the Gabriel affair, I get nothing in return for my emotional exhibitions of my inner consciousness. I confide and confess and smite my brow and beat my breast and demand of love that it shall "*really mean something*".'

Sassoon demanded more than passivity; he craved a serious response to his deep complex feelings: the problem with Philipp was 'he does not *tell* me anything.' No friendship with Sassoon could survive unless it was capable of passing beneath the surface of things. Philipp and Gabriel were not inclined to launch themselves into such depths of emotional commitment. Sassoon admitted to himself in his solitariness at Berchtesgaden that he tended to idealise relationships: 'As usual I have been embracing a dream which turns out to be a dull one – quite different from my first vision of it anyhow.' He was too near the events to make a coherent judgement about his progress since the war and his embarking upon a period of 'new beginnings'. His outward self, he decided, had gone about experiencing things, but had there been sufficient solitude for his inward self to assimilate them so that in the fullness of time they would reappear in his poetry? No, there had not been, and he needed time – 'magnanimous time'.

Then there was the matter of getting away from the past. 'In my present mundane approach to the *inner* solitude, I learn about myself by sympathetic communion with the past and those friends who inhabit it.' During the war and its uncertainties his impulse had been to pack in as much as possible 'before the axe fell. I thought in months. Now I think in years, and life is a more difficult problem. In the war I lived only in emotions; and emotions were the only material for my poetry. And my emotions were not complicated by any elaborate intellectuality.'

Solitude was proving a double-edged sword. He had no clear vision, but there were intimations of an inward journey. The reluctance he felt at the prospect of returning to Munich, to the clamour of Berners' and Schuster's friends and Philipp's acolytes, was rooted in the need to continue along the path of self-knowledge, to be *serious* rather than 'float along on the froth of frivolity and self-indulgence. My own self-indulgence exists, but in a different form; I am fantastically *in earnest* about *everything*.'

On the eve of his departure from Berchtesgaden he was concerned about spending the next two months between Germany and Italy in the company of Philipp. While he was still fond of him, the magic in their friendship had faded and Sassoon knew that inevitably his mood would turn black and that 'tornadoes of tigress ill-temper' would spoil what he genuinely desired to be 'a happy and fruitful and unperturbed' few weeks. His only hope was to insist on having time to himself, using as an excuse the need to work on his poetry. The solitude at Berchtesgaden had been therapeutic; he did not wish to lose any of its benefits through an uncongenial atmosphere or social tensions.

The squalls did not materialise – not, that is, until after their first two weeks in Venice. Philipp, Sassoon wrote on the 13 October, had proved an ideal companion. But, as ever, the entry is qualified. On that same day Philipp, whose politics were of the extreme right, remarked that some of Sassoon's friends he had met in Venice were part of 'a socialist clique', to which Sassoon too belonged. Instead of shrugging off the remark Sassoon took offence: 'His inclusion of me in a "clique" is the most annoying thing he could say. It is part of my weakness and my power that I deeply resent the idea of being in any way involved in a coterie of intellectuals. I am a lonely bird – a proud and wrong-headed one at times, but at least I do insist on my independence.' The reaction quite outweighed the original offence because Sassoon was tetchy before the accusatory comments were spoken. Earlier he had spotted Osbert Sitwell, Emerald Cunard, Francis Meynell and Wyndham Lewis in the piazza. Lewis had come across to speak to him, which annoyed him further.

He then learned that outside the Doge's Palace a film of *The Bohemian Girl* was being made, starring Gladys Cooper with Constance Collier as Queen of the Gypsies. Starring in the male lead was Ivor Novello. The news irritated Sassoon. Novello had found fame in 1916 with his song 'Keep The Home Fires Burning'. In the dug-outs gramophones played it non-stop. Sassoon hated the tune, the lyric and the composer. After the death of Rupert Brooke, the affections of Eddie Marsh turned towards Novello and he devoted himself to helping his career in the theatre. For the next 30 years Marsh rarely missed a day in his company. As they both were friends of Marsh a civilised acquaintanceship between Sassoon and Novello, if not an affectionate one, should have existed, but when Novello approached him and Philipp in the piazza Sassoon cut him dead, an action which embarrassed Philipp. In Rome, some 10 days later when he raised the incident with Sassoon, he was told unequivocally, 'I despise him and all he stands for.' Exactly what Novello stood for Philipp was not told.

Sassoon retained his affection for Philipp but became increasingly critical of his attitude towards modern art, music and architecture. He concluded that Philipp was incapable of 'exploration and surprise'. Brought up to accept certain standards and taste, he held to them with a rigidity that belied his young years. 'I am afraid this intellectual rigidity will develop into ossification, unless something extraordinary occurs to wake him up,' and there was no possibility that Sassoon's views on politics or social affairs would be the agent of such a change. 'No doubt my vanity makes me hypercritical of him. He admires my prestige as a poet (which he probably over-estimates) but he does *not* for one moment admit that all his ideas would be enlarged by assimilating any of my ideas. He doesn't even try to understand what my ideas are. He vaguely classes me as 'a Socialist' who *hasn't* read Goethe, he thinks I am wrong to tolerate Gauguin and Van Gogh and Stravinsky.'

Berchtesgaden had fed Sassoon's sense of vocation and internal resolve to 'prepare his mind for a big effort of creation'. The immediate task was to continue to garner experiences as raw material for his future writing. 'I use people up – suck them dry. And unless they are people who are developing all the time (like Turner), I soon find that I can get nothing from them. At present I feel I can get nothing more from my friendship with P.'

When they parted in early November little mention was made of the future, except that Philipp invited Sassoon to visit him in Berlin. Sassoon neither accepted nor declined. Then he made his way to London, 'happy and contented, and thankful for what has been between my friend and me'.

11

TRAVELS

1923–4

During the opening months of 1923 Sassoon knew that a boundary had been crossed in his mental and artistic journey. The death of Rivers had engendered a degree of seriousness he had not known previously. Alone with his thoughts in Berchtesgaden, that seriousness had forced him to refocus himself on his vocation. In the uncompleted and unpublished fourth volume of his memoirs, he described the journey as being 'unspectacular and private – a period in which I was qualifying myself to become a prose writer, unobtrusively continuing my career as a poet and practising autognosis'. This was also the time when he finally ceased fox-hunting and steeplechasing. Between January and March he made the journey from London to Cirencester at least once every week and the conviction grew that it was wasted time: as 12 months previously, he found the company of the Loders irksome. The decision was helped by the drain on his finances from keeping two horses: the rheumatic Lady Jill and the lightly built, but highly-strung Higham Destiny. Making the break was made more difficult by his genuine enjoyment of horses, riding and being in the Gloucestershire countryside. 'I get more pleasure from my horses than anything else!' he confessed to Phyllis Loder. He was also a good rider and his successes in point-to-point gave a boost to his confidence; successes which he recorded with typical understatement: 'I have won four; three seconds; three thirds – which prove I'm not an absolute mug at it.'

The following day proved that pride, even understated, comes before a fall. On 11 April he was one of 13 riders in a point-to-point. Among the other 12 was the Prince of Wales. Higham Destiny got off to an excellent start, keeping the leaders in view and taking every fence perfectly, despite the heavy going. Reaching the last four from home and with only the Prince and one other in front of him, Sassoon 'felt the mare dying away'. Instinct told him to rein her in, only Higham seemed determined to finish, but reaching the final fence she was clearly 'stone-cold'. 'The result was that she landed in the ditch on the far side and lay on the ground for about ten minutes. I was afraid she'd broken her back, but she was only completely "blown", and finally struggled to her feet and walked away with her ears cocked, none the worse. Norman and Phyllis had come down to the fence, and we toddled up the hill to the paddock, behind the mare led by the groom – a forlorn little procession. The mare falling like that made me realise that there is something rather brutal about racing.'

The next day Higham Destiny proved her full recovery by carrying Sassoon to a meet of the Cirencester hounds. In what appears to have been a breakdown in the usual discipline of such gatherings, the hounds ran amok into the four corners of the Bathurst estate. Sassoon attempted, with Norman Loder, to retrieve the pack and while negotiating a gateway gave his shin and ankle 'an awful bruising ... Rode about for some time, in considerable pain, and got home soaked through, to find that I'd got a nasty hole in my leg.' It was an inglorious end to the Fox-Hunting Man, who, having agreed with Norman to sell Higham Destiny, took his leave of the Loders and, bearing his wounds, journeyed to Garsington, where he spent three weeks convalescing in 'compulsory idleness'.

It was the first week in May when he returned to the house in Tufton Street, whose challenges were no more onerous than those of Garsington and Cirencester. In a way Sassoon was like Higham Destiny – running out of vitality four fences from home. He was deeply conscious of the need to express something of significance in his writing but he could decide upon neither the message nor the appropriate medium. This barren time was alleviated by one bright moment when he met Max Beerbohm on 21 May at dinner in the Gosses' home. Another guest recited some anecdotes about Robbie Ross and touched the chord of remembrance. The conjunction of Ross and Beerbohm underlines how Sassoon's friendships were almost a continual process of replacing like for like. Taking his leave of Max, Sassoon gushingly but with utmost sincerity told him, 'I think you are one of the best authors.' It was the beginning of a long friendship.

In the post the following morning came news from Norman Loder that Higham Destiny had been sold. Sassoon knew that Lady Jill would have to be put down and that it was beyond his means to invest in another horse.

A few weeks later he visited the Loders for the last time in Cirencester, said goodbye to Lady Jill – 'a miserable episode', and played cricket on the lawn with the Loders' little boy, John, doomed to die four years later at the age of 11. In the autumn Norman and Phyllis moved to Ettington, near Stratford-upon-Avon, where they kept Sassoon's riding gear, more as a memory than an earnest of the future. They played no further role in his life until Norman returned to the stage as Denis Milden in *Memoirs of a Fox-Hunting Man*.

Other friendships survived, albeit precariously in the case of Robert Graves. The estrangement from Osbert Sitwell and his brother and sister continued, but so too did Sassoon's fascination with them. Irritation was perhaps the predominant feeling Osbert aroused in Sassoon by always appearing unexpectedly and inconveniently – in a restaurant in Munich or a piazza in Venice; less exotically in the barber's shop or on the doorstep of the house of a mutual friend, and invariably in Piccadilly and St James's. The indefatigable Osbert was firing off his literary salvoes against his contemporaries, many of them friends of Sassoon. In June it was Robert Nichols' work which suffered the blows of what Sassoon saw as Osbert's complete inability to be generous in his appreciation of talents other than those of his own family. He was self-regarding and demanded to be flattered and lauded. Rushing to his friend's defence, Sassoon forgot his own irritation and disapproval of Nichols' bombastic and self-promoting tendencies, which mirrored the weaknesses – perceived, true or otherwise – which he condemned in Osbert. Objectivity was a hindrance in this as in all battles of the self-will and pride.

Sassoon delighted in the cartoon of the Sitwell brothers, which formed a prominent feature in the exhibition of Max Beerbohm's *Caricatures*, then showing at the Leicester Galleries in London. They stand in self-congratulatory pose, resembling Siamese twins, in their case joined at the ego. Osbert described the cartoon to his sister-in-law as a 'rude drawing'. Max's work was, as ever, a brilliant piece of observation, realised through wit devoid of malice. Sassoon and Osbert learnt little from such an approach and descended into tiresomeness, each sending the other silly postcards with even more jejune inscriptions. Sassoon did send one olive-branch to Osbert who replied in similar vein, but the opportunity for reconciliation had passed. For Sassoon, the Sitwellian trio were an echo of that period immediately after the war which he regarded as fruitless and vainglorious. Renewing the link would be retrograde; on the other hand, quarrelling was destructive. Sassoon decided on a policy of polite avoidance which in reality meant that the shadow-boxing continued. In effect the Sitwells were part of Sassoon's acknowledged 'frustration and failure' in human relationships during the first half of the twenties. Another was Robert Graves.

> *June 6* (Derby Day. Grey and drizzly.)
> After dinner I returned to Apple Tree Yard and talked (alone) to R.G. for two hours ... What a contrast R.G. is to O.S! He has all the humanity (and humility) which O. lacks.

Apple Tree Yard was a small mews off Jermyn Street within the vicinity where Sassoon would spy Osbert bearing down upon him. It was the London home and studio of William Nicholson, the father-in-law of Graves. That afternoon Nancy was her usual difficult and distant self, but Robert, 'stimulating as ever', seemed to want the return of cordiality and mutual enterprise with Sassoon. The afternoon and evening at Apple Tree Yard proved to be an interlude and not a revival of the friendship.

Graves was under a great strain, knowing that his marriage was a disastrous misalliance and that financially he was again in serious straits. He was beset with guilt for having killed his fellow man, and, like Sassoon, was subject to horrendous visitations. He was also suffering bouts of acute bronchitis, which were dangerous to his already weakened lungs but he was more resilient in adversity than Sassoon. He became stoical and clung to his old tenet that 'he who endures to the end shall be saved'. Sassoon was also missing the support and guidance of Rivers.

A decisive element in Sassoon's confused behaviour was the absence of a strong guide. Rivers' death the previous year had robbed him of that. The period between his return from America and the demise of Rivers had also been unsatisfactory and confused, but at least Rivers was there. Now that support had been removed – 'I lost him when still much dependent on his influence and advice. He was much the best friend I had, at that time.' Only one person came near to filling the vacuum, Dr Henry Head; but, helpful as that relationship was, Head did not completely fill the void left by his colleague. Even so, without Head and his wife and the sympathetic welcome proffered at Montagu Square, Sassoon would have been even more at sea.

It was to Head that Sassoon wrote on 15 June 1923, 'Here is the volume which has taken 4 years to evolve, print and bind.' This was *Recreations*, a collection of 24 poems – all unpublished in book form except three – and

Sassoon's first new work since *Picture Show* in 1919; *War Poems* in that same year combined poems from *The Old Huntsman, Counter-Attack* and *Picture Show*. As was his way, Sassoon had 75 copies privately printed but no public edition of *Recreations* ever appeared. Some of the poems had been previously published in magazines, mainly in *The Nation and Athenaeum*, and the *London Mercury*, whose Editor, J. C. Squire, had been treated so roughly by the Sitwells. Writing to Squire, Sassoon said: 'I suppose I am a curmudgeonly chap. I can only repeat that the *Recreations* stuff leaves me dissatisfied. I suppose this keeping my work dark is only an obscure form of conceit.'

Recreations contains poems based on his experiences in America and also a satirical chorus against hunting, pretentious concert-goers and other society gatherings Sassoon found distasteful or comical. Other poems describe single unobtrusive moments in the museums and galleries of London. They are quintessential Sassoon – evocative, succinct descriptions of human activity in its unchanging ordinariness. This is especially true of 'In the Turner Room', 'An Old World Effect' and 'The London Mercury'. The tenor of these poems had been set some years earlier when the poem 'On Some Portraits by Sargent' appeared in the *London Mercury* and revealed Sassoon's decision to move away from the vehemence which coloured his war poetry, as explained in *Siegfried's Journey:*

> I had said my say: the stimulus of experience and emotion had ceased. I had it in mind to attempt realistic poems about everyday life. For, although my existence since the war had been undirected and adrift, my literary instinct was sufficiently wide-awake to warn me against allowing the vehemence of my war writings to become a mannerism. In the *London Mercury* I demonstrated my transition to the new style of versifying which I proposed to cultivate. It was a pattern for a series of descriptive pieces in which I assumed a laconic, legato tone of voice.

Those who received a personally inscribed copy of *Recreations* expressed their appreciation both of the gesture and of the contents, but the adjectival tones 'represented a sort of success but rather a dreary one … there is something lulling and dangerous about their acknowledgements of the "charm" etc. They have been polite. I would prefer them to be puzzled and excited.' Pondering these reactions in his restrictive rooms in Tufton Street, Sassoon knew that his latest effort lacked spontaneity. The

Weirleigh: 'The background to all my dreams both pleasant and unpleasant.'

Top: Alfred with his sons. Michael on the left and Siegfried and Hamo on the right.

Above: Theresa with her 'dear boys'. Siegfried at lower left, then Hamo and Michael.

Left: Lady Ottoline
Morrell at home: 'My first
view of her was somewhat
disconcerting.'

Above: The photograph
Sassoon sent to Ottoline
from France, January 1916.

Top left: Edmund Blunden: 'What a blessing little B is.'

Top right: 18 December 1933: 'O, Hester, you must redeem my life for me.'

Above: Heytesbury House: 'When I am forty-nine I will look for that house and when I am in it I will write wise books.'

Top: Sassoon, Hester and George at Heytesbury: 'George brings us together as nothing else can do.'

Above: Sassoon and car. A terrifying partnership.

Right: Siegfried Sassoon, at the end of the day. *'When I'm alone ...'*

poems were careful, neat and dead. How different from the war poems when his passion poured forth in the honesty of direct utterance. These Tufton Street poems had been composed rather than 'given'. Of course he could not write poems in fulsome spirit about his homoerotic feelings – the subject he sometimes described as 'closest' to his heart. Or, if he did, he made sure they did not survive.

Polemical poems in the manner of 'The Case for the Miners', composed two years earlier in the heat of a general strike, held no appeal for him in 1923. Poetry itself had moved on from the pastures, hay-ricks and warbling birds of Eddie Marsh's post-war *Georgian Poetry*. Sassoon had warned Marsh four years earlier: 'The danger with G.P. is that it will become too tidy.' Now, in 1923, he was saying the same thing about his own work. He had refused the invitation to be included in the fifth and final volume of *Georgian Poetry*, published at the end of 1922, being 'entirely out of sympathy with several of the Georgian shavers in the shade of your laurel-tree'.

He was also out of sympathy with those who were 'hooting' Georgian poetry to its grave – the Sitwells but, more importantly, the 'modernists' and in particular T. S. Eliot. Sassoon could make neither head nor tail of *The Waste Land* (1922) and was much comforted when he heard it described as 'literary leg-pulling'. As for Eliot himself, Sassoon considered him uncongenial and a publicity-seeker. It was impossible to attend a dinner-party without Eliot's name being mentioned in oracular terms: 'getting fed up with being told that T.S.E. is the most important modern poet, and that Huxley [Aldous] is first-rate', he noted with irritation in his diary.

Between Osbert, Graves, Eliot and the heat, London was unbearable. Sassoon took himself away to 'silver-green East Anglia' and the Blundens at Stansfield in Suffolk. Soft showers and the country air soon brought tranquillity but all was not well in the Blunden marriage. Mary could not enter fully into the literary scene and had disliked living in the suburbs of London. Moving back to Suffolk eased her problem but created a strain for Edmund, who was forced to travel the slow and tedious route to his London office. When Mary and Edmund met Sassoon at Clare Station, however, all seemed well, although behind Edmund's chirpiness lay tiredness from travel and the financial demands of raising two children. He was a prodigious worker and comprehensive in the subjects he tackled on behalf of the paper, but his remuneration was small. The arrival of Sassoon and the chance to exchange confidences, while he showed his friend around the area, proved restorative, as did the opportunity to travel across the country to Dorset, Max Gate and Hardy. Sassoon had arranged for himself and Blunden to stay at Came Rectory, the former home of the Dorset poet William Barnes, from where they went each day for tea at Max Gate.

This was Blunden's second visit; he had spent a week the previous year on his own getting to know the 'Wessex Wizard'. It was a source of enormous delight to Sassoon to see these two enjoying each other: 'T.H. as charming and alert as ever. It is good to watch him talking while little Blunden listens, intent, respectful, and bird-like.' For Edmund the chance to be with Hardy, and stay in the house of Barnes, fed his delight in all things rural. It would be hard to imagine that they did not discuss the use of dialect in prose and poetry which Hardy featured sometimes in his work, as too did Blunden (to the annoyance of some critics), though neither as much as William Barnes. The echoes of the visit resonated in Blunden's study of Hardy published 20 years later. 'What a blessing little B. is,' recorded Sassoon, reflecting on the days spent in Dorset cycling the lanes in golden weather and thankful for what was now 'four years of flawless friendship'. There was an air of former days when as a young man he had cycled through the lanes of Kent and Sussex, but it could never be more than a hint for him and Blunden. Sadder memories broke the spell, as Blunden observes in *The Shepherd*:

> What mercy is it I should live and move,
> If haunted ever by war's agony?

Much the same feelings preoccupied Sassoon at Weirleigh. Taking advantage of the absence from the house of Michael, Violet and the children, and having popped the Tufton Street kitten into its basket, he spent the last days of summer with Theresa. She had found a new source of comfort – the wireless, which brought music without the bother of travelling to London. The house and its gardens had lost some of its tidiness but none of its charm. Mrs Fenner, who had come as housekeeper during the war, was not someone Sassoon liked or trusted. She was too bossy and intrusive and Theresa indulged these tendencies. (Throughout his life he was always having problems with cooks and housekeepers – but Mrs Fenner does sound on the formidable side!) Apart from a visit to some old friends and a day trip to London, Sassoon spent his time at Weirleigh rummaging in the studio among his pre-war papers. It was time for a good clear-out of thoughts and literary relics, which together with golf-clubs, tennis-rackets and cricket pads accusingly testified to languid days of his 'arrested development and idle existence'.

No such feelings were engendered by Tufton Street. Sassoon was still in his anti-possession period. The two small rooms where he spent nocturnal hours composing his verse and writing his journal were adequate for his needs, but it would have been better if his piano and his music could have been accommodated. It was a real deprivation, a feeling deepened each time its sound ascended to his room as Turner played away unimpeded, with no thought of permission needed or granted, in the same way he had taken Sassoon's pen in Munich. Now the autumn brought the promise of freedom – when the Turners left Tufton Street for the Continent in September and were not to return until November. The house was his – well, almost. Turner had agreed to Edward Shanks, the Assistant Editor of the *London Mercury*, having a pied-à-terre, but that was neither here nor there compared with the prospect of two months' solitude, access to the small downstairs room and use, when he pleased, of the kitchen and the piano. Sassoon was overjoyed when he waved goodbye to the Turners on the doorstep: neither they nor anyone else seeing him that morning would have believed his confession of not wanting a place of his own.

Poetry, of course, remained the priority and within the month he had written nearly 500 lines in the 'legato' mode, mirroring his experiences as an observer of life. Meals were still taken at the Reform and evenings out at dinner-parties and the theatre remained, as too the occasional exhibition. But once inside Tufton Street the public self deferred to the private: 'How delightful to be sitting here, fortified against all intruders! If anyone rings the bell I needn't open the door.' Of course he did open the door and among his visitors was E. M. Forster. 'When I decide to make a friend I persist,' Forster wrote to Sassoon. It was not a central friendship, but nonetheless through their homosexuality there was an understanding of each other's moods and frustrations. Background too united them: upper-middle class, deprived of their fathers at an early age; mothers with whom they seemed to be in an emotional wrestling match – Forster could barely move without informing his mother, even when he was 60 and she touching 90. There was also a reticence, not to say a shyness with regard to other people. Although Forster moved among the gossipy Bloomsberries he was not a gossip, neither was he vindictive. There were elements of the contemplative about him. His biographer, P. N. Furbank, wrote to Stephen Tennant many years later: 'I agree with you in stressing Morgan's inward, mystical quality. He really did live an inner life, as not many people do.'

It was with Forster more than with anyone else that Sassoon discussed what he himself described as 'his problem' and Forster, who declared in an essay that what the world needed was 'not more chastity but more delicacy', knew intuitively where the boundary lay between advice and intrusion. P. N. Furbank also detected in Forster's letters to Sassoon 'a rather avuncular, reproving tone, as though he felt he needed keeping in order'. The letters referred to the early twenties, when Sassoon also needed advice about venturing into prose and about the direction of his poetry. In fact, it was on 14 June 1923 that Sassoon allowed Forster to read his diary for the previous year and also gave him an autographed copy of *Recreations*. Forster, with a first-rate eye for a story, recognised possibilities of transposing the content of the diary into a significant prose work. Forster also read a tentative and incomplete treatment for a novel that Sassoon had penned while on holiday in Porlock Weir with Gabriel in the summer of 1921. He adjudged that effort a failure and coupling it with the diary, wrote to Sassoon: 'You are not (at present) a story-writer, but why not? I wish I could tell you. I can only advise you to try again. The method of your 1921 story has been a failure – diction, power, liveliness all got side-tracked. So I can only suggest that you try an entirely new method. The stuff is certainly inside you – indeed it is "out" in your Journal.'

The writing of memoirs was the subject of a letter Sassoon received from Sydney Cockerell asking his opinion on an accompanying manuscript, the third version of *The Seven Pillars of Wisdom*. T. E. Lawrence and Sassoon had last met around the luncheon table at Max Gate in the summer when Blunden was present. Now in the solitude of a frost- and fog-filled Tufton Street, he immersed himself in the heroic doings in Arabia and reliving the excitement when, as a youth in Kent, he first read C. M. Doughty's *Arabia Deserta*, a new edition of which with an introduction by Lawrence now lay at his elbow. Gradually, Lawrence the man commanded more of his attention than the book. 'T.E.L. is a queer figure in the landscape of my thoughts. His book has impressed him on me as one of the most intensely real minds in my experience. He is an ascetic. And his attitudes are superb, the way he hacks his way down to reality, never sparing himself. My admiration for him grows steadily as I plough through his double-columns of small print, which are like physical experience.'

At the beginning of December, the spectre of the Turners' return cast its shadow over everything. Soon he would be banished to the small rooms and separated from his piano. The downstairs room, whose snug proportions he had so enjoyed, would revert to his untidy landlords. Perhaps he should move on to a place of his own? The idea was appealing. On the evening of 9 December, as he kindled the fire, the door-bell rang and on answering, Sassoon found not the Turners, but the author of *The Seven Pillars of Wisdom*. He could hardly believe that 'the little man (my hero)' was actually on the doorstep. Providence could not have arranged a more wonderful climax to his three months' idyll than this. For over two hours Sassoon bubbled and babbled with excitement, which made Lawrence's stillness even more marked. Sitting in an armchair, Lawrence, small and delicate, made Sassoon feel 'enormous' and very 'protective' towards him. Both Forster and Lawrence possessed the quality of serenity, which controlled the turbulence. Theirs too was the gift of the storyteller, the prose writer for which title Sassoon was striving.

Neither his prose nor his poetry advanced, although by the year's end he had completed nearly 1,500 lines of verse. The polite reactions to *Recreations*, and Graves' lively corrections to the poems in progress and Forster's enigmatic description of some verses as 'pirouettings' left Sassoon downhearted. When the Turners returned he was taken aback to hear talk of the need to move to a bigger house. Two small rooms upstairs were sufficient for him. Ruminating by the fire on the state of his work, all of which he had enjoyed writing, he concluded it was 'bunglings and echoes of the past'. Taking the manuscripts he ripped away page after page, consigning each one to the flames. It was a re-enactment of the conflagration in the studio at Weirleigh, a decade previously. Then Helen Wirgman had looked into the flames and given Sassoon one of her slow sad looks. This time there was no witness as the verses flickered up the chimney. It was Christmas Eve: Sassoon packed his bags and set off for Garsington.

The New Year found Sassoon back in Tufton Street and still in a state of depression. As usual when he was so afflicted, other people became an irritation. Turner, who had been a guide and support, was now an audible irritant; his voice with its querulous cadences carried his views through the floorboards. Other voices were more of a distraction than a nuisance and Sassoon preferred not to join in the company downstairs unless it was someone of the calibre of the poet and lecturer Ralph Hodgson, Henry and Ruth Head and sometimes Ottoline Morrell, who had adopted the Turners and appropriated them for Garsington. During their extended absence,

Sassoon had established a routine whose disruption by them he resented. Mrs Binks, the daily help, having to be at the beck and call of three rather than one, was also touchy, displaying a gift for impertinence. She liked Mr Sassoon – he was neat and tidy. His unusual hours did not worry her, in fact it was all a great help. Since he stayed in bed till the late afternoon, he was not under her feet. She prepared a high tea for him somewhere between three and seven – fish usually followed by a pudding. Later he would stroll to his club or a restaurant for dinner, returning home in the early hours.

Working hours were between midnight and dawn, with cakes and tea bolted down 'as sparrows chirped pert compliments to day'. More often than not he would be retiring to bed as Mrs Binks arrived from Chelsea. They formed an alliance in defence of the routine, Sassoon being adamant that his fish-and-a-pudding was inviolate. He kept his fish and pudding, but Mrs Binks lost her job. Turner had an opinion on everything, which he declaimed with volubility and a dismissive air. Even the beloved Thomas Hardy was not spared. Sassoon began to discuss with friends, discreetly, his growing antagonism to Turner: his affection for Delphine remained unimpaired. Any decision to leave Tufton Street, as some of his friends were advising him to do, would be conditional on it not jeopardising her welfare.

There was also in Turner that element of bombast which irritated Sassoon in Robert Graves and Osbert Sitwell. But he maintained, when comparing Graves with Osbert, that 'Robert has more humanity', by which he meant that Graves never harboured malice but wished to advance the things of good report with 'a few helpful suggestions' which were well meant and honestly spoken. Sassoon trusted his judgement in poetry and Graves' assessment carried weight. What remained unresolved was Nancy. Graves objected to Sassoon's assumption that he could regard himself as a friend of one without being the friend of the other. Not until Sassoon changed his attitude could there be even the smallest hope of them enjoying true friendship again. If only Sassoon would come to stay at World's End, treat Nancy as an equal, all would be well – but not otherwise. Sassoon felt the admonishment and promised that with the return of good weather, he would visit in the true spirit of reconciliation. He also sent a cheque for a hundred pounds to ease the Graveses' financial burden.

Edmund Blunden, whose relationship with Graves veered towards the arctic regions, was much on Sassoon's mind during the first part of 1924.

Blunden's poems were part of Sassoon's reading list and he felt the verses 'deeply consoling and strangely mingled with associations of home and childhood'. He might have added youth and cricket, for in his dreams Sassoon became ambitious for himself and his friend, dreaming that each had scored a century on the pitch at Tunbridge. Few things appealed to Sassoon more than to hear others talk well of 'little B'. When Ralph Hodgson compared favourably Blunden at his best to Oliver Goldsmith, Sassoon was overwhelmed with pride.

He was shocked when, opening his mail on 23 February, he read an invitation to a farewell dinner in honour of 'little B', who, the card informed Sassoon, had been appointed Professor of English Language at Tokyo. Sassoon was puzzled, for when he had discussed Blunden with Hodgson but a month earlier no mention had been made of this development – very odd, especially as Hodgson was also going to Japan to take up a similar appointment. Sassoon wrote at once to Blunden expressing his dismay at the prospect of being deprived of his company for all of three years. Within the week, he was on his way to Suffolk to spend three days with the Blundens. There he learnt that Mary would not be going with Edmund; she refused all efforts at persuasion. Sassoon records in his diary that while he and Edmund settled down of an evening Mary went off to a dance with someone he describes as a 'cad and a bounder'. The Blunden marriage was falling apart. Three weeks later, on 28 March, Blunden waved goodbye to his wife and friends. Sassoon was not on the quayside but enjoying the enchantments of the Hotel Villa d'Este near Milan, thinking tenderly of his mother celebrating her birthday at Weirleigh, and being disappointed by a telegraph message from Rome: 'Impossible. Still hope to see you here – Philipp.' They did not meet. Philipp's following letter pleaded lack of finance and time with the emphasis strongly on the first – as usual.

It had been such a relief to be away from Tufton Street; returning there was a dismal prospect. In fact the months of April and May 1924 witnessed the nadir of Sassoon's creativity – 'I have lived too much in books and have received no new impressions of scenes and events and people.' Complaining thus in his diary and with the bright days of summer now evident in the trees along the Thames Embankment and the flowers in St James's Park, Sassoon felt the need to escape from his smoke-filled room, the noise of the funfair on nearby derelict ground and the incessant banging of Big Ben. Others were solicitous of his well-being and the need for fresh air. Richmond Temple, a pioneer in 'public relations' and one of the smart set that surrounded Frankie Schuster, presented him with the latest sensation in the automobile world – the Gwynne 8 h.p. Sassoon's anti-possession stance made him reluctant to accept but a stance is more pliable than a principle and so with considerable gusto he went down to Schuster's house at Bray, making a sensational entry in a place where sensational entries were the norm.

Temple through his kindness unleashed a driver upon the world whose understanding of cars and the art of driving began at zero and did not progress over the next 40 years. Sassoon was indisputably among the worst and most dangerous of drivers. Friends who survived hair-raising experiences vied with each other for the best story about Sig's maniacal and suicidal tendencies when behind the wheel. Road sense, direction, speed restrictions, elementary safety were matters to which he was oblivious. On one occasion he lit a match to see how much petrol was in the tank – singeing his eyebrows in the process. But the real danger was his belief in himself and his capabilities as a driver. One friend ventured to suggest that an all-round improvement in comfort and safety would be achieved if Sig grasped a fundamental difference between a horse and a car – 'One does not ride a car, Sig.' Bollards on the Bayswater Road were obstacles to be got over rather than around and no one obeyed better than Sassoon the precept of not letting the right hand know what the left was doing. With the arrival of the Gwynne 8 came a 'sense of property and, more importantly, independence'. Life was becoming stale and wearisome even at Bray. 'The Lotus-eating luxury of the Hut; I can no longer work there. Life here [Tufton Street] is arid and hourless. I have difficulty filling up the day. And the Reform Club is a wilderness.' Then there was the continuing deterioration in his relationship with Jim Turner and the half-hearted attempt at patching up his quarrel with Osbert Sitwell, what he called 'ramshackle reconciliations'. News that Philipp, who had promised to come to London for the summer, was now attached to a 'no longer young but once beautiful Baroness in Rome' meant that any possibility of a visit was vitiated. Ralph Hodgson left for Japan and so life became 'empty and arid'. But he had the car.

In his diary 3 July is marked as a day of independence when for the first time he took 'unchaperoned' control of the car. He was beginning to get the hang of it. On 4 July he crashed into a dog-cart but there were no injuries. On 5 July he knocked a cyclist off the road and on to the pavement – again, no harm. He felt himself growing in confidence as a driver and thought fondly of the open road. Since the middle of June

Sassoon had established friendly relations with one of Frankie Schuster's young friends, John Philbin. He had been away in South America for five years doing 'this and that', but was now down on his luck. The Hut at Bray was a roof over his head and Schuster's generosity provided a necessary breathing space. Sassoon liked him, although he later discovered Philbin's talent for exaggeration and make-believe. He was also a good driver and knowledgeable about matters mechanical, rather like Sassoon's brother, Michael, who was given the opportunity to inspect the Gwynne 8, when Sassoon and Philbin visited Weirleigh. Theresa was in a state of panic, that day being the eve of a garden fête at the house. That she should not panic further, the true ownership of the car was not revealed. She had never recovered from her first experience as a passenger, in 1896. Mr Walter Arnold, her neighbour, was one of the first importers of the Benz car from Germany. He was also the first person in Britain to be fined for exceeding the speed limit when driving at eight miles an hour in a two-mile-an-hour area. Theresa agreed to ride with Mr Arnold a short distance, an event which Sassoon and his brothers witnessed with tentative admiration. After one hundred yards Theresa alighted and told Mr Arnold, 'I regard it with the deepest suspicion.'

The high summer days saw Sassoon liberated from London and making a splash with his car at Garsington, Max Gate and Cloud's Hill, the home of T. E. Lawrence. Then to Pembrokeshire and the de la Mares, who were holidaying at Manorbier. All this freedom released a surge of creative energy. While in Pembrokeshire he wrote three poems, 'A Ruined Castle', 'At the Grave of Henry Vaughan' and to complete the trio, 'With de la Mare at Carey Castle'.

Sassoon spent his birthday with Henry and Ruth Head in the Malvern Hills; he could scarely believe the difference the car was making to his life as he drove through the Worcestershire countryside. He attended the Three Choirs Festival in Hereford, where he listened to Elgar's *The Kingdom* and choral works by Holst and Rossini. By moonlight he drove along the Welsh Marches and another day, after listening to a performance of *Messiah*, took the road over Wenlock Edge to Church Stretton. It was a joy to walk the hills of *A Shropshire Lad*, even when the rain came, but it was not unalloyed joy: he had been there before. Almost nine years to the day, in September 1915, he and three others had travelled from their base at Litherland and stayed in the same hotel. One of the three was David Thomas; 'or was it Bobbie Hanmer?' It was a 'vague memory' – vague, but persistent. How unusual for Sassoon not to remember the exact details, especially when David Thomas might be involved. Writing in his diary he describes the moment in terms of 'then and now', how those once loved had faded away and others had taken their places. The entry covered half a page – he tore it out, it was too painful.

The memory was a prelude to thoughts about the immediate future. Where to go next? Pointing the Gwynne 8 towards Tufton Street was not an attractive prospect. 'Gwynning' directionless through the English countryside held a certain appeal. Perhaps he could do that until his budget ran out? But would such meandering yield a harvest of impressions and observations to assist him as a writer and poet? Tufton Street or five days on the open road? Sassoon hesitated no longer. His journey started with no predetermined direction or destination, the pattern emerged as his journey progressed. Taking the road eastward, he drove out of Shropshire and into Staffordshire where, near Lichfield, he recalled playing cricket 20 years earlier. Then a 'vague' itinerary formed in his mind, which would take him through the heart of England to Norfolk. Arbitrariness and vagueness were playing their part; but there were other, more complex impulses at work. This 'vague' itinerary was a return journey. This was Atherstone country, the scene of his fox-hunting days, when Norman Loder was still his hero and where he first met Phyllis. Then the Gwynne took him near to Market Bosworth, past the Rectory where Bobbie Hanmer had lived and his sister Dorothy, with whom Sassoon had so innocently formed an attachment in 1915. Norman, Phyllis, Bobbie and Dorothy and all those others whose lives had touched his were like the people whose memory, two nights before at Church Stretton, had caused him to ponder the transient nature of human relationships.

How does the cord of friendship slacken but the memory strengthen with the years? It was strange now to remember how important had been his friendship with the Loders when they moved to Longthorpe in Cambridgeshire and the Fitzwilliam Hunt. Now in this late afternoon of September 1924, he slowed the car to view the 'the oak-encompassed house'. Five years before, he had stayed at Longthorpe when he was at his most confused and haunted. There, in one of the bedrooms as he waited for sleep, he remembered passing the boundary which separates 'then and now':

> Voices moving about in the quiet house:
> Thud of feet and a muffled shutting of doors:
> Everyone yawning. Only the clocks alert.

Out in the night there's autumn-smelling gloom
Crowded with whispering trees; across the park
A hollow cry of hounds like lonely bells:
And I know that the clouds are moving across the moon;
The low, red, rising moon. Now herons call
And wrangle by their pool; and hooting owls
Sail from the wood above pale stooks of oats.

Waiting for sleep, I drift from thoughts like these;
And where today was dream-like, build my dreams.
Music ... there was a bright white room below,
And someone singing a song about a soldier,
One hour, two hours ago: and soon the song
Will be 'last night': but now the beauty swings
Across my brain, ghost of remembered chords
Which still can make such radiance in my dream
That I can watch the marching of my soldiers,
And count their faces; faces; sunlit faces.

Falling asleep ... the herons, and the hounds ...
September in the darkness; and the world
I've known; all fading past me into peace.

From Longthorpe he continued eastward into Norfolk, where his journey brought him to the village of Edingthorpe. In 1897, Theresa rented the Rectory there for a family holiday lasting two months. Sassoon was approaching his tenth birthday then, now he was 38:

My memories of the place were extremely vague, the landscape was strangely unrecoverable in the light of memory; sad and remote, it looked now, in the grey end of an autumn afternoon. Leaving the car in a farm-lane, I walked across a stubble-field and rediscovered the little church. It had a thatched roof. I hadn't remembered that. Probably I didn't notice that in 1897. The church was locked, but it looked as though it hadn't changed since 1824, except for a new lych-gate, erected to the memory of a young Lance-corporal Muriel (son of the late parson). Somehow that little church, standing in its unkempt graveyard among the stubble and root-fields, had a curious dignity and pathos, which will, I know, haunt me.

On 18 September he was back in Tufton Street, having completed 800 miles in 12 days, which included a visit to the Fitzwilliam Museum to inspect the rehanging of his 'Byronic-style' portrait, commissioned by Robbie Ross and painted by Glyn Philpot in 1917. It was all part of the remembering. The journey was the prelude to his new life as a writer. He had found his subject in the past – his own past.

12

SHERSTON

1925–7

Sassoon was eager to do some preliminary work on his memoirs – at least that was his intention. Starting in earnest, however, was delayed in part by the atmosphere in Tufton Street. He did produce some poems, including 'Evensong in Westminster Abbey'. He wanted to prolong into autumn the wandering, social mood that had typified his summer and this he did, his diary recording a mounting mileage, including a visit to Brighton. In London he frequented the theatre and enjoyed lunching and dining. It was a time too for bumping into old friends. On 28 September, at a flat in Maida Vale, Sassoon spent an evening in the company of Gabriel. They rarely saw one another now, although Gabriel was still on Sassoon's list of those to whom he gave money and remained so for a few more years. It was charity rather than affection – not cold charity, though; the passion had gone but Sassoon remained concerned at Gabriel's increasing degeneracy.

On 1 October, his luncheon guest was Osbert Sitwell. Their estrangement had ended in the summer. Sassoon had always regretted the feud which, on reflection, he acknowledged as ill-judged on his part but excusable because of Osbert's cattiness. On 17 June, Sassoon had spotted Osbert leaving Hatchards bookshop, followed him along Piccadilly and on reaching the Circus drew alongside him, feeling 'an impulse to speak'. They shook hands. Sassoon said, 'I saw you and couldn't help feeling amiable.' Osbert replied with typical insouciance, 'I am always amiable.' They walked together down Waterloo Place and their three-year battle was over.

Reconciliation was the order of the day. Sassoon's lunch the following day, 2 October, was at the Savoy with Ivor Novello. Three days earlier he had been at the Prince of Wales Theatre for a performance of Novello's detective drama, *The Rat*. After the show he went backstage to meet its star, Isabel Jeans. Evidently Sassoon no longer 'despised everything' Novello stood for. This drama of apparent harmony between the two is not available for others to read. Sassoon destroyed the diary record for the last three months of 1924. Speculation and inference are the only guides, plus some later diary entries in 1925–26. It is likely that Sassoon was establishing a relationship, or had even started an affair with Novello, having been given every encouragement by 'dear Ivor', as his friends liked to speak of him. He was a consummate flirt, who collected lovers as he gathered lilacs. In contrast to his lyrics he was devoid of sentiment when bored with a friendship or a romance. Sassoon would not have lasted long.

If he was hurt by Novello's rejection, a substitute soon appeared who would soften the blow. One of Novello's friends was Constance Collier, actress, producer (of *The Rat*, among other plays) and patron of young talent. She was also a friend of Frankie Schuster and a regular visitor to the Hut at Bray. It was there in the summer of 1924 that she and Sassoon began their friendship after which they met in London, sometimes in her home. No doubt Sassoon and Miss Collier discussed Novello and she introduced Sassoon to her other friends and protégés. One young actor, Glen Byam Shaw, was especially regarded by her. She smoothed his way into productions and brought him to the notice of producers by whom he was taken up, including Ivor Novello. Inevitably his youthful looks, gentleness of voice and manner were attractive to Sassoon. Between October and the year's ending, he sent Glen two postcards; a third followed in January. Byam Shaw did not respond to the postcards, though he was amused by them.

Sassoon was not attending to the other writing he had promised himself – his 'prose masterpiece'. He was still excited by the possibility of using his own past as the subject. Such an approach had also been suggested to him by Edmund Gosse. His recommended form was a long autobiographical poem after the style of the Victorian Romantics. A more contemporary approach came from Sam Behrman, his New York friend, who suggested a novel culled from Sassoon's experience of the post-war world, especially the industrial unrest and the challenges to outdated social structures. By 1921 Sassoon had been full of ambition to write a major tome about homosexuality which might prove to be 'one of the stepping stones across the raging (or lethargic) river of intolerance which divides creatures of my temperament from a free and unsecretive existence among their fellow-men'. Even when declaring the idea to himself he knew it was a pipe dream and that such a book on such a theme would not be written for many years to come, perhaps not even in his lifetime. The law of the land precluded any idea of such a publication and the times were not ready for 'another Madame Bovary dealing with sexual inversion'. When he did write his prose 'masterpiece' homosexuality was completely excluded, as were his love affairs. It was E. M. Forster who made the vital connection between a prose work and Sassoon's diaries. The theme of 'then and now' and Forster's suggestion coalesced as Sassoon journeyed across England; but two years would separate the idea and a serious attempt at the task. That attempt would not be made while in Tufton Street.

Meanwhile Sassoon's relationship with Turner was in decline. The friendship and regard he felt for Delphine Turner remained unimpaired. Sassoon knew that she was a victim of her husband's infidelity. Then there were Turner's wild and verbose pronouncements, which over the months rose to excruciating levels of self-importance and fatuity. It was Sassoon's defence of Turner that had ruptured his friendship with Osbert Sitwell three years earlier. Doubts about the wisdom of that loyalty had disturbed Sassoon and already given rise to a desire for reconciliation with the Sitwells. Rarely now did Turner, on returning to Tufton Street of an evening, enter the ground-floor rooms but went straight upstairs, where he spoke a few words to Delphine before going to his own quarters on the top floor. Sassoon did not have to speak to him which was a relief, although when they did come face to face there was never any sign of antagonism. Even so, it was impossible to continue an arrangement where sympathetic contact had ended.

The last day of March brought cause for cheerfulness in the shape of a large wooden box containing 99 copies of his latest privately printed collection of poems, *Lingual Exercises*. The opening poem reflects Sassoon's mood:

> 'When I'm alone' – the words tripped off his tongue
>   As though to be alone were nothing strange.
> 'When I was young,' he said; when I was young …'
>
> I thought of age, and loneliness, and change.
> I thought how strange we grow when we're alone,

And how unlike the selves that meet, and talk,
And blow the candles out, and say good-night.
Alone ... The word is life endured and known.
It is the stillness where our spirits walk
And all but inmost faith is overthrown.

Forty years after its composition, Sassoon wrote: '"Alone" has been one of my most successful poems. I value it because it was the first of my post-war poems in which I discovered my mature mode of utterance (what I call my cello voice).'

His living conditions continued to frustrate him and a final break was inevitable. In July the stage was set for the denouement, in which the main part was played by Lady Ottoline Morrell. His diary entries have the hallmarks of a short story.

On July 4 I wrote 'I saw Turner yesterday at Tufton Street and we talked for half-an-hour, so pleasantly that my secret antagonism seemed rather grotesque.' On July 5 'Last night I read Turner's platonic dialogue on Art, in typescript. It contains an odious travesty of Ottoline, who is described as a sort of Jezebel, whereas I see her as an essentially simple soul under her superficial decoration of aesthetic and intellectual interests.'

On Monday I returned the dialogue with a note urging him to cut out a phrase about 'Lady Caraway's eagerly offered embraces' before he shows it to Ottoline. I added that I wouldn't advise him, as I'd 'no hope that he would avail himself of my advice'.

This evening he replies. 'I expect Ottoline to be intelligent enough to know that one cannot write fiction without embellishments, extensions, and ornamentations of one's original models. I did not attempt to make a portrait of her. She is merely the starting-point of a speculation.'

I have now written, telling him that he is deceiving himself; that he has used the material nearest to his hand; that the 'portrait' is offensively recognisable and that the Morrells will be hurt, and O.M.'s enemies delighted, if he prints it. I felt inclined to add that it will be 'the starting point' – not of a 'speculation' – but of his being permanently cut by the Morrells, whose hospitality has been such a help and enjoyment to him for nearly five years. I am only making this effort to save the feelings of Ottoline (and Delphine). I have lost all faith in Turner, as a writer. He seems to have become an imitator of Aldous Huxley's sophisticated aridities, without any of Huxley's educated clarity. Turner is a poet, imaginative and rather incoherent. This dialogue is neatly written but worthless. If he prints it he will accentuate my hostility to him.

Ottoline, who was unaware of Turner's treachery and full of concern for him and Delphine, sought to save their marriage. Unorthodox as ever, she brought together not the husband and wife but the wife and the mistress. Nothing came of these eccentric efforts. Undeterred, Ottoline gleaned from her talks with Turner, and later with Delphine, that the marriage could be rescued if the Turners had a car. How this conclusion was reached or how it would be efficacious is a mystery. She wrote to Sassoon, who put a cheque for £75 in an envelope, presented it to Delphine with a note promising another £50 later on, and made it clear that he was doing this for her alone. The Turners duly bought a small car. Sassoon was very critical of Turner as a driver for his lacking road sense! As for Turner, he was in a state of bliss: a new car, his marriage saved and his extra-marital activities totally unimpaired.

Sassoon was now desperate to escape from Tufton Street and he knew that if anyone could help it would be Ottoline. He told her his problem and stressed the need for urgency. It was clear to him that spending the months from November through to the following spring working on his poetry and taking initial steps towards a prose work would become impossible if he was forced to stay in Tufton Street. His hopes were raised at the end of August. Ottoline, it seemed, had solved the problem, securing rooms in Mecklenburgh Square in Bloomsbury. Sassoon inspected them and was well pleased. Then he asked about the rent and quickly changed his mind.

'With the intensest relief,' he wrote, 'I escaped from that poisoned house this morning.' His destination was first Highcliffe near Bournemouth, where Ruth and Henry Head gave him their usual warm welcome. So did the Hardys a few days later. Hardy seemed indestructible. He was 85, still writing poetry, and when Sassoon called was correcting the proofs of his latest collection. This visit was the shortest Sassoon ever paid to Max Gate – lunch, tea and then, with Thomas and Florence 'waving cheerily outside the gate, with Wessie in close and tonsiled attendance', Sassoon went to join Frankie Schuster and Adrian Boult for the Three Choirs Festival at Gloucester.

Among the many thoughts which occupied him on the eve of his birthday was the absence of any word from Glen Byam Shaw, the young actor he had met through Constance Collier almost a year ago. Sassoon and Constance were often together, Sassoon calling at her flat and she relying on him as an available and ready escort. News of Glen's acting endeavours formed a natural ingredient of their conversation. From his hotel in the West Country, he decided to send another postcard to Glen. It was a month later that Sassoon received an apologetic reply in which Glen suggested they meet. He also wrote: 'When are you going to give me some of your poems to read? I should love to do so and will promise not to leave them about.' Sassoon was quick to respond and arranged the meeting for the evening of 20 October at the Reform Club. Later at Tufton Street they browsed through Sassoon's collection of books and manuscripts and spoke fondly together of Constance and mutual acquaintances. 'A very successful evening,' Sassoon wrote. 'He seems nice and straight forward, full of charm and good sense.' When Glen left him Sassoon says that he was filled with a sense of peace. He had unburdened himself and wanted Glen to know how much he appreciated such sympathetic understanding.

Dear Glen
The clock has not yet struck one; and I am already writing you a letter! Perhaps that is because I wish you were still here – But it is also to say that I very much enjoyed an evening I'd been looking forward to – although some of the things we talked about were rather awful – weren't they? But you probably understood that it was a relief to me to talk about that subject with someone who could enlighten me, as you could. I hope you don't think me an awful 'mut' after all the things I told you about last winter. Even now I feel a faint horror that I could say, and listen to, such things about I.N. when I remember a year ago and its illusions! But in spite of the lost illusions I still feel that the best thing in life is loyalty to one's friends and this evening has left me with a feeling that I might be able to help *you* along a little. I've always felt you were a person I could trust. At least I *think* I've always felt it now, though one can't be certain!

Glen too wrote a letter expressing his delight and enjoyment of an evening which he 'would never forget'. It was all music to Sassoon, who dashed off another letter full of affection and promise: 'You have no idea how it makes me want to do things for you, and share with you all my solitary thoughts.' Immediately Sassoon took it upon himself to share some of his experiences of life from which, he hoped, Glen would benefit: 'And now I will tell you one of the "things" I have learnt; it is this; never to make excessive demands of people one is fond of; never to encroach on their freedom; to give all one can and to hope in return for their trust.'

These letters from the opening days of their friendship throw a light upon Sassoon's deep paternal impulses through which he sought to raise a relationship 'above mere sensualism'. It is impossible when reading his letters to Glen not to hear the accents of concern for the other person, a protective voice speaking out from its own experience of confusing choices, personal disillusion and vulnerability. It is clear that like Sassoon, Glen had been emotionally bruised by Ivor Novello. This shared experience drew them closer to each other. 'You must try not to feel bitter about "him". I don't, though he outraged and betrayed my decent feelings to an incredible degree.' And in the third letter of that first week of friendship, Sassoon referred again to the torturous experience Glen had suffered at the hands of Novello: 'You must let me try to restore your faith in the niceness of life. Life isn't like that really; you only struck a nightmare patch of it, where standards of decency don't exist and everything is a sham and an evasion of sincerity. Life is damned difficult when you face its fundamental facts. I never began to face them till 1914.'

Glen's reaction to such honest concern was reserved but genuinely thankful that this friendship now begun brought with it the possibility of healing. He also solved Sassoon's immediate problem by finding a flat for him at 23 Campden Hill Square. The flat, upon being inspected, was declared perfect. Its owner, a portrait painter called Harold Speed, appeared a bit of a bore but there was no call for Sassoon to spend time with him. At £150 a year it was everything he needed. There was room for a piano, a good kitchen and if Speed would agree to knocking down a partition wall, two modest rooms could be made into a commodious sitting room and study. In addition, and perhaps more importantly, the flat was only a three-minute walk from where Glen lived.

Leaving Tufton Street, when the moment came, was not without regret. It had been Sassoon's centre for five years, during which he had written the privately printed volumes of poetry. Sassoon caught the moment on the eve of departure in his poem 'Farewell to a Room':

> Room, while I stand outside you in the gloom,
> Your tranquil-toned interior, void of me,
> Seems part of my own self which I can see ...

Light, while I stand outside you in the night,
Shutting the door on what has housed so much,
Nor hand, nor eye, nor intellect could touch, –
Cell, to whose firelit walls I say farewell,
Could I condense five winters in one thought,
Then might I know my unknown self and tell
What our confederate silences have wrought.

Travelling from Westminster to Kensington, Sassoon committed himself to new 'confederate silences', a new friendship and a new and healthier lifestyle. He was out of bed by ten o'clock and ate a combined breakfast/lunch at eleven o'clock. Next came a session at the piano, followed by writing letters before taking a daily constitutional between two and five. The evenings remained much the same as at Tufton Street, being focused mainly on the Reform. His writing, however, remained nocturnal. 'The Power and the Glory', his first poem at Campden Hill Square, was written on 13 December, a week after he moved in. Not that the routine was inviolable. Glen would call of a morning and Theresa, of course, arrived to assure herself that 'dear Siggy' was well, safe and comfortable. Seeing him contented, so she was too, but preoccupied. Her brother, Sassoon's beloved Uncle Hamo, was dying slowly and painfully. The sadness of the moment was relieved by thoughts of Glen: 'The happiness he has brought me is more soothing than anything I've ever known. I am surprised by my own emotional tranquillity. Also I have felt lately a new sense of proportion as regards the trivial details of life. My life seems simpler in construction, and I realise how few are the details which are worth bothering about. This is an internal harmony which I have been striving for since 1918. Or is it the complacency of middle age?'

Despite the cold winter days prior to Christmas, Sassoon and Glen set out for Weymouth and Dorchester. This new companion must be introduced to Hardy. On the evening of their arrival at Weymouth Sassoon read in the paper that Hamo had died. The many visits to Max Gate were always 'sunshine days'; now that circle of happiness was broken. Hardy's friendship with Uncle Hamo and Edmund Gosse stretched back over the decades and the three of them had been solicitous for Sassoon. With a black suit borrowed from Philip Morrell, Sassoon went to Christ Church, Oxford. He placed Hardy's wreath against the trestles beneath the coffin, then sat at the back of the cathedral and thought of that gentle uncle and guardian whose patience he had so sorely tried.

Uncle Hamo had counselled his nephew some years before: 'Do a good day's work; don't be reclusive; go to bed in good time and get up early.' Sassoon could not claim to have followed this rule of life. The opening line of his 1926 diary carries a faint echo of a call to seriousness. He pledged himself to proper application and less gadding about. 'Travel broadens the mind but solitude purifies it,' he wrote, as he refused an invitation from Gerald Berners to spend the spring at his apartment in the Via Varese in Rome. Friends must not distract him from his work and he must learn not to be upset by their attitudes and behaviour. Osbert Sitwell was a case in point. Sassoon regretted the rift and determined to be more friendly and accommodating. He was not going to be unsettled by Turner any more. He missed Blunden, who had another year left in Japan. As for Robert Graves, he was about to sail to Cairo to teach English in the university. It was only a short-term contract but it would help the finances and Nancy would regain her strength and vitality in the hot climate. Graves was still a dilemma to Sassoon and their relationship, which oscillated between friendly and fractious, was an irritation he could well do without. Nancy, he acknowledged, had been much more welcoming during the last year, without any of her feminism having abated. She particularly condemned Turner, citing him as a prime example of male cruelty and selfishness in his treatment of Delphine. Sassoon had to agree. However, he objected to Nancy and Graves sniggering at Ottoline. Their sojourn in Egypt, during which they would have the company of Graves's new friend from America, Laura Riding, meant that the danger of them intruding on Sassoon's solitude was removed.

Sassoon loathed domestic disturbance. It seemed to pervade everywhere – the Blundens, the Turners, the Graveses, it was even poisoning Weirleigh. Michael's family were living off, as well as living with his mother. Sassoon resented this and blamed his brother's indulgence towards his wife, Violet, and her petty-spirited attitude towards Theresa and Mrs Fenner the housekeeper. Sassoon could not visit while that situation existed. He ventured there only when he knew Michael and his family were away or, if unobserved, he could slip into the studio, where Theresa spent most of the day. Each visit she seemed to age; she was suffering bouts of eczema, attributable, Sassoon believed, to the pressures at Weirleigh. The death of Uncle Hamo raised the spectre of his mother's demise: 'I realised what her death would mean to me and how much she has suffered and endured.'

The situation resolved itself when Michael and Violet moved to a new house not a great distance from Weirleigh, but enough to allow Siegfried a greater freedom of access and relieve some of the causes of Theresa's discomfort. But Sassoon needed Weirleigh for reasons other than those of a solicitous son – he needed the Weald and his home so he could tap the vein of remembrance. For memories to be transposed Sassoon needed the physical sensation of the house and countryside where he had walked, bicycled, played cricket, ridden to hounds and watched the Weald change its colour but not its contours. There was no value in grasping at intermittent moments, he needed to return to embrace and possess it. After each visit Sassoon carried manuscripts, music and items of juvenilia back to London.

Sassoon had only one serious doubt during this time: 'Glen is a charming relaxation, but I dread expecting too much of him, knowing too well how soon he might drift away from me and take me for granted.' But Glen was of a different calibre from his other young men. The comparison Sassoon had in mind was probably Gabriel Atkin. He noted in his diary upon moving into Campden Hill Square: 'My bosom's best friend is only a hundred yards away.' Gabriel, his *ex*-bosom friend, was also very close, living in Peel Street, but unaware of Sassoon's proximity. They had last seen each other in October 1924, in Maida Vale, in the flat of a mutual friend. At the time Sassoon was becoming embroiled with Ivor Novello and made no effort to contact him but through an intermediary he sent sums of money which he knew Gabriel would dissipate at the Café Royal, getting drunk, creating an affray and being evicted by the house detectives. He was relying more and more on drugs, a habit he had started as a student in Newcastle. Sassoon had heard a rumour that Gabriel was about to move to France, but he cared little. The sporadic financial assistance continued for a time but Sassoon was reconciled to the fact that Gabriel was 'a hopeless case'.

The quietness of Campden Hill Square during the spring of 1926 gave Sassoon the opportunity to bring together a selection from his two privately printed volumes: *Recreations* and *Lingual Exercises*. The recipients of the private and limited edition had shown them to friends and acquaintances and Heinemann, his publisher, heard very positive reactions, including glowing remarks from the critic Desmond MacCarthy. Sassoon was persuaded to publish this collection of 32 poems under the title *Satirical Verses*. On 28 April *The Times* carried an advertisement and the volume went on sale the following day. It was Sassoon's first publication available to the public in six years. There was little enough in it to remind people of the fierce and protesting war poet.

There were poems, however, of sardonic social observation and political arrows aimed at the snobbish, offensive attitude adopted by the upper class towards the working class. The book reached the shops on 29 April. On 3 May the General Strike began.

Heinemann had organised what Sassoon described to Glen as a 'deluge of publicity'. It was all in vain with everybody's mind on the strike. Glen was appearing in a play in Leeds, a city where there was serious rioting. Sassoon worried about that and the horror of violence pouring out on to the street. 'As you know,' he told the stranded Glen, 'I have the strongest objection to people settling disputes by violent methods.' He also told him that the strike had 'killed the book stone-dead'. Sassoon could see no justification for this crisis and regarded it as more of a general muddle than a general strike. 'My sympathies are all with the workers,' he declared, but he did not believe much would change. The upper classes had it coming to them, of that he had no doubt, and he took a momentary delight in the thought of Sir Philip Sassoon, his cousin, watching his house in Park Lane engulfed in flames. The delight petered out when the possibility suggested itself that the revolutionaries might march from there to Pall Mall and set fire to the Reform.

He was shocked when on 8 May Osbert told him that he had just seen '12 tanks parading down King's Road'. Osbert also told Sassoon that he intended to try to influence Downing Street into settling this unnecessary civil disruption. He intended using his kinship with Lord and Lady Wimborne to bring the factions together for discreet talks. Lord Reading was to be the intermediary between the Wimbornes and the government and Osbert would persuade the railwaymen's leader and Labour MP, J. H. Thomas, to broker the discussions with the TUC. Sassoon, who was present at some of the subsequent meetings arranged by Osbert, became both depressed and outraged at the thought of the miners being beaten by the owners. Sometimes that outrage spilt over and Osbert would have to admonish him for being unhelpful. In an echo of Dr Rivers, Osbert told Sassoon: 'You must try not to think in terms of your emotions but in terms of your intellect.' Sassoon regarded this as 'a wise and helpful saying. I must not make an exhibition of myself' – all of this underlined in his diary.

Osbert's advice may well have been prompted by Sassoon's histrionics when in the house of the Editor of the *Daily Express*, Beverley Baxter. In his memoir, *Strange Street*, Baxter recalls arriving home in the small hours of the morning:

There are two men in the shadow, and when I insert the key they come to my side. It is a relief to find they are two poets, Osbert Sitwell and that gallant eccentric Siegfried Sassoon. They come to my drawing room and explain that they want to end the general strike. I suggest that the difficulties are great because of the temper of the Trades Unions. 'That's right,' said Sassoon, striding up and down brandishing his fists at the ceiling. 'Shoot them down! You're like all the rest.' It was a bad scene with Sitwell almost unnaturally calm and Sassoon riding some tempest of the soul that would not give him peace. The first grisly grey of dawn was breaking over the Thames when they left. Sassoon did not even say goodbye.

Sassoon's record of the encounter does not include the declaiming prophet element and is very uncomplimentary about Baxter. He recognised this bald, heavy-cheeked young man in a golfing suit as someone who wanted to smash the unions. There seemed no hope of harmony and 'In a few days both sides will be beyond the zone of conciliatory meetings.' Within three days of striking that pessimistic note the strike was settled. Sassoon was walking in Kensington Gardens on the afternoon of 12 May when he heard the bells begin to ring a joyous peal, which he recognised as the signal marking the end of the strike. It was like that morning eight years before when he walked in the Oxfordshire countryside and heard the bells ring out the end of the war. As he walked towards the Albert Memorial he decided that it would not be inappropriate to quote 'Everyone suddenly burst out singing'. But, unlike in 1918, not everyone in 1926 was singing the same song.

Glen returned to London from Leeds. Sassoon had not seen him since March. It had been even longer since he had seen Robert Graves, who in the middle of June returned from his time in Cairo with Nancy, their children and his American friend, Laura Riding. Graves had found the members of the English faculty difficult (a feeling reciprocated!). It had been well worth enduring. Nancy had been relieved of the daily care of the children; a first-rate doctor had changed her treatment and Graves had earned a good salary. He was in high spirits when he wrote to Sassoon in August, not from his house in Islip, Oxfordshire, but from rented accommodation in Ladbroke Grove, a stone's throw from Sassoon's flat. He and Laura Riding were living at this address, while Nancy and the children were at the house outside Oxford. Graves said in his letter that it was Nancy who had 'asked Laura and me to leave her the job of running the house all by herself: and come up to Town to write seriously'. It all seemed somewhat of a jumble to Sassoon, who read this letter together with a second letter dated 18 September (Sassoon had spent July to 11 September in Italy and France with the Morrells, hence the delay in receiving the correspondence). The second letter said that Robert and Laura were 'going off together to Austria for a bit: unconventional but necessary and Nancy's idea'. Sassoon was totally confused and confided to his diary, 'From this I can only assume that R and L are living together, and that Nancy wants a quiet life at all costs. Probably they are behaving quite sensibly, but I can't help wondering how it will all end.'

Before Sassoon could reply another letter arrived, this time from Vienna, reaffirming how marvellous everything was. Responding with the minimum of enthusiasm, Sassoon told Graves that if those involved with the arrangements were happy then nothing else mattered. The desultory tone of the letter reflected Sassoon's flagging interest in Graves. How he missed dear little Blunden, whom he now regarded as his only hope among his old friends. 'When will he be back from Japan – next year sometime, I think?' In the meantime there was Glen, and his friendship with the Sitwells was restored. Weirleigh was also accessible now that Michael had moved out. Indeed the relationship between the brothers improved somewhat, but not between Sassoon and his sister-in-law.

On 20 September, a fine and warm Saturday with the temperature reaching 80 degrees, Sassoon set off for Weirleigh. Theresa's recovery of vitality continued, much to the satisfaction of her son. Joining them for tea were two ladies from Sassoon's childhood, May Marchant and her sister Bessie Wormald, whom he describes as 'two people from my remote past – nice simple jolly ladies of the old-fashioned country gentlefolk type'. Like Weirleigh, these two old friends of Theresa were rich in association for him. It and they belonged to his parochial pre-war self. There was a dangerous and subtle appeal which, were he to respond too readily and fully, would overwhelm him and stifle his creative instincts. These journeys to Weirleigh underlined for him the distance between 'then and now'. Travelling to Matfield he expected that the scenes of childhood would have been transformed into something nearer his present experience but on arrival he found that nothing had changed and that he was coming back as a stranger; what he describes as his Enoch Arden complex. The village, the garden, the house, mother, May and Bessie Marchant, New Beacon School, the country around, all evoked memories, each with deep-rooted associations but all frozen in time: 'I go down to Weirleigh and unlock certain dusty cupboards in my mind, and take out the faded manuscripts which belong to mental states which I have outlived and outgrown.' And again, 'I am a visitor from abroad, looking in at windows, and musing on myself as I was in bygone years. I go there alone, and I come away alone. I go into mother's studio and look at the pictures she painted 30 years ago. But there are no new pictures, and never will be.'

Sassoon began writing *Memoirs of a Fox-Hunting Man* in September 1926. He was clear as to its theme and style; the story of a boy growing up, pre-1914, in an upper-class home in Kent. Orphaned, he would be indulged by his Aunt Evelyn, who had a penchant for the eccentric as well as the conventional. Peopled by servants, as Sassoon's circle was in those days, and placed in an idyllic rural setting, the tale would be a chronicle of England at that time, as observed by a young boy crossing the boundary from childhood into youth and adulthood, and how that world impinged upon him. It would be a personal view and by intention a local and limited one, what Sassoon describes as 'keeping within the frame'. There would be no regard paid to the social, political and industrial upheavals of the 1890s or those of the opening decade of the new century. There would be a passing nod to the Boer War and hints that Britain had an Empire, but this would be less important than England having a cricket team. It was about 'remembering and being glad'.

Plainly and anecdotally told, the narration would be in the first person singular and spoken by a young man named, symbolically, George Sherston – George being the archetypal first name for an Englishman, Sherston from a small village on the southern boundaries of the Cotswolds, which would link the character to fox-hunting and point-to-pointing. This was the territory over which Sassoon had often ridden with Norman Loder. But now there was a more recent connection which prompted Sassoon's choice of surname for his alter ego. Sherston Magna was, and remains a rural idyll on the north Wiltshire plain. It was also the land of the Byams, whose name remains on Byam Farm and Byam Cottage: on a white marble memorial in the parish church and on the family tomb alongside the exterior south wall. Their descendant Glen Byam Shaw was the author's muse.

To enable him to use characters from real life without embarrassing either them or himself, Sassoon, as already shown, adopted the device of the alias; Mr Moon became Mr Star, while the solicitor Mr Lousada became Mr Pennett and Tom Richardson became Tom Dixon. Sassoon raided his journals and letters for the main narrative, sometimes altering dates and other small details. *Memoirs of a Fox-Hunting Man* would be a thinly disguised autobiography and would end with the outbreak of the war to which George Sherston would go to face 'the ugly facts of night' in a foreign land, leaving for ever his idyllic life.

Glen Byam Shaw listened to the planned narrative and early extracts. His reaction was enthusiastic. 'G. is going to be an indispensable aid to me in the matter,' recorded Sassoon, who then went on to offer this rather back-handed compliment: 'It is the sort of stuff which he can criticise. If he finds it interesting and amusing I shall know it is all right.' Certainly his sails caught the wind and within a week he had written over 6,000 words. His diary records the number of words written as increasing by a thousand a day. Given that Sassoon wrote in a slow and deliberate way, editing as he went along, the output not only was fast but speaks of a writer completely engaged with his subject. Between 11 p.m. and 4 a.m. he composed, condensed and eliminated. Since 1906 he had kept a diary; by 1926 this had honed his ability to write in that subjective voice essential to convey emotional retrospection. '*Memoirs of a Fox-Hunting Man* will always be your book,' he told Glen. Even with the words and ideas running freely, Sassoon was assailed by doubts about 'building a viable edifice out of these little memories of my early days of sport and simplicity'. Slaying such fears was the singular contribution of Glen who, listening to each new addition, whether visiting the flat or in his dressing-room in the theatre, told Sassoon that the book was going to be an enormous success.

The series of reports to Glen read somewhat like a serialisation: 'You will be glad to hear that Aunt Evelyn and I have got to the Flower Show. I am now 17 and playing in the cricket match: the clock has just struck 12 – but the match has not begun yet. Aunt E has been judging the vegetables in a large hot tent. The total now is 17,000.' By November Sassoon was down in Weirleigh, recovering more diaries and using the 'luxury of loneliness' to mine each one for narrative material. By mid-November it became obvious that there was sufficient material for a sequel. He thought the title of the first volume would perhaps restrict, if not preclude, such a venture. True, the greater part of the book would be about fox-hunting, with supporting themes such as cricket and country pursuits, but the latter part would be about the war. He decided to drop the original title and replace it with the more prosaic *A Tale That Is Told*. Then, and inexplicably, Sassoon suddenly developed writer's block. The ever-faithful Edmund Gosse, reading the incomplete manuscript in the New Year, thought it would become a prose work of significance. In previous years this level of commendation coming from a writer whose own memoir of childhood, *Father and Son*, had been accorded classic status would have sent Sassoon back to his work with a new sense of purpose. Blocked and cast down, Sassoon was convinced that his masterpiece would never be completed, though.

His efforts to produce prose had stifled his output of new verse. Nothing had been composed since April, nine months previously. That he survived this wilderness was due to an oasis of friendship. Blunden's letters from Japan were, he wrote, 'exquisitely penned intimacies – comprehensible to nobody except him and me'. The support of Osbert, Sacheverell and Edith moved Sassoon to declare Edith 'a magnificent woman' and afford Osbert the ultimate accolade in placing his photograph alongside that of Blunden on his mantelpiece. He owned himself 'fortunate to have such wonderful friends'. As for Glen, Sassoon took comfort in this moment of seeming failure to reflect on his success in encouraging his friend into a serious commitment to the stage. Visiting Weirleigh and the Weald he was further depressed by the thought of them as 'the haunts of an empty-minded young man, ignorant of the world, and himself, as emotionally retarded by sexual inexperience and futile athleticism – a discontented young man'.

Into this tortuous syndrome came unheralded a poem:

Nativity

A flower has opened in my heart...
What flower is this, what flower of spring,
What simple, secret thing?

It is the peace that shines apart,
The peace of daybreak skies that bring
Clear song and wild swift wing.

Heart's miracle of inward light,
What powers unknown your seed have sown
And your perfection freed? ...
O flower within me wondrous white,
I know you only as my need
And my unsealèd sight.

'I was a poet when I wrote it – such poems are not written, they write themselves. The process is emotional – intellect isn't used at all.' Such a moment did not raise the gloom under which Sassoon laboured but it did affirm that his vocation had not died. It was a consoling visitation.

Circumstances mundane as well as mystical also made their impact on Sassoon's life, the first of these coming in the form of an obituary notice:

BEER. On 24 April, 1927, at Tunbridge Wells, Rachel, widow of F. A. Beer and daughter of Sassoon David Sassoon of Ashley Park, Walton-on-Thames.

Aunt Rachel, who had held in thrall the young Siegfried as she glided through her magnificent house in Mayfair, who had so stoutly aided the cause of Dreyfus and defied the religious intolerance of her mother, had spent a quarter of a century mentally deranged. She had loved her brother Alfred and been supportive of Theresa and the boys. The estate she left was considerable, being in excess of £315,000, of which her nephew Siegfried, and one suspects her favourite, inherited £50,000. Rather piously he wrote that 'Auntie Rachel's Bradburys' would not induce him to change his way of life: 'I distrust this money. I shall give a lot of the income from it to my mother.' Others would also benefit. The Sitwells were invited to a Continental holiday paid for by Sassoon in September, after he and Glen had spent time on their own in Bayreuth.

'I am 40 years old – remarkably young looking – devoid of literary ambitions, serenely fond of Glen in a way which makes me feel no need for anyone else.' Sassoon was putting on a brave face, knowing that in October Glen would leave for America on a tour that would last a year. He had every intention, therefore, of enjoying warm summer days with him. It was a shock of seismic dimensions when on 25 May Glen wrote to warn him that his contract at the Oxford Playhouse might mean his having to cry off from the holiday, confirming this on 3 June. 'The day disintegrated. Our relationship will be in jeopardy if he fails,' wrote Sassoon. Immediately he wrote to Glen, refusing an invitation to Oxford: 'I would rather not see you, as I should at once begin to make a fuss, which I don't want to do, considering how nicely we have always got on.' Caught in a series of mishaps – he had dislocated his shoulder a few weeks previously, been involved in a nasty car accident and now this Glen upset – his mood was prickly.

Dinner-parties were the last thing on his mind when Osbert invited him to dine at 2 Carlyle Square, Chelsea, to meet four Americans, together with Francis Birrell, Steven Runciman and Mrs Belloc Lowndes. As the table talk grew more and more raucous, Sassoon regretted having said yes, but Osbert was so insistent. The evening marginally improved when the after-dinner guests arrived, including Sacheverell Sitwell, his wife Georgiana, William Walton, Constant Lambert and the Hon. Stephen Tennant, whom Sassoon had not met before and to whom he was not introduced. The whole evening had been a sheer waste of time.

If only he could recover the flow of writing, but the distractions were too many. Then there was his continuing irritation with Glen, who was either impervious to or unaware of the disappointment he had caused:

> 13 June. Letter from Glen saying nothing about Bayreuth – Queer he doesn't realise how much it means to me. He wants me to have supper with him tomorrow but I shall come back here after the Matinée.

Sassoon was working himself up into a frenzy over the matter, which began to affect his sleep; he regretted not having had a set-to with Glen and cleared the air. The Sitwells were very attentive to Sassoon. Sacheverell and Georgiana invited him to the christening of their son Reresby at Lambeth Palace and also to dinner at their home in Tite Street, Chelsea. Sacheverell told him that Stephen Tennant would be there and was, Sassoon records, 'very anxious to make my acquaintance'. At the dinner Sassoon began to play up a bit in excitable talk, mainly he admits, 'for the benefit of S. Tennant, who was obviously a very good audience.' When they all moved on to a party in Berkeley Square, Sassoon watched this epicene creature, consumptively frail with 'affected manners and an ultra-refined voice. But he has a very beautiful face, and is witty and intelligent and well-bred. Of his attractive charm there is no doubt at all.' During the following week, Osbert mentioned Stephen Tennant several times and a dinner planned at Carlyle Square – 'Would you like to come too, Siegfried?'

On the evening of the dinner, as Sassoon arrived at the front door, Stephen Tennant was leaving. He was, he told his host, feeling unwell.

13

STEPHEN

1927–8

'Friendships are like countries on a map,' Sassoon mused in 1927, and toyed with the idea of making a map of his own. Among the most prominent features would be the Land of Elders, featuring a little city called Gosse and a mountain called Hardy. The map would also contain a place called Sitwell Country. Their inclusion in this topographical fancy was evidence of their complete rehabilitation in Sassoon's affection. He was looking forward to their company in Germany at the beginning of September. In Glen's absence Frankie Schuster would be his only companion on the drive to Bayreuth. His annoyance with Glen was hardly fair, seeing that Glen was contractually bound to the O'Fagan Company and was only following Sassoon's advice to take acting seriously; but Sassoon did not like his plans being disrupted. Meanwhile he was meeting some friends of Stephen Tennant. One was Cecil Beaton, whom Sassoon met on 8 July in a flat in Sussex Gardens and dismissed as a 'clever, very affected, effeminate, *arriviste*'. On the same afternoon, at Edith Sitwell's flat in Bayswater, he was introduced to the aesthete Harold Acton, 'a minor poet, who bored me'. On first meeting Glen, and subsequently, he had placed him in a different category from these superficial and self-indulgent people; but perhaps he was not. Sassoon had gone to the expense of buying a Chrysler because he thought the Morris-Oxford which had replaced the battered Gwynne 8 would be too small for three to travel in comfort. All this effort appeared in vain and he feared that Glen would gradually ease his way out of his life. Then the clouds lifted and the doubts dispelled when Glen told Sassoon that he would be able to join him for the first two weeks of the holiday after all.

Sassoon had planned that the route to Germany would include a visit to the battlefields around the Salient at Ypres and its memorial, the New Menin Gate. Arriving there on 25 July, he was filled with anger and disgust: 'The whole wall covered with minute names. The large white, new handsome Gate made me feel bitter about the War. And Ypres – a sightseer's centre! Wrote some lines about the Gate.'

On Passing the New Menin Gate

Who will remember, passing through this Gate
The unheroic Dead who fed the guns?
Who shall absolve the foulness of their fate, –
Those doomed, conscripted, unvictorious ones?
Crudely renewed, the Salient holds its own.
Paid are its dim defenders by this pomp;
Paid with a pile of peace-complacent stone,
The armies who endured that sullen swamp.

Here was the world's worst wound. And here with pride
'Their name liveth for ever,' the Gateway claims.
Was ever an immolation so belied
As these intolerably nameless names?
Well might the Dead who struggled in the slime
Rise and deride this sepulchre of crime.

Listening to Sassoon reading the poem in a recording made 30 years after that visit is to hear anger, especially in the final line. He pauses, takes a breath before 'rise and deride', pauses again after 'this', before letting the whole force of righteous indignation crash on to 'sepulchre of crime'. It is as though with that final breath he might blow the Gate to smithereens. What riled him was 'the nameless names'. For Sassoon the idea that numbers could somehow touch the heart and tragedy of war was an odious heresy. For him, the truth lay in the snatching away of the single life. His anger and grief emanated from the individual loss. He did not turn into Mad Jack when hundreds were being killed around him. The eruption came when the person he loved, the vulnerable, sensitive David Thomas, was taken from him. Printed indelibly upon his memory was the scene when, to the sound of guns and the rain, he watched the body wrapped in a mud-splattered sheet being lowered into the earth, and unforgettably confessed, 'I knew death then.' He *saw* death every day at the Front, but it took the death of Thomas for him to *know* death. The poignancy of these memories intruded on his enjoyment of Glen's company, which was already shortened. Less than three weeks after they had set out, Glen had to return to England.

It was the last day of September before the two men saw each other again – in the flat at Campden Hill Square, on the eve of Glen's departure for America. Both were tense and emotional. Since they met a year previously Glen had brought a degree of stability to Sassoon's life which enabled him to begin his prose work and revise his poetry. Glen, too, found comfort in Sassoon's willingness to listen to, and empathise with his emotional turmoil and lack of confidence. Each met the other's need and as a result their friendship thrived. When Glen left the flat, Sassoon consoled himself with the thought that he had fulfilled the role of protector to a young man who was without guile – unlike Gabriel and Philipp. It was on the following morning, in the privacy of his flat, that the impact of this separation hit Sassoon. He broke down and cried out: 'Don't take him from me.'

The *Memoirs* had remained untouched for 10 months. Progress was laboured with just 600 words written in 10 days but he believed that the writing block would yield in the face of determination and patience. Peace and quiet were also needed, but proved elusive. Blunden had returned from Japan while Sassoon was on the Continent and by October they were meeting for lunch and talk, as in former days. Blunden was going through a wretched time in his domestic life. Three years of separation were hardly conducive to a strong marriage, neither was the lack of fidelity. He had found comfort in Aki Hayashi, a Japanese with impeccable English to whom he became devoted and brought back to England. Mary's allowance from Blunden was generous, considering the resources available, and had given her scope for adventures with her lover, Cyril Keeble. Blunden had not looked forward to his return with the cloud of domestic disagreement hanging over everything. The correspondence between him and Mary over the three years declined into frosty formalities. Writing to Sassoon earlier in the year he warned: 'It is still uncertain what is to happen. I am inclined in any event to live apart. Clare, my daughter, is I think already of Mary's persuasion, and couldn't be trained by me, but I shall want the younger one, John.' After his arrival in England, he first found a flat for Aki Hayashi and then was reunited with his family. Everything changed from despair to hope, as Blunden told

Sassoon: 'Since I last wrote, my troubles have begun to dissolve and my spirits are less tedious. I have seen Mary, her present state and strong affection have persuaded me to resume our life together.'

This reconciliation proved temporary and mutual friends, such as Ottoline Morrell, were concerned and offered help. As in most disputes, people took sides; Sassoon did not, neither was he prepared to interfere, as he wrote to Edmund:

> I have seen too much of this discussing of other people's affairs by people who have too much time on their hands, and I know how pernicious it can become, even when (as in O.M.'s case) the original intention is a friendly anxiety to be helpful. So when O.M. wrote and urged me to advise you to persuade Miss H. to return to Japan, I was at once aware that my flawless friendship [with E.B.] was being threatened. I should like you to show this letter to Mary, so that she can understand that I may be quite open about it all.

Whether or not Blunden expected greater support than this is not known but Sassoon was convinced that such matters should be resolved by candour, rather than plotting and being partisan; while in Japan, Blunden had commenced a volume of memories, *Undertones of War*, and this work continued alongside a mountain of other projects which were needed to pay the bills. Sassoon was generous with his financial help and Blunden gave his thoughts on *Memoirs of a Fox-Hunting Man*. It was not long before they were back in the routine they had established before Blunden left for Japan. Robert Graves was also a caller at Campden Hill Square. He was as busy as Blunden, particularly as a commentator on the literary scene – writing articles and lecturing. With Laura Riding he had written *A Survey of Modernist Poetry*, which contained complimentary references to Sassoon. By the time they met, on 14 October, Graves had completed a biography of T. E. Lawrence for Jonathan Cape. He had written to Sassoon in June asking for editorial help with that project, as well as any thoughts and insights. The industry of Blunden and Graves stood in contrast to Sassoon's moribund efforts with his *Memoirs*, parts of which he read to Graves and Laura. There were reasons other than writer's block contributing to the lack of progress, as Sassoon confided to his diary: 'My emotional adventures have unsettled me altogether as a writer of a 1,000-words-a-night of carefully considered prose.' On 10 October an invitation arrived from Stephen Tennant to a weekend in his country house, Wilsford near Salisbury. 'The weekend at Wilsford will be deliriously amusing,' Osbert assured him. He and his siblings were invited, together with Stephen's circle of friends. Sassoon was not certain about his readiness for this world of bright young people. Writing to Glen in New York he said: 'Have just received an invitation from Stephen Tennant, to stay with him next weekend. Will send you an hour-to-hour account. Don't be surprised if gold-dust falls out of my eyelashes!'

Wilsford stood on a rise and commanded wide and distant views of the Wiltshire countryside. The manor was built for Stephen's parents, Eddie Tennant, Lord Glenconner, and his wife Pamela. Eddie's sister Margot was married to the former Prime Minister, Herbert Asquith. Pamela Wyndham was one of three sisters who were portrayed as the Three Graces in a portrait by John Singer Sargent. She had grown up in a house called Clouds, while Eddie's childhood home was Glen, near Peebles in the Scottish Borders. Their marriage was somewhat unconventional. For many years Pamela had been 'attached' to Sir Edward Grey, later Lord Grey of Fallodon and Foreign Secretary in Asquith's government. Eddie was quite happy with this *ménage à trois*, and when in 1920 he died suddenly, Pamela and Grey married and spent their time between Fallodon in Northumberland, London and Wilsford.

They were not at Wilsford when Sassoon arrived for the weekend. Having lost his way, he made a late entry and was shown into a spacious ground-floor bedroom, used by Lady Grey when in residence. Osbert, Sacheverell and his wife were the only members of the house party he knew well, and William Walton. He had met Cecil Beaton but not the others, who included Rex Whistler and the two Miss Jungmanns, whom their friends called Zita and Baby. Osbert was quite at home, having been a close friend of Stephen's eldest brother Bim, who had been killed in the war. He was also on good terms with Cecil, Rex and the Jungmann girls, they being his admirers and he their inspiration for outraging 'stuffy social conventions'.

At dinner Stephen arranged a seating-plan which ensured that Sassoon was next to him. Sassoon felt like a haggard wreck compared with these young people who were half his age. As some defence mechanism, he began to talk and dominate the table in an effort to dispel any idea that he was a 'tired and middle-aged author'. Stephen, he noticed, seemed to hang on to his words. After dinner came charades. Sassoon took no part but watched the young things robed in sheets pretending to be nuns, then the lights were turned off and the costumes were changed to pyjamas. Up came the lights and on came the music – 'It was very amusing, and they were all painted up to the eyes, but I didn't quite like it.' Not that he let the discomfort show in any way and he was anxious to appear appreciative when Stephen took over the floor for an exotic dance routine. It had been an odd evening and, instead of going straight to bed, Sassoon climbed out through his bedroom window, strolled around the garden and watched the lights go out in the bedrooms. It seemed a lovely place after London.

Sunday was fine and warm and the light was perfect for filming. Cecil Beaton and Stephen had written a playlet for which the party dressed as shepherds. In the afternoon and still in their fancy dress, there was a jaunt in Sassoon's car across the county to the home of Lytton Strachey. An additional guest arrived for dinner, Miss Edith Olivier. She was a contemporary of Lady Grey, 10 years older than Sassoon and 30 years senior to the bright young things, but they all adored her, especially Stephen, Cecil and Rex. The daughter of the Rector of Wilton, near Salisbury, and a graduate of St Hilda's, Oxford, Edith had survived the restrictive upbringing her father had imposed upon her. Like other women before her, she flourished in many directions once the domineering hand of the Victorian paterfamilias was removed. She was friendly with the family of the Earl of Pembroke and lived in the Daye House on their estate at Wilton. Sassoon took to her immediately and she to him.

With the visit drawing to its close, Sassoon was aware that he was being drawn into a situation which was as dangerous as it was desirable. He and Stephen went for a late drive through the lanes around Wilsford – it was, Sassoon recalls, '6.40 a.m. when we returned'. Six hours later they travelled back together to London.

Sassoon had promised Glen an hour-by-hour account of the Wilsford weekend, but he found it difficult to honour his promise fully without betraying his feelings of joy and elation in this new friendship: 'I am torn by my sense of what Glen will think of me if he knew.' When on the following Tuesday he called on Osbert, he tried to avoid any reference to Wilsford but Osbert had been to luncheon with Stephen that day and was full of gossip, which meant the subject was unavoidable. He wanted to share his thoughts with Osbert and explain to him how close he had become to Stephen but he resisted the temptation, not being confident that Osbert was to be trusted. He also suspected that Osbert had his own plans where Stephen was concerned. Next day Stephen called and left a note, hoping Sassoon had recovered from the weekend and proposing they have tea together at the flat the following day. Looking at Glen's photo, Sassoon acknowledged his thankfulness that his long-term lover was in New York: 'Such is human nature! This doesn't mean that I don't love Glen just as much as I did four days ago. It really means I am suffering from Stephenitis.' For the next three months they were inseparable. Sassoon, however, knew that discretion was required. It had come as a shock to Sassoon when Ottoline sent a card, the message on which ended: 'I hear you looked very well as a shepherd on Sunday.' Sassoon guessed that Lytton Strachey had been gossiping. Soon enough their friendship would be an open secret. Stephen saw that the society gossips would fall on them 'like a pack of wolves'. Contrary to the philosophy of the bright young things, he agreed with Sassoon that discretion was a wiser policy than outrage. Neither Edith Olivier, whom Sassoon met for lunch on 25 November, nor Blunden, who came to the flat a week later, mentioned anything untoward about the friendship. Sassoon was pleased that Stephen and Edmund seemed to get on well as they enjoyed tea and toast – 'It was all Charles Lamb-like in my cosy interior as I gazed on my two friends.'

When the end of the year came, Sassoon had written 14,000 words of prose. Unfortunately, they did not mention his alter ego George Sherston but only his new love. The obsession with Stephen had overshadowed the project and Sassoon heard warning notes. Opening his diary for the New Year he resolved to get to grips with *Memoirs of a Fox-Hunting Man*. Stephen must be told that the work took priority over everything else: 'My feelings about S. have changed lately owing to the conflict between my desire to go on with my book and his inability to keep away from me. This has caused me to wake out of my entrancement and to see him with the more critical eye of commonsense. He symbolises all that I should ordinarily regard as idle and pleasure-loving and self-indulgent. Yet he does it all with such grace, and I have realised more and more that he is essentially childish, in spite of his veneer of sophistication.' Not for the first time, Sassoon blamed others for his own lack of resolve.

He was vexed when on 11 January 1928 Stephen arrived just as his writing was flowing again. Stephen had read the first part of Sherston and he wanted Sassoon to know that 'he adored the book and he was jealous of it'. He was back at the flat the following day at noon, before Sassoon had got up – 'I came to tell you about darling Mr Hardy – he's dead.' The news was not unexpected; the newspapers had already carried reports that he was gravely ill. Sassoon was deeply shaken nonetheless and saddened by the thought that only Edmund Gosse was left of his old mentors. He arranged to spend the afternoon with him at the Reform and they talked of Uncle Hamo and Hardy. Sassoon went down to Wilsford with Stephen for the weekend. On Saturday and Sunday he drove over to Max Gate to comfort Florence Hardy: 'I said, "Well Florence," and she replied, "There's nothing to say, is there?" The sand in the hour-glass had run out and the Wizard had departed.' Outside Max Gate was a crowd of reporters and photographers, much to Florence's distress and Sassoon's annoyance. Every paper was full of Hardy and the service at Westminster Abbey on the Monday reminded him of Hardy's greatness. A seat had been reserved for him in one of the front pews but he was late arriving and sat on a bench just inside the west door. He cried all the way home.

Stephen called two days later but Sassoon was in no mood for lightness: 'I sometimes doubt whether he is capable of feeling deeply.' Sassoon continued to feel resentment that this friendship had so interrupted his work. He was cross with himself as much as with Stephen. The following Saturday Stephen left for Germany. He had bought a pale blue and yellow corduroy suit for the Bavarian Alps, which prompted Sassoon to write in his diary: 'I wish he didn't aim so much at a Principal Boy in pantomime ideal.' Stephen was being sent to Germany at the insistence of his mother, who felt his hectic way of life in London would take its toll, perhaps creating a recurrence of the tuberculosis from which he suffered. A small pension was recommended to Pamela by one of her family. Situated near Garmisch, it was run by Walther and Johanna Hirth, a couple impoverished by the German economic recession. They took in paying guests, as well as providing nursing facilities; later they were to become friends of both Stephen and Sassoon. With Stephen out of the way, Sassoon returned to his work on *Memoirs of a Fox-Hunting Man*, which he determined to finish by Easter. He also intended to publish a limited edition of verse, *The Heart's Journey*, in March, followed by an ordinary edition with some extra poems in the summer. It was an ambitious plan requiring discipline and application and freedom from aggravation.

If anyone was likely to disrupt the ambition it would be Robert Graves. At the Reform, Sassoon read an article, with photograph, in the *Sphere* magazine on Thomas Hardy in which Graves assumed an acquaintance with Hardy considerably in excess of the facts. Sassoon was infuriated by this 'vulgar and hasty exploitation of the fact that R.G. had stayed one night at Max Gate in 1920'. This diary entry begins ominously: 'I have never felt hatred for R.G. before.' He had been totally exasperated three days previously when Graves wrote in his usual impervious way that two publishers had approached him to write a biography of Hardy. This indecent haste was galling enough, thought Sassoon, but in the next sentence Graves said that he 'didn't want to be a popular biographer', adding modestly that he was 'not competent to treat of Hardy' and that, apart from T. E. Lawrence, Sassoon was the only person who could undertake the task. He had mentioned this to Jonathan Cape, Graves's publisher, who in turn suggested that he, Graves, should make the offer to Sassoon. This was to Sassoon's mind a presumption too far. It was their second spat in a month; it was about nothing and yet it was about everything. Sassoon made no reply. There was silence between them for two years.

Glen had brought a semblance of balance back into Sassoon's life. So too now did Blunden. His appearance at the flat was always welcomed. Everything changed when he was there: 'He is my ideal brother-poet and writer.' Few had that effect, although Sassoon still enjoyed a good chat with the other Edmund in his life – Edmund Gosse. Hardy had been the subject of their last conversation and how Sassoon might edit his letters. Gosse also liked the way the prose masterpiece was growing and was looking forward to its publication. Suitably encouraged by such marks of confidence and friendship, Sassoon met the deadline, finishing on Easter Sunday, 8 April. He immediately wrote to Glen with the news, then went off to Bray: this was his first visit since the death of Frankie Schuster on Boxing Day. Writing to Glen at the time, he said that he 'didn't feel his death very much – it would be dishonest to pretend I do. But I remembered the pleasant times.' Sassoon was in fact quite judgemental about Schuster, who had left him his collection of poetry books: 'A meagre little collection: I wish he had left me a better feeling about his character. What I learnt from him was mostly negative. How not to live on £8,000 a year.' They were mean comments, considering the generous way Schuster had allowed Sassoon to use the house at Bray almost as his own country cottage as well as the Rolls to go up to town. Sassoon had a weakness for hasty judgements, but this was matched by the virtue of admitting being wrong and, on reflection, reversing his opinions. Sifting through the library and the music, he saw his old friend's character in a better light and acknowledged his earlier remarks as lacking in charity.

On his return to London he began revising. He also decided to change his publisher. Heinemann had not treated him with respect in the last years and now some Americans had moved in there and they showed scant regard, too. He wrote to Richard ('Dick') de la Mare at Faber and Gwyer, later to become Faber and Faber. Dick was only too pleased to take

Sassoon on. Both he and the firm needed a publishing and financial success. After reading the first part of *Memoirs of a Fox-Hunting Man*, Dick knew that Sassoon had delivered a work that would sell, not only because of its literary merit but also because memoirs of the war and novels based on it were in demand at the end of the decade, much as war poetry had been at its beginning.

This commitment honoured, Sassoon was at a loose end. He went down to Weirleigh to see Theresa. It was a grey wintry day, the sort in which neither the house nor its surroundings were attractive. Spring was late and a pall hung over the place. Theresa was full of local gossip, of no interest to Sassoon. He was disappointed that her health was again below par and she was having trouble with her teeth – Sassoon left early. During the week he went to someone with whom he had spoken often since Christmas. Miss Streatherne specialised in arresting hair loss. Stephen had recommended her to Sassoon. The treatments were confidential but the gossip flowed. Miss Streatherne knew what was going on, especially in Stephen's circle. Sassoon was surprised to learn from her that Stephen had an appointment there for the next day. The hair restorer had spoilt the secret. Returning from Faber the following day, having delivered the second part of the *Memoirs*, Sassoon found Stephen in the flat.

The delight in welcoming Stephen home from Europe was deep but not unmixed. During the three months' separation, Sassoon realised how disruptive the enchantment had been to his work. Greater caution and discipline would be exercised in future. Then there was the question of Stephen's fidelity. While in Paris Stephen had contacted a Russian artist, Pavel Tchelitchev, recommended to him by Edith Sitwell, who admired his work. It was the start of a great friendship, which Sassoon suspected was something deeper. How Sassoon found out about the meeting is an unanswered question. It might have been from Edith, to whom Stephen wrote from Paris, or it might have been from Stephen himself who, in recounting his holiday, may have described the meeting with Tchelitchev in terms so enthusiastic that Sassoon's suspicions were aroused, resulting in pangs of jealousy. These he tried to 'relegate to the background' of his heart. He was resolute in one thing – he would not play second fiddle. For the moment Sassoon thought the best plan was to encourage Stephen's dependency on him. Sassoon confessed to himself that the reliance was mutual.

During the first weeks of his return from the Continent, Stephen dived into a round of late-night parties, after which he would call on Sassoon and regale him with the activities of those whom Sassoon regarded as 'silly people whose behaviour really cannot be exaggerated in its folly and extravagance'. Sassoon was concerned that people were talking about Stephen and his circle, believing both to be on the slopes of depravity. What Sassoon knew to be light-hearted ribaldry and exuberance was for others grossly undesirable behaviour. Sassoon defended Stephen by declaring: 'All that is only a mask. All the rest of his character is lovable and witty and intelligent.' Two days later, however, he questioned whether he actually understood young people and their world. He was not interested in either, just in Stephen and Glen. 'I think I am happiest, really, with elderly people because they can talk about the past,' he decided.

One such was Edmund Gosse. Sassoon had spent a memorable evening with him the previous October, two days after his first visit to Wilsford. There he had watched, with embarrassment, the bright young things cavorting in a saturnalia, led by Stephen. Everything in Gosse's house testified to solidity of character and purpose. On leaving 17 Hamilton Terrace that October evening, Sassoon became aware of a life coming to its end and a generation passing away.

Gosse died on 16 May 1928. Sassoon was in the Reform. As he left, Naylor, the night porter, said that the best friendships are those that take time to mature. Sassoon agreed. On the day of the funeral he wrote to Blunden: 'The end of a rainy day and the day of Edmund Gosse's funeral. My heart is heavy today and so is yours. One Edmund is not enough for me in this weary world, and the fact that there were two was an unfailing joy and inspiration.'

The day prior to the funeral, Sassoon went to Preston Deanery, a health farm, to bring Stephen back to London. Stephen wanted to be in the strongest possible health for the rigours of the season. He and Stephen were enjoying their friendship, visiting Weirleigh one day, then on another going to Taplow to see the de la Mares and in the evenings perhaps seeing a play and having dinner. Sassoon's New Year resolution to spend less time with his young lover was proving difficult to maintain.

On the evening of 4 June, while at the Reform, Sassoon was given the message that Mr Shaw had phoned. The message took Sassoon by surprise. Returning the call, he learned that Glen had been back from America for over a week, but had not made contact because he understood Sassoon was away. Sassoon suggested that he call on Glen later, at 10.30. He did not mention that he was with Stephen. This arrangement left just enough time for Sassoon and Stephen to go to the cinema and to get Stephen back to his house in Smith Square. It was a tight schedule but not impossible, though it was past 10.30 when they left the cinema. Stephen then said that he had left his watch at the Reform. This detour via Pall Mall made it impossible to visit Glen, who Sassoon believed would be in bed. But Stephen, on hearing that Sassoon had made this arrangement, insisted he stick to it. He also insisted that he, too, come to meet Glen. Sassoon sought to dissuade him – the last thing he wanted was a duel over him. In the hope that Glen would now be asleep, Sassoon drove home with Stephen to Campden Hill Square. While in the kitchen making tea, Sassoon heard the loud and imperious hoot of his car's horn. Then he heard Stephen's voice resounding across the square: 'Siegfried is on the way down.' Sassoon was in excruciating discomfort. Glen was mystified that after their long separation this was the only welcome Siegfried could muster. Upon reaching the top of the stairs, Sassoon said, 'You'll find Stephen Tennant in there.' For an hour the conversation was stilted; Stephen was trying to be friendly, while Glen, understandably in a huff, left him in no doubt about the antagonism he felt.

Sassoon eventually bundled Stephen into his car and told Glen to drive it to Smith Square, where Stephen was wished a good-night and the car returned to Campden Hill Square. They went into Glen's parents' house, where Glen, according to Sassoon, 'made a slight scene'. In the circumstances, he thought Glen had behaved rather well, although it was 3.45 in the morning before Glen resumed his usual amiability. It was only then that the real reason Glen was so anxious to see Sassoon became clear: he wanted to let him know directly that he had fallen in love for the first time and was going to marry an actress called Angela Baddeley. The irony was that Stephen's brother David Tennant was married to Hermione Baddeley, Angela's sister.

Stephen and his friends were intent upon making the summer of 1928 a memorable one for themselves and for everybody else. Their penchant for publicity meant that they were rarely out of the papers. Among the journalists who wrote about them was Tom Driberg in his William Hickey column in the *Daily Express*. Other writers had their informants at this or that party, all keen to elevate the latest bit of social tittle-tattle into a happening of significance. The bright young things were treading risky ground, especially Stephen, and Cecil Beaton, whose love of make-up and jewellery, mode of dress and address were interpreted as one of the most blatant challenges to the social norm since Oscar Wilde and his friends in the nineties. Reports of pyjama-parties, bring-a-bottle parties and gate-crashing a ball in one of the Park Lane mansions all pointed to a serious disregard for social convention. Before long, the matter got into the press and grew into a major social fracas, with Stephen's name the most prominent.

His mother, on hearing of these things, recognised danger. Her friend Edith Olivier wrote in her journal on 18 July, 'Lady Grey had been warned that it's the beginning of a "Round-up" of Stephen and his foppish friends. She fears he may be suspected of immorality if he continues to be written of in the papers in this company. She was in a panic and wanted me to go at once to London to stop him appearing at David [Plunkett-Green]'s Fancy Dress party tomorrow.' Edith did not go to London but letters were sent to Stephen, and also to Sassoon. One of two reasons explains the inclusion of Sassoon in this correspondence. It was an appeal from Pamela Grey for Sassoon's help to warn off Stephen and to shield him from friends such as Cecil Beaton. There is also the possibility that Pamela Grey may have thought, or may have been encouraged to think, that Sassoon was playing an active part in the escapades. The Greys would certainly have known of the friendship and may have suspected that it was not wholesome. Perhaps in this relationship they feared a re-run of the middle-aged Oscar with the young Lord Alfred Douglas. Writing to him might persuade him to cease these activities. If that was their purpose then they badly mistook Sassoon: he did not take part in any of the escapades nor did he go to the fancy-dress parties. It was reported that he was seen at the Chelsea Arts Ball at the Albert Hall, 'a large group in a fantastic range of chiffon and velvet, showing the Picasso scheme of colourings'. Sassoon was not there. If he was 'spotted' it would have been in the early hours of morning when he drove Stephen home, after spending the entire evening at his flat in Campden Hill Square. Stephen's reaction to his mother's letter was studied indifference. He and his friends were unstoppable – it was as if they knew this would prove to be their last riotous season.

Stephen went to Fallodon in Northumberland to see his mother and Lord Grey. Sassoon joined him. If the Greys had disapproved of the friendship and of Sassoon's influence upon Stephen, it is unlikely that they would have allowed him to visit Fallodon while they were there.

Pamela Grey and her husband approved a plan designed by Sassoon that would put some distance between him and London. He proposed that Stephen and his old nanny, Mrs Trusler, travel by train to Munich and register at Haus Hirth, the pension in nearby Garmisch where Stephen had spent the opening months of the year receiving treatment for his tubercular condition. Sassoon would drive out there and, when Stephen was fully rested, they would go by car through northern Italy to a performance of Edith Sitwell's *Façade* at the Siena Festival of Music. They would motor on to Venice, then return to Garmisch and England. Sassoon would underwrite the whole holiday. Nanny Trusler would help. The Greys suggested that William, one of their trusted servants, should go along too as Stephen's valet.

Stephen, Nanny Trusler and William left for the Continent on 29 August. Sassoon had preceded them, crossing the Channel on 27 August. He felt happy that within a month *Memoirs of a Fox-Hunting Man* would be published, anonymously. Depending on its reception, he would start on a sequel. He enjoyed being on his own in his latest car, a red Packard. A year before, he recalled travelling the same way with Schuster and Glen. Stephen at that time was a peripheral acquaintance, now he occupied the centre. Not that Glen was forgotten. Sassoon wrote to him from Marienbad wishing that he were with them. In that same letter he told Glen of Stephen's infectious enjoyment of everything: 'he is rather child-like in his enthusiasms'. The owners of Haus Hirth, Tante Johanna and Onkle Walther, already had experience in coping with Stephen and now there was William the valet as an additional pair of hands. Of the journey from Garmisch to Italy Sassoon writes of Stephen's pile of luggage. For one who always travelled light, he could not believe the weight and number of Stephen's cases. Some were full of silk shirts, trousers, blazers and shoes. Others contained his bottles of scent and his 30 bottles of cold cream, known as the 'League of Lotions'. They changed hotel each day, when Stephen insisted on all the baggage being brought in from the car and unpacked, and so the journey was a test of stamina for Sassoon, who was also doing the driving. They started to lag behind their timetable.

The main stop was Siena for a performance of *Façade* on 14 September. It was Edith's moment of glory and she wanted to be fêted by her family and friends, as well as composers such as Walton, who had written the music, and Constant Lambert, together with lovers of contemporary music from all over Europe. To be invited was to be honoured. Sassoon drove the car into Siena on a pleasant afternoon, knowing that the performance had been in the morning. Edith was beside herself with rage at what she regarded as a snub and laid the blame on Sassoon. It was beyond comprehension that after the fulsome article of praise she had written about his latest volume of poetry, *The Heart's Journey*, he should be so contemptuous of her work. She refused to see him. The situation was embarrassing because he and Stephen were staying at Montegufoni, the Sitwells' palatial residence. A note was sent up to Edith's room from a penitent Sassoon, craving an audience. After three days and having suffered the glares of the other Sitwells, he was informed that Edith would see him at six o'clock. White lilies were bought and Sassoon entered Edith's room. She was in bed, veiled by a gauze tent of mosquito net. Edith was gracious and extended forgiveness but only after a brusque beginning. Sassoon gave her the lilies and proffered an abject apology. It was a chastening experience. Even so, as he wrote in his diary that evening, some of the old truculence which had coloured the attitude of the youthful Siegfried asserted itself: 'after seven minutes I got her round completely'.

Among the letters awaiting Sassoon's arrival at the villa was one from his mother. She had read *Memoirs of a Fox-Hunting Man* and thought it an excellent piece of writing, witty and a true evocation of those times. Sassoon was moved; it was all the praise he wanted. There was also a special tribute to her being published on 24 September: a limited edition of his poem 'To My Mother', with drawings by Stephen. Five hundred copies were available, numbered and signed by Sassoon. Theresa was on Siegfried's mind as they arrived in Venice. Shortly after his father had deserted her or, to quote Sassoon, 'done a flyer with Constance Fletcher', Theresa had come to Venice on holiday. It was a melancholy thought and in complete contrast to Stephen's ecstatic response to his first view of the city. Looking at him, Sassoon saw the beauty of youth and also its transience, which dismayed him. He doubted whether Stephen would cope with that loss – 'The tragic element in S. is this; that it is impossible, or intolerable, to imagine him as anything but young. I think he realises that himself.' Certainly it was something from which neither Lady Grey nor Nanny Trusler could shield him as they had from most things. Perhaps this was at the root of the tensions that began to manifest themselves. Stephen was, Sassoon thought, indifferent to the plight of others: he lacked even an elementary sympathy. This had been obvious before but in Venice, as he mentioned Blunden's worry and struggle, and Theresa's sad reason for her visit, Sassoon was shocked by Stephen's indifference, the way he responded with 'facile phrases and linguistic precocity – the habit of speech acquired in society, and never at a loss for an epithet'.

The time away from England was drawing to its close and on the return journey Sassoon enjoyed the solitude he had craved for the last few weeks. Stephen and Nanny Trusler travelled by train to Haus Hirth; Sassoon drove unaccompanied. He developed bronchitis and remained a week longer. The others moved on to Paris, to be followed later by Sassoon. His thoughts about Stephen continued: 'My twelve months' experience of Stephen seems to have worked itself through to the end of the volume. I am now interested in trying to influence him towards behaving sensibly.' Their friendship could survive, provided it was moved 'away from mere sensualism'. Sassoon wanted companionship; he doubted if Stephen could provide it – 'For really happy companionship I rely on Glen more than on Stephen, who has yet to prove that his feelings for me are more than physical.' But Sassoon was struggling for his own emotional honesty and knew how deep was his attachment to Stephen: 'Probably I say this about S. because I am afraid of losing him.'

Good news awaited him in Paris: the American publisher Coward, McCann offered £350 for the rights to publish *Memoirs of a Fox-Hunting Man* in the States. This was increased to £500 as other publishers made their bids. Meanwhile, Stephen was on a spending spree. Sassoon told Glen that the bills 'were terribly high'. Knowing Sassoon's dislike of ostentation and extravagance, Glen must have been amused by his friend's reference to the way he, Sassoon, was 'putting on airs and graces' as he ordered the porter to send his car round to the front of the hotel, and how, with the book making money, it was 'merely a matter of months before I shall be swanking about in a Rolls'.

Then there was the heartening news of the critical acclaim for Blunden's memoir, *Undertones of War*. The outlook for the sales was positive. As for *Memoirs of a Fox-Hunting Man*, the sales were nearing 8,000. Blunden's self-confidence was boosted when Sassoon wrote an effusive note of congratulation: 'You and I are popular prose-men now; but let us always remember that Poetry is our heavenly spouse.'

Apart from the occasional hasty word between them and the doubts about the future of their friendship, the three months Stephen and Sassoon had spent together were ending on a high note. Then it was all shattered. A telegram arrived for Stephen saying that his mother had died at Wilsford. Stephen disintegrated and Sassoon would not have coped had it not been for the other pillar in Stephen's life, perhaps the central pillar: Nanny Trusler. It became clear to Sassoon in the following days that, far from the relationship weakening, the demise of Lady Grey meant that Stephen would need him more than ever.

14

QUARRELS

1929–32

Sassoon did not see Stephen again until the New Year, when he travelled down to Wilsford. Stephen had been at Fallodon with Lord Grey and appeared calm, though much subdued. Nanny Trusler had been a tower of strength to him there. Now in Wiltshire there were Sassoon and Edith Olivier to share the burden. Edith, unlike others of Stephen's friends, did not resent the growing influence Sassoon was having on him. From the beginning she noticed 'his quiet apartness', which so few of the others possessed. Knowing of his success as poet and now as prose writer, she admired his willingness to encourage and guide aspiring writers like herself. It was remarkable what he knew about books, their provenance as well as their content. Above all she saw in Sassoon total dedication to helping Stephen regain his health and enjoyment of life. He could be relied upon to see Stephen through this crisis.

Memoirs of a Fox-Hunting Man was selling better than had been predicted. Faber decided to publish an illustrated edition and William Nicholson was commissioned to provide the drawings. Sassoon had called on him before going down to Wiltshire for the New Year. While Nicholson sketched, they talked, among other things about Robert Graves, Nicholson's son-in-law. Sassoon had learned via Glen that what had been a *ménage à trois* – Robert, Nancy and Laura Riding – was now a *ménage à quatre*, an Irish poet named Geoffrey Phipps being the fourth. William Nicholson agreed with Sassoon that Graves had become 'rather impossible'.

Someone else discussed was Max Beerbohm who, Nicholson said, was in town. This set Sassoon talking, Max being his hero as a writer, exceeding even Surtees in the use of wit and observation. Max and his wife

Florence lived in Rapallo, on the coast road between Genoa and Viareggio. Their visits to England were few. Sassoon had sent each of his privately printed volumes to him as a token of esteem. But Max was not a good correspondent and rarely acknowledged a gift. This did not diminish Sassoon's admiration. He did not feel the same warmth towards Beatrice and Sydney Webb, whose portrait Nicholson had just completed and Sassoon was invited to view. On entering the upstairs studio he was taken aback to find, sitting at a small desk, none other than the 'incomparable Max'. They had last met in May 1923 at Gosse's house when Sassoon had declared that in his opinion Max 'was one of the best authors'. Their renewed meeting, at 11 Apple Tree Yard, was the beginning of their friendship, and of Max becoming the arbiter of Sassoon's prose – especially the punctuation. January 9th was a red-letter day: Max and Florence came to Campden Hill Square for tea. They met Stephen, whom they liked; the liking was mutual. This high point encouraged Sassoon to start work on a second volume of Sherston, entitled with monumental unoriginality *Memoirs Continued.*

He also became friendlier with Rex Whistler. In February, Edith Olivier invited the two men to the Daye House for a weekend. Edith adored Rex. As for Rex's feeling for Edith, that might best be described as puppy-love, Edith being more than 30 years his senior. She had a gift for making her home a centre for friendship and a harbour of calm and stability. The contemporary of their parents, she did not inhibit the young and enjoyed their vitality. Edith lived by clear standards of morality which emanated from a deep Christian faith, but she eschewed the judgemental. Cecil Beaton, Stephen Tennant and Rex Whistler warmed to her optimistic personality, as did other young people she came to know in the twenties. The relationship was symbiotic; their gift to her was unconditional friendship that released her talents as a writer. She had always wanted to be published, but her father's suspicion of the arts in general put such ambitions beyond her reach. Now these young people rekindled the dormant ambition. She wrote romantic fiction and was moderately successful. It did not make her a fortune but for one whose financial resources were limited, every penny was a boost. Edith flourished in the last 25 years of her life in a way she could not have imagined.

She may well have inveigled Whistler and Sassoon down from London to help keep their friendship on an even keel. Rex was sensitive to the way Sassoon was monopolising Stephen to the exclusion of those whose friendships with him went back further than his. Even so, the weekend proved a happy affair, although it began with a near tragedy due to Sassoon's reckless driving. He ploughed into a pond, which fronted on to a pub. Infuriated, the owner offered no help, but fetched a billboard, which bore the words THIS POND IS PRIVATE. It was Edith who had to summon help to 'dig out poor Rex and Sieg'.

Whatever his other friends may have thought, Sassoon was determined to support Stephen through his period of grief and Stephen seemed not to object to being monopolised. His dependency grew; some friends noticed it, but if Sassoon knew of other people's resentment, he ignored it. All that mattered was Stephen's health. Actually most people were surprised by Stephen's resilience. The outward appearance was deceptive. There was a recurrence of the TB germ. He was sent back to Haus Hirth for treatment and an extended period of convalescence. As ever, the faithful Nanny Trusler went with him. The Hirths, in particular Tante Johanna, were dedicated to nursing the tubercular and Stephen was much loved by them, while Sassoon was regarded as a hero. Dr Kaltenbach from Heidelberg believed that the best treatment for Stephen was a procedure known as pneumothorax, in which the lung is collapsed in order for it to rest. This, followed by plenty of fresh air, rest and food, brought recovery – sometimes.

In London, working at his book, Sassoon received a letter from Eddie Marsh telling him that he had been awarded the Hawthornden Prize for 1929. He replied: 'Your letter made me sing in my bath. This prose success has astonished me.' The success also brought him a shock when in February he received a letter from a Mr Edgar Newgass, who was somewhat put out by the description of him in *Memoirs of a Fox-Hunting Man*. Sassoon's use of the alias was not always effective. As Tony Lewison he sold the famous 'Cockbird' to Sassoon for the give-away price of 50 pounds. The offending sentence in the book was: 'We marvelled more and more that anyone could be such a mug as to part with him for fifty pounds.' The implication was that Newgass in the guise of Lewison had been taken for a ride.

Dear Newgass,
So glad you liked the book, but I am horrified that you should have identified yourself with 'young Lewison' who was a mere dummy put in to contrast with the livelier character of 'S. Colwood'. If I thought there was any chance of your making such a mistake I would have changed the name of 'Cockbird'. Of course the book is half-fiction

and half-fact, and one is liable to be misunderstood by those who knew the material on which the narrative is based. So for heaven's sake get this idea out of your head.

Newgass was gracious enough to accept the explanation. His mother, who lived in Frant, was an acquaintance of Theresa's; Newgass was at Henley House at the same time as Sassoon and a contemporary of Hamo Sassoon at Cambridge. *Memoirs of a Fox-Hunting Man* elicited another more pleasant letter from Dorothy Hanmer, sister of Bobby and Sassoon's former girl-friend, now wife of the Master of the Grafton Hunt, Harry Hawkins, and living at Daventry, Northamptonshire. She had received a copy and letter from Sassoon, who confessed to having passed her once in Bruton Street in London, but been too unsure of himself to speak: 'I often think of the old days, I think we were both shy in those days! I have just read your book and loved it, it is most awfully interesting, and I think I know more about it even than most people.' But Sassoon's aliases foxed her when she wrote, '"Dick" at Litherland is Bobby of course?' when in fact it was David Thomas.

Sassoon was looking forward to seeing Stephen again at the beginning of April in Germany. Edith Olivier and William Walton went to Haus Hirth a few days before him. The expenses of the ever-impecunious Walton were met by Sassoon, who had paid for his first trip there. They found Stephen in good spirits, having put on a few pounds. Edith wrote in her diary: 'Tante Johanna says the specialist from Heidelberg writes full of hope over Stephen's physical recovery, tho' wondering how any one so heavenly, so *unerlich*, so spiritual, can face this rude world – Thinks him a Fra Angelico or a Botticelli. Is dazzled by his personality. Isn't that marvellous from a German scientist.' On 4 April, after lunch, Sassoon arrived and Edith noted: 'Such a delight. He is most vivifying and so lovable. Everyone here adores him, host and hostess, and he adores them all.' Edith also wrote that 'Stephen's happiness is beyond anything.' On 15 April, Sassoon sent a letter to Glen saying that the doctors had given their permission for him to spend an hour in the afternoon and evening in Stephen's room, that there was no danger of infection and they were 'wonderfully happy'. A week later Stephen celebrated his twenty-third birthday. He came down to a party at lunchtime and opened his cards and presents.

Stephen's health by May had greatly improved. The daily treatments continued and all the signs were good. If there was a cloud in the sky it was Nanny Trusler, whose vitality was showing signs of decline and she was becoming confused. The decision was made by Sassoon to move out of Haus Hirth into a vacant property in the nearby village of Breitenau. They had secured the help of an English nurse called Brambling, and each morning Stephen went to a local convent-cum-hospital for treatment. Everything was idyllic, marred only by Nanny Trusler's condition. Stephen was not aware of the extent of the problem but he knew something was amiss and fretted. The decision was made to send her home to England. It was a sad parting. Although she had long been incapable of lessening the demands made on Sassoon, her presence was important to Stephen's contentment. On her departure, Stephen's dependence on Sassoon deepened, as did Sassoon's commitment to him. Eddie Marsh, as Chairman of the Hawthornden Prize, asked Sassoon by letter whether he would receive the prize in London at the award ceremony. 'I must remain here with Stephen,' was the uncompromising reply. In the event the prize was accepted on his behalf by Edmund Blunden. This most faithful of friends was always solicitous of Stephen and never failed in his letters to send him warmest greetings. In fact, most of Sassoon's friends accepted the friendship. So long as 'old Sig' was happy, so were they.

Theresa's reaction, according to Sassoon's diary for 9 June 1928, was, 'she thinks S. "a dear boy"'. At a later date, probably post-1933, that original opinion carries an amendment: 'she very soon decided otherwise! – divining his essential heartlessness'. It is unlikely that she would have approved of this friendship if she suspected there were sexual aspects to it, but she knew that it was counterproductive openly to oppose her son's actions. There is a letter she wrote to Stephen acknowledging a drawing he had sent her. It is dated 5 May. The year is omitted but likely to be 1928, some eight months after Sassoon and Stephen met.

Dear Mr Tennant,
Thank you so much for the exact and charming drawing of the Gentians. No blue is so splendid. The small ones I do not know. My plants here had some flowers on – but what they need is a blanket of snow over them.
I do hope you have warmer weather than we have here.
It would be interesting to make a set of drawings of the flowers in bloom where you are –
With kindest regards from
Theresa Sassoon

The letter gives the impression that she was struggling to find something to say. It is without doubt an echo of what her son described as his mother's calling voice: 'formality tinged with reserve'. Before leaving for Germany, Sassoon had written to Glen, concerned about Theresa's health. She had, he wrote, 'a slight infection of both lungs. Her eldest sister, Mrs Donaldson, died last night and this will not aid her recovery.' Sassoon had a real fear that Theresa would die suddenly and leave him bereft. Even the slightest cold would awaken foreboding in him. Stephen's fear of losing Nanny Trusler was understandable to Sassoon. At the end of July Stephen was advised to return home. He arrived in time to take his last farewell of the woman who meant as much, possibly more, to him than his mother. She died on 14 August, aged 71. Within nine months Stephen had lost the two most important people in his life: Sassoon now occupied that central place.

Sassoon set himself two aims: to keep Stephen occupied and to prevent his strength being drained by the demands of inconsiderate friends. Providentially the first aim coincided with Stephen's intention to refurbish the interior of Wilsford and redesign some of its exterior aspects. It was symbolic of a new beginning. Sassoon ensconced himself at Wilsford for the rest of the summer and watched over Stephen. He was rigorous about visitors and, in the politest way possible, suggested they postpone their plans for a little while. One such was Rex Whistler, who took it not in best part – understandably so. Sassoon was also cancelling his own obligations to friends and this, in the case of the Sitwells, was cause for spiteful and resentful remarks. The boundary between monopolising and shielding was a difficult one to draw, certainly one that needed tact in its execution. Tact was not one of Sassoon's gifts.

In September Glen was appearing in a new production of Chekhov's *The Seagull*. To give Stephen a respite from the refurbishing at Wilsford, Sassoon wrote to Glen asking him to get tickets for the opening night. Stephen wrote afterwards to Glen in glowing words: 'Your performance seemed like that of a being from another world.' Blunden came to Wilsford, his genial spirit bringing bright moments to the autumnal days. It was through these surprises that Sassoon tried to keep Stephen in a happy frame of mind. It was not totally effective: grief persisted and a depressing heaviness hung about the invalid. Plans had already been laid by Sassoon to take Stephen away for the winter to the warm climate of Sicily, where Sassoon would work on the second half of the memoirs, revise some poems and develop others. Whatever excitement he felt about the trip, it could not have been greater than that on his having persuaded Max to read the manuscript of *Memoirs Continued*. He had asked Max when he and his wife visited Campden Hill, never really believing that Beerbohm would agree. What was more, the Beerbohms had invited Sassoon and Stephen to bring the manuscript in person to Rapallo. However, before they could leave a crisis with a script by another friend occurred, over which Sassoon had to take immediate action.

In the summer the situation in the Graves household in Hammersmith had been a period of high drama verging on farce. Put briefly, Robert and Laura were lovers; Nancy and Phipps were lovers. Laura, however, was in love with Phipps and believed he was in love with her. Robert believed he could be loyal to Nancy without being faithful. Nancy decided to leave Robert and live with Phipps; Phipps had agreed to live with Laura. When the four of them tried to sort out the confusion and duplicity, Laura opened a third-floor window, got out on the ledge, said to the other three, 'Goodbye, chaps' and jumped. Her attempt at suicide failed but Graves himself came under suspicion of attempted manslaughter, the police at first thinking that he had pushed Laura out of the window during the quarrel. Literary London feasted on the incident. Sassoon, who was in Germany with Stephen, had heard the news. He wrote to Glen on 16 June from Garmisch: 'The Graves–Riding episode appals me.' Riding was not only seriously injured; she was in serious trouble with the police for suicide at that time was illegal. She was also in England on a visa. Her illegal action meant she was in danger of being deported. Graves wrote to Eddie Marsh asking him to use his influence with the authorities. Meanwhile Nancy went off with Phipps to Oxfordshire to be with her children. Graves was in terrible state of mind, made worse by a serious shortage of money. His publisher, Jonathan Cape, agreed to Graves's idea of a war memoir to be published towards the year's end. Graves worked at break-neck speed to meet a deadline set for October. The pressure this imposed on him and the other worries had their effect on the finished product; there were serious factual errors and indiscreet references. Anxious to get away from England, Graves and Laura Riding went to France, where they made the spontaneous decision to make a new start in Mallorca. They were living on the island when the book was published in mid-November.

Cape had sent a review copy to Blunden, probably at Graves's suggestion. What Blunden read appalled him. As a reader of war memoirs he wanted accuracy and detail from authors. The war was a unique happening and nothing written about it should detract from that uniqueness. Graves on every count betrayed his calling. Writing to Sassoon, Blunden was savage in his criticism: 'R. G[raves]'s reminiscential neuroses arrived and I began a letter about them to you, but broke off. I don't think a worse *book* was ever flung together. His unreliability, obvious in all passages where I was able to test from my own information, destroys his war scenes. His self-importance and cold use and slaughter of others ruin the possible solace of a personality.' Blunden condemned the 'bombastic and profit-seeking display' that Graves had made of Sassoon's private affairs. Graves had included a poem in letter form which Sassoon had sent him in August 1918; its personal nature and allusions made it mostly inaccessible to the general reader and Sassoon clearly would not have wished it ever to be published. That apart, permission to publish the poem had not been sought. More serious was the reference to Wilfred Owen being accused of cowardice by his Colonel: 'unpardonable and inaccurate' averred Blunden. On Tuesday, 12 November Sassoon went to the offices of Cape and demanded a copy. What he already knew via Blunden paled into insignificance when his eyes lighted upon the content of pages 289/290. Graves, without naming Weirleigh, Theresa or Sassoon, wrote of a visit he made to a wounded fellow officer, who lived in Kent:

An elder brother had been killed in the Dardanelles, and their mother kept the bedroom exactly as he had left it, with sheets aired, the linen always freshly laundered, flowers and cigarettes by the bedside. The first night I spent there, my friend and I sat talking about the War. The talk had excited me, and though I managed to fall asleep an hour later, I was continually awakened by sudden rapping noises, which I tried to disregard but which grew louder and louder. At nearly three o'clock I heard a diabolical yell and a succession of laughing, sobbing shrieks that sent me flying to the door. In the passage I collided with the mother who, to my surprise, was fully dressed. 'It's nothing,' she said. In the morning I told my friend: 'I'm leaving this place. It's worse than France.' There were thousands of mothers like her trying to get in touch with their dead sons by spiritualistic means.

Sassoon recognised the story. Amazingly, for a perceptive reader, Blunden did not, on first reading, connect the extract with Sassoon's mother. He suggested, in an effort to comfort Sassoon, that others would not realise its origin either, but Sassoon was taking no risks. The reviewers were already at work; someone like J. C. Squire, whom he met that morning with a review copy under his arm, was too experienced not to make the connection, especially as the preceding and succeeding paragraphs named Sassoon. He wrote to Cape threatening legal action unless the extract was deleted. Cape knew that the firm could not publish until it conformed. Next day, 13 November, he sent a telegram inviting Sassoon to his office and, with apologies, agreed to his demands. He then wrote to Graves, who in reply expressed surprise that Sassoon was upset but he was quite prepared to be led by Cape. *Goodbye to All That* was published on 18 November 1929, each copy containing pages with blank spaces.

As he left for the Continent, Sassoon was grappling with preoccupations. Stephen needed and demanded constant attention. In the next months this was unlikely to decrease. Graves's book, with its numerous references to Sassoon, vitiated his enthusiasm to continue his own memoirs. Then there was Blunden, who was embroiled in painful discussions about the custody of his children, Clare and John, in anticipation of divorce proceedings. Sassoon had offered to become John's legal guardian, an offer which Blunden welcomed but Mary rejected. Above all, he hoped that his mother would not read *Goodbye to All That*. It was not until they reached Rapallo and Max that these preoccupations receded. 'An enchanting experience,' Sassoon records, 'the hospitality of Mrs Max so perfect. Their liking for me and Stephen so blissfully comforting.' Max peppered their talks with the wry observations of someone who had the measure of the world. There was so much about him which reminded Sassoon of Robbie Ross, that matchless style of the sardonic dandy offering a wave from the other side of the war – 'His style is so complete and so exquisitely entertaining. His leisurely anecdotes are so interwoven with his delicious mimicries and social intonations. Max produces a feeling of having had just enough good wine to make one happy.'

Sassoon was lighter of spirit as he travelled south to Naples and on to Sicily. His poetic voice returned with 'Presences Perfected' and 'We Shall Not All Sleep', both hauntingly beautiful and mysterious, audible only to 'the ears of the heart'. In the drier, warmer climate, Stephen's health improved. This was a mixed blessing. He made demands on Sassoon's time, wanting to explore the countryside and scour the seashore for shells to add to his Wilsford collection. Sassoon, always resentful of time lost, of any distraction or interruption, explained to Stephen that there was a further purpose to their stay on Sicily apart from the restoring of his health. Stephen did not understand. A compromise was reached in which afternoons would be given to Stephen's pursuit of shells, mornings to writing and evenings to relaxation and contentment. As the days passed the island captivated them. For Sassoon it was the finding of 'The Heart's Paradise', a poem he composed in March and which had appeared in *The Nation and Athenaeum* on 5 April:

> At the end of all wrong roads I came
> To the gates of the garden without a name,
> There, till the spell should fail, I found
> Sudden Elysium, strange with sound
> Of unknown birds and waters wild
> With voices unresolved for rest.
> There every flower was fancy's child,
>
> And every tree was glory's guest,
> And Love, by darkness undefiled,
> Went like the sun from east to west.

But that glimpse of Elysium was no antidote to the 'mental inflammation' caused by *Goodbye to All That*; it persisted, it rankled, it intruded upon his thoughts, it seemed to inhibit the ink from running smoothly through the pen. Putting the episode aside was not made easier by the correspondence from Blunden, which picked away at the sore. The letters contained epithets and asides which fell below Blunden's normal conciliatory, genial approach to life in general and people in particular. Imitating Blunden's schoolboy name-calling, Sassoon became silly and juvenile. Names such as von Rubberneck or a new title for the book, *A Welsh-Irish Bull in a China Shop*, did nothing to reduce the temperature.

Blunden was under duress himself and this may account for his perverse behaviour. His marriage was ending and he was working too hard. Sassoon wrote to admonish him for taking on too great a load of reviewing and editing but Blunden needed the income. His persistence in combing over the Graves' matter might well have been a symptom of his frustration with his own tangled affairs. Blunden's letters are out of character: he felt resentment towards Graves for making injudicious statements to Mary about his alleged drinking habits, and Graves's tendency to pontificate on good and bad poetry, including Blunden's – all these grievances created bad feelings between the two. The book opened the floodgates of pent-up resentment.

Leaving a situation half-resolved was not Sassoon's way. This was especially true when feeling wronged or belittled. Neither could he allow those whom he loved or admired to be the victims of calumnies. When roused, Sassoon could be wounding and withering in defence and attack. In the case of Graves these feelings were tempered, but only slightly. Fed by Blunden's letters and by his own nagging annoyance, he decided that he would write to Graves. The letter was restrained in its censuring of the inaccuracies; the spirit was friendly, despite the disappointment. In explaining why he had neglected Graves since 1927, Sassoon was almost apologetic. He emphasised that he too had commitments which were all-consuming and which brought their own worries. With that as a preface he itemised Graves's actions which were responsible for the present state of their relationship, in particular his belittling of Gosse and his vulgar exploitation of Hardy's memory, recounting the spiritualistic activity, Sassoon's alleged comments about his mother's irrational behaviour and his dead brother's unworthiness of his mother's grief. As for the references to the war, the Medical Board and its consequences, Graves's defective memory had betrayed a friendship and portrayed a fiction. If the book confirmed anything at all it was Graves's own self-importance. Naïvely, Sassoon ended the letter: 'It may interest, and even please you to know that, although I made a new will last year, you will still be consoled for my death to the extent of £300 a year tax paid. I have written this letter to relieve my mind, and no reply is necessary. We must agree to differ, especially on matters of "good taste". But I implore you not to write anything more about me.'

It was impossible for Graves not to pick up his pen. Typically he launched forth and forthrightly. Gosse was 'a vain, snobbish old man'. Hardy was 'good, consistent and a truthful man [but] I do not believe in great men'. As for Stephen, 'never met him and you never mentioned him to me'. With some other asides Graves came to what were, to his mind, the cross-currents which disturbed their friendship: 'your homosexual leanings; your jealousy of Nancy; later Nancy being in love with you (which no doubt you noticed and were afraid of); your literary friendships which I could not share; finally your difficulty with the idea of Laura'. Graves's reply had cleverly moved the ground away from the alleged failings of his own book. Finally, with regard to the legacy, Graves was not interested in jam tomorrow. Three years before and during the intervening years he had needed assistance. If he had been helped then, he would not have been forced to write the book in haste and Sassoon, Blunden and others would not now be criticising it at leisure.

Sassoon's response was immediate: an itemised list of Graves's accusations challenged by his own counter-accusations. The correspondence was solving nothing. Like all quarrels it was profitless, even as a cathartic exercise. Graves did not reply – he had made his point and wanted to get on with his work. Thirty years later, in reply to a question about this altercation, Graves said: 'He had quarrelled with me, not I with him.'

In one of those odd coincidences that marked Sassoon's life, Graves's letter reached him on 1 March, the day Sassoon's memoir of the war reached the point where he meets Graves for the first time. In that memoir, Graves is re-named David Cromlech: the first name identifying him as Welsh, and Cromlech being the Welsh word for a Celtic burial chamber or grave. The portrait of Cromlech is not a flattering one: he is greatly disliked by his fellow officers and regarded as truculent by his superiors. Would the portrait of Cromlech have been more flattering had the letter and dispute come later?

Memoirs Continued was completed almost two years to the day after Sassoon finished *Memoirs of Fox-Hunting Man*. At the insistence of Faber, the title was changed to *Memoirs of an Infantry Officer*. Sassoon was not happy with the final chapters – 'If I had written them in solitude they might have been stronger.' But he did not regret the time spent with Stephen, collecting Venus Ear shells and then sitting on the beach cleaning them. As they prepared to leave Sicily, the irritations caused by Stephen and the petty disputes between them slipped into the background. He had been happy – and he was still – but it was a happiness tinged with foreboding.

In Sicily

Because we two can never again come back
On life's one forward track, –
Never again first-happily explore
This valley of rock and vines and orange-trees,
Half Biblical and Hesperides,
With dark blue seas calling from a shell-strewn shore:
By the strange power of Spring's resistless green,
Let us be true to what we have shared and seen,
And as our amulet this idyll save.
And since the unreturning day must die,

Let it for ever be lit by an evening sky
And the wild myrtle grow upon its grave.

During the return journey to England Sassoon was plagued with doubts about the future: 'I dread any human relationship which will make demands on me.' A week later he is more specific, seeing the friendship resolving itself into a conflict 'in which I must choose between giving up my work as a writer or giving up my enslavement to Stephen's possessiveness'. When they reached Paris, Stephen's favourite city, but one which always made Sassoon miserable, they quarrelled: 'A sad ending to our half-year abroad.' Sassoon had always struggled with Stephen's mercurial temperament – childlike and childish. Sentences from the diary speak of the need to handle him carefully, of tearful outbursts because his trustees were counselling more prudence in Stephen's spending, and Sassoon having to coax him back into feeling happy again: 'I am sometimes very clumsy with him, forgetting how easy it is to hurt his feelings. Learning how to manage S., I am being taught not to be egotistical and domineering.'

Stephen went to Wilsford; Sassoon to London. He was happy to see Blunden again, despite the continued pressure under which 'little B' tried to keep together the different strands of his life. And there was cricket! The Australians were touring and an afternoon at Lord's watching them play Middlesex brought relief to troubled spirits. This was the first match he had watched in two years – too long an absence. He wrote – almost in mitigation for such an omission – that he 'had read the scores every day'. He regarded the summer as the season for revising his work, sometimes for re-writing but never for creating. Above all it was the season of freedom, for getting out and about and walking. Weirleigh in June was incomparable. Theresa was in high spirits: Fenner the housekeeper was laid low with phlebitis and nothing reinvigorated Theresa more than having someone in the house ill. Weirleigh, however, now had competition for Sassoon's loyalty – Wilsford. Walking the lanes and across the Wiltshire Downs, he was entranced by their beauty and the solitude offered but Stephen's erratic temperature marred the carefree days of middle June. This was followed by a rapid decline in his energy. Nurse May, who had come to Wilsford to nurse Stephen full-time, brought worse news to Sassoon: the latest sputum test had revealed TB. 'My heart became like a lump of lead.' They waited for Dr Kempe to arrive before telling Stephen. Sassoon wept as he had done 40 years before over his consumptive father. It was Edith Olivier who came immediately and concurred in Sassoon's conviction that Dr Kempe and the others were not taking the situation seriously enough and how much better it would be if Stephen returned to the care of the German doctors and Haus Hirth. Rex Whistler phoned about his visit to Wilsford the following weekend. Sassoon annoyed him by suggesting he stay with Edith at the Daye House. Sassoon suspected that part of Stephen's decline was due to friends encouraging him into too much excitement and activity: 'I have to cope with S.'s friends who all want to come and see him.' Sassoon's instincts were right but the friends misinterpreted his motives. Another dissident was Nurse May, who objected to Sassoon busying himself with matters medical. Edith Olivier began to suspect that Nurse May's objection was based on her own infatuation with Sassoon: 'It is the fury of a woman scorned,' declared the romantic novelist.

'I am going to keep everyone away for the next two weeks if possible,' Sassoon wrote in his diary and he was successful in his efforts. But the style and tone of his letters were too pedantic and ruffled the feathers of old friends like Cecil Beaton:

My Dear Cecil,
It is a great disappointment that your long delayed visit must be postponed. But you will understand how essential it is that Stephen should avoid all excitement and fatigue. He has started his systematic treatment, and until his temperature is down and he has put on a little weight he must be quiet. His life depends on the disease being checked.
  Will you be coming down to camp out in your house? If so you must come over and see us for an hour or two. That would be the best way for you to see S. at first. I have had a most harassing time for the last 8 weeks – The way the doctors behaved was enough to send one crazy! But thank heaven the good doctor has been here at last and we are lucky that only 6 weeks were wasted.
Yrs ever. SS.

The first visitor came a month later – Glen Byam Shaw, who stayed during the first weekend of September. Friends such as Rex and Cecil Beaton were peeved at their exclusion from Wilsford when Sassoon's intimates were given an unimpeded welcome. It was very petty but, as Sassoon learnt, pettiness was characteristic of these relationships. Glen and Edith Olivier realised the sacrifice as well as the effort Sassoon was making to save Stephen. He was even exceeding Stephen's own family in his concern to secure the best medical advice. So involved was Sassoon that he did not recognise the signs of Stephen's selfishness when on 23 September he was told that Stephen had decided to be alone for at least the next 10 days. Sassoon left Wilsford.

He took full advantage of being back in London, dining with E. M. Forster and with Blunden, who was busier than ever at *The Nation*, with the Morrells and the Waltons. All made their enquiries about Stephen. Sassoon was high in his optimism – Stephen had gained nearly two pounds in weight. 'All he needs is rest, air, and food, and freedom from worry,' he wrote after visiting Wilsford on 4 October. In fact things were looking up generally. Dick de la Mare wrote to say that *Memoirs of a Fox-Hunting Man* had sold over 27,000 copies and *Memoirs of an Infantry Officer* had topped 24,000.

Max Beerbohm and William Nicholson encouraged him to start a third volume, based on the post-war years. The possibility had already presented itself to Sassoon who, as a start, had taken the relevant diaries down to Wilsford, believing at the time that he would be spending all the autumn and the winter with Stephen. There were doubts in his mind about 'meddling in the memoirs prematurely'. There were other obstacles, too: 'The parts about love-affairs must of course be separated from the rest. (They make uncomfortable reading.)' They would also be illegal reading. Gabriel Atkin would only feature, if at all, as an acquaintance from the north.

On 8 October he dined at the Reform. Perusing the guest list, he read the name of his erstwhile lover. They met, they shook hands, but Sassoon did not speak to him and that evening only conversed with Gabriel's host, Sir Roderick Meiklejohn, friend of Robbie Ross and resident at Half Moon Street. Sassoon's diary records that Gabriel was looking 'healthy but much coarsened'. He was at the Reform for a private dinner to mark the opening of an exhibition of his watercolours; Sassoon made a point of visiting it. During the five years since last Sassoon had seen him, Gabriel had been a male prostitute first in Lyon and then in the south of France. Sassoon's financial help to him had ceased years before and would only have recommenced had there been evidence of reformation. In 1930 he married Mary Butts, a minor writer and, like himself, careering towards disintegration with the help of drink and drugs. The marriage ended in divorce. By 1936 they were both dead, Gabriel at 39. If Sassoon felt anything for him on that night at the Reform it went unrecorded.

Similarly with Philipp of Hesse, who married Princess Mafalda of Savoy, daughter of King Umberto the Second of Italy. They became two ne'er-do-wells in Fascist Europe, scuttling between Hitler and Mussolini, and on their behalf using their royal connection to make contact with the Duke of Windsor. Having served their masters well, they were sent to Buchenwald, where Mafalda died in 1945 and from where Philipp was released. In his abandoned fourth volume of memoirs, Sassoon recalls friendships with the likes of Gabriel and Philipp as happening at a time 'when sex was making a fool' of him. While in London he also met another couple from his past – Jim and Delphine Turner. He recorded the meeting with a vicious dismissal of Turner: 'Five years ago I parted from the Turners. He is a recognized failure and I am ditto a success.' The entry is an exception to the usual charitable reticence employed by Sassoon when writing about those with whom he had quarrelled. Where his anger did spill on to the page, he usually revised the entry. This one remained unaltered – clearly he meant what he wrote.

Sassoon returned to Wilsford for what he thought would be a prolonged visit but, within four days, on 4 November his diary records: 'Stephen has lost a 1lb – my presence excites him. So we arranged I should stay away until 22 November. We parted with emotion and I went upstairs to pack and caught sight of my white face in the glass. Such scenes are very trying. S wrings my heart. He is so pathetic and childlike.' Stephen was continuing to play cat-and-mouse with him. Sassoon put it all down to another bout of weakness. The week before Christmas, having invited Sassoon for the Tuesday, Stephen sent a telegram postponing the visit by two days, then sent another telegram on the original Tuesday telling Sassoon to 'come at once'. In a hired Daimler, the enthralled Sassoon went to Stephen, who greeted him with complaints of being neglected for so long. Edith Olivier, Walton and his mistress, Imma Doernberg, Princess of Erbach-Schonberg, came to lunch on Boxing Day. They caught only a glimpse of Stephen. As 1930 died, Sassoon stood on the doorstep at Wilsford and listened – 'New Year Bells were sounding clear and peaceful and a drift of a white cloud across the stars.'

In a letter to Glen dated 17 January, Sassoon complained of feeling nervy, a condition he attributed to the constant attention he was giving Stephen and his lack of company. The isolation was of his own doing: his ban on visitors was strictly adhered to and continued to cause offence to many of Stephen's friends. Sassoon believed that the invalid himself did not want visitors and was being 'sensible and self-controlled' about everything; Sassoon was not on his own at Wilsford, nor doing the nursing. Nurse May was there full-time but she and Sassoon continued to be at loggerheads. Stephen observed it all from his bed, probably more than a little pleased that people were fighting over him, but he tired of the diversion and in February decided that Sassoon must leave the manor. It was his second expulsion, for which he blamed the nurse not Stephen, and he fully expected to be back in Wilsford soon and Nurse May out of a job. While waiting for the call, he took himself away to Switzerland for April and May, where William Walton and Princess Imma were on holiday in Asconia. From there on 19 May, he gleefully wrote to Glen that Nurse May had been replaced by Nurse Turnbull. The change of regime brought an invitation for Sassoon to visit Wilsford in June.

When they met he found Stephen little improved in health or demeanour. There was little possibility of rekindling their affair but Stephen invited him to visit again in July. Came the day and came a letter postponing the arrangement, Stephen pleading a chill. The cat-and-mouse game affected Sassoon's brittle temper. 'I've been so disagreeable lately,' he wrote to Glen, who was hoping to see him before leaving for a tour of South Africa, a meeting Sassoon postponed more than once. Another symptom was his inability to settle down to life in the Campden Hill Square flat. He booked into the Hyde Park Hotel; clearly minimalism in furniture and limited space were no longer on the agenda. By the autumn nor was London: he moved out and never lived there again.

In October 1931 he took a lease on Fitz House in the small Wiltshire village of Teffont Magna (Edith Olivier and her sister Mildred had once lived there). Situated on the southern perimeter of Salisbury Plain, it was also within easy distance of Wilsford and Stephen. This was a strange move, when to all appearance their affair was petering out. Sassoon nursed the hope that the embers would flare again. He was not invited to Wilsford but was kept informed of Stephen by the two sisters who tended the gardens there, Beryl and Eileen Hunter, whom he nicknamed 'Really and Truly'. They also allowed him to stable his newly-acquired horses there. To be riding again after nearly eight years was a therapy; being close to Wilsford, even though exiled from it, brought its comfort. But the agony of exclusion was bruising, especially when he heard in November that Rex Whistler had been allowed to visit. Six months had passed since Sassoon had seen Stephen. There was a letter from him in August, a birthday message in September and in December 'a frostily inscribed New Year Card'.

He could find no escape from the pervasive desire to be with Stephen. There had been a distraction when Theresa was taken seriously ill at Christmas and underwent an operation in January. 'The only good result,' he told Glen, 'was that it made me realise how much she means to me and what a wonderful character she is.' His letters to Glen make it clear that he still believed himself to be central in Stephen's life – 'I do not intend to be discarded without a fierce struggle, because I can't help believing that any future he has depends very much on me for its success.' His tone was just as earnest when writing to Max Beerbohm: 'He could never be moderate in anything he did; and as at least half of me is loitering about in his locality waiting for him to get well, I am not an impartial judge of his methods of enduring this dreadful illness. But if only we could do something to help him, obstinate little creature as he is.'

Perhaps he should have followed Cecil Beaton's example and just sent him a bunch of red roses and gone about his own business – but then Stephen *was* his business. Rex Whistler when he visited just indulged his friend with gossip and nonsense. Few if any understood Stephen better than Rex. If only Sassoon could see him again but without that possibility, he could only rely on friends – William Walton, Edith Olivier and the Hunter sisters 'Really and Truly' – for news. Then in August, as a result of persuasion by his cousin Violet Bonham Carter, Stephen agreed to see him. Inevitably their conversations were strained but at the end of the second, on the 19th, there was a trace of the old harmony – not enough, however, to hide from Sassoon that something was terribly wrong.

Stephen's lungs were declared free of tuberculosis but he had become the victim of a more sinister affliction. Sir Henry Head in the light of much that he was told by Sassoon deduced the illness was psychological: Stephen was in the grip of a neurosis. His biographer writes, 'The pent-up emotional stresses of the last years – Pamela's and Nanny's deaths – had been held back to some extent by his affair with Siegfried; as that began to break down, so the trauma of past loss manifested itself.' Stephen had leant on Sassoon but found no release in a relationship that was demanding rather than consoling. Having lived in a world of make-believe, a world created for him by his mother and in which he was indulged by Nanny, he was emotionally incapable of handling reality in two of its most powerful manifestations – life-threatening illness and death.

In October he was admitted to Swaylands, a private clinic in Penshurst, Kent. The Cassel Hospital for Functional Nervous Disorders, as its name suggests, was another Craiglockhart. Sasson visited him there twice in November and three times in February. There was no invitation to visit on 21 April, Stephen's twenty-seventh birthday. Sassoon wrote to Swaylands rebuking Stephen for his tantalising, teasing behaviour, which was destroying their friendship. The rebuke was met with crushing disdain and dismissal from Stephen and delivered via his specialist, Dr T. A. Ross.

Dear Captain Sassoon,

Mr Tennant told me that he received a letter from you, but he had not read it and I do not think intends to. What I am going to say is something I have nothing whatever to do with, except that I have been asked to pass it on to you as a message from him. I do not know why, but since your last visit his feelings towards you have not been what they were. He says you upset him and make him feel ill, and that he cannot see you again. I know that he has done this before, and that you will probably feel he is a very impossible person. He is, of course, not well, and that is about all there is to be said for it. I know also that I have encouraged you to come here in the autumn, because I thought that your visits did him good: but as he says he does not wish to see you now, I can obviously do nothing further in the matter.

Indeed, there was nothing more anyone could do.

15

HESTER

1933–7

'Where did I go wrong?' he asked Edith Olivier. Like Cecil Beaton and Rex Whistler, he knew that he had fundamentally misunderstood Stephen. He had treated him as a child and expected him to behave like an adult. Too late in the day he realised this and wrote to Glen Byam Shaw: 'Stephen wants what is withheld. He is always a victim of his own selfishness and like all people of that type he is always under the impression that he is above criticism.' What Stephen demanded was an audience, to be fêted, applauded, admired, adored, his whims indulged and his beauty constantly affirmed by his worshippers. He was a butterfly who could not be caught, who would not be possessed or dominated. Sassoon was so infatuated that he could not deal with Stephen's capricious nature – 'However naughty he is, one always reverts to adoring him.' But his fatal misjudgement was to believe himself indispensable to Stephen. The reverse was the case – Stephen had become indispensable to him. As a result he failed to see the signals that he was no longer wanted. His presence, once a comfort, had become a demand, that impossible demand on friendship that W. J. Turner had warned him against in Germany. How he might have benefited from the example of Cecil Beaton and Rex Whistler, who sidestepped that error and retained Stephen's friendship. He might have saved himself a lot of agony if he had responded as his mother did. She had said: 'I hear Stephen is in a lunatic asylum – the best place for him.'

Edith Olivier understood how deeply Sassoon was being crushed. She saw him the day the letter arrived from Dr Ross and wrote in her diary that he was 'absolutely broken. It was torture to see Sig's anguish and I could not help him.' She was too wise to offer false comfort and pretend all would be well again; it was over. They drove to Wilsford and took a stroll in the gardens, as if for the last time. The Miss Hunters, Beryl and Eileen, thought they, too, were on the verge of departure, believing Stephen would not return. It was an era coming to an end. Four days later Edith wrote, 'Haunted all night by thoughts of Sig who said he felt as people who kill themselves – people with no future, but he says he won't.'

All in all, 1933 had been a rotten year. At its beginning he had broken his collar-bone when his horse stumbled, throwing Sassoon to the ground, then trampling all over him. Tossing what he thought was an extinguished match into a waste-paper basket he set it and the curtains on fire, and very nearly the house. There were two altercations in his Packard car, the first with the kerb-stones on a sharp corner and the second with a bus, its driver and the local police. The lanes of Wiltshire were not designed for fast cars to challenge buses in overtaking manoeuvres and mudguard-to-mudguard duels. In heated language Sassoon demanded an explanation from the bus driver (notorious for his bad manners, noted Sassoon) as to why he was racing him. Before receiving a reply he accused the man of being 'a bloody fool'. Then he got into his car and drove off, believing the incident concluded. It was not long before the local policeman (a lazy and incompetent man, noted Sassoon) was investigating this further example of Captain Sassoon's questionable ability as a driver. Collusion was in the air (the bus driver and the policeman were close friends, noted Sassoon). But he knew how to stem this corruption of authority. He enlisted the aid of Edith Olivier, whose cousin 'is a great friend of the Chief Constable of Wilts and will get the C.C. to put a stop to all this nonsense. And I suppose the stupid Wilsford P.C. will get it in the neck.' Sassoon was, however, found guilty, fined £6. 9s. 4d. and came within a whisker of losing his licence. Only Toad of Toad Hall excelled him in the combination of righteous indignation and incompetence at the wheel.

Sassoon had burdens enough and was in no mood for more: just the sort of time when Robert Graves tended to appear in one form or another. During the three years' silence between them, he had settled in Mallorca with Laura Riding and, in the village of Deya, enlarged his house and built a road down to the sea. Then the tradesmen reverted to their inconvenient convention of asking for payment. Graves had not budgeted wisely, money was needed quickly but all sources had dried up – all that is except one:

My Dear Siegfried,

I am writing this to you care of Faber and Faber. I don't know your address and have heard nothing of you since our last most rotten correspondence three years ago.

I want to know whether you still have money in any quantity, and accessible and if so whether you can lend me some. I need about a thousand pounds, because I have got into a hole. As I do not consider that our quarrel was in any way final or fundamental and found both of us in a bad state, I naturally turn to you. If you can't do anything about it, at any rate let me know that you get this letter as I want to know at once how I stand.

Robert

The PS was vintage Graves: 'I don't say anything about repayment, but I expect that this is not impossible.' It is also vintage Graves that the first of Sassoon's replies is nowhere to be found but it is obvious from subsequent letters that Sassoon did not oblige. Enlightening rather than elevating, the correspondence created another rash of accusation and counter-accusation. Sassoon could not see the funny side of Graves's dilemma, nor that the whole episode was the stuff by which friendships are cemented, not, as in this case, consigned to a silence of 20 years.

Edith, the support to whom Sassoon looked in these days of mixed fortune, ensured that he had little time to brood. When Stephen returned to Wilsford, news filtered down to Fitz House via the Hunter sisters but Edith persisted in turning Sassoon around to face new directions and meet new people. Among the most important were the Morrisons of Fonthill Abbey. They were political and artistic patrons and discerning collectors. Fonthill was full of rare and beautiful *objets d'art*, manuscripts and books harvested by Alfred and Mabel Morrison. Their son Hugh became MP for Salisbury in 1918. Edith was a staunch Conservative and worked for him in this and subsequent elections. Katharine, their daughter, married a barrister, Stephen Herbert Gatty, who progressed to a knighthood and to the position of Chief Justice of Gibraltar. Edith also introduced Sassoon to the Gatty offspring: Richard, Oliver and Hester. Yet despite her endeavours, Sassoon complained to Glen more than once of feeling isolated. Much of this was of his own choosing, increased by the demands of two collections of poems he was preparing. There was loneliness, also grief, mixed with anger. He took to riding across to Wilsford to exchange news with 'Really and Truly'.

Glen came to stay at Fitz House; Edith and Rex dined there on champagne and caviar. Newcomers to the nearby village of Rockbourne were Lord David Cecil and his wife Rachel. Sassoon was acquainted with David and admired Rachel's father, the writer and critic Desmond MacCarthy. Edith and the Daye House became the centre of a circle similar to Garsington, though less intense. Ottoline came down to spy out the land and see Sassoon. She liked Edith and the people she met at the Daye House but was suspicious of Violet Bonham Carter, who was greatly taken with Sassoon. Violet had been sharp with her cousin, Stephen, for his selfishness and beastliness. She was familiar with the Tennants' mercurial behaviour; her step-mother Margot being one of them. Her letters to Sassoon from Swaylands and Wilsford had been a comfort, in that he liked to know even the bad news but they did nothing to help him break away from the obsession. Edith, on the other hand, was trying to release Sassoon in creating opportunities through which a sense of freedom and a new beginning might emerge.

The highlight of the summer was the Wilton pageant. Held during the first week of June in the grounds of Wilton House, it was a splendid but demanding event, which included full dress rehearsals. Sassoon was on Edith's guest list, as were Glen and Angela Byam Shaw. So too were Richard and Hester Gatty. Edith noted in her diary that Hester looked 'a dream in an oyster silk Caroline dress', while her brother looked 'rather dull as Charles I'. Sassoon appeared somewhat self-consciously as an Elizabethan bard. According to Edith, the weather was 'blazing' and took its toll on many of the participants. Hester Gatty, she noted, had 'retired with a headache to the shade of the riverbank. Sig, however, was very happy. The whole thing has been real fun and has made a huge difference to him.' It was Edith's reward to see him inching his way out of Stephen's shadow and she was determined not to let him slink back into solitariness, which only made him brood and become self-pitying. The Thursday after the pageant she went with him to dinner at Rockbourne. David and Rachel Cecil, newly married, appealed to Edith's romantic instincts. 'A delicious evening of talk – such fun, and all amazing,' she wrote.

Sassoon's spirits were raised when Blunden married Sylva Norman in July. Blunden was settled at Merton College, Oxford, and working on more projects than he had fingers on which to count them. Solace as well as income was the spur. His divorce from Mary had left its mark. Like Sassoon, he needed constant emotional support as much as creative stimulus. Their friendship was part of the emotional reserves upon which each drew. Blunden's busyness robbed them both of much of that support.

Throughout August Edith was constant in her attention. Sassoon spoke openly to her, as he rarely did with women. She had an advantage in that she made no demands on him, sought nothing from him and offered herself as a listener. Above all, she understood the depth of his feelings for Stephen. One evening in August, strolling through the gardens at Wilton, he told her how his feelings for Stephen 'can only end with his life, and he divides people he knows between those who understand this and those who don't.' Edith did not ask him about the implications of such a commitment, or how it might colour, even determine, future relationships but she understood from an earlier conversation that he no longer fretted himself about his ex-lover. He was capable of 'criticising him from the outside'. Stephen had became an 'element in his past life which had made him what he is'.

As one reads extracts from Edith's diary and Sassoon's of this time at the Daye House in the summer of 1933, there is the clear impression of him having caught a glimpse of possible happiness. Again it was to Edith that he confessed how he had enjoyed the summer, the pageant, Ottoline's visit, then Glen and Angela, dinner with David and Rachel and the laughter as Rex propelled Edith recklessly around the garden in a wheelbarrow, nearly colliding with Sassoon's car. But he also knew, as he drove back to Teffont, he was going home to an empty house: 'I need love to light up my existence. Mental friendships are not enough. Emotional companionship is what I need.'

On 5 September, as he drove home he saw a young lady in a pink dress. She was sketching, as indeed she had been two days previously when he had noticed her for the first time. He thought he knew her but could not remember from where. Later they met on the road that leads to the village. After they had exchanged afternoon greetings she introduced herself as Hester Gatty. Then he remembered her from the Wilton pageant. With her brother Richard, she had been a houseguest of Edith. She was now staying at the Black Horse, the inn a few hundred yards from Fitz House. With that minimum of acquaintance he invited her to dinner that evening. 'H.G. has rather a sad face, but is attractive,' he wrote, adding immodestly, 'she is not likely to forget her evening with me – as I was at my best all the time and we got on easily.' In fact so easily that Hester explained she had recently recovered from a nervous breakdown, the result of a failed love affair. Such a display of confidence greatly moved Sassoon and he wrote: 'I felt grateful for her companionship.' They spent the next days together, Sassoon driving her around the countryside during the day and entertaining her at dinner in the evening. On parting he confessed in his diary, 'I felt a strong affection for her,' after which he wrote (one is tempted to say, inevitably) that she needed protecting. The danger signals were appearing.

As the niece of Hugh Morrison of Fonthill Abbey, Hester would not be absent for long from Sassoon's social circle. Edith Olivier had known her since she was a child and, as was Edith's way, had helped her through her earlier romantic trauma. On Saturday, 1 October, at Hester's request, Sassoon drove her home to Ossemsley Manor, arriving there in time for luncheon. He enjoyed the company of Hester's brother Richard and strolled the grounds of what he thought was an ornate, but cluttered Edwardian home. Lady Gatty was very deaf, but 'with a charming, kind face'. The house and its grounds, the family, the ambience nothing like what he had imagined. Hester seemed out of place there. He could not explain why he felt this, but it was one of the questions which preoccupied him as he drove back to the Daye House and to Edith for the weekend. Hester, he recognised, was offering him an escape from his solitary existence but even allowing for her ease of manner and the evident affinity they felt for each other, was it possible that she could be happy with him, a man 20 years her senior? Then there was the question of his homosexuality. He had told her about Stephen – that is about their friendship: discretion and delicacy imposed the boundaries. 'What can I do? I can't say to her, "Look here, I am 47, and I have never had a love affair with a woman. The best thing you can do is never see me again."' Questions and doubts assailed him but more prominent was the feeling that life was 'gently leading' him away from Stephen.

Sassoon was perplexed and continued to be so as he travelled the following week to London to meet Hester. Staying at the Reform, he slept badly, his mind occupied by uncertainties. He determined it was best to tell Hester clearly about his feelings for her, in particular how he saw her as his supreme chance for happiness and that he was convinced that he could make her happy. Then he states in his diary, 'My belief that I am in love with her, physically as well as mentally, has strengthened since Sunday.' They met in the afternoon and talked – at least Sassoon did – about the past six years. Next day, Saturday, they travelled back to Salisbury. Sassoon, now positively garrulous through excitement, told her over and over of his serious intentions. Hester was reluctant to accept his over-complimentary view of her. On reaching Salisbury, they parted but only for a while. That evening at 8.10, as Sassoon precisely records, he arrived at the Daye House to be reunited with Hester. When he saw her any last doubts were vanquished. He knew she was happy and he whispered to himself, 'O, Hester, you must redeem my life for me.'

Edith was in no doubt that 'Sig and Hester would marry'. It was right and appropriate that her home should have played so central a role in it all. She also thought of how that dinner at the Cecils' – David and Rachel being so in love with each other – must have inspired Sig towards marriage. Edith deserved her moment of romantic illusion as much as she deserved the seat reserved for her in the parish church of Christchurch on 18 December. Hester and Siegfried were married in the Lady Chapel. Among the small number invited were Rex Whistler and T. E. Lawrence (at that moment assuming the identity of Aircraftsman Shaw), and Glen was best man. Theresa was not well enough to attend. Sassoon had taken Hester to Weirleigh in October and all was pleasant. Edith, in Theresa's absence, sat in the place reserved for the mother of the groom, admiring the couple she had brought together. She was especially happy for dear Sig. He was quite right in saying it had been a wonderful summer. They had shared so many thoughts and become good friends. She also remembered Stephen.

Ten years previously, on 27 March 1923, Sassoon wrote a prophecy in his diary:

> Some day, when I've settled down and come into a fortune, I will buy a little manor house in a good hunting country and keep three or four 'nailing good performers' and play on a grand piano in a room full of books, with a window looking on to an old-fashioned garden full of warbling birds and mossy apple-trees. When I am forty-nine I will begin to look for that house and when I am in it I will write wise books.

He was in fact 47 when he heard that Heytesbury House, in the village of that name, near Warminster, was up for sale for £20,000. Standing in the Wylye valley on the edge of Salisbury Plain, it had caught Sassoon's eye as he visited the Nicholsons at nearby Sutton Veny. Built in 1700, with a façade and portico added 80 years later, this two-and-a-half-storey gentleman's residence stood sequestered among trees. It had eight principal bedrooms, nine secondary bedrooms, five bathrooms and six main reception rooms. Light falling through the tall windows enhanced the spacious and elegant proportions of the rooms. One, just off the main hall, bore the name of Queen Matilda. It was claimed that the house occupied the site which once was her residence. Sassoon and Hester took possession on 18 May 1934. It was quite a change from the basic accommodation Sassoon had lived in since 1919. For the first time in his life he was a man of property which included extensive parkland, woods and fields. He loved Heytesbury, a home made possible mainly through Aunt Rachel's legacy. As a gesture of gratitude and affection her portrait occupied a place of honour in the library. That room was soon full with Sassoon's collection. Standing there he may have recalled a stanza from his hero Shelley's poem, *Epipsychidion*:

> I have sent my books and music there, and all
> Those instruments with which high Spirits call
> The future from its cradle, and the past
> Out of its grave, and make the present last
> In thoughts and joys which sleep, but cannot die,
> Folded within their own eternity.

Taking possession of the house was a great challenge to the managerial skills of Hester. Not overly endowed with such gifts, she lacked the sense of order and arrangement which Sassoon possessed. If anything, he tended to be too neat and tidy. 'Hester is doing her best,' he would say, defensively. Great excitement and much activity filled the place as they, to quote Sassoon, 'built a little private Utopia'.

One of the first visitors to the new house was T. E. Lawrence. Writing to Geoffrey Keynes, he said he had made 'a raid on Heytesbury. All visitors there intrude, as yet, I think. He and she are like children alone in the world. S.S is abnormally happy. He looks so well, too. Whether it will last I cannot say. The barometer cannot always stand so high.' On her first visit Edith described the place 'as a dream'. Max Beerbohm tussled with nouns and adjectives to express delight: 'This morning I said to Florence, "they are both of them lovely spirits, in a lovely" – and here I paused for the right word and could only think of "bottle", and said "bottle"' and then righted myself and spoke the word I had wanted, "setting" which Florence thought a great improvement. Heytesbury is worthy of you.'

Not least among the joys of Heytesbury was its cricket pitch. Standing at the village end of the park, it became the centre of many a summer. A cricket match was the only occasion when Blunden and Sassoon were in contention for supremacy as their opposing teams squared up to each other. In the summer of 1934 Sassoon played his first game in 14 years. His diary for 30 June records that his team played against Warminster. He got a duck – given out by what he regarded as a travesty of a decision – his only consolation being a victory for Heytesbury by nine runs. Thirty years later, he told Dom Martin Salmon of Downside in detail of this cricketing injustice as he saw it. Salmon maintained it had been for Siegfried's good because he became 'a very difficult batsman to dislodge'.

Sassoon's marriage and the move to Heytesbury marked another boundary. As the years progressed he became less enamoured of town life. Each year since the war he had enjoyed a season on the Continent – Germany, Italy and the south of France. During the 1930s he made only three trips abroad: in the spring of 1934, 1937 and 1938. But nothing pleased him more than to welcome his friends to Heytesbury as his desire to leave his new home fell away to the point where, he boasted to Max, 'I now get my hair cut in Salisbury.' A poem of this period, 'Elected Silence', reveals his mood:

> Where voices vanish into dream,
> I have discovered, from the pride
> Of temporal trophydoms, this theme,
> That silence is the ultimate guide.
>
> Allow me now much musing-space
> To shape my secrecies alone:
> Allow me life apart, whose heart
> Translates instinctive tragi-tone.

If this was, as some suggested, a retreat, it was not from the world and its claims but from the world and its clamour. 'Despite his solitariness he watched the world astutely,' wrote Blunden. Edith Olivier recalled Sassoon speaking of the prophetic role of the poet. It was a role which Sassoon was about to assume.

'The poet can only warn,' said Wilfred Owen. In the decade after the Armistice it was not only poets who recognised the signs of Europe moving towards another war. Prominent among the seers was Winston Churchill, whom Sassoon met at a house party just before moving to Heytesbury. Churchill's attitude towards President Wilson's vision for a new world order and later his opposition to the Labour movement, in particular his actions during the 1926 General Strike, soured Sassoon's opinion of him and, in consequence, the friendship with Eddie Marsh. But he agreed with the warnings Churchill was uttering about the ambitions of the European dictators. It was a sickening blow when in their conversation Churchill confirmed what Sassoon dreaded, that war was inevitable. To allow such a calamity would be to renege on every promise made at every cenotaph and war grave. Yet he had always feared that war would come when he heard the calls for vengeance and reparations drown out the calls for reconciliation and forgiveness. His poem 'Reconciliation', published in *Picture Show* in 1919, is indicative of his response. During his travels in Germany and Italy, he saw and heard more than music and opera. Hyper-inflation created bankruptcy and cast down friends like Onkle Walther and Tante Johanna at Haus Hirth. In Philipp of Hesse he had noticed and recorded the simmering anger of hurt pride that would seek its revenge.

During the decade that ended in a second world war, Sassoon published three volumes of poetry: *The Road to Ruin* (1933), *Vigils* (1934) and *Rhymed Ruminations* (1939). Such is the chronology of publication, but not of composition. Some of the poems in the third volume were written before the first or second volumes were published. Far from being three separate entities, these volumes are a continuum of thought and theme. Sassoon was never arbitrary in his selection of poems for a volume. This is not to deny the integrity of the individual poem, but when Sassoon wrote 'my real biography is my poetry. All the sequence of my development is there,' he is confirming that each poem shares something with the others, in addition to having a life of its own. The poetry is drenched with the thoughts of Frazer's *Golden Bough* and the ethnological and anthropological ideas of Dr Rivers. His influence on Sassoon spills over into the poetry; in *Vigils* the poem 'Revisitation' carries the initials 'W.H.R.R.' in brackets under the title. In using the word 'Vigils', Sassoon conjured up the image of the silent, careful watcher of unfolding events. It is one of his better titles.

A synoptic approach to the three volumes reveals Sassoon's train of thought on man and his destiny faced with what he feared was a war which threatened the continuance of the human race. He did not believe, indeed had ceased to believe before the war, in the Judeo-Christian revelation but retained a belief in the cosmic battle between good and evil fought on man's behalf by angels (Sassoon was a great believer in angels. They fly in and out of his poetry like his favourite Camberwell Beauty).

Neither did he lose his sensitivity to the mystical, what he called his 'religious sense', especially in response to nature. The poet Ralph Hodgson, who had been a frequent caller at Tufton Street, was as influential in this facet of Sassoon's experience as Dr Rivers had been in other aspects – 'R.H. has the most *religious* mind I know. By that I mean he is passionately concerned with goodness. Poetry is the central point of his religion.' Hodgson also possessed an abounding optimism about man's progress which appealed to Sassoon. When in 1924 Hodgson left for an academic post in Japan, Sassoon felt a deprivation equal to the previous loss of Blunden and of Rivers, two years earlier.

In his poetry Sassoon portrays man climbing out of some primordial swamp and through a process of advances and regressions pressing towards some destination of bliss. Edging his way upward, he developed a sense of himself and his destiny. Each generation climbs on the shoulders of its predecessor, reaching a little higher up the face of the rock. Immortality is not individual but rests in the continuance of the species. Generations live on in their offspring, who carry with them the hope and cultural memory of their forebears. Indeed, hope and memories are the rod and staff that comfort them. The climber on the rock is an amalgam of past, present and future, a thread in the kinship of humankind, whose role it is to follow and to fulfil. He learns from the past, navigates the present and ensures the future. War is inimical to hope and an offence against harmonic progress. War is evidence that man has moved in the wrong direction across the face of the rock and entered a gully from which he must retreat. War delays progress. War is 'The Ultimate Atrocity', the title of the fourth poem in *The Road to Ruin*:

> I hear an aeroplane – what years ahead
> Who knows? – but if from this machine should fall
> The first bacterial bomb, this world might find
> That all the aspirations of the dead
> Had been betrayed and blotted out, and all
> Their deeds denied who hoped for Humankind.

With apocalyptic urgency Sassoon's poetry is now directed to this danger. Unlike any other war the next one will be the War of the Great Bacillus, poisonous gases and hideous devastation. The eponymous poem which opens *The Road to Ruin* sounds the alarm:

My hopes, my messengers I sent
Across the ten year continent
Of Time. In dream I saw them go, –
And thought, 'When they come back I'll know
To what far place I lead my friends
Where this disastrous decade ends.'

Like one in purgatory, I learned
The loss of hope. For none returned,
And long in darkening dream I lay.
Then came a ghost whose warning breath
Gasped from an agony of death,
'No, not that way; no, not that way.'

Among the friends who received copies of *The Road to Ruin* and *Vigils* was T. E. Lawrence. Writing to acknowledge the second volume, he told Sassoon that the poems should be read 'slowly and in sequence. These poems are like wood-violets and could be passed over by men in a hurry.' But in the 1930s men were in a hurry. With the world going headlong into another war and ideologies in conflict, the cauldron of politics was boiling over. This was a time for taking sides and raising banners. *The Road to Ruin* – prophetic, sharp and sardonic – had its admirers but *Vigils* seemed anaemic. Sassoon's style, language and content were inappropriate to a generation of poets who were politicised, committed to an ideology – W. H. Auden, Stephen Spender, C. Day Lewis and, to an extent, Louis MacNeice.

What Sassoon achieved in the First World War through a conjunction of poetry and a cataclysmic event was repeated by the Auden generation focusing on the evils of capitalism and the threat of Fascism. Ironically, Sassoon had entered that battle in the previous decade with his prose and poetry expounding and espousing the cause of the Labour movement and the miners in particular. The overture to the Second World War was the Spanish Civil War, which galvanised artists of the Left around the Republican cause. There is no echo of this in Sassoon's work. That his poetry pointed to consequences beyond the moment, seeing as far as the war after next when an aeroplane – a recurring image in the trilogy – would deliver the ultimate atrocity in wiping out the species, brought no honour from the poets and writers of the thirties. Why should it have done? Sassoon was not bringing a unique insight to the times; there were others in literature, politics and science earlier and louder in the field. He was not a solo performer but part of a chorus, though nonetheless valuable for that. *The Road to Ruin* contained only seven poems including the title poem and there is great disparity of accomplishment and effectiveness between them. The weaknesses become more pronounced when these poems are placed alongside the work of the younger poets, and when reading the trilogy as an entity, especially the puerile contents of the oddly entitled *Rhymed Ruminations*.

Sharing the theme of war with *The Road to Ruin* and *Vigils*, it spoke of the poet's bemusement at finding the world again on the verge of destruction and possessed by fear born of an 'air-raid-worried mind':

> We are souls in hell; who hear no gradual music
> Advancing on air, on wave-lengths walking.
> We are lost in life; who listen for hope and hear but
> The tyrant and the politician talking.
>
> Out of nothingness of night they tell
> Our need of guns, our servitude to strife.
> O heaven of music, absolve us from this hell
> Unto unmechanized mastery over life.

Sassoon no longer believed that man, despite his technological sophistication, was progressing. Far from advancing he was going round in circles, repeating his follies. This is the thrust of his poem '878–1935'. It had all happened before, on his own doorstep:

> Here, on his march to Earthundun, King Alfred passed
> No wood was planted then; terraced hill was grassed.
> Now, in the summer, tanks come lumbering down the lane.
> I'd like to watch King Alfred walk this way again.
>
> Then, it was quite correct to hack and hew the Dane,
> And to be levied for a war was life's event.
> Now in a world of books I try to live content,
> And hear uneasily the droning aeroplane.
>
> I'd rather die than be some dim ninth-century thane;
> Nor do I envy those who fought at Earthundun.

> Yet I have wondered, when was Wiltshire more insane
> Than now – when world ideas like wolves are on the run?

Rhymed Ruminations is also an exploration of the individual desire for inward harmony and meaning; a continuation of the themes begun in *The Heart's Journey* and *Vigils*. It expressed Sassoon's gradual disenchantment with his own century and his yearning for a world in which the alliance between man and nature is restored; the world of Blake, Wordsworth and George Meredith. The answer to his quest lay not in the future but in the past; something lost on the way which must be found. His poem 'A View of Old Exeter' was inspired by a painting of the same name by the artist J. B. Pyne. Sassoon closes the poem with the desire to stare and

> Sigh for that afternoon he thus depicted, –
> That simpler world from which we've been evicted

With thoughts like this it is no wonder Sassoon was still perceived as playing in the Georgian band conducted by Eddie Marsh, to whose music nobody was dancing any more, although some might listen in the warm glow of a nostalgic evening. Running almost parallel with the trilogy of poems was *Sherston's Progress* (1936), the final volume of the *Sherston Trilogy*. He had started writing it the previous October. It had been difficult, dealing as it did with his time in Craiglockhart and the last year of the war, that 'dirty trick which was played on my generation and me'. With the clouds of another war gathering, he completed the book on 9 January 1936. He was not joyous – where had all the sacrifice led? There is an unintended irony in the title *Sherston's Progress*. In retrospect it all appeared regression. He told Eddie Marsh: 'It has been a laborious task but it seems to have plenty of vitality – and I feel confident that it will be read with enjoyment.' Rather dejectedly, two days later he wrote again to Marsh, not about prose but about poetry. Heinemann published a regular edition of *Vigils*. It was dedicated to Hester – 'The reviews of *Vigils* have been most peculiar. A new generation of critics has sprung up and they seem to regard me as a dreary back number.' This was followed by the first of another, more directly autobiographical trilogy, the deeply nostalgic *Old Century* (1938). It was all about yesterday: it was escape literature, anecdotes for the end of the day; a sentimental obituary of a defunct era. He resembled one of those characters in Louis MacNeice's 'Autumn Journal':

Close and slow, summer is ending in Hampshire,
Ebbing away down ramps of shaven lawn where close-clipped yew
Insulates the lives of retired generals and admirals
And the spyglasses hung in the hall and the prayer-books
ready in the pew
And August going out to the tin trumpets of nasturtiums
And the sunflowers' Salvation Army blare of brass
And the spinster sitting in a deck-chair picking up stitches
Not raising her eyes to the noise of the 'planes that pass
Northward from Lee-on-Solent.

The rural is the past, it's where the old, the conservatives are. Mean-while, 'the rebels and the young/Have taken the train to town,' says MacNeice. Sassoon had missed that train and was standing on the platform waving his handkerchief, a man so like his epithet of Lord Grey, 'designed for countrified contentments'. This perception of him was a travesty but it says a great deal about Sassoon that he did nothing to correct the image. Perhaps he was comforted by Hardy's word about 'those intellectuals up there in London'. Rejection is not so easily dismissed. Being known only as a 'war poet' and fox-hunting man irritated him but he could not escape the label.

His poetry did, however, find a resonance in the 1930s, becoming an essential and public part of the pacifist organisation, the Peace Pledge Union: the PPU, as it became known, was founded by a gifted former Rector of St Martin-in-the-Fields, London and Dean of Canterbury. The Revd H. R. L. Sheppard was committed to what was called the Social Gospel. Its emphasis was the realisation of the Kingdom of God on Earth. The Labour leader Clement Attlee described it as 'Christianity without the mumbo-jumbo'. It succeeded in forming an easy coalition with non-adherents to the faith, particularly with Socialists. In the middle of the 1930s the pursuit of peace and the avoidance of war became the centre of Sheppard's ministry. Dick Sheppard created an alliance among all those who renounced war as a means of settling international disputes. He had a gift for publicity and prodigious energy. Celebrities were invited to become sponsors and to promote the aims of the movement. Mass meetings were organised and the leading lights, usually three per meeting under the chairmanship of the founder, would tell their audiences that war must be banned from international affairs. Sassoon became one of the first sponsors in 1935. His willingness to assist was helped by the high esteem in which Sheppard was held by Max Beerbohm, who had met him in Rapallo. Max was taken by his gaiety and easy manner. He was, said Max, 'a welcome intrusion' and quite unlike any clergyman he had ever known.

Sassoon was not willing to deliver a speech, believing that his most effective contribution to the cause would be to read some of his poetry. On 14 July 1935 he was among those on the platform at the inaugural night in the Royal Albert Hall. Among the PPU's most prominent members and speakers at its rallies were Bertrand Russell and Vera Brittain. She wrote of how she and others were moved to tears, listening to Sassoon reading of war and its waste, of bravery, suffering and desolation. Extant recordings of Sassoon reading his poems endorse her account of him as an impressive and effective presence on the public platform.

Hester was also having her own moment of glory – that same year her picture appeared in the February edition of *Vogue*. 'I love her deeply and gratefully,' her husband wrote. Revealingly he continued, 'but it is a love that has learned, by previous experience, to safeguard itself – or try to.' On the eve of his marriage he told Eddie Marsh: 'Hester's advent has been such a miraculous happening. She is a perfect angel.' A year later his diary records: 'Protective and possessive love can never realise that it can be a bit boring at times – lovely sweet Hester, why can't you realise this?' He could have been talking about himself. From then on the criticism escalated from the niggardly to the unbearable. By May, following the death of T. E. Lawrence, Sassoon craved privacy: 'Let me have my feelings to myself,' he pleaded in the pages of his diary. In August after Theresa and Michael had paid a visit to Heytesbury – in itself enough of a trial – he found Hester's persistent attention suffocating. It was a never-ending regime of 'captivity and supervision'.

Hester's intrusive manner was part of the nervousness that had impaired her health some years before. Sassoon was not an unsympathetic person nor undemonstrative but he needed freedom from distraction to 'shape his secrecies alone'. There had been excitement when in September Hester became pregnant. She was unwell and spent 10 days in bed. Sassoon was concerned for her but also grateful for solitude. He wrote off to his mother and friends announcing that 'a little Sass is expected next year – and is thought to be five weeks on the way'. Hester had a miscarriage.

His sadness was short-lived. The following March he wrote to Glen with the news that Hester was pregnant again. The letter also mentions that two 'plaintive letters' had arrived from Stephen, who was in America: 'He is trying to get back in his usual style, but I simply can't believe that he deserves any sympathy after the way he treated me. He would do exactly the same again if he had me in his power.' Stephen had written the previous summer but Sassoon had rebuffed the approach. Edith Olivier commended him: 'I know Stephen has a prankish wickedness in him, and would rather like to try his power and see if he could break their happiness.'

On 31 October a telegram arrived at Rapallo announcing: HESTER HAS A SON. BOTH WELL. SIEGFRIED. Having jumped up and down, Max responded with questions: 'What will he be christened? Sherston? Or Hesterus? or What?' Sassoon and Hester had come to London for the confinement, renting 18 Hanover Terrace, next door to the former home of Edmund and Nellie Gosse. On 28 November the baby was baptised George Thornycroft Sassoon in St-Martin-in-the Fields by Dick Sheppard. Edith Olivier, Max and Blunden were his godparents. Rex was there too, as were Osbert Sitwell and an ailing Ottoline. Sassoon was a proud and happy man but, like others, preoccupied about the future.

The previous evening he had made another appearance at the Albert Hall with Dick Sheppard on behalf of the PPU. Before an audience of 8,500 people he asked, in stentorian tones, 'Have you forgotten yet?' The question was originally posed to ex-servicemen reprieved from death; now he posed it to those threatened by devastation. As with so many new movements and causes, the meetings of the PPU were thronged with the converted but the general public preferred to follow their leaders, Stanley Baldwin and Neville Chamberlain.

Returning to Heytesbury, Sassoon turned to his next book, the estate and George – 'My self reborn', as he wrote in the poem 'Meeting and Parting'. Christmas 1936 was, he said, 'the happiest Xmas ever'. Again, writing to Glen in the late spring of 1937, Sassoon told him that George was 'lovelier than ever, and as contented and good humoured as any baby could be'. For the first, but not the last time, Sassoon wrote of his son: 'I feel that my whole future depends on him.' On the eve of their engagement he had said the same thing about Hester.

16

MARRIED LIFE

1937–9

Heytesbury was always at its best on the cusp between spring and summer. In May Theresa arrived to see her grandson for the first time. Her health was indifferent – she was arthritic and suffered bouts of angina. Being unable to climb the stairs at Heytesbury, she stayed at a Warminster hotel and travelled out each day. Nothing, however, could dampen her spirit and Sassoon described her as being 'in splendid form. She is really glorious. It is so nice to see her with George.' Another of Theresa's grandchildren had just left Heytesbury, Michael's son Hamo. His visit had been intended to last only three days but influenza kept him there for three weeks. Sassoon did not mind, since Hamo was his favourite nephew. There had been other guests, warmly welcomed and equally warmly waved goodbye. Hester had a number of little outbursts, which Sassoon put down to her inability to cope.

A month earlier they had been in Italy, staying at Rapallo and welcomed each day to the Villino Chiaro by Max and Florence. Sassoon enjoyed Hester's company, breezily happy and engaged by the surroundings, especially the small church of San Pantaleone. Seven years before he had walked that same way with no assurance of future happiness: 'My whole existence, as a feeling human being, dependent on the whims and caprices of Stephen, and three years of spiritual disintegration ahead of me – had I but known it! No need to explain the difference between then and now!' He was so proud of Hester, who was always at her best with the Beerbohms, and happy that they liked her so much.

Together, relaxed and on holiday, Sassoon hearty and jolly, they appeared a contented couple. Back at Heytesbury their relationship was not as it had appeared in Italy. Three years into married life Sassoon reverted to, if indeed he ever left, the routine and habits of the single man. He began to resent what he regarded as Hester's intrusions and possessiveness; he became almost paranoid, suspecting her of watching his every move, eaves-dropping on his conversations, prying into his correspondence. All his life he had guarded his privacy, made his own arrangements, followed his own timetable. Being married was no reason, as far as he could see, why he need submit all this to discussion, compromise and certainly not permission. He did not want to share all his life with his partner. The onus was on Hester to conform. He expected her to tend to a wife's duties – run the house, entertain the guests, have children and make her husband comfortable. The impact of this philosophy of the paterfamilias made Heytesbury somewhat removed from the little Utopia of three years earlier and T. E. Lawrence's description of a marital idyll. But Lawrence in the days before the wedding had sounded a warning note. He wrote to Nancy Astor that he had spoken with Hester, who was in love with Sassoon but 'in terror of her life of proving inadequate. I tried to cheer her up, without being foolishly optimistic. I liked the foolhardy creature. Fancy taking on S.S.'

Foolhardy but in love, Hester wanted to share in her husband's activities. She may well have been too insistent at times but Sassoon lacked the desire to include her and she was wounded by the exclusion. It was a rejection she could not understand. There is nothing to commend in his behaviour but there was nothing inconsistent in it either. No one was ever allowed to share his secret and ordered world; it was inviolable. The smallest intrusion, the momentary interruption, was repulsed. The clearest picture we have of Sassoon's ideal is his depiction of Aunt Evelyn, who seems to exist entirely for her nephew, her household arranged for his convenience. George Sherston's world was a man's world, so was Heytesbury, and Hester was no Aunt Evelyn.

Inevitably there were outbursts. Embarrassed, Sassoon wrote to cancel an evening in London with Glen and Angela: 'I can only assume that for me to spend an evening with you and Angela is more than Hester can humanly endure! Sad, isn't it, that her love for me should take this form; but we must hope that she will some day arrive at a more sensible way of behaving.' The letter bears the hallmarks of an end-of-term report. It lacked sympathy – it certainly lacked loyalty. There was forbearance but it was the fruit of indebtedness and not of love: 'She has given me George, so I must not take this tiresomeness too seriously.'

In September 1937 Sassoon began Book Two of *The Old Century*, which would recount the years he was at New Beacon School, Marlborough College, cramming at Henley House and failing dismally at Cambridge. He thought he might call it 'Educational Experiences'. Obviously he found titles difficult! He was also finding writing difficult and was taking an inordinate time to complete just a few sentences. 'Last night I spent three hours writing 150 words,' he told Max. He did not hint that part of the problem was domestic distraction: only Glen was privy to the situation. Writing to him on 30 October, Sassoon reported that Hester had been 'angelic of late' but this was due to his 'not allowing anything to happen which might upset her'. She was ill at ease if asked to entertain visitors whom Sassoon knew but she did not. When an old friend and distant relative of Theresa's stayed at Heytesbury, Sassoon reported that he 'was never left alone with her for 5 minutes. Odd, isn't it?' Hester had also taken against theatrical people, which ruled the Byam Shaws out – 'She can't bear to share me with anyone else. Don't imagine that she dislikes you and Angela. It is merely this jealousy of hers. Even this letter will have to be posted surreptitiously, and your reply carefully worded.' Efforts to explain his need for some time on his own, he said, had been unsuccessful.

By Christmas the writing situation had improved. He wrote to Max in a more confident frame of mind about the book, which he had decided to call *The Old Century and seven more years*. The lower case emphasised that this part was a sequel. It never appeared on the spine of the book, only on the title page, and is rarely if ever quoted as part of the title. He did not mention in his letter that the new work was to be dedicated to Max. When the Beerbohms arrived for a visit to Heytesbury in the first week of the New Year the book was not discussed in any detail. That happened in April, when Sassoon and Hester again visited Rapallo and presented the page-proofs for Max's perusal. 'Not many verbal alterations were required,' Sassoon proudly recalled, 'but I was aware of my punctuation being amateurishly unsystematic. For Max punctuation was of prime importance to perfected prose.' *The Old Century* was published in September 1938. 'It is,' wrote Max, 'a wonderous work, a miracle of evocation. I shall always be immensely proud of the dedication.' It became Sassoon's favourite work – 'a daisy of a book', he sometimes called it, or 'a honey of a book and as mellow as an old fiddle'. But it was not the book he had intended to write.

In the Prelude there are two images. The first is of a rivulet flowing from Watercress Well, near Weirleigh, which 'goes running through the wood, talking to itself in the wordless language of water and roots and stones'. The other image came to the child Siegfried as he watched his mother 'making a water-colour sketch of a man sowing'. He combined these images to state his motive for writing: 'The purpose of this book is to tell whither the water journeyed from its source, and how the seed came up.' This new volume was to be, or so it would appear, an exploration of Sassoon's inner life, his growing awareness of himself, how his perception of his environment, the places, people and his relationship to them had developed. But the book is not faithful to this intent. Towards the end of the volume Sassoon gives the reader a new reason for writing: 'My intention in this book has been to commemorate or memorialize those human contacts which supported me in my rather simple-minded belief that the world was full of extremely nice people if only one got to know them.' The focus has moved. Autobiography has become anecdotal rather than confessional, descriptive not revelatory, objective not subjective. Like the tableaux vivants Theresa used to arrange at Weirleigh, *The Old Century* became one sequence after another of groups and individuals representative of the last decade of the Victorian era. There is little if any historical or social context; there is much character description but minimal personal exploration – that has to be inferred. The book became an account of innocent, all-pervasive, all-conquering happiness, a world in which the intrusions of death and domestic misery yield to the optimistic spirit.

Why he changed the emphasis or what made him veer on to a different course is not clear. An educated guess might include his own state of unhappiness: Sassoon was in 1937–38 a disillusioned and disappointed man. His marriage was one factor, the lack of acclaim for his poetry another, but the world sliding into war was the ultimate blow. Of the opening years of the century he said, 'the future then was something to be desired'. Optimism about the future was no longer a foundation on which he could build a philosophy. He turned around and followed the rivulet back to its source. Like Tolstoy, he was going to search for the green stick which marked the place where he had once been truly happy.

In August 1937 he drove to the Norfolk village of Edingthorpe, where in 1897 he had spent a holiday. In 1924, he revisited the place as part of his pilgrimage across England, which had ignited the idea of the memoirs. Edingthorpe, he discovered, was unchanged despite the passage of years. It was not frozen in time but timeless, immutable. There he succeeded, as he so evocatively described in chapter eight of *The Old Century*, in finding not the past so much as himself. The 50-year-old Sassoon made friends again with the 10-year-old Master Siegfried near to the Rectory, which all those years ago Theresa had taken for the summer:

It looked so ordinary, and yet so far away from the present time. And how easily it showed me myself as I once was – a boy in a brown jersey and corduroy shorts bleached by many washings, sitting in the long grass with his knees up under his chin, reading *The Invisible Man*, which he had brought out there because one of his brothers had tried to tell him how it ended and he didn't want to be told. He doesn't look up or move as I stand beside him – that H. G. Wells-absorbed boy with reddish brown hair. He knows nothing of himself, nothing of the delusions and discontents which he must muddle his way out of before he can be looked back on, almost as though he were someone from another life. Reading *The Invisible Man* in its blood-red binding and wondering how the story will end, he doesn't know what he is in for. He can't guess that there will be a war-memorial lych-gate any more than North Walsham church knew that its tower and bells would be blown down by a gale.

Me he does not foresee, with my queer craving to revisit the past and give the modern world the slip. Thus we are together – the boy I like to be remembering and the man he might have liked to be with, could he but have known me, his completed self.

The longing to be that boy again is almost palpable, to be the other side of that terrible war, free from the wound of knowledge, innocent again; to build a bridge of absolution between the boy and the man; to give the modern world the slip and embrace again the simplicities left behind. Heytesbury too was part of that wish. It was redolent of the harmony and felicity Sassoon desired in his own life. He had been conscious of the need in the twenties and had expressed it in *The Heart's Journey* when he says, 'my inward life took shape'.

The two summers which preceded the Second World War were as glorious as the days recounted in *The Old Century*. Conscious that the drift into conflict was inexorable, Sassoon adopted a policy of business as usual. He was not averting his gaze from the fact that armies were again on the move or closing his ears to the politicians; Sassoon remained well informed about what was happening. What he knew was there was nothing he could do about it except to do what a good batsman does, namely to keep his end up and that meant Heytesbury, the family and the village. Of the summer of 1938 he says, 'We've had an idyllically quiet summer, punctuated by cricket matches in which I make fewer runs than I could have wished.' But he could not resist boasting to Sydney Cockerell that he had scored a six the week before and smashed three panes of glass in the pavilion – 'How many poets have done that at my age? Not even Bridges, I think, although he boasted that he once hit several boundaries in one over.'

Blunden came to Heytesbury during the second week of August, his first visit in 14 months. He and Sassoon had met earlier in that summer in Oxford when the Heytesbury XI took on the Barnacles, Blunden's team. Sassoon's life at this point stood in direct contrast to that of his old friend. Blunden was in perpetual motion, writing, publishing, lecturing and broadcasting; ferreting here and there for some rare edition, and keeping in touch with other poets, including the young and modern ones. Blunden loved activity and being at the heart of the literary world. Unlike Sassoon, he did not cut himself off from the places where interesting and new ideas were. He was particularly active in keeping contacts alive with Germany, arranging and attending literary conferences there and welcoming delegates to England. None of these activities, however, was allowed to impede his enthusiasm for cricket – watching it, talking and writing about it, but above all, playing it.

Sassoon as a writer had come to a full stop. It was a struggle to find the motivation to start another literary project, another volume of memoirs carrying on from where *The Old Century* left off and taking his story through to the beginnings of the Great War. Writing to Max at the year's end, he confessed that he had not written anything. He cited the crisis in Europe, caused by Hitler laying claim to the Sudetenland and a general preoccupation with the deteriorating situation. Each morning, he followed the unfolding events in *The Times*, usually while lying in bed enjoying a boiled egg. Hester would invade his musings, anxious to share perspectives with him and gleanings from the political speeches or special reports broadcast on the wireless. She was well informed, probably better than he was, but Sassoon was reluctant to enter into any discussion. This reluctance contributed to more tensions as 1939 came and the last eight months of peace.

The year began with a visit from Max, followed by a visit from Rex Whistler's brother Laurence and his wife, Jill Furze. He was designing the title page for Sassoon's *Rhymed Ruminations*, to be published as a limited edition in July and followed by another edition dedicated to Blunden. Sassoon was looking forward to the spring and summer, not only because of the new volume but in order to see how his plans for the estate had worked out. A lot of time and effort had been spent reclaiming ground and improving the land. When the summer did arrive it brought with it a park smothered in buttercups and thrushes making their presence heard. Hester was happy, pottering around the garden, spending time with George and keeping in contact with her family, especially her brother Richard. During the last six months she had spent only five nights away from Heytesbury, 'so it isn't surprising that I am feeling the strain a bit', complained Sassoon.

He had so looked forward to the summer and was pleased with the estate but he felt hemmed in. What he needed, he told his diary, was somewhere to work undisturbed by wife and child, especially the former. The ground-floor rooms where he would, in normal circumstances, fill the pages of his exercise books were no longer free from his promenading spouse, nor from the wireless to which she listened constantly for news of the European crisis. Her appetite for information was insatiable and driving Sassoon to distraction. At the same time his refusal to discuss the latest development was having a similar effect on her. At midnight on 21 May he decided to resolve his situation by moving up to a room off the first-floor landing where many of his books were already stacked. It was a retreat in every sense but it meant that Hester could listen to her wireless and, if callers came, he could escape to this refuge. He was also going to introduce rigid rules – all interruptions from Hester would be strictly forbidden. He did nothing to implement the plan until she went away. There was no discussion, otherwise she would start suggesting this or that alternative and the whole idea would dissolve into ruins.

Having devised his plan, Sassoon felt much happier. He was as pleased as a schoolboy with a secret. Externally, things took a fine turn when the clouds lifted, the sun cheered everything and the birds were singing wondrously. Sassoon thought that the song of the blackcaps and the warblers especially was sweeter than ever. Regrettably, there was no sound of the nightingale, which rarely came to the Wylye valley. Standing on the lawn and casting his eye around, Sassoon discerned 'an earthly Elysium of heavenly sunlight and evening peace'. In the final weeks of peace he filled his diary with beautiful vignettes of Heytesbury: Hester in a blue linen dress tending the garden in the Long Walk; George enjoying his freedom on the lawn and bringing joy to his grandmother, Lady Gatty; Sassoon riding Huntsman or Sparks in the cool northerly breeze that wafted across the Great Ridge. 'The buttercup yellow acres of the peaceful park were a paradise of day-dreaming indolence, the house standing there as though expecting nothing to happen till haymaking. The whole place looked pluperfect.' References to the tranquillity of the place increased in number and intensity as the war drew ever nearer but Sassoon knew that earthly paradises are not permanent. They come for a moment, a comforting moment whose memory becomes a sustainment in uglier times:

> I love all things that pass: their briefness is
> Music that fades on transient silences.
> Winds, birds, and glittering leaves that flare and fall –
> They fling delight across the world; they call
> To rhythmic-flashing limbs that rove and race …
> A moment in the dawn for Youth's lit face;
> A moment's passion, closing on the cry –
> 'O Beauty, born of lovely things that die!'

Sporting a new cricket blazer – dark blue with gilt buttons, bought at Winchester College sports shop – Sassoon guided the Heytesbury team to a season of unqualified success. A number of top-rate performances from himself made all the difference, or so his diary records. Blunden's team came and were soundly defeated by 106 runs. Sassoon must have had an off-day, for he only scored two. Blunden scraped by with seven but got a nasty cut on his finger, the price paid for not wearing gloves, as was his habit. He was, however, named man of the match for taking six catches behind the wicket – wearing gloves. Sassoon cherished the moments: the house, the park, the walled garden, the smell of mown grass up on the Jubilee plantation and all the wild strawberries clustered about the appropriately named Heaven's Gate. Above all he loved trees, the cedar, the lime and his favourite, the beech. He listened as the wind swept through its branches and it became his 'whispering tree'. He christened one of them:

> I named it Blunden's Beech; and no one knew
> That this – of local beeches – was the best.
> Remembering lines by Clare, I'd sometimes rest
> Contentful on the cushioned moss that grew
> Between the roots. Finches, a flitting crew,
> Chirped their concerns. Wiltshire from east to west

Contained my tree. And Edmund never guessed
How he was there with me till dusk and dew.

Sitting under a beech with Hester and George, Sassoon was roused from his 'day-dreaming indolence' by his surveyor, John Baragwanath. He had a large map of the estate under his arm and brought news of a calamitous decision made by the Wiltshire County Council on behalf of the Ministry of Transport: a bypass was to be built. This meant that a mighty swathe of road would be driven across the cricket ground, the park would be split in half and the drive blocked at the half-point, effectively separating the house from the lodge gate and eliminating access to the village. Sassoon was left in a state of bewilderment. Could such a travesty be allowed? Next day, during a match on the threatened pitch, a mighty noise was heard from the direction of the stables. An enormous branch from one of the beech trees had crashed to the ground on the instant the ball claimed the last wicket of the innings. It was, Sassoon decided, an omen of approaching war and the demise of the cricket ground.

The Tank Corps, based at Warminster, had a passably good XI and was the next team to challenge Heytesbury. During the match on their bumpy and parched Warminister ground Sassoon resolved that he must fight against the accursed bypass. Much of the inspiration to do so emanated from the crisis-point the game had reached. Heytesbury was in danger of losing. It called out the fighting spirit in Sassoon – 'I got 17 not out and played just the sort of innings I enjoy most – every run counting in a crisis. I feel greatly cheered up by this succcess. I don't often get a chance to pull the match out of the fire.' Watching his team, he sensed the need to safeguard the traditions of the village and of cricket. Driving home he met his neighbour, a renowned horticulturist, Dr Hinton, and told him that the battle of Heytesbury was now joined. He announced the news with such conviction that Hinton declared, 'I shall sleep well tonight.' Never reluctant to use his influence or that of others, Sassoon lined up his well-connected family-in-law, recruited prominent friends and spotted an Old Marlburian tie on the County Council. Wanting to appear reasonable, he tramped around spying out possible alternative routes. The signs were hopeful, support for his cause strong; the enemy was divided, County Council bickering with Whitehall over the bill. On the other hand, the War Office was pressing for an improved road between Warminster and Salisbury and the south coast. With war in the offing, this could be decisive.

Sassoon's battle with the planners was, of course, a fight against the despoiling of his estate but he also drew another motive in his diary: 'I would give up all my fame in the outside world rather than lose my cricket and its human significance, wherein I am not S.S. but "the Captain" or "the Guv'nor".' Where 15 years earlier he was eager to raise the banner of revolution, now he believed that the structured society from which he had sprung, whose roots lay in rural, agrarian England, was to be cherished and defended. Watching his team play Devizes, responsible for George while Hester kept the score, he saw clearly what kind of England he counted as civilised. 'Village cricket with my retainers and neighbours, my son and heir (who is my sun and air), my refusal to go away from Heytesbury and take advantage of my fame – what are all these but acceptance of the fact that one's home is all that matters? I care about the people among whom I exist. *They* never go to London. Why should I? And I think that they are beginning to realise that I *am* one of them in the simplicity of my life. Up on the cricket ground the games go on. Smoke goes up from the kitchen chimney of the house. Tea is waiting for us in the garage. It all belongs to me. But the Heytesbury players know that I own it as a sort of trustee.'

Sassoon was romanticising again, proffering ideas which belonged to the eighteenth century and which most thought had expired in the Great War. He does not explain his journey across a wide spectrum of economic and social arrangement – from choosing two-roomed Turnerdom to buying Heytesbury, from lodger to squire in a decade. He was proud of the estate and the improvements: it was a community where the continuity of relationships was secured. He relished the prospect of young Sam Gedge sharing an opening partnership with George while he himself, grown old, watched from the boundary, content to have secured the things of good report for another generation. But it was also the language of someone who has watched the fire slowly reducing itself to embers and whose musings were an attempt to prolong the moment.

Sassoon oscillated between hope and despair. If only he were of an age to defend Heytesbury as he had vowed to defend the Weald in August 1914. He had no role, no contribution to make this time. These were not worries for or about himself, they stemmed from his involvement in other people's futures, especially George and Hester's; it was not only the Nazis and the trouble in Europe that were vexatious, it was the way the world was going. H. G. Wells had come on a visit and mentioned the whole monetary system was bound to collapse. Sassoon immediately understood what that meant for life at Heytesbury – extinction. Such a calamity would quickly make an end to any desire to live – 'As a selfish individual I ask only that I be allowed to keep my beloved home and refuge from the age of barbarism toward which the world seems tending.'

Perhaps he might save Heytesbury by writing articles for American magazines? The fees were high and required less effort than writing further memoirs. His New York friend, Sam Behrman, when he visited Heytesbury encouraged the idea. With the fountain of inspiration reduced to a trickle, why not? Then into his creative gloom would toddle George 'the healer of all my trivial discontents and dullness'. The important thing, Sassoon concluded, was to grasp these moments of intimacy and revisit through George the 'snake-less Eden of childhood'.

Sassoon had managed to transfer his study from the ground floor to the smaller room upstairs. Hester had taken George to see Theresa at Weirleigh. It was a moment of relief and opportunity. She had changed her mind several times about going, being unhappy at leaving her husband when the international situation was so grave. Sassoon lived in hope that she would just disappear for a few days. Solitude, solitude, he craved solitude.

Eventually she went, clutching George, something she continued to do throughout the time at Weirleigh, much to the concern of Theresa. She also clutched the telephone. Each evening she would ring Sassoon and insist on a complete breakdown of his day. On her return relations between them improved – they usually did after a brief separation. Together with George, they went on outings. Dinner in the evening saw Hester attired as though she was going out on the town. She liked Sassoon to dance with her in the room he had vacated. Suddenly she would break off and go to listen to the news, then return and berate him for not paying her sufficient attention and not discussing the issue of war. Much would be required of Hester when the war came. The authorities had already advised her that Heytesbury would be needed to house evacuees from London and she would have to arrange their accommodation and feeding. The prospect did not daunt her, but Sassoon shuddered. How would he survive this further invasion?

At least he found a room of his own. Sitting there in mid-August, signing copies of the limited edition of *Rhymed Ruminations*, window open for relief from the stuffy and sticky night, he was startled when some earth came in at the window. Hester had a tendency for little jokes. Sassoon made the inevitable assumption, moved to the window and was greeted by a voice from his past. Clearly visible in the night by the luminosity of a white coat and white shoes stood Stephen Tennant. Over six years had elapsed since Sassoon had seen him. Stephen had tried several times to re-establish contact but Sassoon had heeded the warnings of Edith Olivier: he had no intention of being hurt again. Only out of courtesy had he sent him a copy of *Rhymed Ruminations* and now through the same prompting he opened the garden hall door. Two days previously the Hunter sisters, 'Really and Truly', had been to Heytesbury for tea. According to their reports Stephen was on the downward slope and regarded by those close to him as a 'mental case'. This was one occasion when Hester's presence was more than welcome. When first told who was there she flared up, but in the quietness of the music room she was calm and polite. Sassoon thought she was, if anything, fascinated by Stephen, as she rather than Sassoon held the conversation together. He felt nothing for their visitor and marvelled he should ever have felt so deeply about him. All he wanted was for him to leave, which Stephen did after an hour. Hester and Sassoon accompanied him to the front gate. As he dived into his small car, he invited Hester to lunch or dinner: 'Siegfried, of course, will be too busy working.' And then he was gone. 'He's good company,' said Hester. Sassoon thought there was little likelihood of Stephen being a danger – 'though he may *become* a nuisance to us'.

A thousand times more welcome than Stephen was the arrival on 22 August of Blunden, together with his wife Sylva and H. E. Donner, a Swede working at Exeter College, Oxford. Arriving at six o'clock, they saw the final overs of a tense – 'edge of the abyss' – match, which Heytesbury won. Sassoon contributed only five runs to a total of 85. He was out to one of those deceptively slow deliveries which always tempted him with the promise of an easy boundary and which he never learnt to resist. Blunden was newly returned from Germany. Their conversation confirmed what Sassoon knew. Blunden was 'strongly imbued with the German point of view, and seems unable to realise the meaning of Nazi aims and methods. It is pleasant to hear someone talking *tolerantly* about Germany but I simply can't agree with his view that their bullyings are justified and that English public opinion is unfair to them. He disregards the essential wickedness of the Nazi Party machine and their avowed intention of imposing their will on the rest of Europe by brute force.' Blunden, like Sassoon, was not a political animal. Barry Webb, Blunden's biographer, writes, 'this was Blunden at his most gullible'. It was also Blunden at his most distraught. He did not think the situation was caused by one man and he knew that more than one man would die fighting it; the spectre of all he had witnessed between 1914 and 1918 happening again was cause of deep bewilderment and distress: 'Oh those endless, endless graves of mere boys.'

It was a spectre that also haunted Sassoon – he had seen enough and wished only for peace. He loathed the idea of war propaganda, lumping together every German as wicked. How could that be true of Walther and Johanna Hirth, who tended the sick with such love? They were among the noblest people he knew. Small children in Germany, young as his own son, would know savage deprivations and Germans as young as his nephew Hamo would be maimed and massacred. 'If war comes, I shall find myself living in a world *gone mad*. Life will become a hymn of hate.' Yet he had reached the stark conclusion that Germany needed 'to be delivered from its present Government; war seems to be the only way of eliminating Hitlerism. Can such things be? Can one endure them?'

One way to endure would be to find something to do, to make some contribution; it did not have to be conspicuous. Given the choice, he would prefer to 'endure in silence' but if he took such a course, he would end up 'dotty'. Back in May he had penned a letter to Eddie Marsh asking him what 'a supposedly influential writer' might contribute if there were a war? 'I would be grateful if you could find an opportunity to show this letter to Winston.' In the event Sassoon remained at Heytesbury, his services were not required. Hester prepared for 18 evacuees and two helpers. The maids began to sew blackout curtains and the wireless reported the inevitable final steps to war. Sydney Cockerell arrived on the last day of August; he had written to ask if he might find a refuge at Heytesbury. His invalid wife was safe in Gloucester and their grandchildren were being settled at Sutton Veny, a stone's throw from Heytesbury. Sassoon liked the idea of the valley, 'empty of nightingales but full of Cockerells'. His arrival brought the added bonus that he could engage Hester in conversation, especially about the European situation, which was the last thing Sassoon wished to do.

On Sunday, 3 September, as he listened to the declaration of war against Germany, Sassoon wrote in his diary that no other course would rid the world of Nazism. The statement did nothing to relieve his depression. He had never thought he would live to see again a world engaged in the slaughter of its youth. Middle-aged men like himself would be safe in their inactivity, safe but not happy – 'Happy are those who are too busy to think! It all makes me wish that the July 1918 bullet had finished me. I can do nothing now, except endure this nightmare.'

17

HEYTESBURY

1939–47

Sasoon began The Weald of Youth, his second volume of autobiography, in the last week of October. The stimulus was the war, or rather his need to escape from it. The newspapers and the wireless poured forth the latest information. At mealtimes Cockerell and Hester would discuss what they had learned. Conversation became circular without any hope of other subjects breaking through. Psychologically, Sassoon could not bear to hear the vocabulary of armed conflict. Hating war, yet recognising the need to fight Hitlerism, created turmoil in him. It also strained his relationship with the Peace Pledge Union, with whose principles of passive resistance he was at variance. Sassoon's poems 'The English Spirit' and 'Silent Service' were published in the *Observer* on 26 May and 2 June 1940. The following October they were included in the first ordinary edition of *Rhymed Ruminations*. Both poems were clarion calls for everyone to rally to the defence of civilisation. The tone is all 'England, Harry and St George'. Lines stating that 'None are exempt from service' and which praised 'Clenched resolved endurance' were unlikely to receive the commendation of the PPU. Discreetly, and couched in the form of 'a friendly enquiry' from the secretary, the matter was raised with Sassoon. His reply and the original correspondence have perished but he was not asked to resign as a sponsor. There was no publicity and the relationship was allowed to lapse. The incident saddened him. Only his absorption in the new volume saved him from deep depression.

This allowed him to escape to the Weald of 1909 and remember being 24, playing a good innings for the Blue Mantles at the opening of the new season; then to journey from Tunbridge Wells to Matfield driving the new dog-cart, 'a very comfortable one, two wheeled, rubber-tyred, nicely varnished and much the same colour as brown sherry'; his cricket bag under the seat while his straw hat shielded the latest edition of *The Academy*, which contained his sonnet 'Villon'. With that picture he opened *The Weald of Youth*, an account of the years from 1909 to that golden evening in 1914 when he looked on the Weald as though for the last time and then went off to defend it. What marvellous years they were, made better when refined by memory. Then Weirleigh, the Studio, his mother were his to enjoy without interruption. He had enjoyed quietness to build a library and write poems about birds and goblins and early mornings; golf and cricket and hunting, too, with the exuberant Gordon Harbord, then off to Warwickshire with Richardson to ride with the Loders; down to London and the flat at Gray's Inn; the ever-busy Eddie Marsh, the lonely Wirgie, the face of Brooke, the voice of Chaliapin and the Russian Ballet – what a time it had been! Recalling them did not depress him: they were the antidote, they were also the therapy. Without the writing, without the memory he would have sunk even further and faster. He was being saved by memory alone.

When not writing, Sassoon was happiest when with George – pushing him around in the pram up to the woods or down Mill Lane towards the station, leaning on the bridge by Mill Farm watching the dab-chicks on the river and the cows coming in at milking time. All this struck the chord of normality. His currency now was the small change of country life – a chat with some of the locals for whom the centre of the universe was Heytesbury and its concerns. Plans for the bypass were in abeyance (and stayed there for 50 years). Cricket at Heytesbury next season was on the mind of Old Bond (Heytesbury's ex-umpire), as he cut the grass below Cotley Hill in a cloud of gnats. At East Hill Farm, he met Jack Awdry and walked with him to West Hill Farm, where White the farmer said that George was very like his father – 'the most tactful remark he could have made. In the soft golden Elysian sunshine it was all countrified and genial, and just what I wanted for George.'

George was everything. Nonetheless even he could quickly become an irritation. When he did so, it was Hester who was blamed. Sassoon unwisely retreated into whisky and hot water. Taken as a nocturnal sedative when alone in his study, this exacerbated his depression. He slept fitfully and woke in a confused state. Nor was the battle of wills between mother and son the kind of welcome to a new day that Sassoon expected.

Twice in one morning the duel spilled over into his bedroom. He closed his eyes and pretended to be asleep: 'All I want to do is to forget – and forget – and have no arc-lights of practical mindedness turned on to my loathing of this Second Great War, by which I am being reduced to an impotent absurdity.' The reduction was from the active soldier and celebrity to the sidelined poet and chronicler of yesteryear. He read his diaries of the twenties and was struck by the variety of his life; rarely inactive, often unhappy and dissatisfied, 'but I never had the feeling of wanting to die that I sometimes have now. What I wanted then was not to become middle-aged. Now I am living the sort of life which would be inactive for a man of 70!' His diary reflects a resigned spirit: 'Spend nothing; do nothing; get through the days with as little effort as you can. Such are my intentions.' It was an admission of defeat, of resigned acceptance.

> Can happiness be mine when the restless body tires,
> And, wearied of the wine of dangerous desires,
> I turn towards heights that shine with unbefriending fires?
> I have looked and understood how happiness recedes;
> Not like the shore we leave at sunset; not by deeds
> Of anger or indifference darkened into death,
> But taken away by time, – O given back like breath.

The poem resounds with the old plea: 'If only things were different.' If only things could be as they once were. Sassoon was feeling sorry for himself and angry with the world. The reaction is understandable: all his life he had come and gone as he pleased, had his own way and on his own terms. Heytesbury was meant to be a continuation of that unlimited freedom. Suddenly and perversely it had gone wrong. To use his words, 'he was tied by one foot to a pram'. Married life and fatherhood proved restrictive: he found few compensations in the first, delighted in the second, but balked at the demands of both. That symbol of freedom, his Humber car, was standing idle and, with petrol rationed, would do so for the duration. Being confined to Heytesbury would not have been an unattractive prospect but it was being overrun by evacuees. He had been told that hundreds of troops would be encamped in the park, and an official had called to say that he and his family might be evicted and the house used by the Army as a training school. This did not happen, but Sassoon knew that he would have been powerless to resist had the plan gone ahead. Coming on top of his distress that war was a necessary evil and the realisation that, while he was a well-known writer, he was no longer an influential one, his ability to cope crumbled. 'Is this being alive? Or is it just killing time? When I wake up tomorrow, I shall wish that I hadn't woken up at all. I shall wake to nothing but boredom and frustration. My mental life is in ruins. I feel self-destructive and defeated.'

The last thing he wanted in the middle of this calamity was for Hester to throw her arms around him, declaring everything was well so long as they had each other. Hester became the whipping-girl – partly deserved, but mostly not. 'What will my married life look like when the war is over?' he asked himself. His diary for the war years suggests an appropriate answer might be: very unedifying. The list of complaints against Hester grew as irritation turned to exasperation, followed by bitter recriminations. To have married at all was a mistake – not because of Sassoon's sexual orientation, which was bi-sexual, not homosexual. He and Hester were sexually compatible. Indeed, one of Sassoon's complaints against her was the refusal to have more children. This was by no means a side issue: he saw it as an example of Hester's besetting weakness – her self-willed defiance of his wishes. Sassoon was patriarchal as well as paternalistic. He expected Hester to be part of his world; he saw no need to be part of hers. There is no evidence that he believed in discussing matters with her, literary, political, social or financial – except the domestic budget. His view about the role of women was made clear when he saw Hester and one of the maids attending to some blackout curtains: 'It seemed to me what they ought to be doing in a crisis, just sitting still and sewing! (and, of course, gossiping!). Nothing can alter the fact that women are only effective when they stick to their appropriate concerns. A woman who knows the boundaries of her province is worth more than rubies. Her power over men is diminished in proportion to her unwarranted interference with what appertains to his masculinity! Nothing infuriates them more than to be told so. But it is one of the fundamental truths of human existence.' If this was his considered opinion, as opposed to an intemperate statement, the marriage had not the least chance of success. Did Sassoon, so much the product of a matriarchal household, revolt against his background? Or was the statement a diatribe against Hester in particular rather than women in general? It is hard to imagine him applying this 'fundamental truth' to Edith Olivier, Helen Wirgman, Ottoline Morrell or Edith Sitwell. Certainly it was never applied to the women whose company he relished and whose intellectual prowess he admired later in his life.

Sympathy was not a quality Sassoon lacked but patience was not his greatest virtue. Hester was inexperienced in those qualities that her husband counted essential in a good wife: knowing how to run an organised household, how to raise a family and how to secure social standing by discreet entertaining. She came from a higher rung of the social ladder than her husband, and Sassoon would have taken for granted that Hester possessed those qualities but even such perceived 'shortcomings' on her part need not have been fatal to the marriage. In the end it was not what she lacked that proved destructive but what she thought she possessed, and what she supposed he needed. It was her 'possessive solicitude' that drove him to distraction. Unlike the other people in his life to whom he turned, Hester was a very bad listener.

Sassoon also failed. Hester had deep insecurities which he did very little to relieve. Nervous and frenetic by nature, she needed reassurance. Her earlier unhappy experience of a broken relationship was something that Sassoon of all people should have understood. And then there was George – 'George brings us together as nothing else can do.' Thus Sassoon wrote when George was three but it was a romantic statement, not a factual one. It might have been true when he was a baby, but by the time he was a young boy it was not. Rex Whistler, visiting Heytesbury on leave from the Welsh Guards, relayed another picture to Edith Olivier, who noted in her diary that the Sassoons' marriage seemed to be 'going on the rocks thro' the adored baby. He's very naughty, maddens Sieg by always being in the way and because Hester cannot manage him, but if she ever corrects him Sieg takes his side against Hester.' Indeed, Sassoon doted on him and describes his feelings when holding him as like 'holding my own life in my arms'. At such moments he did not want Hester around but Hester did not want to be excluded. Far from George bringing them together, he came to emphasise how divergent were their paths.

Both of them were facing their own battles. Hester was overwhelmed by the evacuees, one batch having to be taken away because they were infested with lice and suffering skin disease. She found it impossible to keep within the government allowance for their food. Running the house with reduced staff and taking care of George without the help of a nanny was beyond her competence. The domestic help was down to a cook and a part-time cleaner. Boasting to Max in a letter, Sassoon itemised his contribution to household chores, from washing up to making George 'his vesperal cup of cocoa'. When not engaged in these duties, he was locked away trying to complete *The Weald of Youth*. By Easter 1941 he had written only nine chapters and told Max that his publisher would soon be sending 'frantic telegrams'. His concentration had been disrupted by friends in London asking him to store their valuable books and paintings in Heytesbury. In the park a huge army camp was being built to house 200 vehicles of the Guards Armoured Division. A general was sleeping in a converted bus parked alongside the outhouses, while the Brigadier and his staff were billeted in the dining room. In his letters Sassoon tried to dismiss his difficulties but they were impairing his capacity to cope and his ability to write. Significantly, his contributions to periodicals were nil – the worst since 1932 when he was in another crisis. The best he could hope for was a decidedly better 1942.

The year started well, with a broadcast by Max. 'No words can express what I feel about it. I laughed aloud – but there were tears in my eyes too,' he told Cockerell. By Easter he had completed *The Weald of Youth* and dedicated it to Glen, who was serving with the Royal Scots in India. His favourite nephew, Hamo, had been injured in the North African campaign but the news was positive about them both. He took delight in seeing the hay-making under way with '2 slow horses' and George piling up mounds of grass. He had even got used to the presence of soldiers in the park and enjoyed watching them use the cricket ground of an afternoon.

Forster came to visit in June, followed in July by Eddie Marsh, who spent his visit weeding the flowerbeds and praising *The Weald of Youth*. Cockerell too reappeared in August. Blunden sent him his book on Hardy, in which the dedication read 'To Siegfried Sassoon remembering other days in the homes of William Barnes and Thomas Hardy'. It all seemed so long ago. *The Weald of Youth* was published in October: 10,000 copies were printed and sales so buoyant that a reprinting was required in December. Income from the book was already £900. Sassoon declared to Max: 'What a vulgarly successful autobiographer I am.' The war left its imprint on the new volume – 'The paper and binding of this book conform to authorized economy standards' is printed on the copyright page. The quality of the paper endorses the message: Sassoon was such a stickler for quality. It was another compromise, another little defeat.

The New Year found Hester in the doldrums and Sassoon was washing his own socks. For therapy he scattered Vim over a table and scrubbed it down. He was of tidy mind and orderly habits – a disorganised house was an abomination to him. Hester's cigarette butts in a saucer and the remnants of her coffee in a wineglass pointed to the feeling of demoralisation and unhappiness permeating the house.

Hester's immediate plan involved taking George away to give Sassoon plenty of peace and quiet. She was also genuinely concerned about the effect the evacuees were having on her son. Things reached a peak when George waved an axe in a very threatening way. Sassoon blamed himself; it was just not fair on the boy – 'He was a machine-gun child with a pre-1914 father.' But he could not contemplate the idea of separation from his son, which he suspected was part of Hester's long-term strategy for the years after the war.

To his great surprise an invitation arrived during June from one of his cousins, Sybil, sister of Sir Philip Sassoon and wife of the Marquis of Cholmondeley. The invitation was to dinner in their palatial London house in Kensington Park Gardens to meet Field Marshal Sir Archibald Wavell, who had told her of the pleasure he derived from poetry. He intended to publish an anthology in the autumn called *Other Men's Flowers*. One of the 'other men' and a particular favourite was Sassoon. With the imperious style of that branch of the Sassoons, the invitation carried all the weight of a royal command. Desperate to get away, Sassoon accepted – just for himself. He made good use of his time while in town, shopping for socks and a pair of winter shoes and visiting the National Gallery. Though he failed to get a table for lunch at the Savoy, he did succeed in finding a toy for George. His mind was on Heytesbury: London was a disaster area. The dinner itself was splendid. Wavell became a friend and so, too, did his son. The critic Desmond MacCarthy was also there. He was an admirer of Sassoon's memoirs, as was the other guest, Ivor Brown of the *Observer*, the newspaper in which Sassoon's poems appeared during the war. Brown invited Sassoon to review Wavell's book. Travelling back to Wiltshire he felt the journey had been worthwhile if only for the civilised company and to know that people of the calibre of Wavell, MacCarthy and Brown held him in high esteem.

A week later, on 10 July, came another boost. Blunden arrived with a new companion, Claire Poynting. Blunden's marriage to Sylva Norman was nearing its end, one of the reasons being her unwillingness to start a family. She did not bring to the marriage the warmth that he needed. Claire was reading English at St Hilda's College, Oxford and had attended some of Blunden's lectures. Of infinitely greater importance was her being a knowledgeable student of cricket. Blunden had already written to Sassoon of this new friendship and of the comfort it brought him. The war was a difficult time for him, especially the opening years, when he found it impossible to concede the necessity for conflict at all. Blunden was more fortunate than Sassoon in having someone whose love eased his bewilderment. He wrote: 'If you were to ask how I got through some of the mud and filth and blanks of 1939–40, I should name Claire Poynting.' Sassoon could only be thankful to her for bringing happiness to his friend. When they met at Heytesbury for the first time he liked her, although some of his comments in the diary are open to varying interpretations, from the snobbish – 'a high-tea type of woman' – to the chauvinistic – 'Claire knows how to be unobtrusive.'

How he wished he could have said the same of Hester, who was now talking to Sassoon about a separation. At least she was trying to bring things to a head. As for Sassoon, he decided to be cautious, knowing from experience how unpredictable Hester could be and how next day she might just as easily be discussing their future together. She was also that autumn becoming friendly with Rex Whistler, much to Sassoon's surprise. In September she went to London to dine with him at the Ritz. Sassoon noticed how her appearance had been considerably smartened and she was looking her best. On her return she declared what a lovely time it had been. It was a double blow to Sassoon: his marriage had gone stale and his wife was flirting with someone he knew well. Unable to prevent her from being fond of someone else, he took a philosophical position. It was 'quite understandable and I don't blame her at all. But I was conscious of a dull ache of misery. When I think how different things might have been if she had been more amenable to my influence.' He blamed the war – 'I feel sorry for Hester.' Then an oddly formed question: 'I wonder what Rex thinks about it?' – not 'I wonder what Rex thinks he's doing?' or 'What is Rex up to?' The way in which Sassoon puts the question suggests that Hester was making the running. But was she being encouraged?

Rex Whistler was not a womaniser but photographs of him suggest why they might be attracted to him – there was a gentleness about him; a vulnerability which had appealed to Edith Olivier, also to Sassoon himself. In 1929, after a weekend at the Daye House, Sassoon had confided to his diary that he was 'feeling rather worried about Rex who is showing signs of falling under my spell'. There had been a bit of rivalry between them over Stephen at that time as well. What an irony if, 15 years later, Hester was indeed falling under Rex's spell. Both were 38 years old, all of 20 years younger than Sassoon; they believed life was to be enjoyed. But who made the first move is not known.

With the arrival of autumn, Sassoon started to outline the third volume of his autobiography, *Siegfried's Journey*. Despite the distractions and disappointments, the ease with which his thoughts flowed was heartening. American soldiers were now in command of the park and the fields, destroying the surfaces with huge parking stands. There was little point in worrying about such things: all that mattered was to make progress with his prose work. As for poetry, there was little inspiration. Typical of his thoughts between 1942 and 1944 was 'The Hardened Heart', which describes a journey from the hope of youth to disenchantment in middle age:

> When things were in their pride
> And youth with morning mind
> Went lost and ardent eyed
> Down by the broadening stream,
> How could he think to find
> That life beloved had lied –
> Its promise undesigned
> Discordant to his dream?
>
> While circumstance-led so
> How could he choose but go
> To the music of delight?
> Or how with laughter learn
> On roads of no return
> To numb his heart and know
> The ugly facts of night?

Such themes – part regret, part anger, part disenchantment – coloured the small amount of poetry completed over the next four years.

Siegfried's Journey was progressing. This was in part due to the absence of Hester. She had taken George for a holiday to the home of her brother Richard and his wife Pamela, who lived in Pepper Arden in Yorkshire. Hester had made no definite arrangement about a return date, so it was a surprise when after 10 days away she and George reappeared. She told Sassoon this was due to her having received a letter from Rex, saying he was in London on leave and working on designs for a new production and inviting her to join him. The play could not have been more apt: Oscar Wilde's *An Ideal Husband*. Off she went for two days and when she returned, Sassoon could hardly believe the change in her spirits. 'So much better,' he wrote. 'She needed the break.' Hester was now in full flow and alive with ideas. Some Sassoon did not approve, such as sending George to a preparatory school where he would have to board. However, when she suggested that she and George spend Christmas with her mother, he instantly agreed. The season of goodwill and festivity was muted at Heytesbury. There was no help in the house at all, but Sassoon survived on a pheasant, a couple of eggs, stewed apples and some bottled peaches: 'What more does one want? – only lots of silence till the New Year.'

It was not to be a happy 1944. In the fields 1,500 American troops were preparing for a second front. It was horrible to contemplate what suffering and loss faced so many of them and the thousands of others, spread along the south coast. Despite the presence of the soldiers, Heytesbury House was quiet. Hester and George were staying with Lady Gatty till the end of January; there were no evacuees and the new housekeeper-cum-cook was not due till February. Sassoon had moved his study from upstairs down to the music room. He told Cockerell, 'I have been very cosy with a big fire and everything arranged to suite my taste for simplicity. The outside door-handle of the music room has broken off, so no one can get in when I am inside!'

Thus fortified against the world, he worked on his book but things soon reverted to their dismal and distracting ways. Hester was still pursuing Rex. Sassoon had told Edith of Hester's infatuation. Edith believed that Rex was far too sensible to entangle himself in such a dalliance. Her reaction was the same to another story, this time told her by Hester – Stephen Tennant was trying to re-establish himself in Sassoon's life. Nothing would come of it was Edith's conviction and she would do all she could to prevent Stephen delivering the final stroke to an already-brittle relationship.

Sassoon was pleased to have George home again, but not Hester. The respite from her only served to fuel his wish for them to separate. He had been upset by the death on 1 April of Eileen Hunter, one of the 'Really and Truly' duo who tended the gardens at Wilsford. Within a month her sister Beryl also died. They were his last link with the place and his only fond memory of that most bitter time a decade ago. Now he was deep in unhappiness again.

Hester seemed impervious to the temper building up in Sassoon. Inevitably they rowed, and at such times Sassoon could be deeply wounding. He told Hester to go to her mother's home for an indefinite period. 'Once there,' he wrote, 'I shall refuse to allow her to return, for the good reason that I shall be going on with my writing.' He, too, had been making plans for the future, but until the end of the war he would temporise. 'When it is over, I shall tell her she can go and lead her own life – take a flat in London. I shall refuse to accept any of her income for the upkeep of the place. The alternative would be to have my life and work destroyed by an intractable fanatic.'

He deeply regretted the failure of his marriage. However, analysing the causes of that failure was of no use – 'The years of being plagued by her are over.' Theresa in Weirleigh was, as ever, entirely in agreement with him and he wrote that his mother had 'sized Hester's character up years ago'. What remained a puzzle for him was 'poor old Rex', as he referred to him. Rex was part of the Normandy Landings, which began on 6 June. It was, Sassoon knew, a turning point in the war. Edith Olivier came to lunch on 18 July – she took five chapters of *Siegfried's Journey* to type from Sassoon's long-hand. She told him of her visit to Lady Gatty at Winterbourne Dauntsey, near Salisbury. Being an old friend of Katharine Gatty, of the Morrison family and Hester, she was anxious to help, but what was to be a tête-à-tête had been inhibited by Hester's insistence on being present the whole time. Unlike Theresa, Katharine Gatty took a more objective view of Hester and of 'dear Siegfried'. This cheered him. He did not wish to be gratuitously dismissive of them, but he was indifferent to any blame they might attach to him. Sassoon had told Edith of Hester's generous spirit and artistic ability, but 'she is so self-centred that all these qualities are killed'. Edith's diary confides, 'He hates her whenever he sees her.' Edith had worries, too, especially about Rex out in Normandy. Then there was Stephen, waiting his chance to get into Heytesbury. Despite such oppressive thoughts, lunch 'with Sieg' was a joy, the weather was wonderful, Heytesbury so beautiful; but Rex lay dead in France.

It was a week before the news was confirmed. Sassoon read the report in the *Daily Telegraph*: 'It was the worst pain I've felt since the war began. I somehow felt he would be killed.' In the late afternoon he took the bus to Wilton: Edith had invited him to dine with Sir Frederick Morgan, Chief of Staff to General Eisenhower. She wrote of Siegfried's tenderness: 'He put his arm around me and said "I am always and ever your friend. Be brave – *you are* – and live for us."' Edith gave Sassoon the oil painting Rex had made of Heytesbury House. On 9 August, Hester arrived at the Daye House, dressed in black and white. She had learnt that Rex had not suffered but been 'killed outright *not disfigured in any way*, but his face happy and calm'. Where she got that information from was not revealed.

Sassoon spent his fifty-eighth birthday on his own. Hester and George were in Yorkshire. He had been urged to join them, but declined. A greeting arrived – 'Best love'. Within the week Blunden and Claire arrived. Beaujolais '33 was opened on both nights – Blunden was a Burgundy man. Sassoon continued to approve of Claire. 'She was sensible and well read and doesn't talk too much – a good listener.' Claire recalled that her silence on both visits was caused by being in the presence of the famous. Her other memory, after another visit, is of George 'running around, very active and of Hester a bit fussed – but welcoming and friendly'.

In the autumn George became a pupil at Greenways, a nearby private boarding school. The whole period had been unsettling for him. He asked his father: 'This is my permanent home, isn't it? I don't like temporary houses.' Perhaps Sassoon recalled his own childhood wish: 'I wanted to enjoy my parents simultaneously – not alternately.' But the marriage had passed the point of reconciliation and sunk into petty recriminations and self-righteousness. Only one hope remained, that eventually some civilised accommodation would be reached for George's sake. Sassoon spent Christmas alone in the repossessed library with a roaring fire in the grate, the rest of the house freezing because the central heating had broken down. He caught a chill. Progress on *Siegfried's Journey* was virtually nil, the new cook 'inadequate and unobliging'. Hester, staying with George at her mother's house in Winterbourne, expressed her concern that Sassoon was on his own and wondered how, if separation were the outcome, he would survive. In the present circumstances she was still paying a large proportion of the running costs out of her own income. Lady Gatty wrote to Sassoon suggesting, if it were agreeable to him, she would pay for part of the house to be adapted to provide a self-contained flat for Hester, from where she could 'lead her own life'. Sassoon dismissed this as an absurd suggestion, knowing only too well that Hester could never resist intruding, any more than she had respected his wishes that she stay away from Heytesbury. According to Sassoon's diary, Hester was an especial nuisance on the phone: always ringing up, behaviour that he determined was neurotic. He did not attribute her actions to concern for him. By May, he was considering suing for divorce.

By 4 May Germany was on the brink of surrender. The prospect of peace in Europe was not complemented by any cessation of hostilities at Heytesbury House. When VE Day dawned four days later, the village and the Angel Inn were bedecked with flags and bunting but up at the house Hester was meddling with Sassoon's books and walking, uninvited, into his study to inform him that it was her intention to learn Greek. By now he was so drained that even the ending of the war failed to cheer him. When Hester left – Sassoon got her on the 5.30 bus – he was alone again in his 'lovely house with my joyous and loving son'. Sassoon had made it clear that he was implacably opposed to Hester residing again in Heytesbury. It was now the turn of her mother and brother to take up her cause with Sassoon. Richard Gatty adopted an uncompromising approach, laying the blame squarely on the shoulders of his brother-in-law. Lady Gatty, however, wrote letters to him in May and June, which were at once firm and conciliatory. She knew her daughter too well not to recognise the blame that must attach to her; she pleaded with Sassoon, but also admonished him. Fifty years after they were written, Katharine Gatty's letters are a testament to her graciousness, her genuine fondness for her son-in-law and her deep concern for the future well-being of her grandson, George.

27 May 1945

Dear Siegfried,

I feel loath to trouble you with a letter, but think that perhaps I ought to do so. I understand that (though she would be willing) you still do not wish Hester to stay at Heytesbury at all, not even for some very short visits, and that you continue to wish to live alone.

If you do, you do and that is one thing – but it is quite another matter that you should be in the exclusive enjoyment of all her possessions, and that she should continue to keep up Heytesbury for your benefit, so that all that is left to her is a bare pittance on which it is impossible for her to have an independent life of her own.

For more than a year Hester has done this, but it is most unfair that this situation should be prolonged indefinitely, and now that your book is practically finished the moment would seem to have arrived when things should be gone into. Why has Hester paid the wages of your outdoor staff etc all this time? It is out of consideration for you that she has acted thus, and you do not appear to realise that she has been patient and has tried to help.

Now has come the chance to get a charming house in this village and as you wish to live alone, I was urging Hester to go in for it, but she is still worrying about how you would manage with considerably less financial help from herself and with a lot of her furniture and pictures etc removed. She thinks about your welfare – do you ever give her welfare a second's thought? I don't suppose so – but as she thinks on these lines I put it to you: think over for your own sake what you are doing.

Hester, I repeat, is willing to try again, and she would, in future, not impose herself on you when you were working. Most women would not have *acted* so patiently as she has done in waiting for over a year to see if things would improve. Please do not think that this is meant in any way unkindly, but I wonder if you have faced the possible import of your decision – will you be able to live at Heytesbury?

After all, my dear, I am old enough to be your mother which is why I write like this. My only desire is that you should *both* be as happy as is possible under the circumstances and that Darling George's best interests should always be borne in mind and considered without bias.

With my love, ever yours,

Katharine

Sassoon's reply confirmed his opposition to Hester returning to Heytesbury. He saw every reason for her buying the Grange in Winterbourne. As for the future upkeep of Heytesbury, he was confident he could manage on his own resources. Lady Gatty accepted she could press no further: dying of cancer, she knew that her hopes of reconciliation were over. She tried one more letter (in June) to convince Sassoon of Hester's 'exceeding fondness' for him and her preparedness to have another child then wisely let the matter rest.

Unwisely, her daughter did not. She continued to pester Sassoon. He consulted a friend, Judge Sturges, about securing some legal respite, but when he threatened Hester with the law she only replied: 'Tell Sturges I love you.' She did love him and protested that love to him over and over again. 'Many waters cannot quench love,' she told him. 'But many scenes can,' was his riposte. There were no means, it seemed to Sassoon, to avoid her questioning, which began to carry the insinuation that he was enjoying liaisons. The headmistress of George's school was an early suspect and so too in July was Helen Waddell. This brilliant medieval scholar, translator of the works of Alcuin and author of the historical novel *Peter Abelard* worked as an editor for Constable the publishers. An idea was in the air for a biography of George Meredith. Sassoon visited her at Constable on 19 July and found her 'a splendid person and I intend to cultivate her acquaintance'. That evening Hester phoned: 'What was Miss Waddell like?' Such persistence could only be counterproductive. It hardened

Sassoon's attitude towards her and increased his dislike: 'Behind her put-on amiabilities, I detect a vulturine resolve to get my scalp and all that therein is.'

Sassoon felt entitled to the support of his oldest friends on his side of the argument. He had Glen's, but Blunden showed sympathy towards Hester. Sassoon regarded this as a betrayal. Hester had contacted Blunden and Claire in a plea for help. There was nothing covert about her actions, as she had written to Sassoon telling him of meeting them in London. Throughout the summer that contact was maintained. By October Sassoon was sufficiently upset to write: 'The curtain will come down and silence will ensue – I must cling to Glen.'

He was imposing on Blunden that 'impossible demand' against which he had been warned by W. J. Turner. It is an insight into that same absolutism which had contributed to the destruction of his marriage. When Blunden's first marriage was in the throes of dissolution, Sassoon had loftily written how he regarded the showing of loyalty to one side in such a dispute as totally wrong. Such advice was now forgotten, or disregarded. In his opinion Hester lacked judgement in putting Blunden into the firing-line. Some time later she unwisely quoted a remark of Claire's about Sassoon being jealous of George's affection for Hester – if indeed Claire ever said it. Sassoon saw this as another example of wilfulness.

Others were soon drawn into the battle. Some of Sassoon's closest friends fell short of the mark and were lowered in his esteem, even cold-shouldered. Geoffrey Keynes, whom he had known since 1933 and who had assisted and advised Sassoon in the style and presentation of his work, was one such: 'Geoffrey Keynes is no good where Hester is concerned. Admirable in his way, Geoffrey is a fair weather friend.' Keynes, it must be said, was unwise to describe Sassoon's domestic upheavals as 'mere eccentricities'. Even the devoted and caring Edith Olivier was counted 'a disappointment over the Hester business'. If it was Hester's intention to punish her husband by destroying his friendships then she was succeeding, but there is no evidence that she harboured any such motive. As for Sassoon himself, he appears to have made little or no effort to save the marriage – there was passivity in his response as if he just hoped the whole business, Hester included, would simply go away. Knowing or fearing that she would turn up uninvited on the midday bus, he would take himself and sometimes George off to the woods to avoid having to speak with her. He disliked domestic scenes. Nothing in his background points to his being by nature confrontational. It would be correct to describe him as dismissive of those whom he found uncongenial. His temper he kept to himself – and for the pages of his diary.

On George's birthday Hester entered Sassoon's study and informed him that she had been taking legal advice about custody of George. She was confident any decision would go in her favour. It is inconceivable that she did not know the effect this would have on Sassoon – it was the ultimate threat. When she left, he went around the house removing as many traces of her as he could, including a framed photograph, which he threw into the fire, saying: 'Goodbye and burn.' In November, Hester began an inventory of the house and on the 21st a furniture van arrived and removed all those items to which she laid claim. It meant the greater part of the contents. She left some of the beds, but the green drawing room was empty save the radiogram, one small table, an armchair, the ornaments on the marble mantelpiece and three small pictures. Here, Sassoon would sit on that and subsequent evenings, quite alone, listening to a recording of Adela Verne playing Schumann and Chopin. Hester could have the lot – but she was not going to have George – 'he is my salvation'.

Siegfried's Journey, published on 7 December, sold so well that a reprint was quickly needed. There was a warm and understanding letter from Blunden but Sassoon's reply was guarded. Hester said she would come for Christmas but Sassoon quashed that idea. He and George spent the holiday together; it was, wrote Sassoon, 'one of the best Xmas days I've ever had at Heytesbury'. In January, he was pleased to hear from Harold Nicolson that Constable were keen to proceed with a 'plain account of George Meredith's career and personality'. Sassoon saw this biographical project as a means of keeping himself occupied as well as an opportunity to develop a friendship with Helen Waddell. She was the first of the post-war women whose intellectual capacity and feminine warmth came to mean so much to him.

The breakdown of his marriage, the central importance of his son, the consolation of Nature... these things were part also of Meredith's life, including a profitless time studying Law. It was inevitable that as the biography proceeded, the more the shared experiences broke through to colour the narrative. Writing of Meredith was also to return to Weirleigh and Helen Wirgman murmuring as she gazed across the Weald: 'Darker grows the valley ...' It was about youth and expectancy of life. Concluding the biography, Sassoon writes: 'I was once asked what I meant by saying that I liked the idea of Meredith though I couldn't always enjoy what he wrote. It is that the idea of Meredith means a sense of being fully alive. To be at one's best is to be Meredithian.' Meredith shines through much of *The Old Century and seven more years*. And Meredith is also there in poem number four of *Vigils*, 'Vigils in Spring':

> The night air, smelling cold with spring,
> And the dark twigs of towering trees, –
> When age remembers youth we bring
> Aliveness back to us in these.

> Leaning from windows on the gloom,
> We are one with purpling woods and wet
> Wild violets of our earth in whom
> Aliveness wakes and wonders yet.

> Inbreathed awareness, hushed and cold,
> Of growth's annunciate thrust and thrill,
> We lean from lifetime, growing old,
> And feel your starlit magic still.

Nature had displayed anything but 'aliveness' since the beginning of the year. The house was bitterly cold. A fire in the library and his thick overcoat enabled Sassoon to continue working. Then came the coal crisis followed by power cuts, followed by heavy drifting snow and the whole country slowly grinding to a halt. Every pipe in the house was frozen and Sassoon waited for the thaw and the deluge. He never expected anyone to come and see if he was surviving – but Hester, incredibly, beat a path to his door. Sadly the welcome was as wintry as the weather. Rain began to drip through the library ceiling; Sassoon spread towels over the floor. Then water began to flood the cellar – Sassoon could do nothing about it. Easter came and he walked out into the park and saw a primrose but the relief from dejection was brief. His biography of Meredith was completed but Constable were dragging their feet over publication. He saw little point in doing any serious work with what he described as a 'pseudo Socialist government pouncing on any rewards'. All stimulus in his life had drifted away, friendships had ebbed, there was little point to anything; he was 'just a solitary, methodical, fire-side-loving man, holding the fort against Socialist legislation in a semi-derelict old country mansion'. He was none too keen on some of the estate staff either. Emotionally down, he was almost out: 'How lonely – how lonely – how lifeless – how forsaken.' He began to have dreams about his father. It was strange to be so occupied with thoughts of him after 50 years. These dreams were followed by others, this time of Weirleigh. Then on 11 July, Michael his brother phoned to say Theresa was dead – she was 93 years old. Sassoon decided not to go to the funeral because 'it would only cause me the needless pain of emotion. I just resolved not to indulge in feelings (Hester has cured me of that!).' Hester felt that if he did not go, then she ought. Sassoon forbade her. Theresa's death, he calculated, would release him from an annuity to her of £400. Weirleigh would be sold, the proceeds from which he would have a share in. This 'addition to my income will relieve me of enforced literary work, and enable me to produce my next book at my leisure'. There never was another book of prose.

In September, *Collected Poems* was published. There were few reviews. In November, Blunden and Claire left England for Japan. On Christmas Day Sassoon mourned the collapse of things which had promised so much. He wrote a strange, haunting poem about his greatest disappointment:

The Child Denied

O child I shall not know – heart haunting cry
Troubling the midnight silence in a thought
That like a footstep pauses, passes by
The door that might have opened, might have brought
The face which never lived and cannot die.

Imagined presence, I have sometimes felt
You near me. In the garden I have seen
Shadow and sun delude me that you knelt
Under a beech, playing at what might have been
On some such afternoon of summer skies serene.

Also it seemed you watched me with your brother,
Watched how we two together were so glad,
He unaware of an invisible other
Denied the living laughter, small and sad.
O living ghost – the child I never had.

18

SEEKING

1948–56

Sassoon was irritable. The newspapers carried the announcement that T. S. Eliot had been awarded the Order of Merit and Vita Sackville-West made a Companion of Honour. For all his protestations of indifference to public esteem, he was conscious of his own worth and desired to be recognised but in his scheme of things he wanted the world to come to him rather than he go out into the market place. However, this was not the 1920s and the literary world was no longer beating a path to his door. Max Beerbohm once began a broadcast with the words: 'I am what writers of obituary notices call "an interesting link with the past".' That is how Sassoon was regarded. His work, in particular his poetry, caught few, if any headlines. He was an interesting link with the first war: apart from that there was little attention paid him, certainly no rush to bestow honours. Liverpool University awarded him an honorary Doctorate of Literature in 1931 – the only other honour had long ago floated down the Mersey in 1917. In an attempt to shrug off this indifference he took the view that it was his unwillingness 'to put himself around – unlike Eliot' that was responsible. Writing to Cockerell on the subject at a later date he stated that the prizes went to those who 'make all the necessary contacts'.

Sassoon was particularly irritated by Eliot being honoured. 'Surely it is a peculiar selection,' he wrote to Philip Gosse, son of his erstwhile mentor. (Ironically, if anyone knew how 'to put himself around', it was Sir Edmund Gosse.) Sassoon felt that de la Mare had a stronger claim. He was soon into his stride, telling young Gosse: 'Somehow I've never been able to accept Eliot's poetry, though I realise that it is frightfully distinguished. But in Cambridge, I suppose he is regarded as a cut above Matthew Arnold, and much more important than Hodgson or de la Mare and Housman. I wonder if the Queen will read *The Waste Land* to the King?' Sassoon could be petty. Eliot was not the kind of personality or poet who in any way appealed to him. Direct utterance was a major requirement in securing Sassoon's approval, as too was not being 'intellectual'. He had no time for Modernism and what Sassoon counted obscurity. Eliot, and indeed the leading critics and poets of the day, were outside his circle of acceptance, as he was outside their world.

In his lecture 'On Poetry', delivered in Bristol in March 1939, he had told his audience that for the previous 15 years 'the writing of straightforward and whole-hearted verse has been out of fashion, and indirect utterance has been indulged in to an unprecedented degree. Its most earnest practitioners appear to regard verse-writing as a science, and emotional expression as a scientific exercise.' Of course he was pointing the finger at Eliot. His best barb on this subject was aimed at Edith Sitwell, to whom 'a syllable may be a chromatic semi-tone, but I much prefer to regard it as a unit of pronunciation'. In 1922 he had praised and defended her innovative *Façade*. But he was a revolutiontary then. His war poems had opened new possibilities for poetry but eventually the innovator became the defender of the orthodox. In *Meredith* he writes: 'Poetry is the language of the heart as well as the head.' He saw the relationship between the poet and his reader as 'deep calling unto deep', an experience beyond analysis. This explains his fondness for Robert Frost, Walter de la Mare, A. E. Housman and Ralph Hodgson. It is also the reason why he was admired in turn by Philip Larkin. Although Sassoon expressed discontent with the later stages of Georgian poetry and Edward Marsh's conservative ideas, he was faithful to the principle of intelligibility; what Marsh might have called 'regard for the reader'. Larkin shared that conviction and practised it in his poetry.

Blunden was much more flexible in his attitude to the Moderns. Although he continued to write in his pastoral vein, he was prepared to enthuse over new work. Poetry was for him a living organism, constantly evolving. Not that he approved of everything, but he was willing to investigate. He was ready for anything in the world of verse, including Eliot, whom he liked personally and as a poet. Then there was Graves, who was forever challenging the conventions in both style and content. Sassoon, however, stuck to the known ways and to the known subject – himself.

Since October 1947 he had grappled with the idea of a fourth volume of autobiography. This would follow the story of the young man portrayed in *Siegfried's Journey*, of whom the reader's last glimpse had been in Trafalgar Square in 1920, returned from America ready to make a new start. *Know Thyself* became its working title. Next, he went to the diaries for 1921–25 and began to review those years with a mind to finding a theme. Page after page was filled with possible treatments and peppered with questions as to how he might include this or that episode or this and that person. Should it be chronological or should it be thematic? It is an insight into his method of construction but from its first mention, one thing was clear – a fourth volume would never materialise.

'The vital problem *is what to try and express by the the book. The Old Century* expressed childhood and adolescence. *The Weald* – unsophisticated youth, *Siegfried's Journey* – youth finding its feet, but still undeveloped and bewildered. This one must be an adventure in the gaining of self-understanding.' The pages turned in the diary and the weeks passed and the year changed from 1947 to 1948 but, try as he might, he failed to find his theme. Belief in the project was undermined when he realised how flimsy and undirected his life had been in the twenties. How was it possible to write about such irrelevancies in a world daily under the threat of the atom bomb and the possibility of a third world war between Russia and the West? Who could possibly want to read about a young man 'who couldn't see where he was going'? Sassoon was out of sympathy with that younger self – why should anyone else be interested? 'To be writing with elaborate seriousness about my own problems and character formation in these years would be an absurdity.' Panic set in when he faced the possibility that there would be nothing to occupy his mind after the publication of *Meredith* in the autumn. He went back to the diaries: 'The material is there but I am unable to formulate my plan of dealing with it.'

The past was not only in the diaries. In February Stephen Tennant started writing a flurry of letters to him. Sassoon shuddered as each one arrived. Stephen, now 42, had lost his looks but not his ability to beguile and to outrage, achieving both in the same letter. 'But I dread him; and the mere thought of him being anywhere near George horrifies me,' wrote Sassoon. The Tennant shadow, as he had predicted, would be, if not a danger then certainly a nuisance. At Easter he took George for a holiday in Norfolk, hoping that being with him in a part of England where he had spent his own childhood summer days he would be gripped by a new vitality. It was a vain hope and he could only look with regret on that creativity, now lost, which had marked his prose and poetry up to the completion of *The Old Century* in 1937 – 'Since then I've experienced the double purgatory of Hester and the 2nd World War. My books have been written *in spite of* impediments and harassments, by sheer resolution.' He began to engage in a profitless exercise of counting the cost of domestic chaos: 'Had the last 10 years been prosperous and peaceful, should I have done any better? But I am haunted by the thought of the poems I might have written if the poetry hadn't been battered out of me by domestic disturbances.'

Introspection throughout the summer did nothing to raise his spirits; neither did the arrival of furniture and other items from Weirleigh. He wrote to Max about the old candlesticks that once lit his way to bed in the nineties and 'old clocks which ticked away my days of childhood'. Max also received a postcard from Sassoon in August bearing the postmark Isle of Mull. Sassoon was at Lochbuie, spending a month's holiday with George. He found the scenery inspirational, even in the rain that came every day. Hester's family, the Morrisons, were landowners on the island and she was entertaining the idea of selling her house in Winterbourne and settling in Lochbuie. George could spend part of his holidays there – and Sassoon, too, if he wished.

The toll of the troublesome years began to be exacted. Throughout his holiday he suffered bouts of dyspepsia, which worsened after his return to Heytesbury. It took away some of the pleasure from the publication of *Meredith*. The book did not sell well but he was heartened to receive letters of appreciation from friends. None was more important than the paean of praise from Helen Waddell, who had given him such wise advice on the portraying of the private as well as the public side of Meredith. Waddell was to inspire some of Sassoon's later poetry, 'Awareness of Alcuin' being the most obvious example.

By early October Sassoon was suffering acute abdominal pain and was admitted to the Central Middlesex Hospital in London, where he underwent surgery for the removal of a duodenal abscess. This was his first serious illness in 30 years. At 63 his health was good, but it was being undermined by the accretion of despair. Helen Waddell visited him during his six-week stay at the Middlesex but they did not meet again. Their friendship, conducted mainly through letters, was short-lived for she was succumbing to a degenerative illness. On his return to Heytesbury he led the life of a semi-invalid. The December weather produced strong winds and heavy rain, but in the brief intervals of mild wintry sunshine he ventured for a short walk. George, now a tall 12-year-old, had not been home since 17 October – he missed him. Hester had bought a house in Lochbuie that Sassoon feared would prove a strong 'counterattraction for George'. The solitude of Heytesbury he so loved lost its appeal momentarily and the place wore a dreariness; he was feeling 'old and futureless'. George's return from school for Christmas brought life and activity as it got his father moving around the house and out of his depressing self-pity, but the respite was brief. For the rest of the holiday, George went to stay with Hester at Winterbourne. Sassoon was back in bed with a recurrence of his abdominal complaint. In the middle of January he wrote dejectedly that everything had conspired to knock his mind to pieces.

As in previous bouts of despair, he knew the only remedy was to occupy his mind with work. But what work? Writing a long book was a challenge that filled him with dismay. No longer had he the stamina to meet the strain and the worry of such a task. He did make an attempt at the autobiography and completed a hundred pages with a prelude but he was not in sympathy with the subject any more. The fourth volume of memoirs started to fade away. Although he would return to his notes in later years, by November 1949 the project had all but disappeared and with it the end of any further significant contribution to English prose.

Among those who wrote to Sassoon welcoming the publication of *Meredith* was Rupert Hart-Davis. Edmund Blunden had mentioned him in a letter. In the late forties he was establishing the publishing house which bore his name. His letter conveyed not only compliments on the biography but a request – 'and now please write some more poetry'. The request coincided with Sassoon's own wish 'to concentrate on trying to say something worthwhile in verse'. Sassoon never lost his conviction that life – and his mother – had marked him out for a poet. It had been the sustaining hope in his existence and its ebb and flow determined his moods of buoyancy or depression. Since the publication of *Rhymed Ruminations* in 1939, the output had been meagre – an occasional single poem in the *Observer* or *The Listener* at the request of its Literary Editor, J. R. Ackerley. For the past decade the writing of the autobiographies had consumed his creative energy. By 1948, he felt empty and drained – 'As a poet I am almost extinct.'

J. R. Ackerley, who visited Sassoon in the summers of 1949 and 1950, penned a chilling description:

Siegfried sweet, kind, loquacious, absent-minded, lonely, dreadfully self-centred and self-absorbed. What a sorry and dreary figure he is, this strange lean man, moving about his beautiful estate with rather short staccato steps, slovenly dressed in unbecoming clothes, with a rent more than likely in the seat of his trousers through which a patch of white buttock shows, a loose short-sleeved yellow pull-over draped over his long-sleeved blue flannel shirt, and on his head, with its brim turned down all round, a thirty- or forty-year-old felt hat only held together in its decayed, faded and greasy parts with safety pins. His hat, of course, is a symbol; it is the past, his old life when he was famous and young and sought-after, before he grew old and forgotten and was put out to moulder and gather dust upon the shelf. He clings to it therefore – making it a sardonic joke.

Ackerley also recorded his impressions of Hester in the months before she finally moved to Mull. He felt sorrow for her, but not sympathy: a 'woman trying to hold on still to something she had lost through emotions beyond her control, making tea-table conversation to a husband in whose face and manner aversion and distaste are only too plainly writ'. He felt that Hester's unease at the table emanated from her suspicion that Sassoon had already soured Ackerley's mind against her. It was not an easy situation for a stranger but Ackerley, whose own life was dominated by his sister, could probably understand better than most. He also noted the passion with which Sassoon talked about George and the depth of his emotional reliance on him. Ackerley questioned in his mind the wisdom of such an all-consuming intensity. His most penetrating comment, quoted by his biographer Peter Parker, goes to the heart of the matter: 'Dear Siegfried has taken a wrong turning somewhere. There is no happiness in self, self as a permanent diet is melancholic and poisonous, it kills, one dies, as he is dying, talking away about his lost fame, his loneliness, his domestic affairs – his age-worn face turned sideways, sightless, towards the window.' The image is powerful – turning his face towards the window when he might so easily have turned his face to the wall. In a moment of irony Ackerley employs the word 'sightless'. Within a few years the word would be used by Sassoon to describe his transformed existence, the 'joy of sightless seeing'.

Rupert Hart-Davis writes of Sassoon: 'Although he only occasionally knew it, he had always been looking for God.' But it was only after the completion of the memoirs and *Meredith* that he specifically expressed his

309

deepest longings, 'crying out for the living God *in me*'. From this time to the end of his life he turned his whole attention to the exploration of man as spirit and to questions about God. In his diary he described it as being the study of a 'thoughtful human being against the background of nature and the universe. And the achievement of faith in spiritual guidance from beyond apparitional existence of flesh.' Fifteen years earlier in 1933 he had posed:

> That question which concerns me most – about
> Which I have entertained the gravest doubt –
> Is, bluntly stated, 'have I got a soul?'
> And, soulhood granted, while millenniums roll,
> Will it inhabit some congenial clime,
> Detached from thoughts indigenous to Time, –
> Anonymous in what we name 'the Whole'?

In his 1948 poem 'An Asking', 'the Whole' is addressed as:

> Primordial Cause, your creature questions why
> Law has empowered him with this central I;
> Asks how to carnal consciousness you brought
> Spirit, the unexplained of sovereign thought;
> And whence your influent essence quickened first
> In hungry heart, the brain's unscienced thirst.
> My heritage I ponder. Who was he,
> In geologic gloomed pre-history,
> That glimpsed beyond his death environed cave
> The soul – a star – a gift he yet might save?

This is the subject of his poetry – man as spirit, living in the world but having a destiny beyond the world. It was this destiny that occupied him with increasing intensity from 1949 and which he came to regard as the only thing that really mattered. This became the raw material of the poems and his diary. Expressed as questions or as articulated desperation, this was part of his 'human cry for salvation and my reaction against the modern denials of religious faith'. He had lived too long and seen too much to believe that man unaided would be anything other than a disaster.

Elsewhere

Let Congresses consider how to avoid
These bomb abominations being employed
In suicidal conflict – how
To unannihilate the future now

Since nothing that one man can think or say
Could be effective in the feeblest way,
He for appeasement of his tortured mind,
Must look elsewhere to be
Defended and befriended and resigned
And fortified and free.
Elsewhere. The indestructible exists
Beyond found formulas of scientists.
Our spiritual situation stood the same
In other epochs when
To thwart all ministries of mercy came
The arrogant inventiveness of men.

The prophetic voice is still there in some of the poems but it is a fading voice. The poems are much more the voice of the Psalmist and the anguished cry of Job, 'Oh that I knew where I might find Him.' Increasingly he adopted the language and metaphors of the Bible as he began to move away from his obscure anthropological vocabulary and ideas. More and more his gaze became inward and personal, distilled through the poetry written mainly from 1948 onwards. The stream began to flow again through the parched channel.

Sassoon was preoccupied with matters other than those Ackerley and others perceived to be troubling him. He had determined to keep his own counsel, finding his own way through the thickets or, as he expressed it, 'just muddling on by instinct'. He had also decided to revert to solitude. Without peace and quiet there was no possibility of hearing the inner voice. When writing in *Siegfried's Journey* of his busyness in the twenties he regretted that the time spent in flitting like a bee from one flower to another had, unlike the bee's, been completely unproductive. The start of his search is marked with his stated recognition that 'quietude is essential to human endeavour'. In *Siegfried's Journey* he quotes from the writings of the seventeenth-century divine Norris of Bemerton. Bemerton was a small parish, not far from Heytesbury, where George Herbert had served as priest from 1630 until his death in 1633. 'I think it advisable for every man that has sense and thoughts enough, to be his own companion (for certainly there is more required to qualify a man for his own company than for other men's), to be frequent in his retirements as he can, and to communicate as little with the world as is consistent with the duty of doing good, and the discharge of the common offices of humanity.'

Sassoon's poetry and life took on the hue of this philosophy. 'In a Time of Decivilisation', a poem written in 1947, he craves 'stillness, man's final friend'. In poem after poem over the next four years, the theme was developed. Sassoon became by his own admission 'the Hermit of Heytesbury'. It was a reversion to type but also an admission of his need. Turning in on himself he sought answers and assurances about life after death. Sassoon felt old and tired – he resented both – he wished for youthfulness again, 'the glow and glee of boyhood skating ponds'. He wanted no part 'in an age of values lost'. He wanted the warmth of yesterday and the innocence of childhood but he must now face 'the circumstances of growing old and teaching myself to submit to it philosophically and learn what I can from the process'. His mood was morose, owing in part to the literary world's perception of him, although he believed that the public's response to his work was as positive as ever. On 20 January 1950, his chafed spirit confided in the diary:

> I was thinking this evening that my inward grumblings and discontents about the Eliot literary autocracy are entirely personal. If I weren't a poet, I shouldn't bother about it at all. I respect Eliot as a literary expert (though his early poems are the only ones I've ever been able to enjoy). What I resent and take to heart is having his immense importance perpetually rubbed in to me by the professors, with implications that I am of no importance at all. It is the penalty of not being an intellectual poet. Lyrical poetry is now vitually forbidden – (though 'the general public' still prefer it.)
>
> At one time I regarded it as certain (and so did T. E. Lawrence) that I should be made into one of the Grand Old Men of English Letters. And even now, on what I have achieved, and the success of my prose books, I am quite adequately qualified for such a pedestal. It now seems probable that my concluding years will be

what they are now – established reputation – not talked about in literary circles – out of sight, out of mind – 'O, is he still alive,' sort of thing. But I seem unlikely to produce anything more which will stir up interest in me.

It seems incongruous that Sassoon in the critical years between 1948 and 1956 did not acknowledge that he was walking the same path as Eliot, who was but a short distance ahead of him. *The Four Quartets* (1935–42) echo with all that Sassoon himself was asking in the trilogy he published between 1950 and 1953: *Common Chords, Emblems of Experience* and *The Tasking*. In 1956 these were published by Faber and Faber in a volume called *Sequences*. Eliot had his office in Faber and yet not a word nor letter passed between them. Was it all merely the conventions of a publishing house, Richard de la Mare being Sassoon's editor, so Eliot and Sassoon never needing to communicate? So it appears. Maybe it was another example of Sassoon's reluctance to put himself about?

In the past Sassoon had enjoyed a number of father-figures but in these years he did not share his burden or perplexity with anyone. The chill in his friendship with Blunden closed that path. Nor did he reveal to Glen Byam Shaw how deep and urgent was his quest. His letters to Glen are unrestrained in their comments on Hester, his love for George and the joy he found in climbing and walking with his son on the Isle of Mull – but there is nothing in them about his latest preoccupation. The stark quality of the Argyllshire terrain, softened by the summer light, prompted thoughts of worlds not made with hands.

He and George enjoyed their August holiday in Lochbuie but it was tinged with regret on Sassoon's part. At the end of it, George would start as a pupil at Oundle School in Northamptonshire. The distance between them would be greater and the move marked another step in George's growing up and, his father feared, their growing apart. Circumstances meant that he could only see his son for part of the school holiday: Hester would insist on his spending time with her on Mull.

In October Sassoon was cheered by having enough poems ready for a private printing. *Common Chords*, with its 18 new poems, gave voice to his deepest need for peace and the gift of stillness to continue his pilgrimage but the opening poem, 'Release', is a riposte to the 'intellectuals', scientific and literary:

One winter's end I much bemused my head
In tasked attempts to drive it up to date
With what the undelighting moderns said
Forecasting human fate.

And then, with nothing unforeseen to say
And no belief or unbelief to bring,
Came in its old unintellectual way
The first real day of spring.

As he collated the manuscript he was conscious again, as he had been at the year's beginning, of the need to talk with someone about his doubts and seekings; not about his poetry but about being 'spiritually minded'. It seemed like a repeat of 1913, when he 'muddled along on his own trying to be a poet'. Who could he talk to? When Helen Waddell had sent her book *Stories from Holy Writ*, he confided to his diary: 'If only I could talk to her – she would do me the world of good – one of the biggest people I know.' That was at the beginning of the year – now at its end he felt isolated. He was also peeved. A letter arrived on 3 December offering him the honour of being a Commander of the British Empire. It was just not good enough. He was disappointed and, he conjectured, so too would his friends be when the New Year's Honours list was published. But he went ahead and accepted, and before long his friends wrote effusively of their delight. For once Hester struck the right note: he should have been made a knight – 'like William Walton'.

At Heytesbury Sassoon faced 1950 feeling quite incapable of coping with his circumstances. Life had become an empty experience: George back at school, few callers at the door and even fewer visitors to stay. He was fortunate to have secured a good housekeeper and cook, Mrs Benn, who arrived in 1949 and stayed a decade – a record. As for poetry, there was much that he wanted to express but still no impulse to write. His explanation for this decline in inspiration and increasing lethargy was being stranded in his 'sexagenarian solitudes'. Sassoon tended to exaggerate his loneliness, greeting those who called with the pathetic complaint that 'No one calls to see me' and its variant in letters, 'Haven't seen a soul for weeks.' After such dirgeful openings he would proceed to name names, repeat and quote conversations. He took a perverse revenge on the years in pretending to be older than he actually was. If there was any comfort it came from his belief in what he described as 'presences' –

the recalling through memory of departed friends for whose thoughts and words he himself was the ventriloquist – an idea he pursued in his poem 'Solitudes at Sixty':

> Sexagenarian solitudes, I find,
> Are somewhat stagnant, motiveless and slow:
> Old friends arrive; but only to my mind,
> Since their earth-farings ended years ago.
> Beloved or valued ghosts, these reappear
> At my peculiar prompting. Known by heart,
> Finite impersonations, learnt by ear,
> Their voices talk in character and depart.
>
> They, once my wise and faithful, have no being:
> No supersensual agency can bring
> Those presences from silence and unseeing:
> They dwell secure from world's importuning.
> Meanwhile myself sits with myself agreeing
> That to be sixty is no easy thing.

Sassoon took to his bed, only getting up between three and six each day. Influenza complicated the bronchial tightness which caused him discomfort. Exploring 'the cosmos of Miss Austen' helped him back to some semblance of vitality, as did the first signs in late February that spring was near and the summons to Buckingham Palace to receive his CBE. He was the only literary man in the line and, dressed in his pre-war blue suit, the only one not in black. Lord Clarendon called his name, making it sound like 'Sickfreed Sassoon'. Vintage Siegfried is the best description of his diary entry for the day: 'I think the King was pleased to see me, as my writings are liked by the Queen and I was undoubtedly the most famous person there. He spoke nicely with a charming, genial smile, "I am glad to see you here – I suppose you are as busy as ever?" With a strong feeling for him I said, "God bless you" in a low voice as he shook my hand.' Despite the disappointment at not being given a more illustrous decoration, the ceremony boosted his spirits. He wrote to Max, saying: 'I emerged into the Mall feeling rather cheered up by it all.' The therapy was given greater potency by the good news from Australia that England had won the first Test match. Statistic-conscious as ever, Sassoon noted, 'first win since 1936'.

But all these boosts were temporary and the events peripheral to the 'quest for spiritual illumination'. His thoughts were evolving. The basic pantheism reflected in his poetry and the impersonal nature of the universe were no longer enough, he needed a personal response. Like the traveller in de la Mare's poem 'The Listeners', Sassoon was asking, 'Is there anybody there?' Amusingly he comments on being 'left alone with my efforts to make friends with God, who doesn't appear to be a forthcoming conversationalist. Too busy with that Universe of His I suppose.' But he took comfort that this was the nature of the spiritual life, a slow struggle; a series of matches struck in the dark – 'Perhaps I am in the dark night of the soul.' Sassoon had long ago discovered and been deeply engaged by the Metaphysical poets. Henry Vaughan and George Herbert were old and familiar sources to him, the former in particular being the poet of loss and of childhood. In August 1924, when he visited the grave of Vaughan in Llansantffraed, Powys, he wrote of:

> the skull that housed white angels and had vision
> Of daybreak through the gateways of the mind.

and of how:

> this lowly grave tells Heaven's tranquillity
> And here stand I, a suppliant at the door.

A quarter of a century later, Sassoon was still a 'suppliant at the door' but with an intensity not known before. His poem 'Redemption', which concludes *Common Chords*, is plaintive in spirit:

> I thought; to the Invisible I am blind;
> No angels tread my nights with feet of flame;
> No mystery is mine –
> No whisper from that world beyond my senses.
>
> I think; If through some chink in me could shine
> But once – O but one ray
> From that all-hallowing and eternal day,
> Asking no more of heaven I would go hence.

Reading the manuscript of *Common Chords* in an attempt to reconsider the poems' 'effect and significance', Sassoon was disturbed by the thought of people judging them to be 'a curious withdrawal from sensory existence – a concentration of mind on unphysical reality and refutation of aliveness'. His worries were justified: that is how all his last poems were judged by the majority. He was also dissatisfied with his lack of progress; partially due to God's obstinacy and partially to his own limited spirituality, 'a man alone with a self which asks awareness of God, but only gets as far in his mysticism as saying that He *must* be there'.

Private copies of *Common Chords* were sent to friends. On 9 August came the all-important word from Helen Waddell. Her commendation and elucidation caused Sassoon to see the poems as portraying not only his own struggle for illumination, but the intrinsic nature of that quest: 'You do not know what you have done and I have not the words to tell you. The soul's dark cottage in these poems has not only let in the light through chinks that time has made: it has itself become a light shining in the darkness.' Through such words Sassoon realised that those who criticised his work were of less consequence than those who would be helped by it. Thus he overcame his reluctance to publish this and the subsequent volumes.

Dear old Eddie Marsh approved the volume but from a different angle: 'Nobody has so well rendered the ambiguity of the times we live in.' Who but a civil servant could have thought of such an inoffensive word as ambiguity? Sassoon was not surprised. He knew Eddie too well to expect him to 'approve the spirituality' of his work. Helen Waddell was the only one, he felt, who grasped the essence of what he was aiming at: 'Her letter is all I want. Helen's words have given me the feeling of being able to sit back with my task achieved. Others will feel as she does about the poems.' Five years previously he had written in his journal: 'I suppose some day a lot of clergy will discover that I am a religious poet.' Waddell confirmed his vocation – he did not wish to be any other kind.

He had another wish, 'someone to talk to instead of this dreary journal'. Solitude he enjoyed, indeed he thrived on it, but loneliness depressed him. Turning the pages of his journal and transcribing the contents, he was reminded of those who had 'slipped out' of his life. If there was sadness at the loss it was momentary – 'Blunden is the only one whose loss I regret and Glen who from 1925 has been nothing but a blessing.' He had not lost Glen's friendship, but had been deprived of it by theatrical and travelling commitments. Blunden's friendship, however, was sorely missed. When Laurence Whistler visited Heytesbury, old friends and faces were on the agenda, including Blunden. As Whistler took his leave, Sassoon told him how much he needed 'little B' and that he was 'very lonely'.

In May 1950 Blunden had returned to England from his three-year professorship in Japan. He had also returned to his former post at the *Times Literary Supplement*. There had been no contact between him and Sassoon since 1947. They had not quarrelled but had become estranged through the circumstances of Sassoon's marriage. For his part, Sassoon had resolved to let Blunden and Claire enjoy their friendship with Hester, they having decided to whom they would be loyal; he was not going to quarrel with them. Whistler informed Blunden of the affectionate terms with which Sassoon had spoken of him – the ground was laid for reconciliation. An exchange of letters in the spring of 1952 restored the bond of friendship but Sassoon in his diary wrote of Blunden: 'He acted unwisely and made it impossible for me to feel friendly towards him. I suppose I mean more to him than he now does to me.' Sassoon could be so unbending and severe.

Stephen Tennant called at Heytesbury at the end of January 1952. Outwardly Sassoon had mellowed towards him. Certainly Tennant was made to feel welcome and no doubt made himself at home as their conversation progressed. Sassoon recorded his enjoyment of their afternoon together and their talk but he knew to his cost 'how deceptive these charming, superficial selfish people are'. Osbert Sitwell came into that category. In May Sassoon met him for luncheon at the Reform. On the surface it was all pleasant but Sassoon was not comfortable – in fact, he had never been truly at ease with any of the Sitwell trio. Osbert was now *Sir* Osbert, having inherited the title on the death of his father, Sir George, in 1943. He had written to Sassoon in June 1951 proposing to clear an old loan of £7,500, on which he had been paying Sassoon 5 per cent interest. In that same letter he told Sassoon that he was off to Oxford, where Edith was receiving an honorary doctorate: 'The Sitwells are prime examples of what can be achieved by organized pushing (Eliot is another).' Sassoon now wanted nothing to do with any of them and their friendship, like their opinions, he discounted.

Blunden was different and was invited down to Heytesbury, where the talk continued virtually non-stop for two days. He had received a special copy of Sassoon's most recent volume of poems, *Emblems of Experience*, and was particularly taken by 'A Fallodon Memory', which commemorates Stephen Tennant's stepfather, Lord Grey. 'A noble poem,' Blunden called it. Sassoon felt a tinge of regret that Blunden and other recipients seemed not to enthuse over the religious poems in the volume. Resignedly he wrote: 'I suppose people prefer poems about something definite, and close to everyday life. They don't want my spiritual self-communings – (though Helen Waddell does).' That entry marks a turning point in Sassoon, not deliberate on his part but in consequence of his turning from one world view to another. Waddell was the first member of his new circle. One poem, 'The Need', in *Emblems of Experience* has overtones of the idea of an elect, a faithful remnant:

> Speak through the few,
> Your light of life to nourish us anew,
> Speak, for our world possessed
> By demon influences of evil and unrest.
> Act as of old,
> That we some dawnlit destiny may behold
> From this doom-darkened place.
> O move in mercy among us. Grant accepted grace.

Sassoon wanted to be identified with those who shared in such prayers for a world redeemed. They were to be his friends, and not only those living but those who had shared the vision. He had found such communion with George Herbert and Henry Vaughan. In his poem to the medieval scholar Alcuin he found another:

Awareness of Alcuin

> At peace in my tall-windowed Wiltshire room
> (Birds overheard from chill March twilight's close)
> I read, translated, Alcuin's verse, in whom
> A springtime of resurgent learning rose.
>
> Alcuin from temporalities at rest,
> Sought grace within him, given from afar;
> Noting how sunsets worked around to west;
> Watching, at spring's approach, that beckoning star;
> And hearing, while one thrush sang through the rain,
> Youth, which his soul in Paradise might regain.

The translation mentioned in line three was the work of Helen Waddell in her volume *Mediaeval Latin Lyrics*. These connections of friendship forged by a common desire were to become what Sassoon called 'sustainments'. It was notionally the communion of saints, but he was far from recognising it as such. He was still floundering, still muddling along trying to construct his own private system of religious belief. It was tragic that Helen Waddell's mental and physical decline should cast the shadow of deprivation at this moment. Sassoon had many father figures in his life but, Dr Rivers apart, he only ever had mother-confessors of whom Helen Waddell was one. He needed her to be his eyes in the wilderness: 'Helen's disappearance was a catastrophe for me.'

In May 1953 Sassoon travelled to Cambridge. He liked the city and the colleges and was tempted to make it a centre for himself. People he liked were there – Philip and Anna Gosse, Geoffrey and Margaret Keynes. There was every likelihood George would gain a place at King's. Somewhat to his surprise, but also to his enormous delight and satisfaction, his old college, Clare, decided to make him an honorary fellow. Nearing half a century since his first and not-successful encounter with academia, Sassoon looked fondly on the River Cam and the punts to whose temptations he had yielded so readily in 1906.

Cambridge also meant cricket at Fenners and how well timed was this visit with the university team playing a home match. Blunden, exiled in London, had encouraged Sassoon, if any encouragement were needed, to visit the ground and to make the acquaintance of a promising batsman, Dennis Silk. He did not mention that Silk had been primed. 'I remember clearly the gaunt, handsome stranger in moth-eaten blue blazer and faded trilby hat who marched up to the pavilion with a long hazel staff in his hand. He looked up at the rows of seated spectators and said in a tone of inquiry and a little awkwardly: "Dennis Silk?" I identified myself and he said simply: "Siegfried Sassoon."' Blunden was perceptive. Although he knew full well the melancholic spirit which ran through Sassoon's personality, and that he was given to periods of withdrawal, nonetheless he believed that his present state pointed to another need – for new friendships, and the companionship of younger people. Blunden was right: the friendship flourished unalloyed for 13 years. It got off to a good start when Sassoon learnt that Silk's father was Rector of Renishaw and therefore responsible for Osbert Sitwell's spiritual welfare! There would be other friendships, too, which revived Sassoon's spirit of youthfulness.

In September 1953 Archie John Wavell, son of Field Marshal Earl Wavell, was posted to the School of Infantry at Warminster. Sydney Cockerell encouraged communication between Sassoon and the young Wavell, who had succeeded his father to the title. Wavell wrote to

Cockerell: 'I long to meet him as I have always enjoyed his poems, and then he was such a good friend of T. E. Lawrence and Wilfred Owen, two of the people whose writings I have much admired. He has beckoned me to come along and asks me to treat his library as a refuge from soldiering.' The meeting took place on Sassoon's sixty-seventh birthday and Wavell wrote again to Cockerell: 'As he saw me coming along the drive and walked towards me I could not believe this was a man of sixty-seven. He began in clipped, nervous unfinished sentences – and I felt shy too – but as the evening went on I could watch his fine face and neck in profile. I think he is lonely, he says the winters are very long without anyone to talk to when his boy is away at school.' Sassoon was impressed with Wavell and wrote to tell Cockerell: 'What an admirable fellow he is. I urged him to come over as often as possible, and he really did me a world of good.'

To have formed new friendships helped Sassoon to accept the departure of Blunden in September for a professorship in Hong Kong. It is doubtful whether he would have turned to his old friend for guidance in his search for spiritual illumination but the loss of Blunden's visits to Heytesbury for cricket matches and long conversations was a significant deprivation. Young Wavell helped with his visits. Sassoon enjoyed discussing books and writers with him, much as he enjoyed 'instructing young Silk about literature and life in general'. In November, however, Wavell departed for Africa and the troubles in Kenya with the Mau-Mau.

It was winter again and the year's ending – not Sassoon's favourite season. He turned to his poems, arranging them for another volume, which he decided to call *The Tasking*. Writing of the poems, composed during 1952–53, 'I would say that they are merely an exhibition of the spiritual and intellectual shortcomings of a man trying to find things out for himself – attempting to formulate his private religion step by step, in hopes that it may be of some slight service to a period which appears to have rejected religious beliefs in favour of psychology and scientific research.'

Sassoon was unwell again with serious bronchial congestion but in reasonable spirits, even completing a poem, 'The Making'. He wrote to de la Mare, thanking him for the splendid gift of his latest poems. Then on Boxing Day news came that Archie John Wavell had been killed in Kenya. Sassoon was stupefied by the news – the death of a young man on active service triggered horrendous nightmares. 'The worst thing that happened in 1953 was Archie Wavell's death,' he wrote some years later. 'His religious-mindedness seemed a life line thrown to me – as with Helen Waddell.' He wrote to Cockerell: 'For the loss of such an incalculably valuable young life it is hard to think up consolations. He made me feel I had gained a wonderful new friend. Though knowing I might not see him again for 18 months, the thought of being able to communicate with him was a real comfort in my solitude.'

Sassoon returned to *The Tasking*. The title is a description of the challenge he had set himself. He also felt that he was being compelled by some inward force to search and know himself. The task was hampered by thoughts of his own ignorance of matters spiritual. All this concentration on his soul while the world was in turmoil seemed a perverse undertaking. Like Jacob he was wrestling with some angel and oscillating between giving up the fight and saying, 'I will not let you go ere you bless me.'

The Tasking

To find rewards of mind with inward ear
Through silent hours of seeking;
To put world sounds behind and hope to hear
Instructed spirit speaking:

Sometimes to catch a clue from selfhood's essence
And ever that revealment to be asking;
This – and through darkness to divine God's presence –
I take to be my tasking.

In March 1954 he wrote the poem 'Faith Unfaithful', which he described in 1960 as his 'last word' on the search. After this he 'just went blindly onwards, clinging to the *idea* of God, unable to believe that salvation applied to *me*, though firmly convinced of the existence of a spiritual world and a heaven above. Again and again in these past years, I have asked myself how I endured it, so unendurable it seems in retrospect. Was it some kind of dark night of probation?' *Be still and know that I am God* was the counsel which, in a footnote to the poem 'Renewals', he says was his 'most often repeated words from Scripture'.

I said to fitful mind –
Put discontents behind;
Be silent and grow still.

Common Chords, Emblems of Experience and *The Tasking* were combined to make a single volume with the title *Sequences*. On 6 November 1956, 3,000 copies went on sale to the general public. There was no rush to buy the volume; the reviews ranged from mild to harsh. Sassoon had expected the reaction, believing most people wanted him to continue writing in the mode of the *Memoirs*: '"What a pity he can't write more about fox-hunting," the public will say.'

19

ULTIMATE SPRING

1957–67

Margaret Mary McFarlin was recovering from a bout of flu when, in January 1957, her friend Lola Dmitrieff gave her an advanced birthday present of *Sequences*. As a student at Liverpool in the 1920s she had read and admired Sassoon's poetry and now, delighted by the gift, she settled down to read its contents in her room at 23 Kensington Square. 'I read the book through, my amazement growing at the complete change in tone from his earlier works. I had studied his War Poetry in my student days: knew and loved his memoirs of Sherston and especially *The Old Century* and *Siegfried's Journey* – and I felt an insistent urge to write and tell him that I would pray that he would, as he writes in *The Tasking*, "through the darkness divine God's presence". I obeyed the urge, wrote a very short letter and sent it c/o Faber and Faber.'

Sassoon replied by return on 10 January:

Your message came like a blessing from above; and I have carried it about in my mind all these last two days, much comforted in spirit. When your gracious kindness impelled you to write it you did not know the good you would do me.

So I must explain that I am always very much alone here during the winters; and since my book was published early in November, I have seen no one, and yours is only the second letter I have received about it. (Most of my friends read the poems in their privately printed editions, and wrote to me then.) And the 'professional reviewers' do rather take the heart out of one with their uncomprehending generalisations. They are not interested in my modest 'progress of the soul'.

In my solitudes I have meditated much about the poems and their effect on thoughtful readers for whom I have unlocked my heart. And silence surrounded me. From this you will now realise what a consolation it was to read your words.

It is, of course, always my best reward to hear that my writings have been enjoyed and have made me new friends. Hundreds of good people have written to tell me so. But – the knowledge that I am to be remembered in your prayers – what greater gift can I receive than this? Does not the man who wrote 'Faith Unfaithful' need them? He does indeed.

You must not, however, think of me as subdued by melancholy. In *The Tasking* I was 'putting myself through it', so to speak facing the rationalist point of view (which my soul instinctively rejects) and striving to – but, O dear – you know what I was striving to do. Millions of souls have done it, but they don't write poems about it, as a rule.

When I wrote 'spiritual' poems in the past they were only emotional attitudes. Of late years I have had to think it all out for myself unemotionally. And the state of the world hasn't aided optimism, has it? It seemed as though the world were pervaded by evil, and the powers of darkness really showing their hand.

To you, probably, my little speculations and inquiries about my Maker will seem quite childlike. But I do seek the Divine Light with my whole being. 'Held to what infinite heart – heard by what immanent ear?' Please write to me again; and tell me what you think of my gropings, but you must not trouble yourself if this is asking too much of you. Your letter was the 'the answered orison'.
Yours most gratefully,
SS

The admission of ignorance in matters spiritual and the gratitude for being included in the prayers of the writer were due to the fact that she was the Reverend Mother Margaret Mary of the Convent of the Assumption. Her second letter to him posed questions of belief but more than catechising him she won his trust through a shared delight in poetry, Robert Browning and Thomas Hardy. Challenged, he found found replying very difficult. He got into a muddle trying to explain his feelings; he wanted to be honest and 'to say only what might help you to help me. I can only tell you how safeguarded you have made me feel. Can it be that you have awakened me to a new start on my road to the celestial city? That is what it has felt like.' The correspondence became a constant flow of question and answer. 'I urged him to pray – prayer being the mainspring of my own life,' recalled Mother Margaret Mary. Sassoon felt that his flood of outpourings was an imposition and he ought to fend for himself and continue the search unaided. He would have done so, but something had changed since that first letter, some 'invisible influence – a peace of spirit – a sense of healing'. By Eastertide he knew he had crossed a boundary and reached:

> the calm verge
> Of some annunciation that should bring
> With flocks of silver angels, ultimate Spring
> Whence all that life had longed for might emerge.

Between 19 and 21 April his assurance of deliverance, of hope fulfilled, became the inspiration for the poem 'Deliverance':

> No comfort came until I looked for light
> Beyond the darkened thickets of my brain.
> With nothingness I strove. And inward sight
> No omen but oblivion could obtain.
> He spoke. He held my spirit in His hand.
> Through prayer my password from the gloom was given.
> This Eastertide, absolved, in strength I stand,
> Feet firm upon the ground. My heart in heaven.

Almost 40 years before, he had stood in a trench in France, 'staring across at the enemy I'd never seen. Somewhere out of sight beyond the splintered tree-tops of Hidden Wood a bird had begun to sing. Without knowing why, I remembered it was Easter Sunday. Standing in that dismal ditch, I could find no consolation that Christ was risen.' Within the week, on 23 April 1957, he presented himself at the convent in Kensington Square for his first meeting with Mother Margaret Mary. 'His appearance gave the impression of a very alert army man! Tall, wiry, nervy, with a peculiar manner of talking in bursts of speech and often barely intelligible. When he sat, his long legs were jumpy; he was fidgety – unwinding and winding his handkerchief round his fingers: lighting eternally his beloved pipe: fixing one's eyes with his own green-grey ones, then looking away but missing nothing. We talked about everything and he read me "Deliverance". He had his first Benediction – and when the Angelus rang at 12 o'clock he heard it said for the first time.'

As to what happens at conversion nobody can explain – except that there is a before and after; the crossing of a border: a moving between states – darkness to light; chaos to order and everything made new. Sassoon in the spring of 1957 was aware of an 'instant release'. His puzzlement was why he had taken so long to understand that it was not an intellectual argument but just unconditional surrender.

At Christmas 1949 he was filling his diary with questions about the 'Immanent Will' and 'Prime Cause': the survival of the soul, questioning whether belief in God made any difference to happiness and whether, if there is a God, He cared anyway about insignificant human beings who were daily becoming even more insignificant. On and on goes the diary entry with no paragraph breaks. And then, having piled up this list of agonies, complexities and intellectual enigmas, he writes, 'I suppose unquestioning faith is the only solution. "Just as I am, I come to Thee" and so on.' But he did not act upon this insight. In retrospect he poked fun at himself going round in circles, 'just muddling on by instinct'. Reading the work of John Henry Newman he surmised in a letter: 'I wonder what effect it would have made if someone had given it to me ten years ago. Everything I needed is there, waiting for me! All clear as daylight. And as simple as falling off a log – just unconditional surrender.'

> This, then, brought our new making. Much emotional stress –
> Call it conversion; but the word can't cover such good.
> It was like being in love with ambient blessedness –
> In love with life transformed – life breathed afresh, though
> yet half understood.

The final decade of Sassoon's life was 'learning to understand that other half'. Mother Margaret Mary remained his guide but she did not instruct him in the faith. A vital part in Sassoon's conversion experience was the impact made when he read a letter sent from Hilaire Belloc to Katharine Asquith. Sassoon was seized by its contents: 'The Faith, the Catholic Church, is discovered, is recognised, triumphantly enters reality like a landfall at sea which first was thought a cloud. The nearer it is seen the more it is real, the less imaginary: the more direct and external its voice, the more indubitable its representative character, its "persona", its voice. The metaphor is not that men fall in love with it: the metaphor is they discover home. "This was what I sought. This was my need." It is Verlaine's "Oh Rome – oh Mère!" And that not only to those who had it in childhood and have returned, but much more – and what a proof – to those who come upon it from over the hills of life and say to themselves, "Here is the town."' Sassoon wrote of that moment: 'Belloc's magnificent words settled it, once and for all. "That's done it," I said. My whole being was liberated.'

Sassoon knew Belloc and had visited him with Sydney Cockerell in June 1919, when he impressed Sassoon with 'his brilliant powers as a talker and the gusto of his human companionship'. He also knew Katharine Asquith of Mells in Somerset. Although his social network in his final years was not extensive, it was tightly woven. He had been introduced to her through the Bonham Carters, who were neighbours of Sassoon at Stockton, halfway between Heytesbury and Salisbury. Lady Violet and in particular, her daughter Cressida were very fond of Sassoon and regular visitors. Katharine had married Lady Violet's eldest brother, Raymond Asquith, who was killed in action in 1916. Her only brother Edward Horner also died in the war.

Such losses made an instant bond between Mells and Heytesbury, a bond strengthened by the friendship with the Bonham Carters. Katharine had embraced the Catholic faith in 1924. The Manor House at Mells is some eight miles from the Benedictine abbey at Downside, which became, after Katharine's conversion, central to life at Mells. It was at the Manor House that one of the outstanding religious minds of the twentieth century lived for the final years of his life, Monsignor Ronald Knox. Sassoon met him while still on his quest but he never asked Knox for assistance. Only once did Sassoon hint at his search for enlightenment when, at the end of some general conversation, in his usual self-deprecating way he told Knox that he was 'only a child in knowledge and understanding. He smiled and pressed my arm.' Knox had received a copy of *The Tasking* from Sassoon. When acknowledging the gift Knox was reserved – 'reticent' is Sassoon's description of the letter – but he would never rush in. He did, however, in 1955 mention Sassoon to his friend at Downside, Dom Hubert van Zeller, suggesting they should meet – 'You will find it difficult at first to know what he is talking about, but every bit is worth keeping.'

Ronald Knox and Mother Margaret Mary were known to each other.

She wrote to Knox suggesting that he might instruct Sassoon and guide him through the months until his reception into the Church. It was an incalculable loss to Sassoon that such guidance was not forthcoming, for Knox was dying of cancer. On 30 May Sassoon travelled the 15 miles to Downside for his first instruction with Dom Sebastian Moore. It was clear to Sebastian that Sassoon was already well prepared. He was struck by the qualities of the mystic, which manifested themselves in his stillness and in his vocabulary. Sassoon was received into the Church on 14 August 1957 at Downside and received his first communion the following day. Ever after he counted the abbey church as his first spiritual home and the community as one part of his family.

As in all things, Sassoon wanted his conversion and reception to be private. It came as a shock to him when a reporter from the *Sunday Express* arrived at Heytesbury. Sassoon declined to be interviewed, pleading the personal and private nature of what had happened. His innocence led him to share part of his story with the reporter, believing that, having requested privacy, the request would be respected. He contacted John Junor, the Editor, requesting nothing be printed. His heart sank when the *Sunday Express* carried the story. Matters were made worse when Sassoon wrote a letter to *The Times* explaining that what had been published was his 'expostulation against my most sacred intimacies being exhibited as newspaper publicity'. Junor refuted this in a follow-up letter to *The Times*: 'I can understand Mr Sassoon's desire to avoid personal publicity. I cannot accept as an "expostulation" an interview which occupied four closely written pages in shorthand.'

Sassoon wrote to Glen that 'it was a nightmare come true. I can only hope that few people who respect me will have seen this horror which I brought on myself by being so simple minded.' Unfortunately for him, not all his friends were happy that they had to discover his conversion through the papers. The correspondence between him and Philip Gosse was brittle, as it was with Geoffrey Keynes. Sassoon told no one in advance, not even George or Glen, or Dennis Silk. Most were pleased for him when they eventually knew, but Sassoon's tendency to secrecy and, it might reasonably be added, his imperviousness could be disconcerting to those who loved him. While having lunch with Blunden and Claire in Salisbury in 1957, Sassoon took his handkerchief from his pocket. Something fell from the handkerchief; it was a rosary. Claire later recalled how Sassoon, clearly embarrassed, put it back in his pocket without saying a word. Blunden had been with Sassoon at Mells the year before, on 5 July, at the last meeting between Sassoon and Knox but that is how Sassoon had pursued his spiritual quest, telling and asking no one.

One happy outcome from the publicity was a letter from Robert Graves. As ever with Graves, the letter was not straightforward but it was well meant and Sassoon was pleased to respond:

> All I need say now is that I experience peace beyond anything I could have hoped for – not through my formal submission to R.C. dogma, but through the grace of faith which came to me after prolonged perseverance in prayer and through the help I received from a very holy Catholic.
>
> I was not at all bothered by the re-issue of *Goodbye*, and hope it will remind the present generation of what 1914–18 was for those who endured it. I think the reason for my being so upset in 1929 was that I was in a great state of mental fatigue and worry with writing *The Infantry Officer*. All that you wrote about me was entirely generous – beyond my deserts.

It was a happy way to end the year, which had also brought him the Queen's Medal for Poetry.

Writing to Dom Philip Jebb of Downside, grandson of Hilaire Belloc, Sassoon declared his ambition now was to be of spiritual help to others. He liked the idea of being used, and proposed that the poet is 'an instrument being played'. In Sassoon's case this did not mean much new poetry – or prose for that matter – but it did mean discipline in his private devotional life and being 'open to all that God wants me to understand'. His letters became a compendium of religious insights, all expressed in a spirit of excited discovery, and very often rediscovery of truths cast away: 'First beliefs remain.' A new emphasis on his Jewish ancestry also became evident, to which he ascribed the prophetic hue of some of his poetry. More and more he was given to reflection on the years that the locust had eaten; his journey full of 'significances' which now he saw as God's promptings and providential leadings. He constantly ends paragraphs of these recallings and the road to conversion with the exclamation: 'It just had to happen, didn't it?' Driving home from Downside one afternoon he felt compelled to stop the car, go into a field and lift his arms in praise for so great a deliverance. It was the same impulse that led him to spend time on his own in the abbey church, sobbing deeply.

The account of his conversion is contained in his poem 'Lenten

Illuminations', published in the *Downside Review* in the summer of 1958, which marks, he wrote, 'my farewell to conversion happiness'. It was time to move on. He distrusted fame and had learnt to bridle emotionalism. Rivers had shown him that at Craiglockhart, and time had taught him the cost of being 'a Vesuvius of impulsiveness'. He acknowledged that much of his poetry in the 1920s and 30s – *The Heart's Journey* and *Vigils* – was nothing more than 'undirected and emotional aspirations which ended in the spiritual desolation that preceded my conversion'. In the past year he had learnt obedience and submission. It was hard at his age to bend to 'inflexible authority' but he recognised this as a need. His life needed order, which he sometimes called direction. John Henry Newman's sermons helped him to understand that acceptance of the Christian revelation was not a question of the emotions, nor of the intellect, but the submission of the will to God. Sassoon put it neatly in a letter at the end of 1959: 'Not so many treats now and plenty of Taskings.'

That letter was sent to another Benedictine community, Stanbrook Abbey near Worcester. Dame Felicitas Corrigan, OSB, was the organist there and an authority on liturgy, but she was also steeped in religious literature. Her contemporary at Liverpool and in holy orders was Mother Margaret Mary. The occasion for writing to Sassoon was the result of his friendship with Sydney Cockerell, who had been friendly with the former Abbess of Stanbrook, Dame Laurentia McLachlan – indeed some 750 letters passed between them starting in 1907 and concluding in 1953. Sassoon knew not only about this friendship but also about the Stanbrook Abbey Press, owning a copy of the Stanbrook Carols and the Little Breviary. Cockerell had also sent him a copy of Dame Felicitas's book *In a Great Tradition*. By the end of October 1959, letters were passing between Heytesbury and Stanbrook, and would continue to do so for the next eight years. Sassoon was enthusiastically writing to Dame Felicitas of how 'everything fitted together': how his life had been 'completely transformed', and that Stanbrook had 'joined Downside in my midnight prayers – all the Doms and Dames who have been kind to me'.

He liked his priest in Warminster and the church of St George. When the bronchial complaint affected him in the winter, the priest would come on a Monday to celebrate. Sassoon liked the idea of taking communion on his own, being a rather 'uncongregational' sort of worshipper, a thought with which he opened 'Lenten Illuminations':

Not properly Catholic, some might say, to like it best
When no one's in the cool white church that few frequent ...

The 'cool white church' was the abbey church of Downside, dedicated to
St Lawrence and whither Sassoon would retire – 'huffing and puffing' –
after a cricket match. It was as a result of playing for the Ravens, as the
Downside team was called, that another link in the 'Catholic family' chain
was forged. Writing to Dame Felicitas in July he said: 'I was bowled to by
a boy named Galsworthy – great-nephew of the great J.G. Last Friday at
Vespers at our church I noticed a charming looking grey-haired lady. As I
went out she gave me a very sweet smile of apparent recognition, and she
turns out to be the boy's aunt.' Sassoon counted such meetings as having
been 'arranged by Our Lady of Consolation'. Muriel Galsworthy became
a close friend and astute observer of his final years. She sometimes felt like
a sister to him and occasionally like Aunt Evelyn, having to sit and listen
or fetch a book but never allowed to decide the topic of conversation. 'He
was never happier than when people called to greet him,' she recalls. 'He
was particularly good with young people and once gave a tea-party to a
crowd of noisy convent girls from Sidmouth – he chuckled as he told me
of it.'

It mattered to him that what he had discovered and that which had
brought joy should be made known through his own poetry and that of
others. Writing to Katharine Asquith, he mentions the work of a young
schoolmaster, also a convert, whose poetry – it seemed to Sassoon – was in
the best tradition of religious verse. Ian Davie had sent him some 30 poems
– 'all very good', he commented. He was particularly taken with a longer
work, *Piers Prodigal*: 'most lovely in all ways and timeless in utterance and
clarity,' he told Katharine. With tenacity, Sassoon succeeded in getting the
work published. The friendship was strengthened when Ian Davie – who
recalls Sassoon as a 'radiant complexity' – was appointed to Marlborough
College, from where he could easily visit Heytesbury. In the closing years
of his life Sassoon greatly enjoyed young people, especially if they had a
'religious sense' and were 'good fun'. He took a real interest in their lives
and was full of encouragement. Ian Balding, a friend of Dennis Silk, who
went on to become the trainer of the Queen's horses, was in the sixties a
considerable amateur jockey. Sassoon records how he switched on the
wireless to hear commentary on the Gold Cup, in which young Balding
was riding the favourite: 'Ian, riding a waiting race and all seemed well,
but he fell half-way round.'

For once, and in the face of incontrovertible evidence, Sassoon accepted the result with good grace, which was unlike his reaction to umpires who unjustly sent young Silk from the wicket. In such cases he was 'absolute for friendship'. Each one of these three young men reflected an aspect of the young Sassoon – the poet, the horseman and the cricketer. His interest in the lives of young people was, he said, 'doing my stuff'. Muriel Galsworthy said poignantly, 'I think his encouragement of young people was part of his memory of all those young men who never made it past 1918 – he was very angry about that to the end of his life.'

As for music, his other passion, that was enriched through his friendship with Heather Lewis, a young music graduate with a talent for composition and an appreciation of the nuances in Sassoon's poetry. Her being the close friend of Ian Balding and the sister of Tony Lewis, former captain of Cambridge University cricket team, could only enhance Sassoon's affection for her. She composed settings for some of his poems, 'A Chord' being particularly evocative. Sassoon was moved by its haunting resonances, as he was by her setting of 'A Prayer to Time'. He relished the sound of the piano and the sensitive chords filling the room. It was all so reminiscent of Helen Wirgman hauntingly playing Beethoven at Weirleigh in the summer's late evening 50 years before, and of the breeze blowing through the Aeolian harp high in the crab-tree, which touched him to 'a blurred and uncontrolled chord of ecstasy'.

When Dennis brought his future wife Diana to Heytesbury, Sassoon was entranced by her and happy for him. She remembers being terrified at meeting the famous poet but was disarmed by his charm. 'The Ds' – as he always after referred to them – like Glen and Angela Byam Shaw, were at the centre of his affections. They were his 'sustainments', as were Mells, Downside and Stanbrook. There is a sense in which the description of Sassoon as a hermit has been exaggerated: the years leading up to his conversion were desolate but this ended in 1957. Perhaps he was too ready to encourage the idea of his 'withdrawal from the world'. His diaries and letters do not endorse his elected isolation but abound with references to a final decade brimful with happiness, activity and friendships.

Muriel Galsworthy was one of many who were invited to tea at Heytesbury, a high point in Sassoon's day, which took on all the intricate symbolism of a Japanese tea ceremony. 'Come and have tea on Wednesday,' he would say as they left the church in Warminster: 'I'll come and fetch you in the car.' Miss Galsworthy accepted the invitation to tea but always refused the offer of conveyance. 'I never really recovered from my one and only trip in his car and always made my own arrangements, fearing that my next Mass would be a Requiem.' Sassoon enjoyed such humour. Muriel was convinced that the reason she was so often invited was on account of her Galsworthy connection but more especially because 'I was a good listener and I think he needed an audience.' How perceptive of her to identify the same truth about Sassoon as Dr Rivers had, the penchant for monologue rather than dialogue. Once he was into a train of thought he did not like to be deflected. Dennis Silk noted that he would ignore any interpolation and proceed as if he had not noticed it; then all of 20 minutes later he would pick up the question, weaving it seamlessly into his talk. Dom Hubert van Zeller wrote of his exuberance: 'With Siegfried in full flood it was difficult to come away with more than a cupful at a time. To change the metaphor he was like a juggler sending up a dozen glittering objects at once. He would toss them at you, and you'd be lucky if you caught a few before they fell, when others would already be in the air.' This exuberance was not present on first acquaintance. His loquaciousness was always the result of his being familiar and comfortable with the listener. When he made his first visit to Stanbrook his sentences were as Archie Wavell had described them, 'rapid, jerky and unfinished'.

This visit to the abbey was to meet the Abbess, Dame Felicitas, and speak to the Community. He was also there to discuss the content of a volume of some of his verse in a Stanbrook Abbey Press edition. *The Path to Peace*, Dame Felicitas noted, was a collection, 'which includes several recent poems hitherto unpublished. Although observing no chronological order, a designed sequence traces his spiritual pilgrimage from the somewhat dreamy pantheism of youth through long years of lonely seeking to life breathed afresh in acceptance of the gift of faith.' Dame Hildelith, whose talent had brought such repute to Stanbrook editions, was heartened and probably surprised at the meticulous interest Sassoon took in the production process. Dame Felicitas continues: 'Dame Hildelith joined us, and almost an hour passed in printing discussion. S.S. became the taut, critical connoisseur. No sooner had she passed a specimen of paper and printing to him than the strong, nervous, sensitive hands were testing the texture, noting the watermark, colour surface – and usually dismissing the sample with some short, devastating remark! He was always right, too.'

When Sassoon received his first copy of *The Path to Peace* he wrote to Dame Felicitas declaring the publication to be his 'coronation as a

Catholic'. He felt as bound to Stanbrook as the leaves in the volume. Remembering his experience with the *Sunday Express*, he wrote: 'I have no wish for the book to be written about anywhere. Appreciation from a real Catholic magazine would be in a different category. But public journalism – no! As you say, the book is sacramental.' The volume was also his gift of thanks to Mother Margaret Mary.

Sassoon's abiding regret was the inability of Hester and George to understand the great joy which religion had brought him. He longed to share with them his thoughts and his poetry. It was a deprivation of which he complained in letters to Mells and Stanbrook. Hester came to Heytesbury from her home in Mull to fill the gap when the housekeeper was on holiday or when Sassoon was ill, and always for Christmas. It was with a faint heart that she was welcomed and a relieved spirit bade goodbye. While the visit lasted she fussed and bothered and interfered – at least that is how Sassoon regarded her activities. Muriel Galsworthy met her at Heytesbury and thought her a very kind and gentle person, 'but not very well organised'.

The relationship between husband and wife improved, partly owing to their leading separate lives at either end of the country. Sassoon admits to a fondness for Hester and regretted the sad years of discord. Unfortunately he did not see them as due to some of his own intransigence and domineering attitude. As late as 1962 he was still attributing the disasters to Hester's wilfulness. For her part Hester remained committed to Sassoon's well-being and probably to the marriage; while he became increasingly indifferent to the demands of the estate and the maintenance of the house, Hester made valiant efforts to keep Heytesbury in a state of good repair. Sassoon may well have counted such involvement as interference but such tasks required attention. Mother Margaret Mary also remembers Hester as a gentle, kind person, who called on several occasions to talk to her at the convent. Each time she expressed her gratitude that Sassoon had found contentment.

According to Sassoon, religion for Hester meant the outdoors – 'God is everywhere.' The Church of England had one great merit, she thought, 'you did not have to believe anything definite.' Freedom from dogma appealed to her. She saw little point in organised religion, telling Sassoon that 'God is too big for that sort of thing – mankind has always made the mistake of likening God to itself.' Sassoon saw little point in pursuing the matter with her: 'It is impossible to have a reasonable discussion with her – she just airs her omniscience as though uniquely inspired.' Sassoon did not entertain the thought that Hester might just have been exercising her right to think for herself.

Hester did have a tendency not so much for plain talking as for thoughtless blabbering. On one occasion she told Sassoon that his celebrity 'causes George discomfort'. Nothing could have wounded him more. 'Oh, family,' he wrote, 'why can't you be more familiar with the things that have brought me blessedness?' In particular he wished this for George. Their relationship, Sassoon felt, was no longer as close as it had been – Sassoon worried about his son and became apprehensive for him. He asked himself many times, 'What do I have to offer Hester and George? My family life is there, of course. But it has pathetically little to offer me, and I can do nothing for George and Hester except leave them my possessions. The things that are important and alive for them are only half-real to me. And my own significances mean nothing to them. I don't feel much needed.'

Religion became a serious bone of contention, not only between Hester and Sassoon but between Sassoon and Hester's brother, Richard Gatty. His daughter Jessica seemed to be coming under the religious influence of her Uncle Siegfried but the Gattys were not, understandably, well disposed towards their brother-in-law and resented his treatment of Hester. Nonetheless, invitations to visit their home at Pepper Arden near Richmond in Yorkshire were forthcoming. In 1958, unusually for Sassoon, he accepted their invitation for a summer visit. Jessica was deputed to entertain him and show him around. Sweet, intelligent and without personal ambition, she was inclined to the vocational and the caring professions but was unclear as to the way forward, although religion was not part of the answer – if anything, it was a complication. She remembers that, as she and Sassoon walked in the garden, 'Siegfried took a petal in his hand and in a William Blake way asked, "How can anyone doubt that a great mind is behind this beauty?" The comment was ordinary enough but I was deeply affected by it. In a very real sense Siegfried became my godfather.' She came under the influence of Mother Margaret Mary, now at Richmond, and Mother Clare at Kensington Square, eventually being received and later joining the Sisters of the Assumption. Sassoon's letters to Katharine Asquith and Dame Felicitas provided a running commentary on Jessica's progress. Hester was angry, Richard vituperative, Sassoon overjoyed, while Jessica – thrown headlong into the ministry of reconciliation – assured everyone that all would come right in the end. Sassoon was touched when Jessica wrote: 'Even if my family aren't particularly grateful (which I don't think is completely the case) for you taking an interest in me, I am!'

Spring and summer were the seasons for visitors to Heytesbury. Foremost among them was Edmund Blunden, who in 1964 had returned from Hong Kong at the end of his seven years there. He made visits to England during that period, five in all, and tried to see Sassoon each time. The letters between them were as constant as their friendship. Blunden was in some difficulty trying to raise money to buy a house. He wanted to settle in East Anglia, near Cambridge if possible, and did eventually secure a property in the village of Long Melford in Suffolk with the assistance of Sassoon. The years abroad had not been kind to Blunden. A photograph of him taken in 1956 when placed alongside one from a decade later makes clear that the toll had been considerable. Sassoon was convinced that Blunden had not received the honour due to him and his work. Rupert Hart-Davis had collated a comprehensive edition of his poetry, *Poems of Many Years*, in 1956 – the year in which he also received the Queen's Medal for Poetry. The output had been prodigious – poetry, biography, reviews and translations – hardly an area of literature seems untouched by him. In addition to all this, there was his dedication to teaching and the encouraging of his students. At Heytesbury he was freed from these concerns and could relax with Sassoon as they watched the 'best of all games' being played on the home pitch, or listened to a Test match on the wireless in the shade of the portico and the wafting aroma of Sassoon's tobacco.

There were not many summers left for them. Sassoon cared less than Blunden about the ebbing of his creative powers, although haunted by the thought that perhaps he had another 'Lenten Illuminations' in him. He was not averse to a trip away, to Stratford-upon-Avon for a new production – a rare treat indeed, or to London for a meeting of the Royal Society of Literature. His presence there was due to Rupert Hart-Davis and a friend whose acquaintance was made when he visited Heytesbury in May 1960. Sir Alan Lascelles, one-time Private Secretary to Edward VIII, George VI and Queen Elizabeth, was a devotee of Sassoon's work and played host to him in his home in Kensington. It was through Lascelles that Sassoon met, on 15 July 1964, 'that undoubted man of genius, David Jones'. It was an auspicious date for Jones, who on that day, he told his host, nearly 50 years before had been evacuated to England, having suffered serious wounds during the assault on Mametz Wood.

While grateful to friends and always acknowledging their kindness,

Sassoon was not enamoured of these events and complained discreetly of boredom. His letter to Dame Felicitas recounting those three days in London is an insight into Sassoon's sometimes studied world-weariness and his sharp powers of social observation.

The Lit. Society dinner was the usual fatiguing worldliness, but I sat next to J. Betjeman, who is a kindred spirit and almost too stimulating. Next day David Jones came to lunch with the Lascelles – a pathetic, helpless seeming little man – ultra-sensitive. I talked to him alone for one and a half hours, and worked hard. He was a private in the 15th R.W.F. and wounded at Mametz Wood. His Battalion relieved ours after my day out bombing the Prussian Guard – Have you tried reading him? Father Sebastian specialised in *The Anathemata* – quite beyond me. *In Parenthesis* is an important war record – but doesn't reach me like *Undertones of War*. That afternoon – 6–7 – I was conveyed to 2 cocktail parties! At the Austrian Embassy I shook hands with Prince Schwaszenburg, but it was very loud and boring and we only stayed 15 minutes. The other was quieter – a much married lady, daughter of Mrs Willie James who used to entertain King Edward (and was one of the Duke of Windsor's girls). Two drawing rooms plastered with priceless Impressionist paintings. I took refuge in a cosy chair, knowing nobody, until Sybil Cholmondeley was announced, and pounced on me particularly – I hadn't seen her for twenty years, but she was effusively affectionate. And almost at once asked my assistance and advice about her eldest grand daughter, aged 16½, who wants to become a Catholic. I could only suggest the Assumption Convent, as Kensington Square is only a few minutes' walk from the Cholmondeley chateau in Palace Gate. A lively girl, apparently – was sent away from Wardour Castle School for knocking down the Matron. I get more and more Newman minded about the world and don't trust it a yard.

When one remembers the recipient of these observations, a slight suspicion arises that Sassoon was playing to the gallery. But he recounted the same burden to Katharine Asquith: 'I try so hard to cope with the world in my agedness, weary though I am of most of it – and try to be Mercutio for those who come here.' It was all a strain, nothing more so than the family Christmas – 'all food and fussifications – and being a factotum'.

Signs of frailty sharpened when, with 1965 barely established, Sassoon collapsed. The cause, according to Hester, was 'his years-old duodenal ulcer'. His extremity became her opportunity and throughout January she fussed and bothered over him. Writing to Mother Margaret Mary on 8 January, Sassoon was in a perky mood and fulsome in his praise of Hester: 'I am still a bit wobbly on my feet but feel immensely refreshed in *mind*; and it is elysium, not to be obliged to make any effort about anything. The best thing of all is Hester's happiness in ministering to my every need.' In a previous letter he had remarked that 'it was providential' that Hester was there; how she 'was waiting on me hand and foot', and that, 'Hester is at her best at such times, and her over-anxiety is inevitable, though a little fatiguing. H. is much better and less '"to me-ish" ' about religion. I gave her 2 poems, which made a big effect. She is reading Felicitas's "To Any Christian". She really does seem to understand more, and to be more interested in R.C. ways and means (and less know-all).'

For her part, Hester wrote to Dame Felicitas that 'Life must be taken at a slower pace and his friends can no longer expect him to be active on the cricket field: that will have to stop now.' Hester's concern was that he should attend to the questions of inheritance – she was financially more astute than Sassoon. He was reluctant to entangle himself in temporalities, even when George suggested death duties might well mean selling Heytesbury. He had made what he considered all the necessary arrangements. George would take care of the rest, of that he was confident.

In February the University of Oxford offered him an honorary D.Lit. He feigned reluctance but was pleased. Muriel Galsworthy recalled Sassoon's enthusiastic description of his big day at Oxford and how the congregation in the Sheldonian had so warmly applauded him. But 'he hinted that he would have liked to have received the O.M. like Uncle Jack, Thomas Hardy and Walter de la Mare'. The honour is limited to 24 members and is in the sole gift of the sovereign. A vacancy was created by the death of T. S. Eliot. Sassoon told Mother Margaret Mary that Alan Lascelles, 'will now, I strongly suspect, be pestering the Palace to award me the O.M. in place of T.S.E. Would that make me any happier? I almost dread the possible prospect.' In the event no invitation was forthcoming.

'The way is growing very wearisome,' he told Dame Felicitas at the start of 1966. He was racked with rheumatism, his vitality reduced and he had lost much weight but his spirit was strong and he was overjoyed when Blunden succeeded Robert Graves as Professor of Poetry at Oxford. 'He will now be recognised properly. An exceptionally modest man has been given his due.' Dennis and Diana Silk, Ian Davie and Muriel Galsworthy were 'very loyal and attentive, but the key word to my present existence is passivity. I submit to the long littleness of life dutifully. But the central me dwells elsewhere: what Newman calls the accidents of life no longer interest me, I have immortal longings in me.'

In May he was admitted to the Lansdown Hospital in Bath, where he underwent a prostate operation: 'The ward sister is an R.C. and a Newman devotee.' He was quite irrepressible and told Muriel Galsworthy that when asked if he was ready for his injection, he had replied: 'I have no objection to an injection.' Dennis and Diana came to see him, as did Glen. Two years had passed since they had been together and 40 years since they first met. Sassoon was also pleased to see George, from whom he had felt estranged for nearly a decade but now 'he is nearer to me than for years past'.

June saw him back at Heytesbury. There were letters from Hester up in Scotland, reminding him that he was on the verge of being 80. The poet and radio producer Charles Causley took arrangements in hand for a celebratory volume, subscribed to by friends and admirers, comprising eight poems reflecting Sassoon's religious quest and certainties. *An Octave* was a gesture both affectionate and admiring, which moved him. The 'delicacy and good sense' of Causley's introduction was noted in a letter sent to the Abbess of Stanbrook, as too was his amazement at the pile of letters and telegrams covering the table in the library on 8 September – 'I almost dread the impact of all this acclamation, which had exceeded my expectations. But I have prayed to be enabled to see myself as I truly am.'

Proven Purpose

Because I have believed, I bid my mind be still.
Therein is now conceived Thy hid yet sovereign Will.
Because I set all thought aside in seeking Thee,
Thy proven purpose wrought abideth blest in me.
Because I can no more exist but in Thy being,
Blindly these eyes adore; sightless are taught new seeing.

The Stanbrook Abbey Press marked the birthday with an illuminated extract from Sassoon's birthday gift volume, 'To Mamsy 1897'. He was filled with happiness as he remembered walking to Watercress Well with Theresa and wrote to Dame Felicitas: 'The world was a pleasanter place when I was young and "there was no war on".' The card accompanying the Stanbrook gift carried the inscription: 'Homage on his eightieth birthday to Siegfried Sassoon who even to serene old age has kept the heart of a child.'

Far off in earliest remembered childhood I can overhear myself repeating the words 'Watercress Well'. I am kneeling by an old stone well-head; my mother is standing beside me and we are looking into the water. Many a half-hour's pilgrimage we made from our house to Watercress Well which, after having been one of my 'favourite places to go', now becomes a symbol of life itself in an opaque and yet transparent beginning. From that so intensely remembered source all my journeyings now seem to have started. If I were to go back and look for it I might find that it has vanished; but in my thoughts it is for ever the same. Around and above it whisper the woodland branches; time's wavering shadows are falling across the glade; but there will be no sunset for that pictured afternoon. Light as a leaf, a robin drops down and decides to have a drink. I look again; the robin is not there. The well-head is alone with its secret energy of life. My mother and I are voices out of sight, for we are half-way across a breezy meadow, leaving behind us Watercress Well and the rivulet that goes running through the wood, talking to itself in the wordless language of water and roots and stones.

The birthday celebrated, Sassoon dreaded the cold days and long nights of winter. Visitors were few; he had no project to occupy this time of monotonous hibernation but he was not, he assured everybody, 'spiritually arid'. Any efforts to engage his attention in worldly matters, especially the house and the estate, were repulsed: 'I cannot conform to the futility and tediousness of the things I have to discuss with those around me.' Fortunately, Mr Armitage, the estate manager, whom he never failed to praise, shouldered the burden. He wanted peace and quiet, although he kept a daily eye on the world as reported in *The Times* and watched the horse racing on television. Muriel Galsworthy was a constant visitor and sat patiently listening to Sassoon's latest insights and there was a stream of letters from admirers, many writing in response to the public edition of *An Octave*. He was touched by a letter from the son of a soldier, who was killed at Passchendaele:

Dear Mr Lindley,

Does it surprise you to hear that your letter has given me as deep contentment as any that I have received about my poetry? You see those eight poems are something apart from any others I have written – and have, for me, an ultimate significance. That they should have brought you the spiritual aid you tell me of is indeed a wonderful reward. I feel as strongly as ever about the madness of war. And the 1914 war seems to be more insane the further it recedes in history.

Sassoon could never close his mind to 'the world's worst wound', neither did he close his door on those who called to pay their respects, people who enjoyed reading his books and wanted to thank him, or one old soldier for whom he cracked open a half-bottle of champagne. Above all, his heart never failed where there was need of comfort. A letter he wrote to Rupert Hart-Davis, whose wife Ruth had died suddenly, overflows with human warmth in an attempt to bind up the wound: 'One thing I can offer you – my deep and devoted friendship. I beg you to turn to me for solace, reduced though I am in energy and activity. There is nothing I wouldn't give to redeem your desolation.'

This, his last summer, was not the brightest and the hours of the afternoon seemed long as he lolled in a chair. Mrs Humphries, a Heytesbury neighbour, popped in for a chat after tea: 'telling me what she's watched on T.V. and how her family has been occupying itself – a recital to which I can contribute little except "Is that so?"' Mr Armitage called regularly but Sassoon was tired and the tiredness was all-pervasive. His sense of humour did not leave him nor did his perverse self-regard. He chose to read *The Diary of a Nobody* and told Dame Felicitas that it was 'very appropriate to my daily existence which fails to remind me that I am regarded as a Somebody! I'm always content to be left in peace.' On 16 July, he wrote to Mother Margaret Mary complaining of his summer solitude and inactivity and of being 'tyrannized by my old tummy'. This was his last letter to his spiritual benefactress. A month later she received a letter from Dr Falk, Sassoon's physician: 'He has asked me to write to you. He would very much like to see you and to have your help, because he is, alas, hopelessly ill with an inoperable abdominal cancer. He knows the full facts, and accepts wonderfully the truth that there is nothing we can do that can alter the outcome.' She wrote to Sassoon and promised to come to Heytesbury – which she did on 26 August, together with Jessica, his niece.

Rupert Hart-Davis had already visited: 'I spent several days with him. By then he was all skin and bone, and lying in his large bed, he looked like a saint in a mediaeval painting. One day he said to me, "My poems are all right, aren't they?" "Yes, Sieg, they're fine." "Would you say every one was a bull's-eye?" "No. Many are bulls, some inners, some magpies, some outers, and a few miss the target altogether." His ravaged frame shook with laughter.'

Muriel Galsworthy came to say goodbye. Sassoon, she recalled, was in a very large bed; his pyjama coat-sleeves somewhat threadbare. He asked her to fetch his marked copy of *Morte d' Arthur*. He gave exact instructions as to where the volume was to be found. He was a man of order and neatness to the end. There was no personal goodbye from Hester – she had suffered a seizure and was in hospital in Oban. George arrived and his presence was a great comfort – more than anyone else, probably.

Dom Philip Jebb of Downside, on taking his leave of Sassoon, told him: 'We would all be praying for him but that he must not forget to pray for us. He was most indignant and asked how he could ever forget to pray for any of us – ever. Then he said he was sorry not to be in better form, and I said (what was true), I had never known him more in top form. His eyes went all bright in their deep, deep hollows and he said: "Behind this frail little body I am in the best form." I left him to the angels and the memory has filled me ever since. I have never had difficulty in making the resurrection part of life; but he brought Heaven into the room with his gentle eagerness and for the first time I feel an actual enlargement from death, which is quite extraordinary.'

Siegfried Sassoon died on 1 September 1967 and was buried at Mells in Somerset.

AFTERWORD

This afterword springs from the discovery of a manuscript containing some unpublished poems. Accompanying the document is a letter from Sassoon dated 1 January 1953.

> Since Xmas I have been making a little M.S. for you, which I now send. To whom else should I send it? You must try to tell me whether my little selection from what I've done lately is good enough to add to the previous ones. All I know is that the verse is scrupulously tidy, & that it represents what you called my devotions.

The recipient of the letter and manuscript was Henry Major Tomlinson, a friend of some 30 years' standing, whom Sassoon called Tommy and referred to as H.M.T. He was born in 1873, in the East End of London. After the Great War he was literary editor of the *Morning Post*, coinciding with Sassoon's tenure of a similar post at the *Daily Herald*. Tomlinson later became a successful travel writer and novelist. He never lost his cockney accent nor developed any pretensions: this is what appealed to Sassoon. Tender-hearted, he possessed a sympathetic ear, which is ironical given that he suffered from impaired hearing. Sassoon told Edmund Blunden on the death of Tomlinson in February 1958: 'We must be thankful for all those years of H.M.T. with us. Particularly in the last ten years and more, he sustained me greatly by his letters.'

In the decade referred to, Sassoon wrote the religious poetry, which was published in three volumes: *Common Chords* (1950), *Emblems of*

Experience (1951) and *The Tasking* (1954). The manuscript sent to Tomlinson on New Year's Day 1953 contains 14 poems written in the author's neat and unique calligraphy and carries the title 'Wonted Themes'. It is, in fact, the original version of *The Tasking*, which would eventually contain 24 poems, only 9 of which came from this newly discovered manuscript. In 1956 *Common Chords, Emblems of Experience* and *The Tasking* were published as a composite volume under the title *Sequences*. Sassoon sought Tomlinson's advice on that project too, as he told Dame Felicitas Corrigan in a letter dated 27 March 1962. Appropriately and deservedly, *Sequences* was dedicated to H. M. Tomlinson.

APPENDIX

PEOPLE AND PLACES IN SASSOON'S BOOKS

reproduced by permission of the compiler
Carole Noakes
and the Matfield and Brenchley Historical Society
(first published in *Siegfried Sassoon: A Centenary Celebration at
Brenchley and Matfield in Kent*, July 1986)

FICTION	FACT
George Sherston	Siegfried Sassoon
Aunt Evelyn	his mother Theresa Sassoon
The House	Weirleigh, Matfield
Tom Dixon	Tom Richardson
Mr Star	Mr Moon
Dumborough	Eridge
Amblehurst	Lamberhurst
Hopkilns	Beltring
Finchhurst	Frant
Denis Milden	Norman Loder
Village	Matfield
Sibson	Stevenson
Mrs Shotney	Mrs Hussey
Squire Maundle	Morland
Baldock Wood	Paddock Wood
Ballboro	Marlborough
Bearded collector	Smith

Butley	Brenchley
William Dodd	William Hodges
Richard Puttridge	J. G. Philpott
Jack Barchard	R. E. Marchant
Bob Ellis	Bob Lowres
Sam Batinwick	Sam Elphick
Bill Sutler	Will Butler
Ned Noakes	Edwin Lambert
Parson Yalden	Canon Leigh
Major Carmine	Major Terry
Miss Pattons	Misses Hollands
Captain Huxtable	Capt Ruxton
Miss Maskell	Miss Horrocks
Ashbridge	Maidstone
John Homeward	Tom Homewood
David Cromlech	Robert Graves
Joe Dottrell	Joe Cotterill
Dick Tiltwood	David Thomas
Kinjack	Major Stockwell
Barton	E. L. Greaves
Mansfield	N. Stansfield
Ormand	E. L. Orme
Allgood	Marcus Goodall
Flook	Molyneaux
Captain Leake	Kirkby
Nutwood Manor	Chapelwood Manor, Nutley, Sussex
Lord and Lady Asterisk	Lord and Lady Brassey
Markington	H. W. Massingham
Thornton Tyrell	Bertrand Russell
Ralph Wilmot	Ralph Greaves
Marshall	M. Robinson
Stonethwaite	Jim Linthwaite
Jowett	Howitt
Whiteway	Harold Whitfield
Bond	John Law
Velmore	Vivian de Sola Pinto
Durley	Julian Dadd

NOTES

CUL   Cambridge University Library
FC   Dame Felicitas Corrigan, OSB
SS   Siegfried Sassoon
SSPP Dame Felicitas Corrigan, *Siegfried Sassoon: Poet's Pilgrimage*
All Sassoon poems quoted are to be found in the *Collected Poems*, unless noted below.

Sassoon's Unpublished Diaries, 1926–56 are in the Hart-Davis Collection, Cambridge University Library.
Sassoon's letters to Glen Byam Shaw are in Cambridge University Library.
For full bibliographical details see the Select Bibliography.

Chapter 1 Weirleigh *(pages 1–15)*
Early family reminiscences are quoted from *The Old Century* unless otherwise noted.
Sassoon's letters to Dame Felicitas Corrigan are in a private collection.

1   'Sassoon is the name': SS to FC, 25.6.65.

3   'You are right about my inheritance': SS to FC, 9.11.66.

3   For further family background see Roth, *The Sassoon Dynasty*, and Jackson, *The Sassoons*.

4   'girls would have thought of themselves as advanced': Manning, *Marble and Bronze*.

9   Gerard Manley Hopkins: Manning, *Marble and Bronze*.

14 'We were as different': *Kent Messenger*, 7.9.67.

Chapter 2 Teachers *(pages 16–37)*
Weirleigh childhood and schoolday reminiscences are quoted from *The Old Century*, unless otherwise noted.

16 FC on SS: *SSPP*.

18 'my childhood was not altogether': *Memoirs of a Fox-Hunting Man.*

19 'I have a copy': SS to FC in *SSPP*.

20 On his early poetry: *The Old Century*.

20 'There lay the lake': *More Poems*, 1897, quoted in *SSPP*.

21 'I remember gazing': *Siegfried Sassoon 1886–1967: a Centenary Celebration at Brenchley and Matfield in Kent.*

27 'I believe I was my mother's favourite': SS to FC, 25.6.65.

29 'The Extra Inch': *Cricket*, xxii, 9.4.1903.

35 'state of rapt afflatus': SS to FC, 30.5.62.

35 'Swinburne was the main influence': *ibid*.

35 Rupert Hart-Davis, Introduction to *Diaries, 1915–1918*.

35 'Not a bad start': SS to Dame Hildelith Cumming, OSB, 14.9.62.

36 SS to Hamo: Manning, *Marble and Bronze*.

Chapter 3 Poet and Sportsman *(pages 38–59)*
Reminiscences of Sassoon's sporting friendships and early days in London are quoted from *The Weald of Youth*.
The correspondence between SS and Edward Marsh is in the Berg Collection, New York Public Library.

38 'a real library': *The Old Century*.

39 'most of my serious reading': *ibid*.

39 'knew his books so well': Dennis Silk, Guinness Lecture, Salisbury Festival of Arts, July 1994.

39 'If only the Studio': *The Old Century*.

43 Gosse to SS: 28.3.08. Charteris, *The Life and Letters of Sir Edmund Gosse*.

43 Hamo to Gosse: Manning, *Marble and Bronze*.

43 Gosse to Hamo: *ibid*.

44 SS to Cockerell: Cockerell, *The Best of Friends*.

46 SS to Edward Carpenter: 11.7.11, Sheffield City Libraries.

47 Gosse to SS: 5.12.09. Charteris, *The Life and Letters of Sir Edmund Gosse*.

48 'musical, grandiloquent and mindless': FC in *SSPP*.

51 'An Ode to Music', *The Antidote*, 21.2.13.

52 Marsh on Georgian Poetry: Marsh, *Rupert Brooke*.

Chapter 4 War *(pages 60–86)*
SS to Edward Marsh: the Berg Collection.
Accounts of joining up and life at Litherland are quoted from *Memoirs of a Fox-Hunting Man*, unless otherwise noted.

64 'very much a man dedicated to

67 death': SS to Edward Marsh.

67 SS on Cockerell: *Siegfried's Journey*.

68 Raymond Asquith: Jolliffe, *Letters of Raymond Asquith*.

70 Douglas's prosecution: Borland, *Wilde's Devoted Friend*.

70 SS on Ross: *Siegfried's Journey*.

72 Diary from the trenches: *Diaries, 1915–1918*.

72 'The War changed Sassoon': Hart-Davis, *Praise from the Past*.

73 'What I have written': SS to FC in *SSPP*.

74 'I went to visit C Company Mess': Graves, *Goodbye to All That*.

74 SS on Graves: *Memoirs of an Infantry Officer*.

74 Graves on SS's poetry: Graves, *Goodbye to All That*.

75 'my inner life': *Diaries, 1915–1918*.

75 'Men marching by': *ibid*.

77 Gosse to Ottoline Morrell: Morrell, *Ottoline at Garsington*.

77 Ottoline Morrell's correspondence with SS: *Siegfried's Journey*.

77 'I wondered if I should ever see': Morrell, *Ottoline at Garsington*.

78 'The mare brought me home': *Diaries, 1915–1918*.

78 'the great idea of religion': *ibid*.

78 'brief lights soon burnt out': *ibid*.

79 'About half past ten': Graves, *Goodbye to All That*.

80 SS on death of Thomas and his own subsequent behaviour: *Diaries, 1915–1918*.

81 'I was angry with the War': *Memoirs of a Fox-Hunting Man*.

81 'Down in the craters': *ibid*.

82 'like coming back to life': *Diaries, 1915–1918*.

82 'The bullet and the bayonet': *ibid*.

82 'Whatever my private feelings': *Memoirs of an Infantry Officer*.

85 'I chucked four Mills bombs': *Diaries, 1915–1918*.

85 'If I'm lucky': *ibid*.

85 'The Hamner engagement': *ibid*.

85 'In him I thought': *ibid*.

Chapter 5 Garsington *(pages 87–105)*
88 'I intend it as a commentary': *SSPP*.

90 'His coming had fallen': Morrell, *Ottoline at Garsington*.

90   'beginning to realise as horrible': *ibid.*
91   'How had Uncle Hamo': *Siegfried's Journey.*
92   'Although I didn't': *ibid.*
92   'explained the situation': Graves, *Goodbye to All That.*
93   'Siegfried and his friend': Morrell, *Ottoline at Garsington.*
94   'At Garsington the war': *Siegfried's Journey.*
94   'That this should have an unsettling effect': *ibid.*
96   'What in earlier days had been drafts': *Memoirs of an Infantry Officer.*
98   'I heard from old Birrell': *Siegfried's Journey.*
98   'The spirit and purpose of the war': *ibid.*
98   Gosse to SS: Charteris, *Life and Letters of Sir Edmund Gosse.*
99   'Mr Gosse has written': Manning, *Marble and Bronze.*
99   Gosse to Hamo: *ibid.*
100 'My brain is pitifully': *Diaries, 1915–1918.*
103 'He doesn't know for what': *ibid.*
104 'The dead bodies': *ibid.*
104 'The Front Line was behind us': *Memoirs of an Infantry Officer.*

Chapter 6 The Statement *(pages 106–17)*
106 'The floor is littered': *Diaries, 1915–1918.*
107 Hardy to SS: 8.5.17. Hardy, *Collected Letters.*
107 SS to Hamo: Manning, *Marble and Bronze.*
108 'dying fifty yards from their trench': *Diaries, 1915–1918.*
109 'I am making this Statement': *ibid.*
110 'Possibly what I disliked': *Siegfried's Journey.*
111 'Soldiers conceal': *Diaries, 1915–1918.*
112 'antithesis of an officer and a gentleman': *Memoirs of an Infantry Officer.*
112 'For him the Church': *ibid.*
113 'I am writing you this private letter': *Diaries, 1915–1918.*
115 SS to E. Marsh: 7.7.17. Berg Collection.

115 Marsh to SS: *Diaries, 1915–1918.*
115 Ross to SS: *ibid.*
115 'So I trundled': *Memoirs of an Infantry Officer.*
116 'the poor little thing': *ibid.*
117 'everyone was mad': Graves, *Goodbye to All That.*

Chapter 7 Craiglockhart *(pages 118–38)*
118 'a gloomy cavernous place': *Sherston's Progress.*
119 'It was very jolly': *Diaries, 1915–1918.*
119 'The Pentland Hills': *ibid.*
119 'He was forced': *Hansard, 30.7.17.*
120 SS to Hamo: Manning, *Marble and Bronze.*
120 'a great many of them': *Diaries, 1915–1918.*
127 'He liked me': *Sherston's Progress.*
127 Swinnerton on Rivers: Swinnerton, *A London Bookman.*
122 Rivers on SS's condition: Imperial War Museum, and *Siegfried's Journey.*
122 'I am no exception': *Sherston's Progress.*
122 'There was never any doubt': *ibid.*
124 'were improvised by an impulsive': *Siegfried's Journey.*
124 'my definite approach': *Sherston's Progress.*
125 SS on Gordon Harbord: *Diaries, 1915–1918.*
125 Geoffrey Harbord to SS: 13.9.17. Imperial War Museum.
126 'a sham and a stinking lie': *Sherston's Progress.*
120 SS meets Owen: *Siegfried's Journey.*
128 'It dawned on me': *ibid.*
128 'Seeing you again': *Diaries, 1915–1918.*
129 'Those men so strangely isolated': *Siegfried's Journey.*
129 'I have told Rivers': *Diaries, 1915–1918.*
130 'sweat your guts out': *Siegfried's Journey.*
131 'It isn't worth you coming': *Diaries, 1915–1918.*
131 'When I arrived': Morrell, *Ottoline at Garsington.*

132 'My own comprehension': *Siegfried's Journey*.

132 'He is a man': Morrell, *Ottoline at Garsington*.

132 'officer and gentleman': *Sherston's Progress*.

133 SS's New Year resolutions: *Diaries, 1915–1918*.

135 'there's some merit in the war poems': 16.7.18. Woolf, *Letters*.

135 'The news caused me consternation': *Siegfried's Journey*.

136 'Who is Siegfried Sassoon?': Gilbert, *Churchill*, vol 4.

136 'I said goodby to Robbie': *Siegfried's Journey*.

137 SS on T. E. Lawrence: *ibid*.

138 'I was walking in the water-meadows': *Diaries, 1915–1918*.

Chapter 8 Aftermath *(pages 139–56)*

139 On Victory celebrations: *Siegfried's Journey*.

141 'Blake said that a tear': SS to FC, 12.11.61.

141 Bartholomew to E. T. Dent: CUL.

142 SS to E.T. Dent: CUL.

143 SS on Theresa: *Siegfried's Journey*.

144 'That the Reds': *ibid*.

145 'Despotism and cruelty': Graves, *In Broken Images*.

147 'There is nothing intellectual': Osbert Sitwell in catalogue to the Atkin exhibition at the Laing Gallery, Newcastle, 1940.

148 'The life of a literary editor': *Daily Herald*, 2.4.19; see also *Siegfried's Journey*.

148 SS as crusading columnist: *ibid*.

149 'a small privately printed book': *ibid*.

149 Blunden to SS: Webb, *Edmund Blunden*.

149 SS to Blunden: *ibid*.

150 'Little Blunden': *Diaries, 1920–1922*.

152 'He is one of the rare people': *ibid*.

153 Gosse to SS: 5.7.19. Charteris, *The Life and Letters of Sir Edmund Gosse*.

153 The American tour: *Siegfried's Journey*.

1558 Behrman to Rupert Hart-Davis: CUL.

Chapter 9 Tufton Street *(pages 157–72)*
Sassoon quotations are from the *Diaries, 1920–1922*, unless otherwise noted.

159 'Then the ceiling lights': 22.1.20. *New Statesman*.

165 'Here lies Lord Berners': Amory, *Lord Berners: the Last Eccentric*.

166 Life at Renishaw: O. Sitwell, *Laughter in the Next Room*.

Chapter 10 Friendships *(pages 173–85)*
Sassoon quotations are from the *Diaries, 1920–1922*, unless otherwise noted.

173 'he was absolute for friendship': Dennis Silk, Guinness Lecture, 1974.

181 'dear old Eddie': SS to FC, 28.7.65.

Chapter 11 Travels *(pages 186–202)*
Sassoon quotations are from the *Diaries, 1923–1925*, unless otherwise noted.

186 'unspectacular and private': CUL.

189 SS to H. Head: 15.6.23. Quoted in Keynes, *A Bibliography of Siegfried Sassoon*.

190 SS to J.C. Squire: *ibid*.

190 'I had said my say': *Siegfried's Journey*.

191 SS to Eddie Marsh, 11.7.22. Berg Collection.

193 E. M. Forster to SS: Forster, *Letters*, vol. I.

194 'not more chastity': Forster, *Two Cheers for Democracy*.

194 'a rather avuncular': Furbank to Tennant, Hugo Vickers Collection.

194 'You are not at present a story-writer': Forster, *Letters*, vol. I.

199 'I regard it with the deepest suspicion': *The Old Century*.

Chapter 12 Sherston *(pages 203–20)*
Sassoon quotations are from the *Diaries, 1923–1925*, and the unpublished 1926 Diary, unless otherwise noted.

204 'one of the stepping stones': *Diaries, 1920–1922*.

206 SS on 'Alone': SS to Dame Hildelith

Cumming, 27.2.64. Stanbrook Abbey.

211 Hamo to SS: Manning, *Marble and Bronze.*

214 'asked Laura and me': Graves, *In Broken Images.*

Chapter 13 Stephen *(pages 221–36)*
Sassoon quotations are from the unpublished 1927 and 1928 Diaries, unless otherwise noted.

223 E. Blunden to SS: Webb, *Edmund Blunden.*

229 SS to Blunden: *ibid.*

233 'Lady Grey has been warned': Olivier, *Edith Olivier from her Journals.*

236 'merely a matter of months': *ibid.*

236 SS to Blunden: Webb, *Edmund Blunden.*

Chapter 14 Quarrels *(pages 237–55)*
Sassoon quotations are from the unpublished 1929 and 1930 Diaries, unless otherwise noted.
Edith Olivier quotations are from *Edith Olivier from her Journals.*

239 'Your letter made me sing': SS to E. Marsh, Berg Collection.

239 SS to E. Newgass, CUL.

240 Dorothy Hawkins to SS: CUL.

241 'I must remain here with Stephen': SS to E. Marsh, Berg Collection.

241 Theresa Sassoon to Stephen Tennant: Hugo Vickers Collection.

244 'An elder brother': Graves, *Goodbye to All That.*

247 Correspondence between SS and Graves, February 1930: Graves, *In Broken Images.*

250 SS to Cecil Beaton: CUL.

255 Dr T.A. Ross to SS: Hoare, *Serious Pleasures.*

Chapter 15 Hester *(pages 256–72)*
Sassoon quotations are from his unpublished 1933–37 Diaries, unless otherwise noted.
Edith Olivier quotations are from *Edith Olivier from her Journals.*

258 Graves to SS: May 1933. Graves, *In Broken Images.*

263 T. E. Lawrence to Geoffrey Keynes: 6.8.34. Lawrence, *Collected Letters.*

264 Dom Martin Salmon on SS the cricketer: in conversation with the author, 8.8.91.

264 'Despite his solitariness': 3.9.67. *Observer.*

267 'poems like wood-violets': Lawrence, *Collected Letters.*

270 'Christianity without the mumbo-jumbo': Harris, *Attlee.*

271 Beerbohm on Sheppard: Cecil, *Max.*

271 'Hester's advent': SS to E. Marsh, Berg Collection.

Chapter 16 Married Life *(pages 273–85)*
Sassoon quotations are from his unpublished 1937–39 Diaries, unless otherwise noted.

274 Lawrence to Nancy Astor: Lawrence, *Collected Letters.*

275 'Last night I spent three hours': SS, *Letters to Max Beerbohm with a few answers.*

275 'Not many verbal alterations': SS speaking on a memorial broadcast for Beerbohm, BBC Home Service, 22.8.56.

275 'a wondrous work': SS, *Letters to Max Beerbohm with a few answers.*

275 'a daisy of a book': Dennis Silk in conversation with the author.

276 'the future then was something to be desired': SS to FC.

277 'my inward life took shape': SS to FC, 16.2.62.

278 'How many poets have done that': Cockerell, *The Best of Friends.*

285 'a supposedly influential writer': 3.5.39. SS to E. Marsh, Berg Collection.

Chapter 17 Heytesbury *(pages 286–303)*
Sassoon quotations are from his unpublished 1939 and 1942–47 Diaries, unless otherwise noted.
Edith Olivier quotations are from *Edith Olivier from her Journals.*

290 'vesperal cup of cocoa': 26.1.42. SS, *Letters to Max Beerbohm with a few answers.*

291 'No words can express': Cockerell, *The Best of Friends.*

293 Blunden to SS: Webb, *Edmund Blunden.*

297 Claire on Hester and George: in conversation with the author.

298 Katharine Gatty to SS: CUL.

303 'The Child Denied': unpublished poem in CUL.

Chapter 18 Seeking (pages 304–23)
Sassoon quotations are from his unpublished 1947–54 Diaries, unless otherwise noted.

304 'to put himself around': 31.10.49. Cockerell, *The Best of Friends*.

304 SS to Philip Gosse: 8.1.48, Brotherton Collection, Leeds.

307 'old clocks which ticked away': 28.6.48. SS, *Letters to Max Beerbohm with a few answers*.

308 'and now please write some more poetry': Hart-Davis Collection, CUL.

309 Ackerley on the Sassoons: Parker, *Ackerley*.

309 Rupert Hart-Davis of SS: Hart-Davis, *Praise from the Past*.

310 'cried out for the living God in me': SS's own handwritten annotation to his poem 'Resurrection' in a copy of *Sequences*.

315 'I emerged into the Mall': 28.2.51. SS, *Letters to Max Beerbohm with a few answers*.

317 Helen Waddell to SS: August 1951, Stanbrook Abbey.

320 Dennis Silk on first meeting SS: Guinness Lecture, 1974.

320 A. J. Wavell on first meeting SS: Cockerell, *The Best of Friends*.

321 'instructing young Silk': SS to Cockerell.

311 SS on Wavell's death: SS to FC, 5.8.69; and to Cockerell: Cockerell, *The Best of Friends*.

322 'just went blindly onwards': SS to FC, 5.8.69.

Chapter 19 Ultimate Spring (pages 324–43)
Quotations from Muriel Galsworthy come from her conversations with the author, September 1992.

324 'I read the book through': Notebook of Mother Margaret Mary, CUL.

324 SS to Mother Margaret Mary: 10.1.57, CUL.

326 'to say only what might help': 17.1.57, *ibid*.

326 'Deliverance': is published only in *SSPP*.

326 'His appearance gave the impression': Notebook of Mother Margaret Mary.

327 'I wonder what effect': SS to FC, 5.8.60.

327 'This, then, brought our new making': *Lenten Illuminations*, Downside Review Publication, 1958.

327 Belloc to K. Asquith: Speight, *The Life of Hilaire Belloc*.

328 'his brilliant powers': *Siegfried's Journey*.

328 'You will find it difficult': Hubert van Zeller to FC, 12.3.72.

330 SS to Graves: 7.12.57, CUL.

330 'an instrument being played': SS to FC, 31.10.59.

331 'undirected and emotional aspirations': *ibid*, 9.12.59.

331 'not so many treats': *ibid*, 31.10.59.

332 'joined Downside in my midnight prayers': *ibid*.

332 'I was bowled to': *ibid*, 4.7.60.

332 SS on Davie's poems: SS to Katharine Asquith, 29.5.60. Mells Papers.

332 Davie on SS: in conversation with the author.

332 'Ian riding a waiting race': SS to FC, 27.4.63.

334 'With Siegfried in full flood': Hubert van Zeller to FC, 12.3.72.

334 'Dame Hildelith joined us': *SSPP*.

334 'coronation as a Catholic': SS to FC, 29.11.60.

335 Hester's religion: SS to FC, 30.12.61–January 62.

336 Sister Jessica Gatty on SS: in conversation with the author, 16.8.92.

336 'Even if my family': CUL.

336 'The Lit. Society dinner': SS to FC, 5.8.64.

338 SS to Katherine Asquith: 22.12.64. Mells Papers.

340 'the ward sister is an R.C.': SS to FC, 25.5.66.

340 'he is nearer to me': *ibid*.

340 'delicacy and good sense': SS to the
Abbess of Stanbrook, 9.9.66.

340 'I almost dread': *ibid*.

341 'Proven Purpose': written on
18.9.64, first published in *SSPP*.

341 'the world was a pleasanter place':
SS to FC, 9.11.66.

341 'Far off in earliest remembered
childhood': Prelude to *The Old
Century*.

341 'I cannot conform': SS to FC,
13.12.66.

342 SS to Mr Lindley: quoted in *SSPP*.

342 SS to Rupert Hart-Davis: 21.2.67.
Hart-Davis, *Halfway to Heaven*.

342 'very appropriate to my daily
existence': SS to FC, 9.5.67.

342 Dr Falk to Mother Margaret Mary:
13.8.67, CUL.

342 'I spent several days with him':
Hart-Davis, *Praise from the Past*.

SELECT BIBLIOGRAPHY

WORKS OF SIEGFRIED SASSOON

POETRY

Poems, 1906
Orpheus in Diloeryum, 1908
Sonnets and Verses, 1909
Sonnets, 1909
Twelve Sonnets, 1911
Poems, 1911 ·
Melodies, 1912
The Daffodil Murderer, John Richmond, 1913
Discoveries, 1915
The Old Huntsman and Other Poems, Heinemann, 1917
Counter-Attack and Other Poems, Heinemann, 1918
Picture Show, Heinemann, 1919
Recreations, 1923
War Poems (The Old Huntsman, Counter-Attack and Picture Show), 1923
Lingual Exercises, 1925
Satirical Verses (Recreations and Lingual Exercises), 1926
The Heart's Journey, 1927
The Road to Ruin, 1933
Vigils, 1934
Rhymed Ruminations, 1939
Sequences, 1956
Lenten Illuminations, Downside Review, 1959

The War Poems, ed. Rupert Hart-Davis, Faber & Faber, 1983
Collected Poems, 1908–56, Faber & Faber, 1961

PROSE
Memoirs of a Fox-Hunting Man, Faber & Faber, 1928
Memoirs of an Infantry Officer, Faber & Faber, 1930
Sherston's Progress, Faber & Faber, 1936
The Complete Memoirs of George Sherston, Faber & Faber, 1937
The Old Century and Seven More Years, Faber & Faber, 1938
The Weald of Youth, Faber & Faber, 1942
Siegfried's Journey, 1916–1920, Faber & Faber, 1945
Meredith, Constable, 1948

DIARIES
Diaries, 1915–1918, ed. Rupert Hart-Davis, Faber & Faber, 1983
Diaries, 1920–1922, ed. Rupert Hart-Davis, Faber & Faber, 1981
Diaries, 1923–1925, ed. Rupert Hart-Davis, Faber & Faber, 1985

Unpublished Diaries, 1926–56, Hart-Davis Collection, Cambridge
University Library

LETTERS
Siegfried Sassoon, Letters to Max Beerbohm with a few answers, ed.
Rupert Hart-Davis, Faber & Faber, 1986

Geoffrey Keynes, *A Bibliography of Siegfried Sassoon*, Rupert Hart-
Davis, 1956

Bernard Adams, *Nothing of Importance*, Strong Oak Press, 1988
Mark Amory, *Lord Berners: The Last Eccentric*, Chatto & Windus,
1998
Pat Barker, *Regeneration*, Viking, 1991
Beverley Baxter, *Strange Street*, Hutchinson, 1935
Max Beerbohm, *Letters of Max Beerbohm, 1882–1956*, ed. Rupert Hart-
Davis, Oxford University Press, 1981
Simon Blow, *Broken Blood: The Rise and Fall of the Tennants*, Faber &
Faber, 1987
Edmund Blunden, *Cricket Country*, Collins, 1945
Edmund Blunden, *Undertones of War*, Penguin, 1982

Maureen Borland, *Wilde's Devoted Friend: A Life of Robert Ross, 1869–1918*, Lennard Publishing, 1990

Sarah Bradford, *Sacheverell Sitwell: Splendours and Miseries*, Sinclair-Stevenson, 1993

David Cecil, *Max: A Biography*, Constable, 1964

Evan Charteris, *The Life and Letters of Sir Edmund Gosse*, Haskell House, 1973

Sydney Cockerell, *The Best of Friends: Further Letters of Sir Sydney Carlyle Cockerell*, ed. Viola Meynell, Rupert Hart-Davis, 1956

Dame Felicitas Corrigan, *Siegfried Sassoon: Poet's Pilgrimage*, Gollancz, 1973

Dame Felicitas Corrigan, *Helen Waddell: a biography*, Gollancz, 1990

C. S. Dessain, *John Henry Newman*, Oxford University Press, 1980

J. Dunn, ed. *The War the Infantry Knew*, P.S. King, 1938

Leon Edel, *Bloomsbury, A House of Lions*, Hogarth Press, 1979

B. Ifor Evans, *English Literature Between the Wars*, Methuen, 1948

Penelope Fitzgerald, *The Knox Brothers*, Macmillan, 1977

Michael Foot, *The History of Mr Wells*, Doubleday, 1995

E. M. Forster, *Two Cheers for Democracy*, Edward Arnold, 1951

E. M. Forster, *Selected Letters*, ed. Mary Lago and P. M. Furbank, Collins, 1983, 1985

Paul Fussell, *The Great War and Modern Memory*, Oxford University Press, 1975

Martin Gilbert, *The First War*, Weidenfeld & Nicolson, 1994

Judy Giles and Tim Middleton, eds., *Writing Englishness, 1900–1950: An Introductory Sourcebook on National Identity*, Routledge, 1995

Robert Gittings, *Thomas Hardy: The Older Hardy*, Heinemann, 1978

Victoria Glendinning, *Edith Sitwell: A Unicorn Among Lions*, Weidenfeld & Nicolson, 1981

Lyndall Gordon, *Eliot's New Life*, Oxford University Press, 1988

Richard Perceval Graves, *Robert Graves: The Assault Heroic, 1895–1926*, Weidenfeld & Nicolson, 1986

Robert Graves, *Goodbye to All That*, Cape, 1929

Robert Graves, *In Broken Images: Selected Letters of Robert Graves, 1914–1946*, ed. Paul O'Prey, Hutchinson, 1982

Thomas Hardy, *Collected Letters*, Vols 5 and 6, ed. Richard Little Purdey and Michael Millgate, Clarendon, 1978

Kenneth Harris, *Attlee*, Weidenfeld & Nicolson, 1982

B. H. Liddell Hart, *History of the First World War*, Macmillan, 1992

Rupert Hart-Davis, *Praise from the Past*, Stone Trough Books, 1996

Rupert Hart-Davis, *Halfway to Heaven: Concluding Memoirs of a Literary Life*, Sutton Publishing, 1998

Christopher Hassall, *Edward Marsh: Patron of the Arts*, Longman, 1959

Dominic Hibberd, *Wilfred Owen: The Last Years*, Constable, 1992

Philip Hoare, *Serious Pleasures: The Life of Stephen Tennant*, Hamish Hamilton, 1990

Alistair Horne, *Macmillan*, Macmillan, vol I, 1988, vol 2, 1989

Walter E. Houghton, *The Victorian Frame of Mind*, Yale University Press, 1957

Stanley Jackson, *The Sassoons*, New York, Dutton, 1968

John Jolliffe, ed., *Life and Letters of Raymond Asquith*, Collins, 1980

Ronald Knox, *The Hidden Stream: A Further Collection of Oxford Conferences*, Burns Oates, 1952

Angela Lambert, *Unquiet Souls: The Indian Summers of the British Aristocracy, 1880–1919*, Macmillan, 1984

T. E. Lawrence, *Collected Letters*, ed. David Garnett, London Reprint Society, 1941

Jeanne MacKenzie, *The Children of the Souls*, Chatto & Windus, 1986

Louis MacNeice, *Collected Poems*, Faber & Faber, 1966

Elfrida Manning, *Marble and Bronze: The Art and Life of Hamo Thornycroft*, Trefoil Books, 1982

Edward Marsh, *The Collected Poems of Rupert Brooke with a Memoir*, Sidgwick & Jackson, 1918

Jan Marsh, *Edward Thomas: A Poet for His Country*, Elek, 1978

Matfield and Brenchley Historical Society, *Siegfried Sassoon 1886–1967: A Centenary Celebration at Brenchley and Matfield in Kent*, 1986

Martin and Mary Middlebrook, *The Somme Battlefields: A Comprehensive Guide from Crécy to the Two World Wars*, Viking, 1991

Paul Moeyes, *Siegfried Sassoon, Scorched Glory: A Critical Study*, Macmillan, 1997

Ottoline Morrell, *Ottoline at Garsington, 1915–1928*, ed. Robert Gathorne-Hardy, Faber & Faber, 1974

Nicholas Mosley, *Julian Grenfell: His Life and the Times of His Death, 1888–1915*, Holt, Reinhart, Winston, 1976

Edith Olivier, *Edith Olivier from her Journals, 1924–1928*, ed. Penelope Middleboe, Weidenfeld & Nicolson, 1989

George Orwell, *The Road to Wigan Pier*, Left Book Club, 1937

Wilfred Owen, *Collected Letters*, eds Harold Owen and John Bell, Oxford University Press, 1967

Peter Parker, *The Old Lie: the Great War and the Public School Ethos*, Constable, 1987

Peter Parker, *Ackerley*, Constable, 1989

Andrew Pinnell, ed., *Siegfried Sassoon: A Celebration of a Cricketing Man*, MakingSpace, 1996

The Poetry Review, ed. Arundel del Re, January 1912

J. B. Priestley, *English Journey, 1933*, Heinemann, 1934

Huw Richards, *The Bloody Circus: The Daily Herald and the Left*, Pluto Press, 1997

R. Ellis Roberts, *W.R.L. Sheppard: The Life and Letters*, John Murray, 1942

Robert H. Ross, *The Georgian Revolt: Rise and Fall of a Poetic Ideal, 1910–22*, Faber & Faber, 1967

C. Roth, *The Sassoon Dynasty*, Robert Hale, 1941

Michael Schmidt, *Lives of the Poets*, Weidenfeld & Nicolson, 1998

Miranda Seymour, *Ottoline Morrell, Life on the Grand Scale*, Hodder & Stoughton, 1992

Martin Seymour-Smith, *Robert Graves: His Life and Work*, Hutchinson, 1982

Martin Seymour-Smith, *Hardy*, Bloomsbury, 1994

Michael Shelden, *Orwell*, Heinemann, 1991

Dennis Silk, *Siegfried Sassoon*, Compton Russell, 1975 (Guinness Lecture at Salisbury Festival of Arts, 19 July)

Jon Silkin, *Out of Battle: The Poetry of the Great War*, Oxford University Press, 1972

Edith Sitwell, *Selected Letters of Edith Sitwell*, ed. Richard Greene, Virago, 1997

Osbert Sitwell, *Laughter in the Next Room*, Macmillan, 1949

Osbert Sitwell, *Noble Essences*, Macmillan, 1950

Richard Slobodin, *W. H. R. Rivers: Pioneer, Anthropologist, Psychiatrist of the Ghost Road*, Columbia University Press, 1978

V. de Sola Pinto, *The City That Shone*, Hutchinson, 1969

Robert Speight, *The Life of Hilaire Belloc*, Hollis & Carter, 1957

Jon Stallworthy, *Wilfred Owen: A Biography*, Chatto & Windus, 1974

Frank Swinnerton, *A London Bookman*, Secker, 1928

Frank Swinnerton, *The Georgian Literary Scene*, Dent, 1946

Michael Thorpe, *Siegfried Sassoon: A Critical Study*, Oxford University Press, 1966

Ann Thwaite, *Edmund Gosse: A Literary Landscape*, Secker & Warburg, 1984

Barry Webb, *Edmund Blunden*, Yale University Press, 1990

H. G. Wells, *Mr Britling Sees It Through*, Cassell, 1916

Theresa Whistler, *The Imagination of the Heart: Life of Walter de la Mare*, Duckworth, 1993

A. N. Wilson, *Hilaire Belloc*, Hamish Hamilton, 1984

Jean Moorcroft Wilson, *Siegfried Sassoon: The Making of a War Poet*, Duckworth, 1998

Virginia Woolf, *Letters of Virginia Woolf*, ed. Nigel Nicolson and J. Trautmann, Hogarth Press, in six vols, 1977–84

Virginia Woolf, *The Essays of Virginia Woolf*, ed. Andrew McNeillie, Hogarth Press, 1986

Philip Ziegler, *Osbert Sitwell*, Chatto & Windus, 1998

INDEX